Distributional Impacts of COVID-19 in the Middle East and North Africa Region

MENA DEVELOPMENT REPORT

Distributional Impacts of COVID-19 in the Middle East and North Africa Region

Johannes G. Hoogeveen and Gladys Lopez-Acevedo, Editors

WORLD BANK GROUP

MENA Development Report Series

This series features major development reports from the Middle East and North Africa Region of the World Bank, based on new research and thoroughly peer-reviewed analysis. Each report aims to enrich the debate on the main development challenges and opportunities the region faces as it strives to meet the evolving needs of its people.

Titles in the MENA Development Report Series

Distributional Impacts of COVID-19 in the Middle East and North Africa Region (2021) edited by Johannes G. Hoogeveen and Gladys Lopez-Acevedo

The Reconstruction of Iraq after 2003: Learning from Its Successes and Failures (2019) by Hideki Matsunaga

Beyond Scarcity: Water Security in the Middle East and North Africa (2018) by World Bank

Eruptions of Popular Anger: The Economics of the Arab Spring and Its Aftermath (2018) by Elena Ianchovichina

Privilege-Resistant Policies in the Middle East and North Africa: Measurement and Operational Implications (2018) by Syed Akhtar Mahmood and Meriem Ait Ali Slimane

Jobs or Privileges: Unleashing the Employment Potential of the Middle East and North Africa (2015) by Marc Schiffbauer, Abdoulaye Sy, Sahar Hussain, Hania Sahnoun, and Philip Keefer

The Road Traveled: Dubai's Journey towards Improving Private Education: A World Bank Review (2014) by Simon Thacker and Ernesto Cuadra

Inclusion and Resilience: The Way Forward for Social Safety Nets in the Middle East and North Africa (2013) by Joana Silva, Victoria Levin, and Matteo Morgandi

Opening Doors: Gender Equality and Development in the Middle East and North Africa (2013) by World Bank

From Political to Economic Awakening in the Arab World: The Path of Economic Integration (2013) by Jean-Pierre Chauffour

Adaptation to a Changing Climate in the Arab Countries: A Case for Adaptation Governance and Leadership in Building Climate Resilience (2012) by Dorte Verner

Renewable Energy Desalination: An Emerging Solution to Close the Water Gap in the Middle East and North Africa (2012) by World Bank

Poor Places, Thriving People: How the Middle East and North Africa Can Rise Above Spatial Disparities (2011) by World Bank

Financial Access and Stability: A Road Map for the Middle East and North Africa (2011) by Roberto R. Rocha, Zsofia Arvai, and Subika Farazi

From Privilege to Competition: Unlocking Private-Led Growth in the Middle East and North Africa (2009) by World Bank

The Road Not Traveled: Education Reform in the Middle East and North Africa (2008) by World Bank

Making the Most of Scarcity: Accountability for Better Water Management Results in the Middle East and North Africa (2007) by World Bank

Gender and Development in the Middle East and North Africa: Women in the Public Sphere (2004) by World Bank

Unlocking the Employment Potential in the Middle East and North Africa: Toward a New Social Contract (2004) by World Bank

Better Governance for Development in the Middle East and North Africa: Enhancing Inclusiveness and Accountability (2003) by World Bank

Trade, Investment, and Development in the Middle East and North Africa: Engaging with the World (2003) by World Bank

All books in the MENA Development Report series are available for free at https://openknowledge.worldbank.org/handle/10986/2168.

Contents

5 Djibouti: Refugees More Vulnerable Than Nationals 117

Bilal Malaeb, Anne Duplantier, Romeo Jacky Gansey,
  Sekou Tidiani Konaté, Omar Abdoulkader Mohamed,
  Jeff Tanner, and Harriet Mugera

Part II: Middle East and North Africa Microsimulations 139

6 Tunisia: Poorest Households Are the Most Vulnerable 141

Deeksha Kokas, Abdelrahmen El Lahga, and Gladys
  Lopez-Acevedo

7 West Bank and Gaza: Emergence of the New Poor 163

Romeo Jacky Gansey, Alia Jane Aghajanian, and Jawad
  Al-Saleh

Boxes

Figures

Tables

Foreword

The Middle East and North Africa (MENA) region has been suffering from long-term structural challenges, including low GDP growth; low employment, especially among youth and women; a low human capital index; many state-owned enterprises; a large informal sector; poor foreign direct investment inflows; a weak investment climate; poor participation in global value chains; and rising levels of debt. These preexisting conditions, which are reflective of the fragile condition of the social contract in many countries in the region, have amplified the negative effects of COVID-19.

Globally, poverty has been declining since the early 1990s, but a deceleration in the rate of decline in the MENA region could be observed even before the pandemic hit. COVID-19 not only slowed the decline further but also reversed the gains made for the first time in the past three decades. This report aims to inform policy makers about the consequences of a health crisis that is moving at lightning speed. It adds value by analyzing newly gathered real-time primary data collected through phone interviews complemented by microsimulation techniques. The key questions this report endeavors to answer are: How does COVID-19 affect the welfare of individuals and households in MENA, and what are key issues that policy makers should focus on to preserve hard-won gains in alleviating poverty and inequality in the region?

This report finds ample evidence that COVID-19 may result in a major setback on the poverty front in the MENA region. Although stringent work closures have begun to be relaxed in many countries, the measures have caused substantial economic slowdowns and continue to have a widespread impact. The COVID-19 pandemic has disproportionately affected the welfare of poor households, amplifying existing inequalities.

The report shows that the uneven impacts of the pandemic are driven by a range of factors, including differences in characteristics of jobs and occupations, the nature of employment contracts, and the ability to do some tasks from home. At the root of the problem has been sizable income loss, in large part due to work stoppages that began early in the pandemic. These stoppages led to significant job losses, with a significant share of MENA firms reporting that they reduced their share of permanent employees (17 percent in Algeria and 14 percent in the West Bank and Gaza).

Even so, the share of MENA firms that laid off workers is less than that in regions like Latin America and the Caribbean and Sub-Saharan Africa. Firms in MENA have been trying to hold on to their permanent workforce, attempting to adjust by providing leave (often without pay), reduced work hours, lower salaries, and fewer temporary workers. This tightening can be seen in part in the decline in the intensity of work that is reported by households across the region.

The drop in income and living standards throughout MENA has been most intensely felt by the poorest. In four rounds of phone surveys (mid-May to mid-October 2020), the bottom 40 percent in Tunisia reported being the most affected by those drops compared with prepandemic levels. A similar pattern is found in the Arab Republic of Egypt. The evidence points to a severe decline in household welfare as the pandemic unfolded, a decline that is often not reversed but extended beyond the end of restrictions on individual mobility.

This publication is a reminder that the pandemic is not over and that it will have long-lasting consequences. By identifying the socioeconomic impacts and other distributional effects on welfare from COVID-19, decision-makers will be better placed to design appropriate responses to the pandemic and prepare for future crises and disasters.

Nadir Mohammed
Regional Director, Equitable Growth, Finance and Institutions
Middle East and North Africa Region
The World Bank

Acknowledgments

The preparation of this report was led by Johannes G. Hoogeveen (practice manager, Poverty and Equity Global Practice) and Gladys Lopez-Acevedo (lead economist, Poverty and Equity Global Practice). The core team also comprised Omar Abdoulkader Mohamed, Alia Jane Aghajanian, Federica Alfani, Jawad Al-Saleh, Aziz Atamanov, Gildas Bopahbe Deudibe, Dorra Dhraief, Anne Duplantier, Abdelrahmen El Lahga, Romeo Jacky Gansey, Deeksha Kokas, Sekou Tidiani Konaté, Bilal Malaeb, Eduardo A. Malásquez, Stuti Manchanda, Vasco Molini, Harriet Mugera, Minh Cong Nguyen, Dan Pavelesku, Marco Ranzani, Jaime Alfonso Roche Rodríguez, Laura Rodriguez, Pablo Suárez Becerra, Jeff Tanner, and Matthew Wai-Poi.

Chapters 3 and 7 benefited from the support provided by the Norway West Bank and Gaza Single Donor Trust Fund and from the input of peer reviewers, namely Javier Sanchez-Reaza and Sebastian Saez.

The team is also grateful to Laura Wallace for her skillful editing.

The cover illustration for this report was conceptualized and executed by Alejandro Espinosa of Sonideas.

About the Editors and Contributors

Editors

Johannes G. Hoogeveen is practice manager of the Poverty and Equity Global Practice at the World Bank. He currently works in the Middle East and North Africa region and has published edited volumes on data collection using mobile phones and data collection in fragile states. Hans has published academically on poverty measurement, survey design, education, nutrition, statistics governance, informal insurance, and land reform. Earlier in his career he was manager at a local nongovernmental organization, Twaweza, in Dar es Salaam, Tanzania, where he led a unit strengthening citizen accountability through feedback mechanisms. He holds a PhD in economics from the Free University in Amsterdam.

Gladys Lopez-Acevedo is a lead economist and a program lead in the Poverty and Equity Global Practice at the World Bank. She works primarily in the Middle East and North Africa Region of the World Bank. Gladys's areas of analytical and operational interest include trade, welfare, gender, conflict, and jobs. Previously, she was a lead economist in the World Bank Office of the Chief Economist in the South Asia Region, as well as senior economist in the World Bank's Poverty Reduction and Economic Management Vice Presidency and in the Latin America and the Caribbean Region at the World Bank. She is a research fellow at the Institute of Labor Economics, Mexican National Research System, and Economic Research Forum. Prior to joining the World Bank, she held high-level positions in the government of Mexico, and she was a professor at the Instituto Tecnológico Autónomo de México (ITAM). She holds a BA in economics from ITAM and a PhD in economics from the University of Virginia.

Contributors

Omar Abdoulkader Mohamed has been working since 2009 at the National Statistics Institute as a statistician economist. He currently holds the post of director of economic statistics and national accounts. He has acted as a consultant in various socioeconomic studies and worked on the targeting strategy of the cash transfer component of the Integrated Cash Transfer and Human Capital Building Project (PITCH) on behalf of the Djibouti Ministry of Business and Solidarity. He holds a statistician engineer degree and a master's in development economics, with an economic policy management specialty.

Alia Jane Aghajanian is a poverty economist with the World Bank. Her research interests are in the microeconomic impact of conflict, particularly understanding how social networks and cohesion can be affected by communal and civil violence. Her work focuses on data collection and capacity building to improve the quality and use of statistics. She received her PhD from the Institute of Development Studies at the University of Sussex.

Federica Alfani is an economist in the Poverty and Equity Global Practice at the World Bank. She has been in charge of several research projects in the fields of poverty, rural development, and labor markets. Previously, she worked at the International Fund for Agricultural Development and the Food and Agriculture Organization of the United Nations. She holds an MA in development economics and international cooperation and a PhD in economics from University of Rome, Tor Vergata.

Jawad Al-Saleh is chairman of assistance for developing statistical programs with the Palestinian Central Bureau of Statistics. His work experience covers social statistics, especially living standards; monetary poverty and multidimensional poverty; the labor force and informal employment; and food security. He holds a master's in international economic integration from PAVIA University, Italy, and a master's in applied statistics from Birziet University, Palestine.

Aziz Atamanov is a senior economist in the Poverty and Equity Global Practice at the World Bank. He has been working on poverty measurement, poverty, gender, distributional, and labor analysis in many economies, including Belarus, the Islamic Republic of Iran, Jordan, the Kyrgyz Republic, Lebanon, Moldova, Tajikistan, Turkey, the West Bank and Gaza, and the Republic of Yemen. He also established and co-led the Middle East and North African Team for Statistical Development of the

World Bank. Currently, he leads the poverty program in Uganda. He holds a PhD in development economics from Maastricht University.

Gildas Bopahbe Deudibe is a consultant at the World Bank and a PhD candidate at the University of Clermont Ferrand in France. He joined the World Bank in 2017 and has worked in the Poverty and Equity and Macroeconomics, Trade and Investment Global Practices. His research interest includes environmental macroeconomics, poverty measurement and analysis, and global value chains. He received his MSc in statistics and applied economics from African Statistical Schools in Côte d'Ivoire and Cameroon.

Dorra Dhraief is a general engineer in statistics and the director of household consumption statistics at the National Institute of Statistics of Tunisia. From 2004 to 2009, she was responsible for the quarterly employment survey, and since 2010 she has led the National Household Budget, Consumption, and Standard of Living Survey. She has been in charge of several research projects in the field of poverty.

Anne Duplantier is a development economist and consultant at the World Bank in the poverty department for the Middle East and North Africa region. She has experience in data collection in the field and has held lecturer positions at Sherbrooke University. Anne recently contributed to three waves of the COVID-19 survey in Djibouti to estimate the impacts of the pandemic on Djiboutian households. Her research interests include education, labor economics, and migration in developing countries. Anne holds a PhD in development economics from the University of Sherbrooke in Canada and a master's degree from the Center for Studies and Research on International Development in France.

Abdelrahmen El Lahga currently works in the faculty of economics and management of the University of Tunis. He does research in labor economics, microeconomics, and development economics. He holds a PhD from Louis Pasteur University in Strasbourg.

Romeo Jacky Gansey is a consultant in the World Bank's Poverty and Equity Global Practice. He works on implementing COVID-19 phone surveys in the region, along with conducting various poverty analyses, such as investigating the distributional impacts of the pandemic. His primary research interests are in impact evaluation, poverty, and health in developing countries, as well as migration and economic development. His previous work includes an estimation of the distributional impacts and efficiency of taxation on households in the Democratic Republic of

Congo, an impact evaluation of the malaria program in Mainland Tanzania, and an econometric assessment of vulnerability to poverty. He holds a PhD in demography and population studies from the University of Pennsylvania and a master's in public policy from Duke University.

Deeksha Kokas is a consultant in the Poverty and Equity Global Practice at the World Bank. Her current research covers trade, poverty, jobs, and digitization. She has been extensively researching the labor market adjustment process in response to globalization shocks. She has also worked on finance and private sector issues as part of the World Bank's Development Research Group and Trade and Competitiveness practice. Outside the World Bank, she has experience in conducting impact evaluations as part of J-PAL South Asia. She received a master's in economics from University College London.

Sekou Tidiani Konaté is a statistician and analyst in epidemiology. He worked at the National Statistics Institute of Djibouti (INSTAD) as an expert statistician from 2002 to 2020, then as director of coordination, cooperation, statistical planning, and communication since 2021. He also teaches courses in statistical practices at the University of Djibouti. He is a founding member and currently secretary general of the Djiboutian Evaluation Association.

Bilal Malaeb is a poverty economist at the World Bank for the Middle East and North Africa Region. He works primarily on poverty, inequality, and migration issues. Previously, he worked as a postdoctoral researcher at the University of Oxford and the London School of Economics. He holds a PhD in economics from the University of Manchester.

Eduardo A. Malásquez is an economist in the Poverty and Equity Global Practice at the World Bank, where he leads the poverty programs in Saudi Arabia and the West Bank and Gaza. Eduardo has also been collaborating with the Global Solutions Group on markets and institutions for poverty reduction in the analysis of the distributional impacts of competition policies. His research interests focus on applied microeconomics, in particular in the fields of development and empirical industrial organization. He holds a PhD in economics from the University of Illinois at Urbana-Champaign and an MA from the University of the Pacific in Lima, Peru.

Stuti Manchanda is a consultant at the World Bank. She is currently pursuing a PhD in public policy and global affairs at Nanyang Technological University, Singapore, and also holds an MSc in local economic development from the London School of Economics and Political Science. She is a published author and has previously worked with policy makers and civil servants from the government of India. Her research interests include development economics, comparative political economy, public opinion and behavioral public policy, and environmental sustainability.

Vasco Molini is a senior poverty economist at the World Bank for the Maghreb. His main scientific interests are income distribution, inequality, and conflicts. He has published on these topics in various international peer-reviewed journals, including *World Development, Journal of Development Economics, Review of Income and Wealth*, and *Food Policy*. He holds a PhD in development economics from the University of Florence and a postdoctoral degree from Free University in Amsterdam.

Harriet Mugera is a senior data scientist with the United Nations High Commissioner for Refugees–World Bank Joint Data Center on Forced Displacement. She joined the World Bank in 2015 as an economist with the Development Data Group and is the focal person on migration and data-related issues of the forcibly displaced. She has expertise in survey instrument development, field operations, data quality control, and analysis of household and survey data. She also contributed to the drafting of the International Recommendations on Refugee Statistics and the *Manual on Refugees and Internally Displaced Persons*. She holds a PhD in economics from the University of Trento, Italy, and was a visiting fellow at Cornell University.

Minh Cong Nguyen is a senior data scientist in the Poverty and Equity Global Practice at the World Bank. His research interests include poverty, inequality, welfare measurement, small area estimations and imputation methods, and data systems. He currently leads the Middle East and North Africa team for statistical development. Previously, he co-led the Data for Goals team, worked for the Europe and Central Asia team for statistical development, the Sub-Saharan Africa Region, the South Asia Region, the Human Development Network, and the Private Sector Development Network. Minh holds a PhD in economics (applied microeconometrics) from American University.

Dan Pavelesku is a consultant in the Poverty and Equity Global Practice at the World Bank. He has successfully implemented several research projects in the fields of poverty, social protection, subsidy reforms, and labor market. For the past four years, he has worked mainly in the Middle

East and North Africa region, including Algeria, Morocco, and Tunisia. He holds a master's in economics and has contributed to several World Bank research reports and publications.

Marco Ranzani is an economist in the Poverty and Equity Global Practice at the World Bank, in the Middle East and North Africa Region. His research focuses on labor markets, poverty, and inequality. Previously he was a consultant for the Poverty Reduction and Economic Management Anchor; a researcher at Understanding Children's Work, an interagency research cooperation initiative involving the International Labour Organization, UNICEF, and the World Bank; and a postdoctoral fellow at the University of Bergamo, Italy. He holds a PhD in public economics from the Catholic University of Milan, Italy.

Jaime Alfonso Roche Rodríguez is a consultant in the Poverty and Equity Global Practice at the World Bank. His research focuses on trade, poverty, and labor market distortions. He is also an economist at the Mexican Central Bank, conducting macroeconomic analysis for the support of monetary policy committees. He holds a BSc in economics from Tecnológico de Monterrey and an MSc in international finance from Rennes School of Business.

Laura Rodriguez is an economist in the Poverty and Equity Global Practice at the World Bank, where her work focuses on poverty and distribution in the Mashreq countries, particularly in Jordan and the Islamic Republic of Iran. She is interested in studying the impacts of shocks on countries' poverty and well-being and in the measurement of inequalities, especially the gaps for disadvantaged groups. She holds a PhD in economics from the University of Manchester in the United Kingdom and was previously a researcher at the Overseas Development Institute.

Pablo Suárez Becerra is a consultant in the Poverty and Equity Global Practice at the World Bank. He currently works on projects related to Saudi Arabia and the West Bank and Gaza. Previously he worked on a joint World Bank project with UNICEF on the global estimates of extreme poverty for children. He holds an MA in economics from Brown University and a BA from Universidad del Pacífico in Lima, Peru.

Jeff Tanner is a senior economist in the Poverty and Equity Global Practice at the World Bank. In his current assignment as a member of the secretariat of the World Bank–UNHCR Joint Data Center on Forced Displacement, he serves as a technical adviser on data collection and analysis of displaced populations across the globe. Previously, he was a senior economist with the Global Financing Facility and the Independent Evaluation Group. He has also served as a staff economist at the Millennium Challenge Corporation. He holds a master's in public administration in international development from Harvard University and a PhD in applied economics from the RAND graduate school.

Matthew Wai-Poi is lead poverty economist at the World Bank for East Asia and the Pacific and co-leads the World Bank's global research on distributional impacts of fiscal policies. He has worked extensively on East Asia and the Middle East and was previously based in Jakarta. His work has covered poverty and inequality, the middle class, barriers to female labor force participation, forced displacement, and targeting of social assistance. He holds a PhD in economics from Columbia University and degrees in law and business.

Abbreviations

CPI	consumer price index
FAO	Food and Agriculture Organization (of the UN)
FCS	Food Consumption Score
FDI	foreign direct investment
FIES	Food Insecurity Experience Scale (of FAO)
ID4D	Identification for Development
GIC	growth incidence curves
HEIS	Household Expenditures and Income Survey
HFPS	high frequency phone survey
IDA	International Development Association
IFPRI	International Food Policy Research Institute
ILO	International Labour Organization (and International Labour Office)
KRI	Kurdistan Region of the Republic of Iraq
LFS	labor force survey
MENA	Middle East and North Africa
NGO	nongovernmental organization
OECD	Organisation for Economic Co-operation and Development
PCBS	Palestinian Central Bureau of Statistics
RAPS	rapid assessment phone survey
RDD	random digit dialing
SCI	Statistical Center of Iran
SRHCS	Syrian Refugees and Host Communities Survey
TD	Tunisian dinars
UNDP	United Nations Development Programme
UNESCO	United Nations Educational, Scientific, and Cultural Organization
UNICEF	United Nations Children's Fund
UNRWA	United Nations Relief and Works Agency for Palestine Refugees in the Near East
WEF	World Economic Forum
WFP	World Food Programme

Overview

Introduction

Even before COVID-19 arrived in the Middle East and North African (MENA) countries in March 2020, the region had been facing a number of serious socioeconomic challenges, which were amplified as the pandemic spread. Over the past two decades, MENA has recorded a low annual growth rate of about 1.4 percent per capita, below that of its peers. There has been a doubling of extreme poverty (those living on less than US$1.90 a day), from 2.4 percent in 2011 to 4.2 percent in 2015, in part fueled by conflicts in Libya, the Syrian Arab Republic, and the Republic of Yemen. Even food insecurity has been on the rise.

Other factors also tore at the social fabric—notably, an unconducive business environment and the absence of quality jobs, very high levels of unemployment (especially among youth), and atypically low female labor force participation, with many engaged in the informal sector. These factors limit people's opportunities and affect life satisfaction, which unlike all other regions globally was already declining prior to the pandemic. In 11 out of 14 MENA countries for which data are available, life satisfaction in 2019 was lower than in 2010.

COVID-19 is not the first crisis to affect the region. In fact, it is the fourth to hit MENA in the past decade, following the Arab uprisings, the 2014–16 decline in oil prices, and the 2019 resurgence of protests in countries that had escaped the first wave in 2010–11. The COVID-19 crisis differs from the others because of its broad impacts and its distributional consequences, which have varied across countries, reflecting the region's diverse economic makeup of high-, middle-, and low-income countries and economies; those heavily dependent on oil exports; and those marked by fragility, conflict, and violence-related vulnerabilities.

By February 2021, almost 6 million people in MENA were infected with COVID-19, with the highest number of cases in the Islamic Republic of Iran (figure O.1). Health care expenditures have jumped, people have lost jobs and income, and businesses have been disrupted.

1

FIGURE O.1

The Islamic Republic of Iran Tops the List in Highest Number of COVID-19 Cases

Total number of COVID-19 cases in MENA, end-February 2021

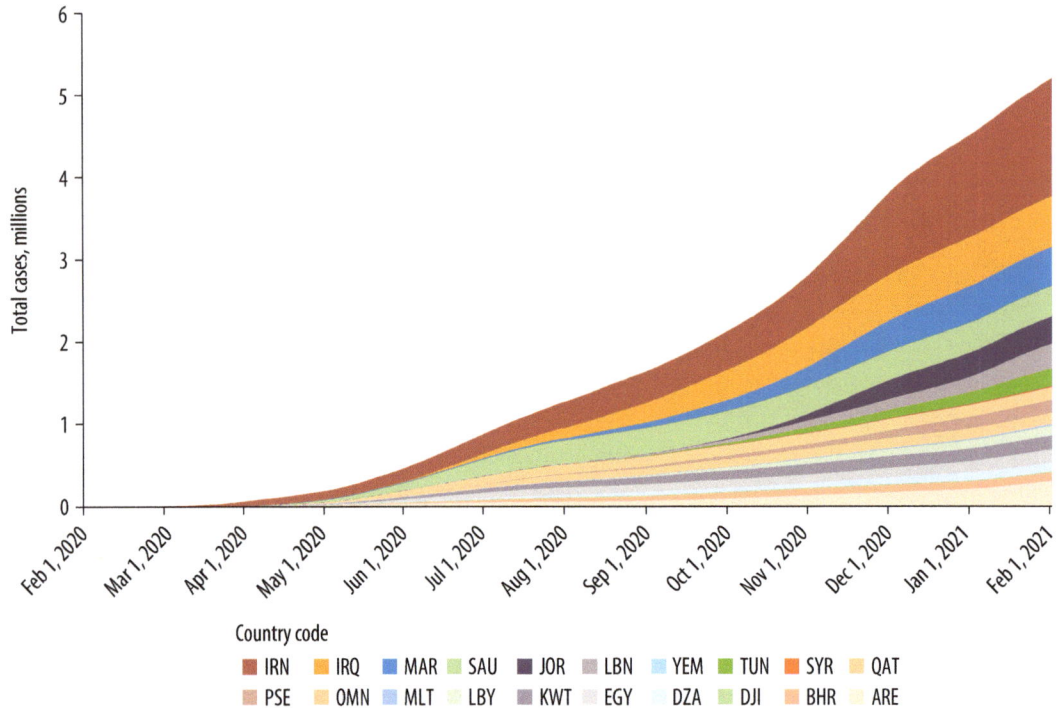

Country code

IRN · IRQ · MAR · SAU · JOR · LBN · YEM · TUN · SYR · QAT
PSE · OMN · MLT · LBY · KWT · EGY · DZA · DJI · BHR · ARE

Source: Our World in Data (database), https://ourworldindata.org.
Note: MENA = Middle East and North Africa.

MENA's output in 2020 is estimated to have fallen by more than 5 percent, with recovery unlikely until 2024 or 2025. Meanwhile, the economic cost of the pandemic in the region is estimated at about US$227 billion (World Bank 2021), and fiscal support packages are averaging 2.7 percent of GDP, putting further pressure on MENA's already weak fiscal position.

Compounding matters is the increasing evidence that the negative effects of COVID-19 are being borne by those who, prepandemic, were already disadvantaged and vulnerable. The January 2021 Global Economic Prospects forecast estimates that between 7 million and 8 million people in the region will fall into poverty.

Against this backdrop, this report asks: How does COVID-19 affect the welfare of individuals and households in MENA, and what are the key issues that policy makers should focus on to enable a quick and sustained economic convalescence? It aims to inform the debate about what policy makers should do in light of a health crisis that is moving with lightning speed. It adds value by analyzing newly gathered primary data in the region—largely through telephonic surveys, which represent an unprecedented data collection effort to produce real-time information on the socioeconomic impacts of the pandemic and the associated economic crisis on households and individuals. These surveys are complemented by projections carried out though microsimulations that allow the assessment of impacts on poverty and inequality.

The following are the report's four key messages:

- COVID-19 has had unequal impacts, often affecting the poor and vulnerable disproportionately. The results suggest (a) a substantial rise in poverty, (b) greater inequality, (c) the emergence of a group of "new poor" (those who were not poor in the first quarter of 2020 but have become poor since), and (d) changes in the labor market at both the intensive (how hard people work) and extensive (how many people work) margins.

- Besides the pandemic, some countries are struggling with (a) inflation, (b) macroeconomic crises, (c) food insecurity, and (d) fragility and conflict (with large refugee populations).

- There is a risk that recoveries will further increase inequality, given that the informal sector, in which many less well-off people work, tends to recover more slowly.

- More pandemics will occur, along with bigger, more frequent climate change shocks; hence, there is a need for better protection of people and livelihoods and greater resilience.

Given that the region faces various degrees of pandemic-related challenges, as well as other reform challenges, policy interventions will need to be tailor-made for each country. The report's assessments on changes in employment, income, consumption, living standards, and inequality should help guide policy makers and other stakeholders to design policies to minimize escalations in poverty and to provide income and social support to those who were worst hit, albeit with fiscal prudence. Top policy options center on stepping up vaccination programs, resuscitating economic activity, rethinking the approach to the informal sector, boosting resilience to future shocks, and improving data quality and transparency. In a sense, this crisis offers MENA a rare opportunity to correct structural imbalances while battling a pandemic.

An Innovative Approach to Taking MENA's Pulse

COVID-19 has affected, and continues to affect, poverty and inequality through four channels, which factor in monetary and nonmonetary

FIGURE O.2

COVID-19 Affected Poverty and Inequality through Four Channels

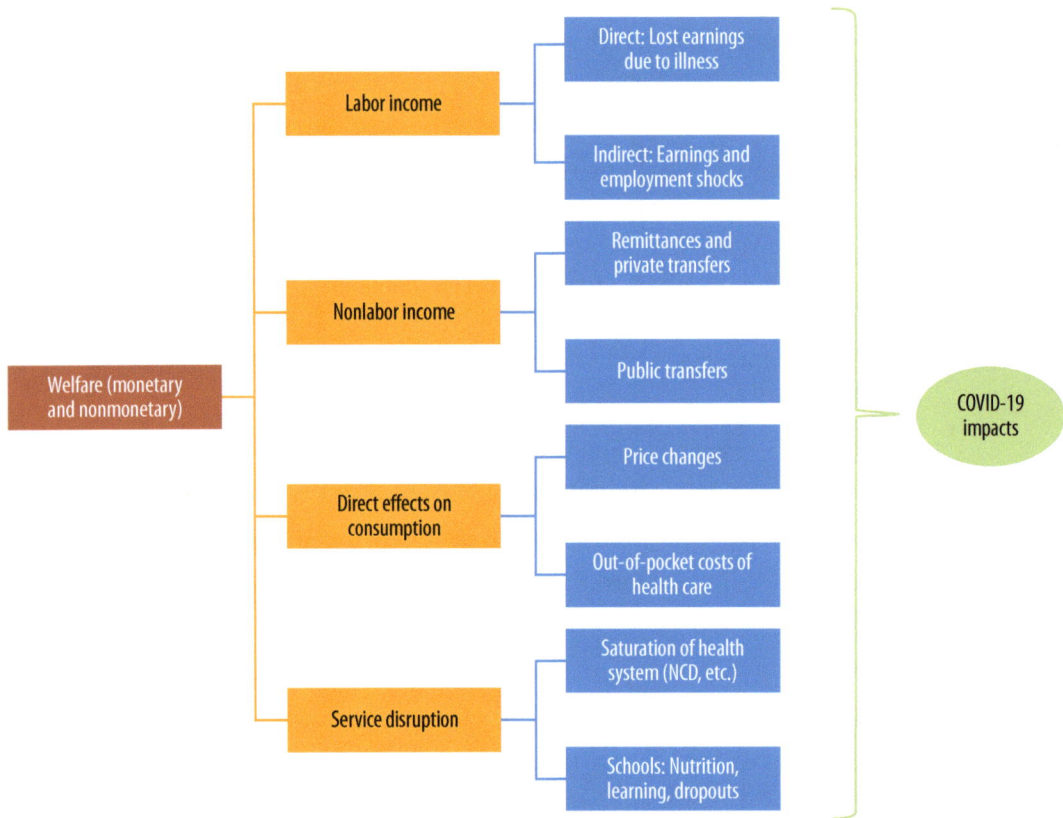

Source: World Bank 2020.
Note: NCD = noncommunicable diseases.

approaches to analysis (figure O.2). The first is the labor income channel, which includes both direct loss of earnings as a result of illness and indirect impacts on earnings caused by employment shocks, such as reduced work and reduced wages. The second is the nonlabor income channel, which pertains to loss of remittances, public transfers, and support payments. The third is the consumption channel, which is directly affected by price changes and sudden out-of-pocket expenditures on health care in the absence of insurance. The fourth channel is through service disruption, which covers nutrition (for example, because of the unavailability of certain food items) and learning.

Of these four channels, labor income is particularly important in this report, because sanitation and lockdown measures directly hamper economic activities, causing a loss of jobs or restricted work activities. Those who lack a steady flow of income—the unemployed or those not actively engaged in work—can be adversely affected not only by costs of food but also health care and education, which in turn have long-run consequences for the labor force. The labor income channel also holds great significance for the poor and bottom 40 percent of the distribution, who rely on wages or self-employed income and lack savings or alternative support.

This report uses two methodological approaches—telephonic surveys and microsimulations—to take the pulse of how households in MENA have been faring during the pandemic, especially in terms of labor income and overall welfare.

Telephonic surveys. The first approach presents analyses from multiple rounds of high-frequency telephonic surveys that take stock of the situation in various countries at different points in time. These surveys were conducted between April and December 2020. In some countries, they were done in the earliest months of COVID-19, in others during the height of the lockdown, and in still others after lockdowns ended, adding more depth to the results.

The interviews, which were conducted with adult household members, facilitate an understanding of self-reported changes in welfare (income, access to services, jobs, and food security). The data pertain to multiple countries and economies: Djibouti, the Arab Republic of Egypt, Iraq, Lebanon, Libya, Morocco, Tunisia, and the West Bank and Gaza. Results from many of these phone surveys can be found on the COVID-19 Household Monitoring Dashboard and the COVID-19 Business Pulse Survey Dashboard,[1] which provide an insight into the socioeconomic impacts of COVID-19 on households and individuals across regions. An advantage of these surveys is that they reflect people's experiences directly. A disadvantage is that the surveys are unable to answer questions, at least directly, on the consequences of poverty and inequality. For that, we rely on microsimulations.

Microsimulations. The second approach employs microsimulation techniques to arrive at estimates under different assumptions and scenarios. Each simulation uses a slightly different approach, but generically speaking, each one combines information on GDP growth projections by sector, using household survey data—especially the job characteristics of respondents—to impute the loss of employment and income. This calculation, in turn, allows the simulation of the impacts of COVID-19 (or of the mitigation measures) on consumption, poverty, and inequality. In this report, the simulations pertain to the Islamic Republic of Iran, Lebanon, Tunisia, and the West Bank and Gaza.

Besides the telephonic surveys and microsimulations, this report draws heavily on routine country surveys: national household surveys; national surveys on the budget, consumption, and household standard of living; labor force surveys; and household expenditure and income surveys. For refugee information, the data come from World Bank surveys of refugee and host communities. In addition, the COVID-19 Business Pulse Survey Dashboard and the COVID-19 Household Monitoring Dashboard provide information about both the impact on the operations of firms during the pandemic and the public support they have received. In this overview we selectively draw on the various surveys to corroborate evidence on labor patterns obtained from households. The surveys were conducted in the MENA region between July and August 2020 and are available for firms in Algeria, Djibouti, Jordan, Morocco, Tunisia, and the West Bank and Gaza.

Message 1: COVID-19 Is Hitting Some Groups Harder Than Others

The report's first message underscores the uneven nature of the pandemic's impacts, with some groups experiencing hardship more than others. What is particularly worrisome is that in MENA—the only region that has been experiencing rising levels of poverty since 2013—our assessment has found ample evidence that COVID-19 aggravated poverty in the region and increased preexisting inequalities.

How the Labor Market Has Adjusted

At root, the problem affecting the labor market is income loss, in large part because of work stoppages that began early in the pandemic. For MENA as a whole, the average work stoppage is about 23 percent—similar to other regions, except for Latin America, which is close to 50 percent. These stoppages led to significant job losses, with a significant share of MENA firms reporting that they reduced their number of permanent employees (for example, 17 percent in Algeria and 14 percent in the West Bank and Gaza). Even so, the share of MENA firms that laid off workers seems to be less than in some other regions, such as Latin America and Sub-Saharan Africa.

Overall, firms in MENA have been trying to hold on to their permanent workforce by making adjustments at both their intensive and extensive margins—including through more leave (often without pay), reduced work hours, lower salaries, and fewer temporary workers. This tightening can be seen, in part, in the decline in the intensity of work that is reported by households and can be found throughout MENA. During wave 1, the decline was most pronounced in Egypt, where 76 percent of those who worked the week before the survey reported that they worked less than usual, followed by Tunisia, where 66 percent worked

FIGURE O.3

Intensity of Work Fell Sharply throughout MENA during the Early Months of COVID-19

Change in intensity of work, by share of all workers (%)

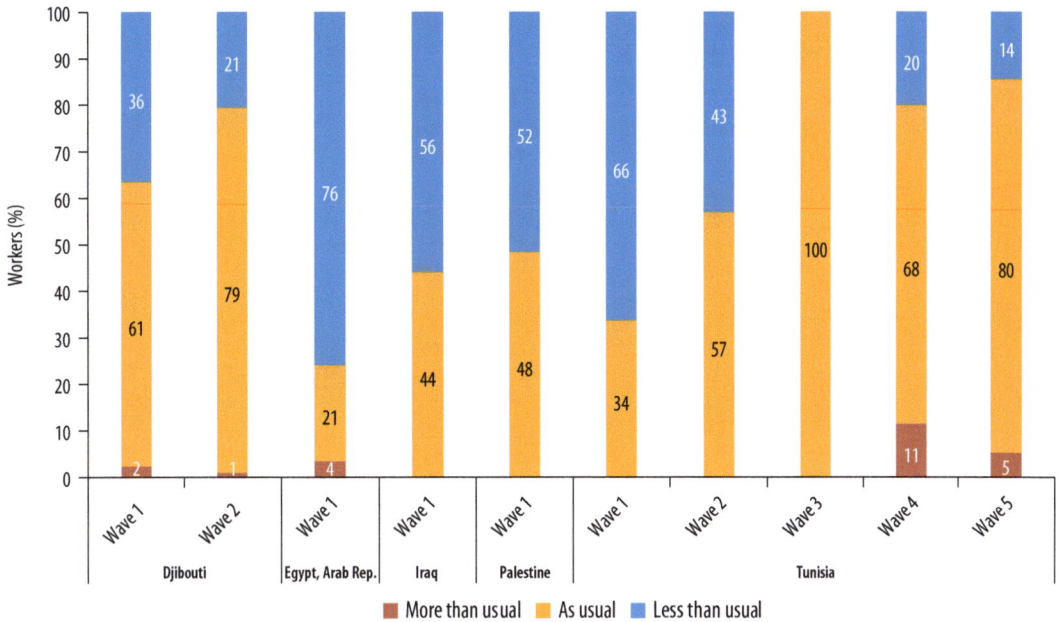

Source: MENA Harmonized Database of High Frequency Phone Surveys.

less (figure O.3). In fact, all but one of the countries surveyed were above 50 percent during wave 1.

The impact of the pandemic is further corroborated by trends in hours and wages reported in the Business Pulse Surveys: 14 percent of firms in Tunisia reported fewer working hours; 40 percent of firms in Morocco and Tunisia reported being forced to grant leave to their workers; and Tunisian firms reported a decrease in wages of 16 percent. Noteworthy, though, is that at the regional level, the percentage of firms citing fewer hours is the lowest in MENA (9 percent) and the highest in Sub-Saharan Africa (42 percent). Similarly, the percentage of firms reporting lower wages is the lowest in MENA (12 percent) and the highest in Sub-Saharan Africa (31 percent).

An exception seems to be the West Bank and Gaza. Not only did 20 percent of previously employed main income earners lose their jobs during COVID-19, but many of those who remained employed saw their incomes decline as they ended up working less or not at all. Even those who continued to work full time (35 percent of workers in the West Bank and 50 percent of workers in Gaza) ended up being paid less than before the pandemic (figure O.4).

FIGURE O.4

Lower Engagement in Work Meant Lower Incomes in the West Bank and Gaza

Share of households faced with lower income during lockdown, by main income earner's engagement in work activities (%)

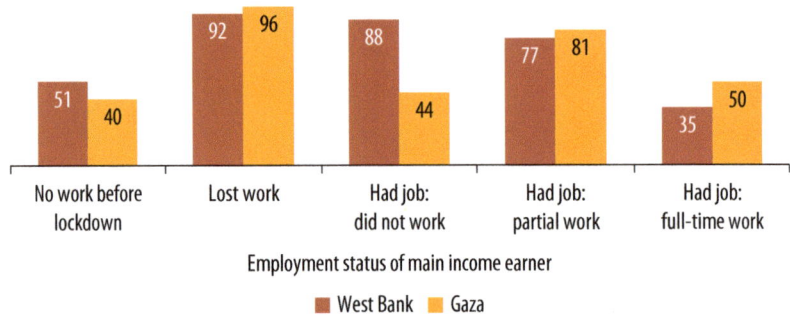

Employment status of main income earner

■ West Bank   ■ Gaza

Source: World Bank staff calculations based on the Rapid Assessment Phone Survey 2020.

Data from the COVID-19 Household Monitoring Dashboard also demonstrate that the speed of recovery can be fast. In Tunisia, 54 percent of respondents in October 2020 reported that they were currently employed (a month after the lockdown had ended), compared with 22 percent in May 2020 (at the height of the lockdown). Other countries corroborate that the recovery can be speedy. In October, 77 percent of Djiboutian respondents reported having a current job, compared with 59 percent in July. In Iraq, employment recovered from 61 percent in August to 69 percent in October. Nonetheless, recovery was never complete, a fact that is confirmed by the Business Pulse Surveys, which show a persistent decline in total sales for firms. This shortfall, combined with a prolonged pandemic episode, now poses a risk of long-term job loss for MENA firms.

Impact on Poverty and Inequality

The drop in income and living standards throughout MENA has been most intensely felt by the poorest. In Tunisia, the bottom 40 percent reported being the most affected compared with prepandemic levels in four rounds of phone surveys (mid-May to mid-October 2020) (figure O.5). The evidence points to a severe decline in household welfare as the pandemic unfolded, and it extended well beyond the end of restrictions on individual mobility. A similar pattern was found in Egypt during waves 1 and 2, with the bottom 40 percent of households being most affected.

Living Standards Drop the Most from Prepandemic Levels for Tunisia's Bottom 40 Percent

Household-level self-reported change in living standards, by prepandemic quintile and survey round

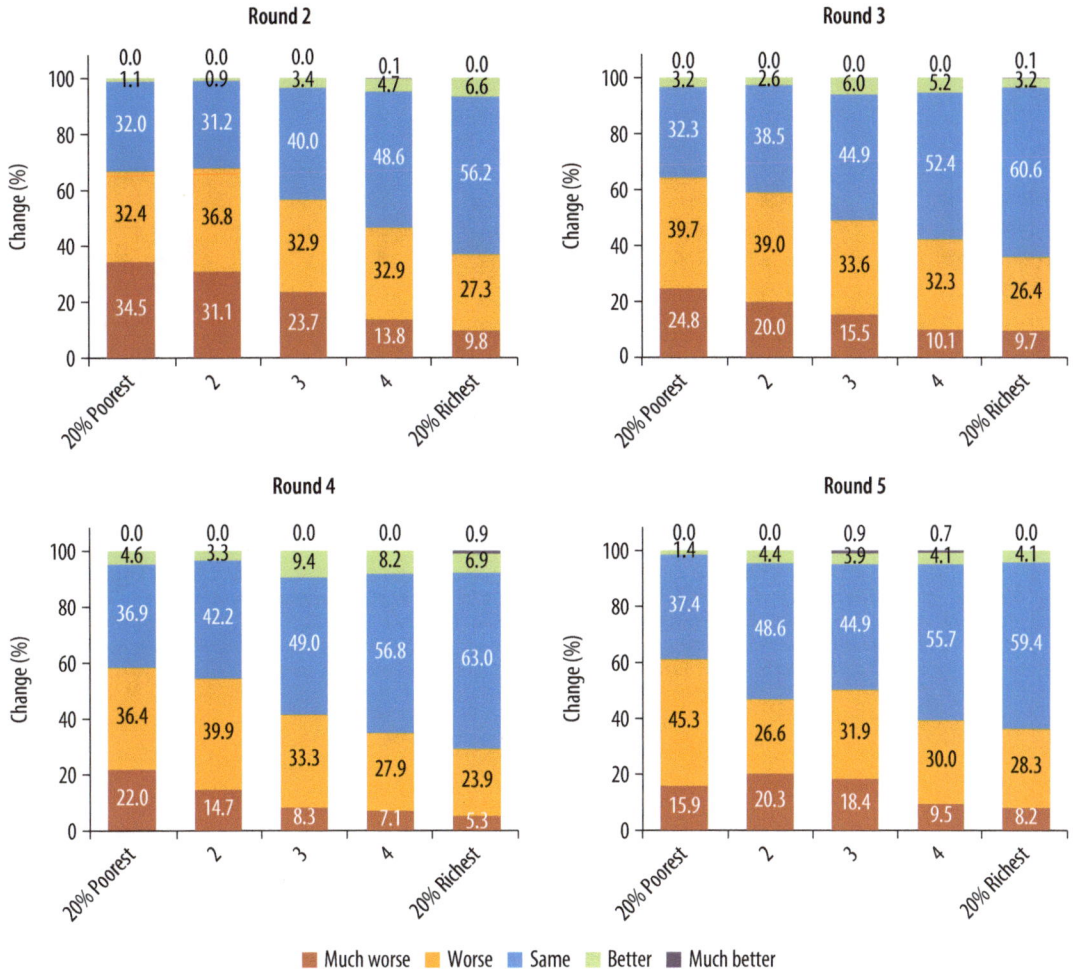

Source: Data compiled from the Enquête téléphonique auprès des ménages pour étudier et suivre impact du COVID-19 sur le quotidien des Tunisiens (survey conducted by the National Institute of Statistics and World Bank).
Note: Round 2 was conducted from May 15 to 21; round 3, June 8–15; round 4, June 22–30; and round 5, October 4–16.

Given that a loss of income feeds both directly (lost earnings due to illness) and indirectly (earnings or employment shock) into poverty and inequality, this report is able to estimate poverty levels in the four sample countries and economies using microsimulations to see changes from 2019 to 2020 (table O.1). The results show that poverty rates in MENA will increase significantly (depending on the country or economy, anything between 5 and 35 percentage points), particularly in countries like

TABLE O.1

Microsimulations Estimate Generalized Rises in Poverty and Inequality

		Tunisia	Islamic Republic of Iran	West Bank and Gaza	Lebanon
Latest estimates from survey data	Survey year	NSHBCSL 2015	HEIS 2018–19	PECS 2016–17 and LFS 2016–20	SRHCS 2015–16
	Poverty	National poverty is 15.2 percent in 2015.	National poverty is 15.2 percent in 2018–19.	National poverty is 29.3 percent in 2016.	National poverty is 27.4 percent in 2011.
	Impacts of poverty	In 2020 poverty is projected to rise by 7.3 percentage points (to 22.5 percent) in the optimistic scenario and by 11.9 points (to 27.1 percent) in the pessimistic one.	In 2020, poverty is projected to rise by 20 percentage points to 35.2 percent, with income loss and inflation each accounting for 10 points.	In 2019, poverty rose to 32.8 percent for the West Bank and Gaza. In 2020, it is projected to rise to 34.9 percent. This breaks down into a rise from 53.0 to 59.2 percent for Gaza, and from 13.9 to 19.2 percent for the West Bank.	In 2020, for nationals, poverty is estimated to rise by 13 percentage points, and for 2021 by an additional 15 percentage points. For refugees, the increase is an estimated 39 percentage points in 2020 and 52 percentage points in 2021.
	Impacts on inequality	Gini index rises from 37 to 39 percent in scenario 1 (optimistic) and to 41.4 percent in scenario 2 (pessimistic).	Gini index rises from 41 to 43 percent.	Gini index rises from 33 to 34 percent.	Not available.

Source: NSHBCSL = National Survey on Household Budget, Consumption and Standard of Living; HEIS = Household Income and Expenditure Survey; PECS = Palestinian Expenditure and Consumption Survey; LFS = Labor Force Survey; SRHCS= Syrian Refugees and Host Communities.
Note: For Tunisia, in the optimistic scenario, activity is assumed to recover gradually as caseloads decline and social distancing efforts are relaxed, enticing households to increase consumption of contact-intensive services; in the pessimistic scenario, COVID-19 outbreaks persist, restrictions on movement are extended or reintroduced, and disruptions to economic activity are prolonged.

the Islamic Republic of Iran, Iraq,[2] and Lebanon, where COVID-19 is compounding other economic ills, and that inequality will widen rapidly.

The phone surveys demonstrate that the degree of losses varies across households, based on socioeconomic characteristics like wealth, gender, employment sectors, nature of employment contracts, and location (urban or rural). Poorer people are particularly vulnerable for two reasons: they face a greater risk of exposure to infection and the economic effects of COVID-19 affect them disproportionately. The phone surveys bear this out. Poor people are more likely to live in cramped conditions, with worse options for preventive measures such as regular handwashing, and they have less money to spend on masks or gloves. They are more likely to live in multigenerational households, which increases the transmission risks to vulnerable elderly who cannot be isolated from interactions with others in the homes. When they work, they are more likely to be engaged in client-facing activities and less likely to receive adequate protective equipment. They also tend to have more underlying health conditions.

The most vulnerable (those in poor or almost-poor households) have been employed in sectors that have felt the highest impact of the pandemic: extractive industries, tourism (including hotels, cafes, and restaurants), retail trade, transport, commerce, and construction. These are the sectors where, typically, informal daily-wage earners or those on contractual (temporary) jobs are employed and where the options of telecommuting or remote working are not available. Women and refugees have been more severely affected by job losses than men and nationals. In Djibouti, 7 percent of refugees living in urban areas reported losing their job relative to the previous week, versus 3 percent for nationals. This outcome exacerbates existing vulnerabilities, as it adds to the 25 percent of refugees who were not working (compared with 11 percent for nationals).

Message 2: COVID-19 Is Just One of the Severe Socioeconomic Challenges Facing the Region

The report's second finding highlights that—making matters worse— COVID-19 is occurring at a time when many countries are grappling with other severe problems, such as inflation, macroeconomic crises, food insecurity, fragility, and conflict (with large numbers of refugees to host), as in the following examples:

- In Lebanon, economic loss has been estimated at a quarter of its 2019 GDP due to COVID-19, but mostly because of the generalized economic collapse. Price levels shot up to about 145 percent by end-2020, and even higher—around 402 percent—for food price inflation (figure O.6), largely because of Lebanon's import dependence and currency devaluation, on top of the pandemic's effects.

- In the Islamic Republic of Iran, GDP per capita growth was –7.0 percent in 2018–19 and –7.7 percent in 2019–20, although some recovery is expected for 2020–21. Inflation, which had started to drop from its 2018 spike, rose again in 2019/20, hitting 41.2 percent, and is continuing to climb.[3] Because many key staples are imported, food prices are especially exposed. Inflation, combined with income loss during the pandemic, is driving up poverty (figure O.7).

The pandemic has increased households' level of stress about access to food, especially for the poorest, raising questions about potentially serious malnutrition problems ahead. In the West Bank and Gaza, 65 percent of households reported worries about not having enough food to eat, as did 40 percent in Djibouti, and 33 percent in Tunisia. This worry is not surprising, given that they are grappling with challenges related to labor

FIGURE O.6

Lebanon's Inflation Has Soared, Especially for Food Prices

Monthly changes in inflation in Lebanon for 2020 (%)

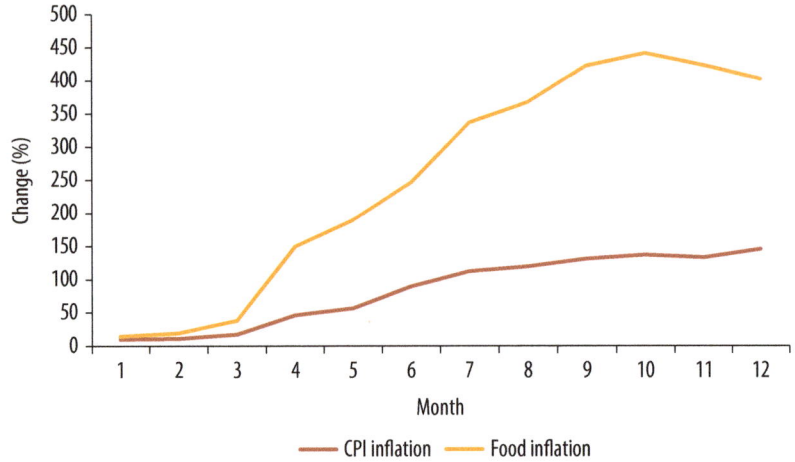

Source: World Bank calculations based on Consumer Price Index (CPI) 2020 data from Central Administration of Statistics, Lebanon.

FIGURE O.7

Islamic Republic of Iran's Inflation, on Top of Income Loss, Further Increases Poverty

Simulated impacts on poverty, changes (%)

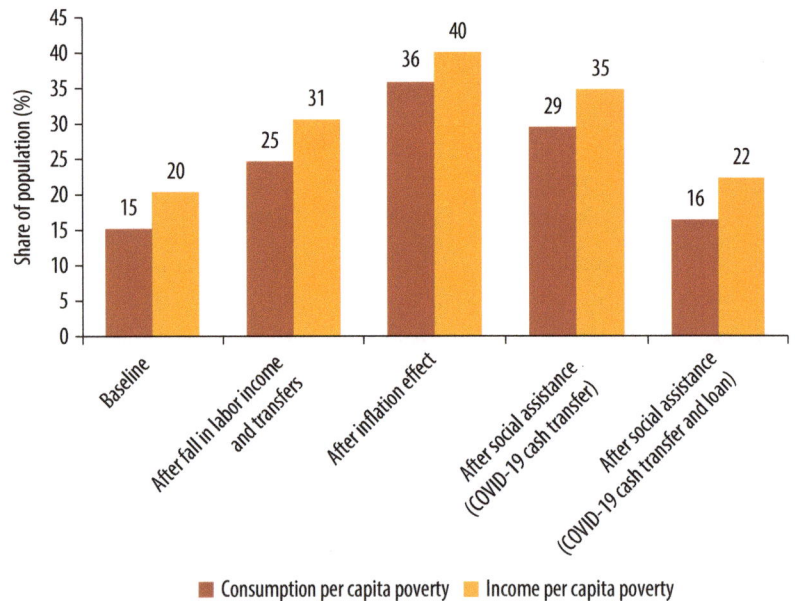

Source: World Bank calculations based on HEIS 2018–19.
Note: Simulations use per capita poverty rates (US$5.50 2011 PPP).

force participation and uncertainty about when the pandemic might end. Moreover, in the West Bank and Gaza, 43 percent of households reduced their food intake because of not enough resources; in Djibouti and Tunisia, the numbers were 27 percent and 15 percent, respectively.

A further complication arises for MENA countries struggling with conflict and/or hosting large numbers of refugees, with nationals doing far better than refugees. In Djibouti, phone surveys (December 2020 through February 2021) show that while the situation is generally improving for the national households, refugees in refugee villages face worse employment conditions than those living in urban areas or than urban nationals. They were less likely to be employed prior to the pandemic, were more likely to lose their job during the pandemic, and do not exhibit similar signs of recovery.

Message 3: Economies Are at Risk of Unequal Recovery

The report's third message points to a risk that over the next few years, as economies in the region recover, some groups and segments of society will fare better than others. Before the lockdown, per capita GDP was estimated to be about US$14,000 in the region, then dropped to a little above US$13,000 during 2020, and is expected to take up until 2024 or 2025 to bounce back to US$14,000.

Moreover, given the uneven distributional effects of COVID-19, there is a substantial risk of an unequal recovery, whereby many of the disadvantaged and vulnerable—especially those in the informal sector without any social or health insurance—will be left behind. Plus, even once the recovery is under way, poor and vulnerable people will continue to experience the effects of prolonged income shocks and diminished job opportunities. The previously unemployed will reenter the job market with fewer skills, more debt, and worse health. There will also be intergenerational consequences, mostly through the education channel. Children of poor and vulnerable households will pay the highest price, and learning disruption associated with school closures now will lead to human capital loss and higher educational and income inequality in the future.

Thus, it is crucial to get a head start and tamp down the amplification of negative effects on the well-being of the disadvantaged and vulnerable. One way to do this is through measures that are targeted to ensure inclusion of the poor in the road to recovery and to avoid inequality in the recovery process. In Tunisia, for example, the government introduced a range of measures early in the pandemic, including measures to help (a) needy families (granting TD 50 and TD 60 in April and May 2020, respectively, to 260,000 households); (b) families with limited income (giving 370,000 households TD 200 in April and May 2020); (c) families caring for a person without family support (giving 779 households TD 200 in April 2020); (d) those with low retirement pensions (giving 140,000 households TD 100 in April 2020, increased to TD 180 in August); and (e) a combination of these (excluding families with limited income, giving 301,149 households TD 200 in May 2020). These programs mostly targeted around 140,000 to 370,000 households. The microsimulations show that although poverty is expected to rise from 13.7 percent before COVID-19 to 20.9 percent after COVID-19, mitigation measures would hold the increase to 20.2 percent (table O.2). Such measures are also likely to help in restoring trust and a social contract between citizens and the state in MENA countries. However, Tunisia's case raises the question of how MENA countries' proposed (or current) mitigation measures could be strengthened to make a greater impact on reducing the expected increase in poverty.

A second way to prevent the amplification of negative effects on the disadvantaged and vulnerable is through public assistance. So far, pro-poor public assistance has been used to mitigate the negative impact of COVID-19 on household welfare—reaching around 10 percent of households in Egypt (wave 1) and as many as 37 percent in Djibouti (waves 1, 2, and 3 of phone surveys) (table O.3). But MENA has not been able to expand social and economic protections enough to adequately soften the blow. As a result, although some of the most vulnerable (including refugees) that were already beneficiaries of social transfers ended up being relatively protected during the crisis, many of the new poor failed to obtain any coverage.

To help firms overcome the pandemic and avoid bigger disruptions in the labor market, governments and policy makers have granted public support, largely in the form of wage subsidies. For MENA overall, the

TABLE O.2

Mitigation Measures Are Estimated to Decrease the Impact of COVID-19 in Tunisia

	Before COVID-19	After COVID-19	After mitigation measure	Difference (without mitigation measure)	Difference (with mitigation measure)
Extreme poverty	2.9	7.4	6.9	4.5	4.0
Poverty	13.7	20.9	20.2	7.3	6.5
Poverty gap (lower)	0.5	2.0	0.7	1.5	1.3
Poverty gap (upper)	3.2	6.4	4.2	3.2	1.0
Inequality	37.0	39.5	39.2	2.5	2.2

Source: EBCNV 2015 (Enquête Nationale sur le Budget, la Consommation et le Niveau de Vie des Ménages).
Note: Simulations are based on the announced measures, because there is no access to information on actual spending under these measures. For Tunisia, in the optimistic scenario, activity is assumed to recover gradually as caseloads decline and social distancing efforts are relaxed, enticing households to increase consumption of contact-intensive services. In the pessimistic scenario, COVID-19 outbreaks persist, restrictions on movement are extended or reintroduced, and disruptions to economic activity are prolonged.

TABLE O.3

Public Assistance in Djibouti, Egypt, and Tunisia Is Being Targeted at the Poorest

Public assistance by quintiles, by share of population (%)

		Quintile based on PMT score					
		1	2	3	4	5	Total
Djibouti	Wave 1	49	37	33	28	0	37
	Wave 2	37	37	30	25	0	32
	Wave 3	30	30	28	20	0	28
Egypt, Arab Rep.	Wave 1	17	9	8	5	3	10
Tunisia	Wave 1	35	25	12	10	5	15
	Wave 2	25	22	10	11	6	13

Source: MENA Harmonized Database of High Frequency Phone Surveys.
Note: For the Arab Republic of Egypt, public assistance refers to the national cash transfer program, Takaful and Karama. PMT = proxy means test (used to proxy income).

share of firms receiving or expecting to receive support was 25 percent, which compares well with other regions. Although MENA is below Europe and Central Asia, at 46 percent, and East Asia and Pacific, at 28 percent, it is above others (South Asia, Sub-Saharan Africa, and Latin America and the Caribbean), which are at less than 20 percent. However, the Business Pulse Surveys suggest that the support is reaching only a minority of firms (figure O.8), mostly from wage subsidies.

A third way to keep negative effects on the disadvantaged and vulnerable from being amplified is through greater use of digital technology, given the changing nature of work in MENA and the rest of the world. Because of the imposed social confinement, several jobs have demanded an acceleration in the process of digitizing activities and incorporating remote working schemes. However, the Business Pulse Surveys point to much more progress on the use of digital platforms than on digital sales.

For digital platforms, firms surveyed reported an overall 11 percent of employees working remotely at the time of the interview. Moreover, in Jordan, 38 percent of firms reported having started or increased the use of digital platforms, followed by 32 percent in Tunisia, 30 percent in Morocco, and 23 percent in the West Bank and Gaza, giving MENA economies an overall average of 31 percent of firms. This level is close to that of South Asia and a bit ahead of both Sub-Saharan Africa and Europe and Central Asia, but behind East Asia and Pacific (figure O.9, panel a).

However, MENA fared less well in terms of its share of monthly sales using digital platforms (only 4 percent). By country, both Jordan and Tunisia were at 4 percent—a reflection of either the type of firms or industries or less country focus on going digital. MENA's level is

FIGURE O.8

MENA's Public Support Was Chiefly in Wage Subsidies

Share of firms that received support, by type of support (%)

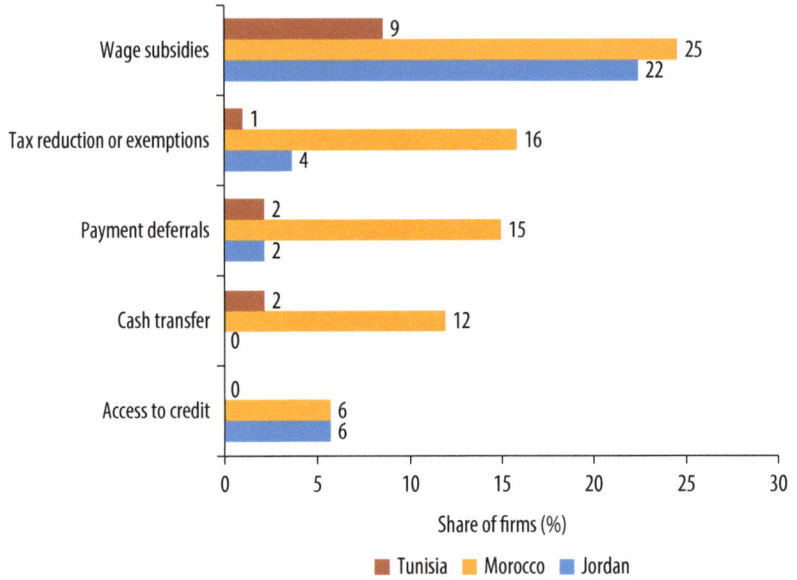

Source: World Bank COVID-19 Business Pulse Survey Dashboard.

FIGURE O.9

MENA Steps Up Use of Digital Platforms and Eases into Digital Sales

Use of digital platforms in response to shutdowns, by region

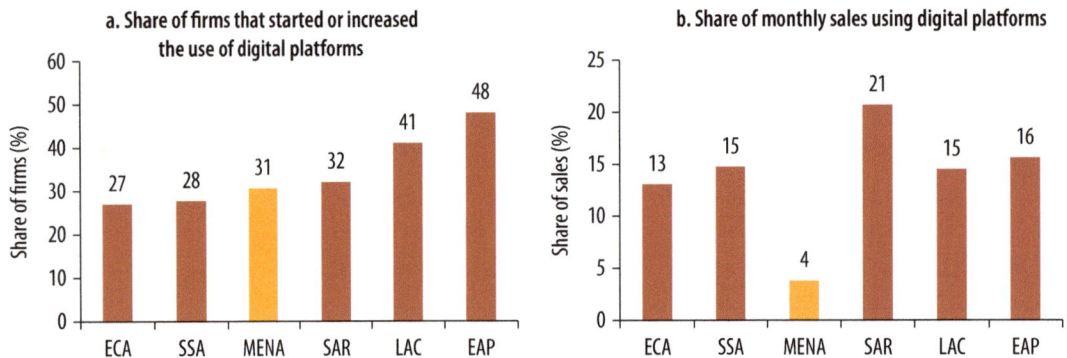

a. Share of firms that started or increased the use of digital platforms

b. Share of monthly sales using digital platforms

Source: World Bank COVID-19 Business Pulse Survey Dashboard.
Note: EAP = East Asia and Pacific; ECA = Europe and Central Asia; LAC = Latin America and the Caribbean; MENA = Middle East and North Africa; SAR = South Asia; SSA = Sub-Saharan Africa.

far below the average of firms in all other regions, which ranged from 13 percent in Europe and Central Asia to 21 percent in South Asia (figure O.9, panel b). That said, MENA's low ranking highlights a large opportunity area in the changing nature of work in the region.

Message 4: The Region Must Be Better Prepared for Future Shocks

The report's fourth message is that as the global community starts to put COVID-19 in its rearview mirror, it does so with the knowledge that this pandemic is not over, nor is this the last one it will need to contend with. Climate change, for instance, is bound to bring with it more severe and more frequent weather events. Thus, by identifying the socioeconomic impact and other distributional effects on welfare from COVID-19, we will be better placed to ensure that future crises and disasters do not result in setbacks for hard-won gains in alleviating poverty and inequality.

It is beyond the scope of this report to make detailed recommendations for MENA countries and economies. But it is evident from our results that one critical element will be resuscitating economic activity to unlock the region's potential, with a focus on a more conducive environment for the private sector and entrepreneurship. Another critical element is rethinking the approach to the informal sector, which engages a majority of MENA's labor force but lacks formal contracts and insurance. In addition, three program areas stand out for countries to prioritize.

First, step up vaccination programs. In the short run, this is a top priority for MENA countries to help contain the pandemic, stimulate the economy, and protect spending on other routine health services—especially for the poor and informal workers who lack social and health insurance. Key hurdles include securing and administering vaccines to a majority of their populations, given limited vaccine manufacturing capacity and limited fiscal space. Little help can be expected from private insurance. This challenge means that vaccination programs need to be efficient and transparent. In Lebanon, for instance, reports of cronyism in the vaccine rollout have raised concerns about its fairness, which could harm international aid for financing its vaccination program (Cornish n.d.). On the other hand, the vaccine rollout in Morocco has expanded significantly, with 26.7 percent of the population fully vaccinated by July 2021 (Roser and Ortiz-Ospina 2021).

Second, boost resilience to future shocks. This focus is essential to prepare MENA for future crises and disasters. The phone surveys reviewed for this report suggest that countries with more elaborate registration systems (like Djibouti or Morocco) were able to provide better targeted assistance. Similarly, subpopulations (such as refugees) covered by existing assistance systems have been found to be more protected against shocks caused by COVID-19 than populations at large. These findings suggest that one tool that deserves attention is Identification for Development (ID4D). Facilitated by digital identification (like civil registration), ID4D is designed to help people access services through digital identification systems. It can help build an inclusive database and better identify and target beneficiaries by addressing issues such as poverty, gender equality and female empowerment, inequality, financial inclusion, health insurance coverage, and safe migration. Such a tool would be particularly helpful in MENA, given that it is difficult to track and account for activities and workers in the informal sector, not to mention maintain official records and evidence.

Third, improve data quality and transparency. Improved data and transparency are urgently needed to inform decision-making about the economic recovery and to improve resilience to future shocks. Good policies cannot be made in a vacuum and without evidence. They require publicly accessible data and engagement with stakeholders. During the pandemic, the absence of data was strongly felt by leaders who did not know which sectors were most affected or which citizens were most vulnerable, yet they were forced to make decisions on that scant evidence. The crisis also underscored the importance of real-time data collection to facilitate timely response actions from governments.

This report aims to contribute to the data and evidence needed to inform recovery efforts. It does so in part by drawing on phone surveys implemented across the region, often in response to the crisis, in a remarkable data collection effort. Even so, the overwhelming sentiment remains one of data scarcity. More than 18 months since the onset of the pandemic, disaggregated information on the number of infected, hospitalized, or vaccinated people is almost impossible to obtain—as is up-to-date information on the socioeconomic impacts of the crisis. Given the region's long period of underinvestment in statistics, this lack of performance is unsurprising. However, now more than ever this low statistical capacity must be urgently addressed, and MENA now has a rare opportunity to seize the moment and do so.

Notes

1. COVID-19 Business Pulse Survey Dashboard (https://www.worldbank.org/en/data/interactive/2021/01/19/covid-19-business-pulse-survey-dashboard); COVID-19 Household Monitoring Dashboard (https://www.worldbank.org/en/data/interactive/2020/11/11/covid-19-high-frequency-monitoring-dashboard).

2. Iraqi simulations are not included in this report, but a paper coproduced by the World Bank and UNICEF finds that the initial lockdown and a sharp decline in oil prices increased the national poverty rate by 7 to 14 percentage points in the summer of 2020, from 20 percent in 2017. With the gradual opening of the economy and improved oil prices, poverty receded slightly by the end of 2020 and remained 6.7 percentage points above the 2017 level (under a mild scenario) (World Bank and UNICEF 2020).

3. World Bank data (https://data.worldbank.org/indicator/NY.GDP.PCAP.KD .ZG?locations=IR; https://data.worldbank.org/indicator/FP.CPI.TOTL .ZG?locations=IR).

References

Cornish, Chloe. n.d. "Lebanon's Queue Jumping Affair Threatens World Bank Vaccine Lifeline." *Financial Times*. https://www.ft.com/content/55d802dc -d5d4-424e-9c55-7dde3a0f7f50.

Roser, Max, and Esteban Ortiz-Ospina. 2021. COVID-19 Data Explorer (published online at OurWorldInData.org), https://ourworldindata.org /explorers/coronavirus-data-explorer.

World Bank. 2020. "Poverty and Distributional Impacts of COVID-19: Potential Channels of Impact and Mitigating Policies." World Bank, Washington, DC. https://www.worldbank.org/en/topic/poverty/brief/poverty-and -distributional-impacts-of-covid-19-potential-channels-of-impact-and -mitigating-policies.

World Bank. 2021. "MENA Economies Face Rapid Accumulation of Public Debt; Strong Institutions Will Be Key to Recovery." Press release, April 2, 2021. https://www.worldbank.org/en/news/press-release/2021/04/02 /strong-institutions-will-be-key-to-mena-recovery-amid-rapid-accumulation -of-public-debt.

World Bank and UNICEF (United Nations Children's Fund). 2020. "Assessment of COVID-19 Impact on Poverty and Vulnerability in Iraq." UNICEF, New York. https://www.unicef.org/iraq/media/1181/file/Assessment%20of%20 COVID-19%20Impact%20on%20Poverty%20and%20Vulnerability%20 in%20Iraq.pdf.

CHAPTER 1

Setting the Stage

Gladys Lopez-Acevedo, Stuti Manchanda, and
Jaime Alfonso Roche Rodríguez

Key Messages

- COVID-19, the fourth crisis to hit the Middle East and North Africa (MENA) in the past decade, is expected to have a significant socioeconomic impact on the region, along with large distributional consequences.

- Already, growth and welfare challenges have intensified: output in 2020 is estimated to have fallen by more than 5 percent in MENA, and 2021 forecasts suggest 7–8 million people will fall into extreme poverty.

- This is occurring in a region that has long been grappling with structural vulnerabilities, such as high unemployment among youth and women, inequality in education, low participation in global value chains, and a large informal sector.

- Lockdowns and workplace closures have contracted economic activity and widened inequalities by disproportionately affecting the poorest households, those who are largely employed in informal sectors, lack health insurance, and are more prone to infections as a result of cramped living conditions.

- Given that GDP per capita is unlikely to return to its pre-COVID-19 level before 2025, policy measures for the short run and long run need to be designed through a lens of equity, inclusion, and fiscal caution.

Introduction

The COVID-19 crisis is the fourth crisis to hit the Middle East and North Africa in the past decade, following the Arab uprisings, the 2014–16 decline in oil prices, and the 2019 resurgence of protests in countries that had escaped the first wave of protests in 2010–11 (Muasher and Yahya 2020). This crisis differs from the others because of its overall socioeconomic impact and its distributional consequences. Already, it has exacerbated a series of problems that characterized the region before the crisis—high shares of inactivity, especially among youth; inequality in education; high levels of informality; and large gaps in economic opportunities for women. In 2020, during the pandemic, about 80 percent of informal private sector employees and 68 percent of self-employed reported reduced work in many MENA countries, according to World Bank phone surveys.

The incidence and spread of the pandemic have inevitably affected the socioeconomic conditions in the region, derailing progress and intensifying economic woes. Increasingly, the evidence shows that the negative effects of COVID-19 are being disproportionally borne by those who, prepandemic, were already disadvantaged and vulnerable (Hill and Narayan 2020; Oxfam 2021). Using April 2020 growth forecasts from the World Economic Forum, Lakner et al. (2020) estimated that an additional 4 million people are expected to fall into extreme poverty in MENA as a result of the pandemic. The June 2020 Global Economic Prospects (GEP) forecasts raised this estimate to 5 million, and the January 2021 GEP forecasts further raised this estimate to 7–8 million.

Especially worrisome is that it will take many years before the region's economic activity springs back to pre-COVID-19 levels. Per capita GDP in MENA, which was estimated to be about US$14,000 before lockdown, dropped to just a little above US$13,000 during 2020 and is expected to take the next four or five years (by 2025) to bounce back to US$14,000. Meanwhile, the economic cost of COVID-19 in MENA is estimated at about US$227 billion. Further, infection rates have intensified, exerting greater pressure on health care, and fiscal support packages across MENA averaged 2.7 percent of GDP, adding to fiscal pressure.

At the global level, mortality from the pandemic stands as high as 2.6 million as of March 2021 (Schellekens and Wadhwa 2021). COVID-19 induced extreme poverty—the difference between poverty rates with the pandemic and without the pandemic—and is estimated to rise by about 88–115 million people compared with prepandemic levels. And lockdowns and mobility restrictions have accelerated economic recession and led to steep downgrades in growth projections. In 2020, worldwide economic output is estimated to have contracted by about 4.4 percent (IMF 2020). And economic projections confirm that extreme poverty will increase across the globe as a result of COVID-19 impacts, rising to as many as 150 million people by 2021, and upend the global trend toward less poverty.

Toward the end of 2020, David Malpass, president of the World Bank Group, stated in the foreword to *Poverty and Shared Prosperity 2020: Reversals of Fortune* that the pandemic is expected to cause more than 1.4 percent of the population to fall into extreme poverty, which will set back poverty reduction efforts by three years. As the report noted, COVID-19 increased poverty by 8.1 percent in 2020, compared with 2019. Furthermore, the poverty rate is expected to increase by about 1.4 to 1.9 percentage points (baseline scenario to downside scenario) in 2021 (Lakner 2020). However, this seems to be an underestimation for the MENA region, where estimates suggest a much higher increase in poverty (for example, 7.3–11.9 percentage points in Tunisia, 20 percentage points in the Islamic Republic of Iran, 13 percentage points for host communities in Lebanon, and 39 percentage points for refugees in Lebanon).

For MENA, a big part of the recovery problem is that even before the pandemic hit, countries in the region had been struggling with many structural issues, as evident in MENA's annual GDP growth rate of 1.4 percent over the past two decades—a level that was low relative to other regions. It has faced low employment, especially among its young population (close to 30 percent unemployed); its role in global value chains has been limited to low value added goods (and heavy dependence on oil exports); and its large public sector and bureaucracy have failed to provide a conducive business environment. Even food insecurity has been on the rise; in 2019, more than 30 percent of the global total of food insecure people (43 million of the 135 million) were in MENA.

Complicating matters is the fact that each country faces varying degrees of threats as well as reform challenges, necessitating tailor-made policies. In part, this variation reflects the fact that the region is a mix of high-income countries (Bahrain, Kuwait, Oman, Qatar, Saudi Arabia, and the United Arab Emirates); upper-middle-income countries (the Islamic Republic of Iran, Iraq, Jordan, Lebanon, and Libya); some lower-middle-income countries and economies (Algeria, the Arab Republic of Egypt, Morocco, Tunisia, and the West Bank and Gaza); and some low-income countries (the Syrian Arab Republic and the Republic of Yemen). In addition, although some have a heavy dependence on oil exports (Algeria, Gulf Cooperation Council countries, and the Islamic Republic of Iran), others have either a preexisting financial crisis (the Islamic

Republic of Iran and Lebanon) or protests and social unrest (Algeria, Lebanon, and Tunisia). Moreover, some are marked by fragility, conflict, and violence-related vulnerabilities, such as (a) high-intensity conflict in Libya and Syria, (b) medium-intensity conflict in Iraq and the Republic of Yemen, (c) social fragility in Lebanon and the West Bank and Gaza, and (d) spillover effects in Jordan and Lebanon. Furthermore, the region remains prone to climate risks, such as water scarcity, coastal flooding, desertification, and famine.

Against this backdrop, key questions for the region are: How does COVID-19 affect the welfare of individuals and households in MENA, and what are the key issues that policy makers should focus on to enable a quick and sustained economic convalescence? This report attempts to help answer these questions by focusing on the pandemic's impact on welfare. It furnishes impact estimates for different economic sectors and households across distribution classes, and it throws light on the channels through which they have been affected in different countries. Of the 19 countries and economies in MENA, this report focuses on those with available household-level data: Djibouti, Egypt, the Islamic Republic of Iran, Iraq, Lebanon, Libya, Morocco, Tunisia, and the West Bank and Gaza.[1]

Since the onset of COVID-19, many statistical agencies have started collecting data to assess the socioeconomic impacts of COVID-19 on households. One of the report's innovations lies in drawing on this household-level primary data, collected during the peak of the pandemic (as opposed to firm-level data) to facilitate an understanding of self-reported changes in welfare. Findings from many of these surveys can be found on the COVID-19 High Frequency Survey Global Dashboard.[2] In addition, the report uses microsimulations to assess not just the overall macroeconomic impact but also distributional implications on welfare and poverty in the selected MENA countries.

A key message of this report is that COVID-19 has created an economic slump and increased poverty and inequality, which will require both immediate short-run measures as well as long-term policy supports with an eye on equity and inclusion.

COVID-19-Induced Shocks

More than 5 million people had COVID-19 infections in the MENA region as of early February 2021. Among MENA countries, the Islamic Republic of Iran had the most confirmed cases, with about 1.5 million, followed by Iraq, and Morocco (figure 1.1). Governments in the region have moved quickly to contain COVID-19 since March 2020 by

FIGURE 1.1

The Islamic Republic of Iran Tops the List in Highest Number of COVID-19 Cases
Total number of COVID-19 cases in MENA

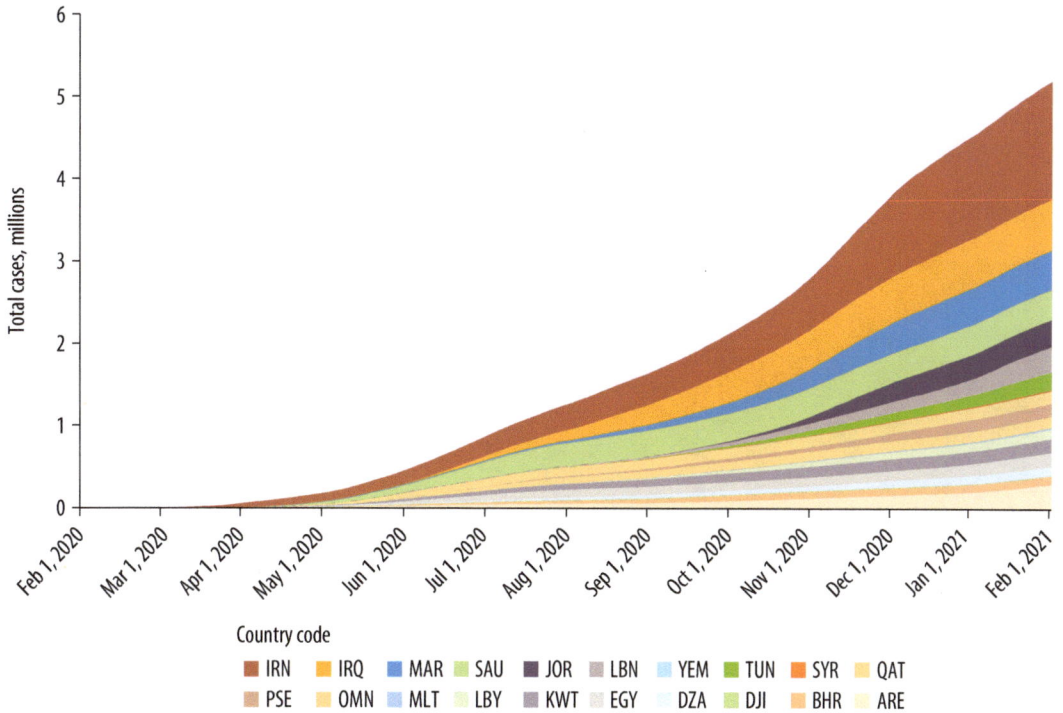

Source: World Bank calculations based on data from Our World in Data (Roser and Ortiz-Ospina 2021), https://ourworldindata.org/coronavirus
-data.

developing strict containment measures, which were implemented in the very early stages of the pandemic. These measures helped to limit the first wave of infections and were gradually reduced from June onward for some countries. In other countries, such as Lebanon and Morocco, more restrictions have been applied, leading to a higher stringency index than at the start of the pandemic (figure 1.2).

So far, the pandemic has triggered multiple demand and supply shocks to the economies of MENA. On the demand side, the worldwide lockdown disrupted demand for MENA exports, of which crude oil happens to be an integral component. Moreover, with a glut in the oil market, crude oil prices plummeted to a low of US$20 per barrel in April 2020, although a price rebound started in the summer and by early February 2021 was back up to pre-COVID-19 levels. Also problematic has been a disruption in tourism, which in many countries in the region is an important source of employment. On the supply side, some workers fell ill,

FIGURE 1.2

Stringency Index across Countries in MENA Shows Big Variations in Size and Timing of Containment Measures
Average stringency index

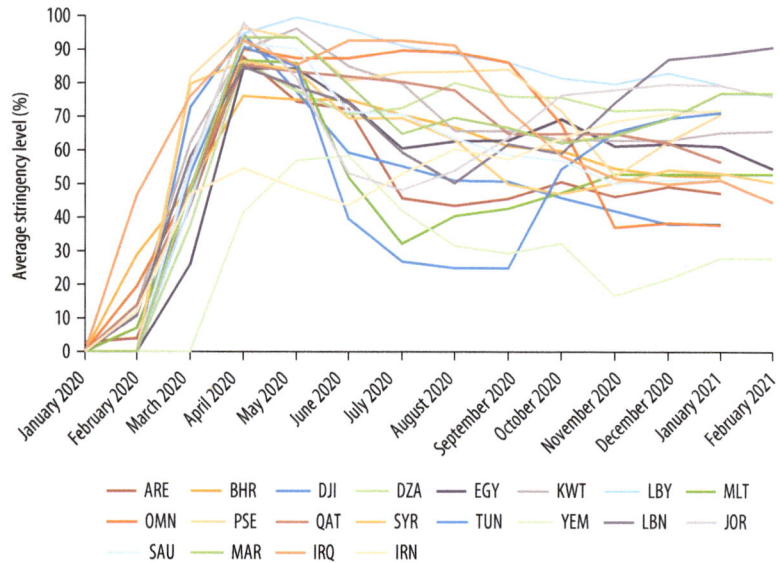

Source: World Bank calculations based on data from Our World in Data (Roser and Ortiz-Ospina 2021), https://ourworldindata.org/coronavirus-data.
Note: The stringency index is a composite measure based on nine response indicators, including school closures, workplace closures, and travel bans, rescaled to a value from 0 to 100 (100 = strictest). If policies vary at the subnational level, the index is shown as the response level of the strictest subregion. December data represent only until 10th of the month.

while others faced reduced mobility because of social confinement measures imposed by governments. These disruptions hit the self-employed and those in the informal sector in contractual jobs the most. Supply chains fell short because of disruptions in transportation and businesses, thereby heavily hampering economic activity.

Stringent workplace closures have been relaxed in many countries, but the current measures continue to have a widespread impact. Overall, about 80 percent of MENA's workers currently reside in countries with some sort of workplace closure measure in place (figure 1.3). This share reached a peak of more than 90 percent for a period of five months from April to September 2020, then slowly declined until end-October, after which it started to increase slightly again. Specifically, lockdowns of workplaces for all but essential workers (that is, the most stringent of possible measures) continue to affect a sizeable share of the global workforce. As of end-2020, almost 20 percent of the region's workers were living in countries with such lockdowns. More recently, the most stringent workplace closure measures have begun to be targeted at highly infected

FIGURE 1.3

Workplace Closures Are Still Widespread

Share of MENA region's employed in countries and economies with workplace closures (%)

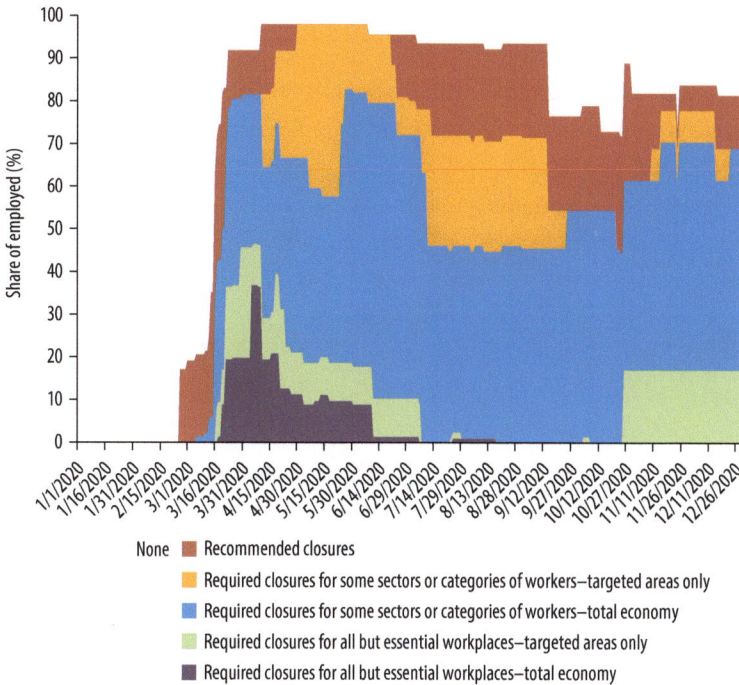

Source: ILO 2021.

areas in countries, rather than covering a country's entire economy. A further 50 percent of the region's workers were living in countries with required workplace closures for some sectors or categories of workers (again, with this type of closure increasingly being targeted at specific areas within a country), while just 10 percent of workers were living in countries that have only recommended workplace closures in place.

With a long period of workplace closure coupled with an already high unemployment rate in the region, opportunities and productivity for workers continue to be dismal. A recent study from the International Labour Organization (ILO 2021) reported that, in the region, the total estimated decline in working hours in 2020 was 9.1 percent, equivalent to 9 million full-time jobs, assuming a 48-hour work week. No labor force survey data covering the impact of the COVID-19 crisis were available in ILO data repositories for any country in the region at the time of producing the estimates.

The pandemic has disproportionately affected the welfare of poor households, amplifying existing inequalities. Those in self-employment and sectors where work cannot be done from home have been afflicted with either loss in employment or loss in income. Furthermore, those prone to catching the infection (those in poor households living in high-density areas and in cramped conditions) are also likely to suffer loss of income as a result of sickness, or have lower disposable income on account of unexpected out-of-pocket health care expenditures. Restrictions on labor mobility and disruptions in supply chains have created a shortage leading to food price inflation. And estimates show that, despite some variations across MENA countries, prices for some main staples have increased by more than 20 percent. Further, school disruptions also affect the poor households most, as they lack digital technological resources to access education.

But the inequality-increasing effect of COVID-19 should not come as a surprise. In fact, past pandemics, such as SARS, MERS, H1N1, Ebola, and Zika, exacerbated inequality, and the effects did not fade over time (Barro et al. 2020; Beaunoyer, Dupéré, and Guitton 2020; Bowleg 2020; Furceri et al. 2020).[3] Furceri et al. (2020) find that pandemics have caused the Gini index to increase by 1.25 percentage points, on average, in the five years following their occurrence. In addition, COVID-19 affects educational opportunities in a way that most affects children from the least advantaged households. UNESCO (2020) estimates that the global progress made on children's access to education in the past 20 years will be reversed by the effects of the COVID-19 pandemic, resulting in increased poverty and inequality.

What is different with COVID-19 is the scale of the pandemic and hence its impact. Also, it is not completely over and continues to dampen economic activities to some extent. Thus, the sanitation and containment measures, by dampening demand and supply, have prompted a slowdown in MENA's economic output, which the World Bank estimates dropped by more than 5 percent in 2020 (World Bank 2021). The resulting loss of disposable income and welfare is pushing more people below the poverty line. While MENA has been able to curb extreme poverty, there is widespread economic insecurity, given that more than 40 percent of the population have incomes below US$5.50 per day (at 2011 PPP). Moreover, MENA is the only region that has been experiencing rising levels of poverty since 2013 (figure 1.4). And its middle-class population has been stagnant at 15 percent since 2011. At the same time, the region's chronic low growth continues to be slower than its population growth— a situation that not only creates unemployment but also makes it tough to reap the benefits of a demographic dividend.

FIGURE 1.4

MENA Is the Only Region with Increasing Poverty since 2013

Trends in poverty rates at the US$1.90-a-day poverty line, by region, 1990–2018

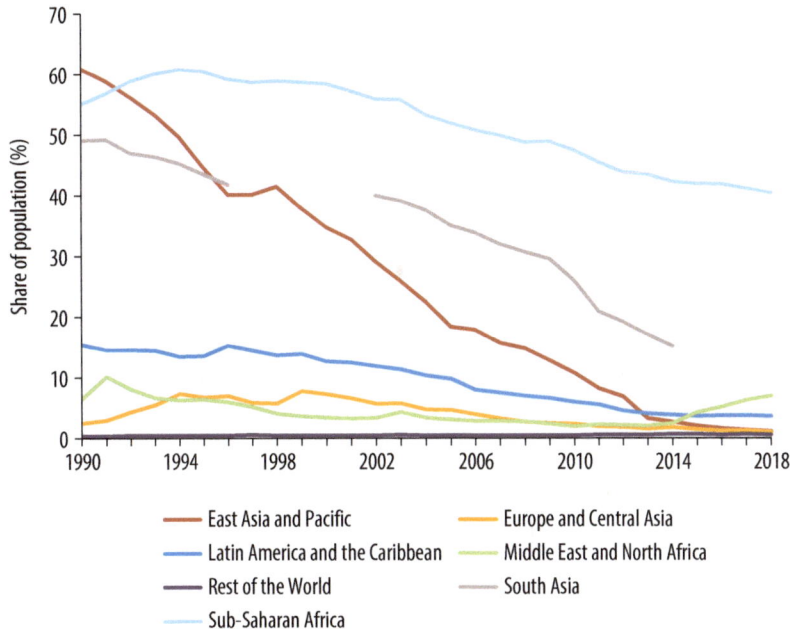

Source: World Bank 2020; World Bank calculations using PovcalNet, http://iresearch.worldbank.org /PovcalNet/povOnDemand.aspx.
Note: Data from 1997 to 2002 and from 2014 to 2018 are not available for South Asia.

In the aftermath of the COVID-19 crisis, as it has widened inequalities and exposed vulnerabilities, estimates suggest that it is the worst crisis in the past three decades to have derailed the path toward global poverty goals. There are likely to be long-lasting effects on the labor market as well. For example, some evidence in this report suggests that even when stringency measures have been relaxed, it has not resulted in a complete resumption of work by all (see chapter 2). Moreover, with coverage of many social support programs being low or slow (such as in the Islamic Republic of Iran), it is important to caution that the crisis is ongoing and will continue to be felt, in part because vaccination rates in most countries in the region are still low.

Therefore, both containment measures and a plan for recovery matter significantly for MENA, which has been persistently trying to improve its performance relative to other regions. Loss of jobs and income, insufficient social protection, mounting public debt, rising poverty, and high and rising unhappiness have exposed structural issues that require policy attention both immediately and in the medium to long run. Building back better should offer the poorest and most vulnerable the opportunity to regain what they have lost. Labor market, social protection, and health and education policies should be (re)considered through a lens of equity and inclusion, and designed in a way that productivity and welfare are improved in a progressive way. In a sense, this crisis offers MENA a rare opportunity to correct previous structural imbalances while battling a pandemic.

Preexisting Structural Problems

To better deal with these COVID-19-induced shocks, it is important to understand the long-standing structural issues that have faced MENA: low GDP growth; low employment, especially among youth and women; low human capital index; large state-owned enterprises; a large informal sector; poor foreign direct investment (FDI) inflows; a weak investment climate; and poor participation in global value chains. These problems have amplified the various impacts of COVID-19 and are impediments to a long-term growth path.

So far, the growth rate in MENA has been modest when compared with other regions. From 2000 to 2019, MENA (excluding high-income countries) registered annualized GDP per capita growth of 1.4 percent, a little above the growth rate of 1.2 percent in Latin America and the Caribbean (figure 1.5). East Asia and Pacific (EAP) ranked the highest with 7.2 percent, followed by South Asia and Europe and Central Asia. However, MENA had a GDP per capita of US$4,174, more than double South Asia's US$1,933 and Sub-Saharan Africa's US$1,645. But with widening inequality and growing poverty during the pandemic, the economic outlook is grim. In October 2020, the International Monetary Fund projected MENA's real GDP to drop by 4.1 percent in 2020, 1.3 percentage points more than expected in April of that year (IMF 2020).

Employment among MENA's working-age population remains low, with more than half unemployed. Although rising labor productivity has been driving economic growth in the region, MENA's employment levels are dismal. In terms of output per worker, the region was third in 2017, at US$15,812, after Latin America and the Caribbean (US$18,684) and Europe and Central Asia ($19,219) (figure 1.6, panel a). However, it ranked the lowest in employing its working-age population, at 39 percent, behind South Asia at 49 percent (figure 1.6, panel b). In the lead were East Asia and Pacific and Sub-Saharan Africa, at more than 60 percent. In addition, MENA suffers from a low human capital index, with an average of 0.57 (relative to 0.48 in Sub-Saharan Africa, 0.59 in East Asia and

FIGURE 1.5

MENA Is among the Lagging Regions in GDP Per Capita Growth

Annualized GDP per capita growth, 2000–19

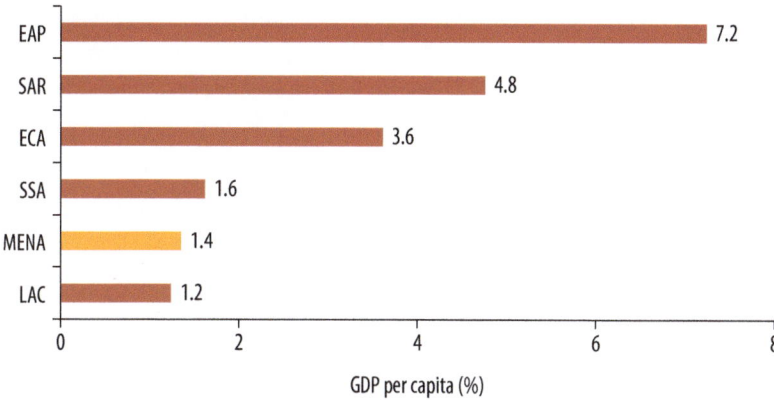

Source: World Bank Institute, https://data.worldbank.org/indicator/NY.GDP.PCAP.KD.
Note: EAP = East Asia and Pacific; ECA = Europe and Central Asia; LAC = Latin America and the Caribbean;
MENA = Middle East and North Africa; SAR = South Asia; SSA = Sub-Saharan Africa.

FIGURE 1.6

Labor Productivity in MENA Is Good, but Employment Share Is Very Low

Output per worker and employment-to-population ratio, workers over age 15

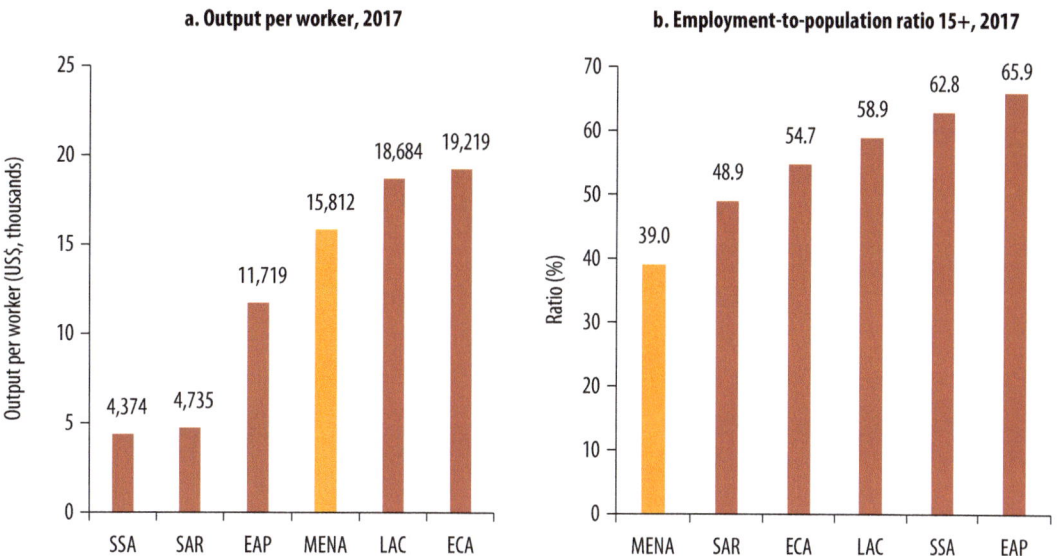

Source: Panel a: World Development Indicators database, excluding high-income countries, https://databank.worldbank.org/home. *Panel b:*
World Development Indicators database, https://data.worldbank.org/indicator/SL.EMP.TOTL.SP.ZS.
Note: EAP = East Asia and Pacific; ECA = Europe and Central Asia; LAC = Latin America and the Caribbean; MENA = Middle East and North
Africa; SAR = South Asia; SSA = Sub-Saharan Africa.

Pacific, and 0.69 in Europe and Central Asia. Post-COVID-19, this could mean amplified disadvantages for those unemployed who may need more policy support.

MENA has a relatively low degree of participation in global value chains, with the non-oil-producing countries concentrated in low value added goods. In the past two years, MENA's exports have shown a sharp decline. In terms of foreign value added in exports, the United Arab Emirates, Djibouti, Jordan, Lebanon, and Tunisia match or exceed the average of upper-middle-income countries, at more than 20 percent in 2018. Other countries—including Algeria, Bahrain, Egypt, the Islamic Republic of Iran, Iraq, Kuwait, Oman, Qatar, Saudi Arabia, and Syria—are lower than the average of low-income countries, while Morocco is just over the average. Given its geographical proximity to Europe, MENA can exploit its advantageous location in sourcing its supply chains after the pandemic.

MENA also suffers from the problems of large state-owned enterprises, a large informal economy, poor FDI inflows, and a weak investment climate. A large public sector presence has hindered the business climate in the region and instead fostered an informal economy. From 2005 to 2010, the share of nonagricultural employment in the informal economy was high in MENA, ranging from 31 percent in Syria, to almost 46 percent in Algeria, 51 percent in Egypt, 57 percent in the West Bank and Gaza, and 78 percent in Morocco. The large public sector and bureaucracy have failed to provide a conducive business environment, thereby discouraging FDI inflows. In 2019, FDI net inflows as a percentage of GDP were lowest in MENA and East Asia and the Pacific, at 1.3 percent. At the top was Latin America and the Caribbean, at 3.1 percent (figure 1.7). In terms of the Doing Business Index for MENA, United Arab Emirates is the best performer—16th out of 190 economies—whereas Libya and the Republic of Yemen are some of the worst (186th and 187th, respectively). Among the others, only Bahrain (43rd) is among the top 50, and Morocco comes close (53rd).[4]

Poor labor market outcomes especially affect women and youth. In 2019, MENA was on the lowest rung in terms of the female labor force participation rate, at 17.8 percent, with South Asia just above it at 23.4 percent (figure 1.8).[5] In contrast, Latin America and the Caribbean employed more than half of working women. Similarly, MENA recorded the highest youth (ages 15–24) unemployment rate, at 27.7 percent, much higher than the 17.7 and 17.8 percent in Latin America and the Caribbean and Europe and Central Asia, respectively, and 20.1 percent in South Asia (figure 1.9). Even before COVID-19 arrived, the International Labour Organization (ILO 2020) estimated that youth employment has been continuously declining, with the young working-age people three

FIGURE 1.7

MENA Is at the Lower End of FDI Net Inflows

FDI inflows as share of GDP, 2019

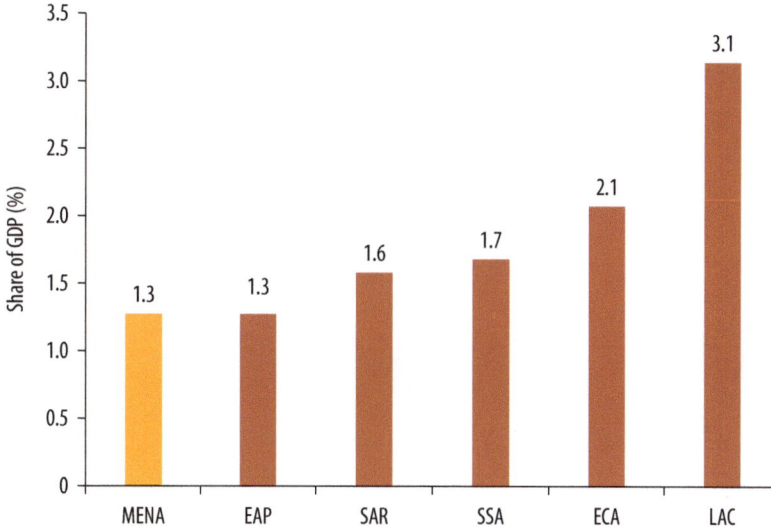

Source: World Bank Institute, https://data.worldbank.org/indicator/BX.KLT.DINV.WD.GD.ZS.
Note: EAP = East Asia and Pacific; ECA = Europe and Central Asia; LAC = Latin America and the Caribbean;
MENA = Middle East and North Africa; SAR = South Asia; SSA = Sub-Saharan Africa.

FIGURE 1.8

MENA Is at the Bottom in Terms of Female Labor Force Participation

Female labor force participation rate, 2019

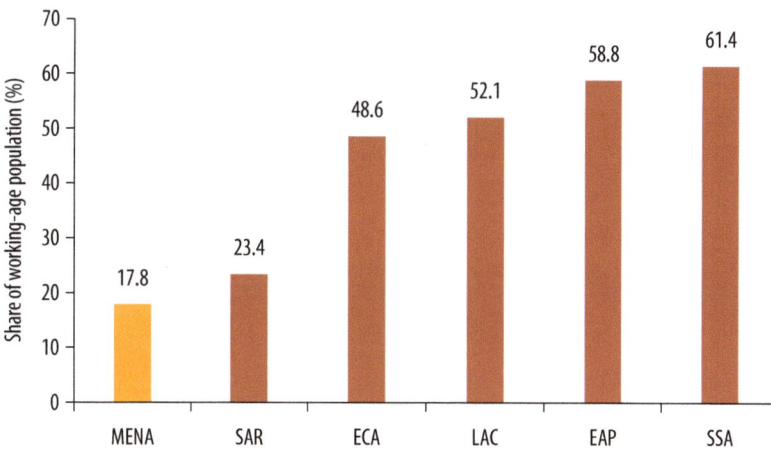

Source: World Bank Institute, https://data.worldbank.org/indicator/SL.TLF.ACTI.FE.ZS.
Note: EAP = East Asia and Pacific; ECA = Europe and Central Asia; LAC = Latin America and the Caribbean;
MENA = Middle East and North Africa; SAR = South Asia; SSA = Sub-Saharan Africa.

FIGURE 1.9

MENA Also Has Highest Youth Unemployment

Youth unemployment as share of the labor force, 2019

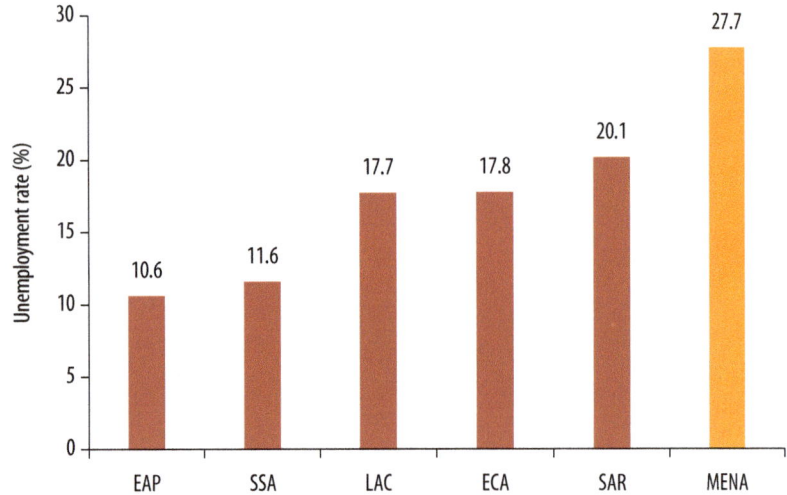

Source: World Bank Institute, https://data.worldbank.org/indicator/SL.UEM.1524.ZS.
Note: EAP = East Asia and Pacific; ECA = Europe and Central Asia; LAC = Latin America and the Caribbean;
MENA = Middle East and North Africa; SAR = South Asia; SSA = Sub-Saharan Africa.

times more likely to be unemployed than older working-age people (above 24). Graduating youth and other young people of working age (15–24) will now also have to contend with a labor market made worse by the pandemic, possibly with long-term consequences.

Roadmap and Value Added

Over the years, much work has been conducted to better understand the economic challenges of MENA and to better inform policy. Governments of various countries in the region have initiated policy reforms and continue to push for higher growth and development. However, many structural issues—notably, poverty and inequality—remain top-priority items and are getting worse with the pandemic. This report aims to inform the debate about what policy makers should do in light of a health crisis that is moving with lightning speed. It adds value by analyzing newly gathered primary data in these countries, complemented by projections carried out through sophisticated simulation techniques. Because shocks such as pandemics create both immediate disasters as well as long-run effects, the compilations also account for long-term perspectives. The report thus lays the foundation for designing policies backed by updated data and estimates.

The first methodology presents analyses from multiple rounds of high-frequency telephonic surveys that take stock of the ground situation in various countries. These surveys were conducted during the peak of the pandemic (from April to December 2020) by state agencies in collaboration with the World Bank. One of the report's innovations lies in using this household-level primary data (as opposed to firm-level data) to facilitate an understanding of self-reported changes in welfare. The phone survey data pertain to multiple countries and economies, including Djibouti, Egypt, Iraq, Lebanon, Libya, Morocco, Tunisia, and the West Bank and Gaza. Given the time-sensitive developments, as well as to ensure a timely assessment, smaller but nationally representative samples were conducted.

The second methodological approach employs various microsimulation techniques to arrive at estimates under different assumptions and shock scenarios. Simulations complement the analysis by helping to assess the overall impact on the economy and differential welfare impacts that may not be measurable through surveys because of limitations in data collection and dynamic pandemic conditions. This report also innovates by sometimes combining the phone survey data with the simulations.

While one approach builds on primary and time-sensitive data, the other is based on macroeconomic projections and an array of estimates. Together, these approaches provide a robust understanding of the possibilities of outcomes and range of impacts on different sectors and distribution classes that policy makers will need to account for. As there are likely to be long-term consequences on well-being and social mobility of those disproportionately affected, these estimates can also aid an understanding of policies needed to reduce the long-term impacts of this economic shock.

The two approaches perform a complementary task of corroborating each other's results (see box 1.1)—that is, how responses from self-reported changes in employment, income, and welfare correlate with micro-to-macro simulation estimates, based on sectoral projections. At the same time, each methodology presents some trade-offs. While the phone surveys inform the on-the-ground situation through self-reported responses of households or individuals during the crisis period, microsimulations help to estimate the changes in welfare indicators relative to precrisis levels, as well as to guide estimates for the postcrisis period. Both have their own merit. One provides real-time updates on the socioeconomic situation of households, and the other provides more specific estimates on the well-being of households, which could help to delineate time trends in different sectors to assist policy makers in designing specific policy responses (see box 1.1).

BOX 1.1

Tunisia: Using Phone Surveys and Microsimulations to Paint a COVID-19 Picture

Phone surveys present real-time evidence from the ground (such as income and living standards) while microsimulations try to quantify the overall expected effects for the economy (such as poverty and welfare). How the two approaches corroborate each other can be illustrated with the case of Tunisia.

As the pandemic unfolded, five waves of phone surveys were conducted. The self-reported results indicate that about half of the households saw living standards deteriorate compared with the pre-COVID-19 period, particularly among the poor and the bottom 40 percent. Those hardest hit include informal workers—especially in the private sector or self-employment—in construction, manufacturing, accommodation and food services activities, and transport. The surveys also show that the deterioration in welfare was caused by job and income loss along with higher food prices.

These findings are corroborated by the microsimulations. Using pre-COVID-19 administrative data, the first exercise simulates the impact on consumption, poverty, and inequality using labor income and consumption. The second exercise simulates price effects to determine the change in disposable income. The third

exercise identifies high-risk sectors (tourism, textiles, mechanical and electrical industry, transport, commerce, and construction), which are also the industries where a large number of poor and vulnerable are likely to be employed.

The microsimulations project an increase in poverty ranging from 7.3 percentage points (a more than 50 percent rise) in the optimistic scenario to 11.9 percentage points (an almost doubling) in the pessimistic scenario. They also add value by estimating the degree to which government compensatory measures can mitigate some of the losses: poverty would increase an estimated 6.5 percentage points in the optimistic scenario with mitigation measures as opposed to 7.3 percentage points without it.

Put together, the two methodological approaches not only support each other's findings but also indicate trends or furnish estimates such that they build on each other to provide a more robust picture. In Tunisia's case, these combined results would give policy makers a better idea of which segments of the population need to be targeted (and in which sectors), along with the potential effects from mitigation measures and policies.

Lessons from this exercise also highlight the crucial role that administrative data can play for such analysis and estimates. Administrative records are less likely to be susceptible to biases relative to specially administered surveys. Moreover, the former may be collected as part of an actual state support program or exercise and be more accurate, continuous, low-cost, and granular in nature. On the other hand, one-off surveys are very helpful tracking tools in such crisis situations and provide glimpses of the socioeconomic situations of households, although they may lack the consistency of administrative data. The upshot of this data exercise is that policy makers need a combination of different tools and data, administrative records, more frequent national surveys (like labor force surveys), and even infrequent phone surveys to track the well-being of households.

This report is divided into two parts, which differ by analytical approach: Part I is based on direct observation of the impact on welfare through evidence from phone surveys. Chapter 2 assesses the unequal impact that COVID-19 has had on households across multiple countries and economies in MENA, with a focus on jobs, earnings, health care, social protection, and welfare distribution. Chapter 3 examines the effect that the pandemic has had on the welfare of the population of the West Bank and Gaza, especially jobs, income, and food insecurity. Chapter 4 examines the decline in living standards of Tunisians during the pandemic, which continued even after the lockdown measures had been lifted. And chapter 5 explores the trends of recovery in Djibouti households since the onset of the pandemic—including a subsample of refugee households, which includes refugees and asylum seekers from other countries.

Part II builds on various welfare simulations. Chapter 6 continues the analysis of Tunisia, using phone surveys and microsimulations, to probe the anticipated impact on poverty and value of government mitigation measures. Chapter 7, which focuses on the West Bank and Gaza, explores the impact on poverty and inequality, with microsimulations that rely on microdata (including phone surveys). Chapter 8, which focuses on the Islamic Republic of Iran, assesses the distributional impact of COVID-19-induced inflation and loss of income on welfare and poverty, along with the value of government compensatory measures; but in the absence of phone surveys, it relies on household survey data from before the pandemic. And chapter 9 looks at the impact of the pandemic on poverty for Syrian refugees and the host community in Lebanon, with simulation tools that use pre-COVID-19 survey data and household income and consumption data.

The report's assessments on changes in employment, income, consumption, living standards, and inequality should help guide policy makers and other stakeholders to design policies to minimize escalations in poverty and to provide income and social support to those worst hit, while exercising fiscal prudence.

Notes

1. Algeria, Bahrain, Djibouti, Egypt, the Islamic Republic of Iran, Iraq, Jordan, Kuwait, Lebanon, Libya, Morocco, Oman, Qatar, Saudi Arabia, Syria, Tunisia, United Arab Emirates, West Bank and Gaza, and Republic of Yemen.
2. The World Bank's COVID-19 Household Monitoring Dashboard provides 93 harmonized indicators on 14 topics, allowing users to compare and analyze how COVID-19 impacts vary across countries over time and by industry sector and regions. Data can be downloaded for further analysis at https://www.worldbank.org/en/data/interactive/2020/11/11/covid-19-high-frequency-monitoring-dashboard.
3. Among the past pandemics, the most widespread one was H1N1 (swine flu), with more than 6 million confirmed cases across 148 countries and about 19,000 fatalities. Excluding H1N1—which spread across all regions—the other four events are mostly confined to specific regions: (a) SARS (2003) and MERS (2012) in Asia; (b) Ebola (2014) in Africa; and (c) Zika (2016) in the Americas. In terms of average mortality rates (deaths from confirmed cases), Ebola and MERS were the most fatal, followed by SARS, Zika, and H1N1.
4. Data are from World Bank's Doing Business Indicators (database, accessed July 4, 2021), http://www.doingbusiness.org.
5. Female labor force participation rate is the sum of both women working and unemployed women actively looking for a job as a share of the working age population.

References

Barro, Robert J., José F. Ursúa, and Joanna Weng. 2020. "The Coronavirus and the Great Influenza Pandemic: Lessons from the "Spanish Flu" for the Coronavirus's Potential Effects on Mortality and Economic Activity." NBER Working Paper 26866, National Bureau of Economic Research, Cambridge, MA.

Beaunoyer, Elisabeth, Sophie Dupéré, and Matthieu J. Guitton. 2020. "COVID-19 and Digital Inequalities: Reciprocal Impacts and Mitigation Strategies." *Computers in Human Behavior* (111): 106424.

Bowleg, Lisa. 2020. "We're Not All in This Together: On COVID-19, Intersectionality, and Structural Inequality." *American Journal of Public Health* 110 (7): 917. doi:10.2105/AJPH.2020.305766.

Furceri, Davide, P. Loungani, J. D. Ostry, and P. Pizzuto. 2020. "Will Covid-19 Affect Inequality? Evidence from Past Pandemics." *Covid Economics* 12(1): 138–57. https://voxeu.org/article/covid-19-will-raise-inequality-if-past-pandemics-are-guide.

Hill, Ruth, and Ambar Narayan. 2020. "Covid-19 and Inequality: A Review of the Evidence on Likely Impact and Policy Options." Working Paper. Centre for Disaster Protection, London.

ILO (International Labour Organization). 2020. *Global Employment Trends for Youth 2020: Technology and the Future of Jobs*. Geneva: International Labour Office.

ILO (International Labour Organization). 2021. ILO Monitor: *COVID-19 and the World of Work*, 7th ed. https://www.ilo.org/global/topics/coronavirus /impacts-and-responses/WCMS_767028/lang--en/index.htm.

IMF (International Monetary Fund). 2020. *World Economic Outlook, October 2020: A Long and Difficult Ascent*. Washington, DC: International Monetary Fund. https://www.imf.org/en/Publications/WEO/Issues/2020/09/30/world -economic-outlook-october-2020#Full%20Report%20and%20 Executive%20Summary.

Lakner, Christoph, Nishant Yonzan, Daniel Gerszon Mahler, R. Andres Castaneda Aguilar, Haoyu Wu, and Melina Fleury. 2020. "Updated Estimates of the Impact of COVID-19 on Global Poverty: The Effect of New Data." *Data Blog*, October 7, 2020.

Muasher, Marwan, and Maha Yahya. 2020. "A Coming Decade of Arab Decisions: The Day After." Digital magazine, Carnegie Endowment for International Peace. https://carnegieendowment.org/2020/09/09/coming-decade-of-arab -decisions-pub-82506.

Oxfam. 2021. "The Inequality Virus: Bringing Together a World Torn Apart by Coronavirus through a Fair, Just and Sustainable Economy. Methodology Note." Oxfam Methodology. Oxfam International. https://oxfamilibrary .openrepository.com/bitstream/handle/10546/621149/tb-inequality-virus -methodology-note-250121-en.pdf.

Roser, Max, and Esteban Ortiz-Ospina. 2021. COVID-19 Data Explorer (published online at OurWorldInData.org), https://ourworldindata.org /explorers/coronavirus-data-explorer.

Schellekens, Philip, and Divyanshi Wadhwa. 2021. "Relative Severity of COVID-19 Mortality: A New Indicator on the World Bank's Data Platform." *Data Blog*, March 11, 2021. https://blogs.worldbank.org/opendata/relative -severity-covid-19-mortality-new-indicator-world-banks-data-platform.

UNESCO (United Nations Educational, Scientific, and Cultural Organization). 2020. "2020 Global Education Meeting, Extraordinary Session on Education post-COVID-19," October 20–22 (online). Final report, UNESCO Digital Library, https://unesdoc.unesco.org/search/ca7b75d1-fecc-4f82-9df8 -9ee2828ab4cf.

World Bank. 2020. *Poverty and Shared Prosperity 2020: Reversals of Fortune*. Washington, DC: World Bank. doi:10.1596/978-1-4648-1602-4.

World Bank. 2021. "Middle East and North Africa." In *Global Economic Prospects*, January 2021, 89–111. Washington, DC: World Bank. http://pubdocs .worldbank.org/en/356361599838768642/Global-Economic-Prospects -January-2021-Analysis-MENA.pdf.

Part I: MENA Phone Surveys

CHAPTER 2

Unequal Impact of COVID-19 on MENA Households

Minh Cong Nguyen, Gildas Bopahbe Deudibe, and Romeo Jacky Gansey

Key Messages

- In the midst of the COVID-19 pandemic, high-frequency phone surveys conducted in many countries and economies in the Middle East and North African (MENA) region offer a snapshot of the impacts on households in several key areas: jobs, earnings, health care, and social protection.

- COVID-19 has economically affected households along the entire income distribution, with more severity for those in the bottom 40 percent.

- Workplace closures continue to disrupt labor markets, leading to losses in working hours, job losses, and work stoppages, which vary with job sector and household profiles.

- Once lockdown measures are lifted, many return to work and start earning an income again. Yet not all return to work, and for those who do, incomes earned are lower than before. In addition, those in the bottom 40 percent are less likely to fully recover.

- The pandemic has increased the level of stress about access to food—such as in Djibouti, Gaza, Lebanon, and the Republic of Yemen, where food insecurity is widespread. Food insecurity affects the most vulnerable in particular, and especially the poor.

Introduction

As the full scale of the impacts from COVID-19 continues to unfold, high-frequency phone surveys (HFPSs)—conducted in many MENA countries and economies during the pandemic—offer a snapshot of the impacts on households in several key areas, including jobs, earnings, health care, and social protection. Between April and December of 2020, Djibouti, the Arab Republic of Egypt, Iraq, Lebanon, Libya, Morocco, Saudi Arabia, Tunisia, the West Bank and Gaza, and the Republic of Yemen implemented one or multiple waves of data collection by phone. For eight of these —Djibouti, Egypt, Iraq, Lebanon, Libya, Tunisia, the West Bank and Gaza, and the Republic of Yemen—we were able to obtain the microdata, which are explored in this chapter. These phone interviews represent an unprecedented data collection effort aimed at producing up-to-date information on the socioeconomic impacts of COVID-19 and the associated economic crisis on households and individuals in the region.

COVID-19 affects household welfare through nonincome and income channels. Household income can be reduced when sick household members are unable to work. More importantly, COVID-19-induced lockdowns can limit the ability to work, and reduce the intensity of work, resulting in lower income for many households. The crisis also reduced nonlabor incomes such as remittances, while its impact on government transfers is ambiguous: some households may receive increased welfare benefits because of the crisis, but others might lose existing advantages because governments are aligning their spending with reductions in revenue collection.

The pandemic's impacts on household welfare that occur through nonincome channels, such as increased health spending due to ill-ness, reduce disposable income and limit resources available for other consumption goods. Also, because lockdowns have caused schools to close, students' learning experiences have been disrupted. And worldwide disruptions in production and transport services contributed in many places to higher prices of basic items such as food, thus lowering living standards.

This chapter reports highlights of the results of phone interviews with households conducted in 2020. It focuses on six areas: employment, work intensity, earnings, access to health care, access to food security, and social protection. The findings show that the impact has been unequal. Although all households have been affected, those at the bottom 40 percent of the welfare distribution have been hit the hardest.

How Phone Surveys Are Done

In the absence of the ability to conduct face-to-face interviews, due to the risk of infection, surveys done over the phone have been shown to be a valuable, albeit imperfect, alternative. In the absence of other data, these interviews provide critical socioeconomic information necessary to understand the challenges facing households during the pandemic (see table 2.1). Though the contents of the phone surveys differed from country to country, topics typically covered include labor market experiences, access to health care, food security, and reception of public assistance—along with standard sociodemographic variables (such as gender, age, and level of education). However, the availability of socioeconomic characteristics varies by survey. For example, the gender of the breadwinner is not reported in the Tunisia survey, while wealth status is not provided in the survey conducted in the West Bank and Gaza. Thus, results are presented contingent on the availability of information.

The HFPSs covered in this chapter were designed to be nationally representative and were implemented by National Statistical Offices or partner agencies like the World Food Programme, or commissioned to private sector entities. Sampling methods and procedures differ by country, but all final data have weight variables to adjust for nonresponse rates among subgroups of the population. Libya is the exception. No sampling frame exists, making it impossible to design sampling weights. In Djibouti, Morocco, Tunisia, and the West Bank and Gaza, the surveys were conducted on a subsample of the most recent nationally representative living standards survey, while in Egypt, Iraq, Lebanon, Libya, and the Republic of Yemen, a random digit dialing (RDD) approach was used. Response rates varied: in Tunisia they were relatively high while in Egypt they were relatively low, a difference that likely stems from Egypt's reliance on the RDD approach. Because respondents have no previous contact with the survey team when RDD is used, despite careful advertisement many prefer not to participate, concerned that the survey is a telemarketing attempt. There are other limitations inherent in phone surveys, such as network coverage or response bias (see box 2.1).

In addition, the stringency and duration of lockdown measures vary among countries, as does the timing of the phone surveys relative to the period when the most stringent lockdown measures were implemented (figure 2.1). In Djibouti stringent measures were implemented for a relatively short period of time, following which they tapered off rapidly. In Iraq, by contrast, stringent lockdown measures were maintained for months. In Tunisia strict lockdown measures came in two waves, whereas

TABLE 2.1

Phone Surveys in the MENA Region Were Heterogeneously Implemented According to Each Country's Data Characteristics

Selected characteristics of eight phone surveys implemented in the MENA region

Country	Sample size	Response rate (%)	Completed interviews	Female breadwinner (%)	Timing of the survey	Timing of the lockdown	Implementing agency	Construction of welfare indicator
Djibouti, wave 1	2,082	71	1,486	28	July 7–22, 2020	March 23–May 17, 2020	National Statistical Office	Proxy means test
Djibouti, wave 2	—	85	1,460	—	September 20– October 18, 2020	—	National Statistical Office	Proxy means test
Djibouti, wave 2	—	70	1,947	—	December 20, 2020– February 2, 2021	—	National Statistical Office	Proxy means test
Egypt, Arab Rep., wave 1	—	57	2,039	10	April 27–May 9, 2020	March 17–April 24, 2020	Baseera (Egyptian Center for Public Opinion)	Asset-based index quintile
Lebanon, wave 1	—	NR	2,335	—	July–August 2020	July 30–August 10, 2020	World Food Programme	n.a.
Lebanon, wave 2	—	NR	3,354	—	September– October 2020	October 4–12, 2020	World Food Programme	n.a.
Lebanon, wave 3	—	NR	4,203	—	November– December 2020	November 14–30, 2020	World Food Programme	n.a.
Libya, wave 1	530	NR	521	NR	April 4–May 9, 2020	NR	World Food Programme	n.a.

(continued on next page)

TABLE 2.1

Phone Surveys in the MENA Region were Heterogeneously implemented According to Each Country's Data Characteristics (*continued*)

Selected characteristics of seven phone surveys implemented in the MENA region

Country	Sample size	Response rate (%)	Completed interviews	Female breadwinner (%)	Timing of the survey	Timing of the lockdown	Implementing agency	Construction of welfare indicator
Libya, wave 2	—	NR	996	NR	October 3–November 13, 2020	NR	World Food Programme	n.a.
Iraq, wave 1	—	NR	1,621	—	August 8–28, 2020	—	World Food Programme	n.a.
Iraq, wave 2	—	NR	1,621	—	September 1–25, 2020	—	World Food Programme	n.a.
Iraq, wave 3	—	NR	1,623	—	October 1–30, 2020	—	World Food Programme	n.a.
Iraq, wave 4	—	NR	1,629	—	November 1–25, 2020	—	World Food Programme	n.a.
Iraq, wave 5	—	NR	1,614	—	December 1–25, 2020	—	World Food Programme	n.a.
Iraq, wave 6	—	NR	1,651	—	January 1–25, 2021	—	World Food Programme	n.a.
Morocco	2,350	NR	—	NR	April 14–23, 2020	March 16–May 29	Higher Planning Commission	n.a.
West Bank and Gaza	9,910	81	8,621	11	June 27–July 14, 2020	March 22–mid-May	National Statistical Office	n.a.
Tunisia, wave 1	1,360	77	1,032	—	April 29–May 8, 2020	March 22–May 8	National Statistical Office	Consumption aggregate from previous survey

(continued on next page)

TABLE 2.1

Phone Surveys in the MENA Region were Heterogeneously implemented According to Each Country's Data Characteristics *(continued)*

Selected characteristics of seven phone surveys implemented in the MENA region

Country	Sample size	Response rate (%)	Completed interviews	Female breadwinner (%)	Timing of the survey	Timing of the lockdown	Implementing agency	Construction of welfare indicator
Tunisia, wave 2	1,339	67	899	—	May 16–24, 2020	—	National Statistical Office	Consumption aggregate from previous survey
Tunisia, wave 3	1,339	63	837	—	June 6–16, 2020	—	National Statistical Office	Consumption aggregate from previous survey
Tunisia, wave 4	1,339	59	789	—	June 25–July 4, 2020	—	National Statistical Office	Consumption aggregate from previous survey
Tunisia, wave 5	1,339	53	714	—	October 3–16, 2020	—	National Statistical Office	Consumption aggregate from previous survey
Yemen, Rep., wave 1	—	NR	4,290	NR	June 1–30, 2020	NR	World Food Programme	n.a.
Yemen, Rep., wave 2	—	NR	4,289	NR	September 1–30, 2020	NR	World Food Programme	n.a.

Source: World Bank data.
Note: NR = not reported by the implementing agency; — = not available; n.a. = not applicable.

BOX 2.1

Limitations of Phone Surveys

Phone interviews have turned out to be a valuable alternative to primary data collection using face-to-face surveys, particularly during the pandemic. In normal circumstances, these surveys would be a useful complement to other ways of collecting data, but they would not replace face-to-face surveys, because phone surveys come with a number of limitations.

First, areas or respondents with limited network coverage or no access to phones, typically the poorest segments of the population, will be under covered in the sample.

Second, indicators that are measured at the individual level (such as employment and unemployment) may be biased because of respondent selection. Especially in countries where high-frequency phone surveys (HFPSs) are sampled from an existing nationally representative (prepandemic) survey, the respondent is often the head of household, and thus some statistics (such as employment rates) would differ from those estimated by a conventional labor force survey, which collects information from all household members.

Third, women tend to be under represented because they are less likely to be the head of household, or, in instances where a random digit dialing approach is used, they are less likely to own a phone or respond to an unknown caller.

Fourth, the length of a phone interview is limited, making it challenging to design

an effective survey because the number of questions that can be asked is small and because the questions need to be short and precise for easy comprehension. One implication is that, in many instances, the ability to consider distributional impacts is limited. That occurs because the phone surveys lack the ability to generate estimates of poverty (as doing so would require a long list of consumption questions for which these surveys lack sufficient time). To estimate distributional impacts, proxy variables would have to be calculated (such as wealth quintiles) from the limited information on wealth that is collected in the phone surveys themselves. However, phone surveys that draw their samples from preexisting welfare surveys could derive the pre-COVID-19 poverty status.

Fifth, sample sizes are typically relatively small—often less than 1,500 people—to allow for a rapid turnaround, with the exception of the West Bank and Gaza survey, with more than 9,000 observations. Small sample sizes make it more difficult to break down results by subgroups.

Despite these limitations, phone surveys have demonstrated their ability to collect high-quality data. Their agility and the ability to collect data rapidly, without the need for personal presence by an enumerator, makes phone surveys a valuable tool for specific situations, such as emergencies, dangerous situations, or situations in which the respondent is mobile.

FIGURE 2.1

Work Stoppages Vary by Severity of Lockdown and Timing of Phone Survey

Trend of stringency index and share of workers who stopped working

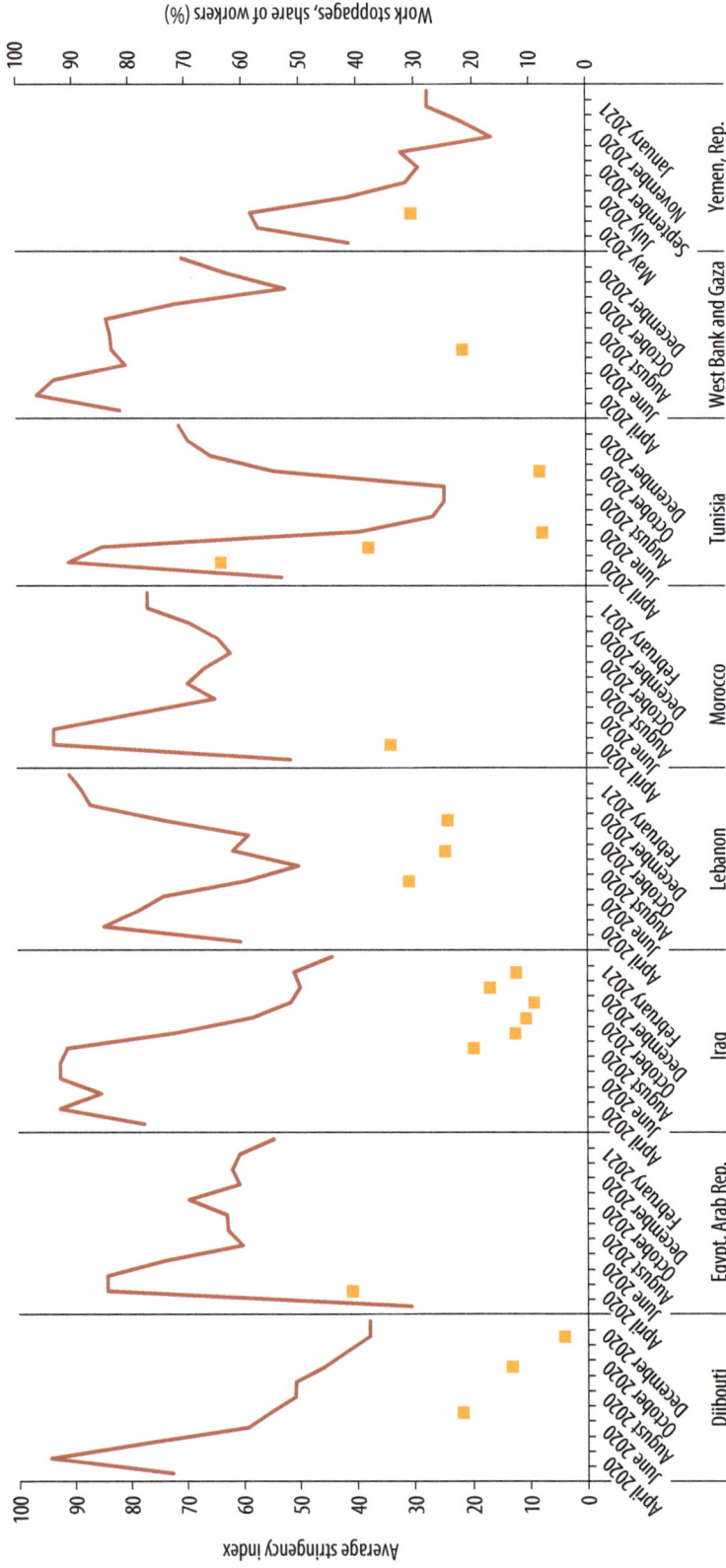

Source: MENA Harmonized Database of High Frequency Phone Surveys and World Bank calculation using data from Our World in Data (Roser and Ortiz-Ospina 2021).
Note: The stringency index is a composite measure based on nine response indicators, including school closures, workplace closures, and travel bans, rescaled to a value from 0 to 100 (100 = strictest). If policies vary at the subnational level, the index is shown as the response level of the strictest subregion. December data span only until the 10th of the month. Orange squares represent work stoppages (right y-axis).

in the Republic of Yemen, lockdown measures remained relatively mild. In some instances, like Tunisia, where five survey rounds were conducted, the consequences of at least the first wave of lockdown measures could be monitored relatively closely. In other instances, such as Djibouti, the surveys came after the lockdowns were implemented. This intercountry variation offers valuable research opportunities to explore how lockdowns affect socioeconomic outcomes. In this chapter, the level of ambition is more modest, as we limit ourselves to presenting the variation in socioeconomic outcomes and describing some emerging patterns.

Impacts on Employment: Work Stoppages

Before the pandemic, many countries in MENA were already struggling with persistent high levels of unemployment. Once the pandemic struck, employment opportunities were further depressed. One of the questions asked by nearly all COVID-19 phone surveys centers on the impact of the pandemic on employment.

Among the countries and economies sampled, a great variation in outcomes is observed, with work stoppages being much higher in some countries than others. During wave 1 of the lockdown, Tunisia topped the list, with 64 percent of its workers forced to stop working, followed by Egypt with 41 percent (figure 2.1). At the bottom are Djibouti with 25 percent, the West Bank and Gaza with 22 percent, and Iraq with 15 percent.

One possible reason for these differences is the variations in these countries' economic structure. Another is that the initial phone survey in Tunisia was conducted during a period when the economic lockdown was at its strictest. Indeed, as the lockdown eased, one observes a rapid decline in work stoppages in Tunisia. The percentage of workers who stopped working had decreased by half during wave 2 and declined sharply to less than 10 percent in the latest waves (wave 4 and wave 5, conducted 4 and 5 months later, respectively). For Egypt the high rate of work stoppage precedes the moment when the most stringent lockdowns were implemented. Yet mobility data suggest that by the time of the survey, citizens had already voluntarily reduced their movements; and as in Tunisia, the Egypt survey coincides with the height of the (de facto) lockdown. In contrast, in Djibouti, Iraq, and the West Bank and Gaza, the phone surveys were completed largely after deconfinement.

The HFPS results thus suggest that (a) at the height of the economic lockdowns, when mobility was severely restricted, (about) half of those who worked prior to the pandemic stopped working; and (b) once the lockdowns were eased, many, but certainly not all, returned to work. Both findings are supported by figure 2.2, which suggests the presence of a strong positive correlation between the stringency of the lockdown and the degree of work stoppages, as well as by the fact that once the lockdown measures eased, some 10–20 percent of workers continued to experience work stoppages.

These work stoppages took a significant toll on households along the entire income distribution, and especially those at the bottom. This can be seen in all the surveys, even though their approach to identifying the poorest or most vulnerable differs. In Iraq, where the surveys were done after the lockdowns had eased substantially, the unemployment rate among those with secondary education remained elevated by 11 percentage points, while for those with less than secondary education it had increased by 20 percentage points. In Djibouti, which like Iraq

FIGURE 2.2

Some Work Stoppages Continue Even after Lockdowns Ease

Correlation between the stringency index and work stoppage

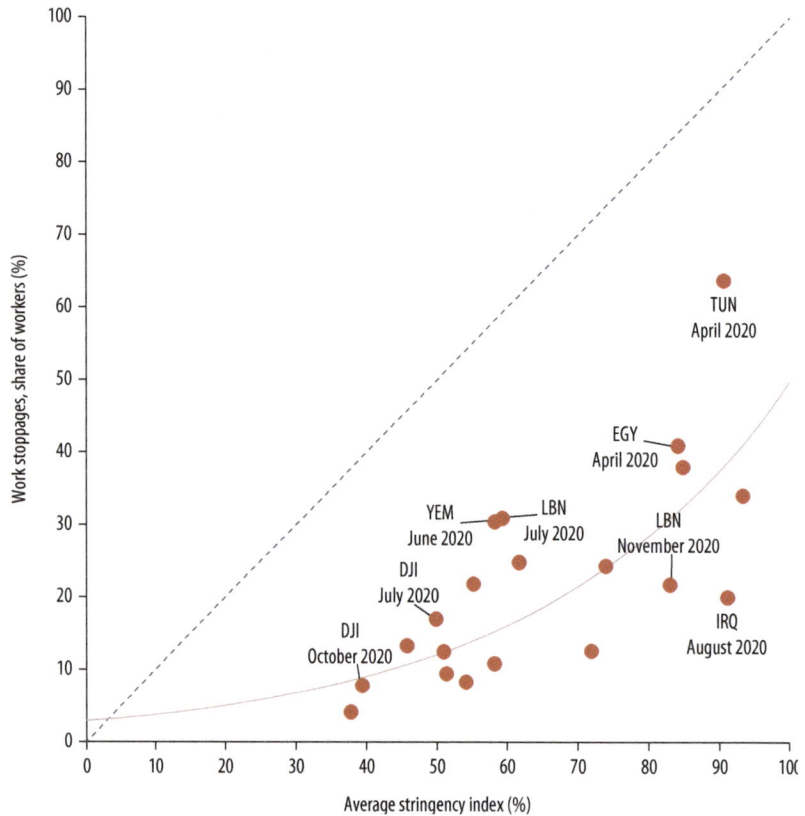

Source: MENA Harmonized Database of High Frequency Phone Surveys and World Bank calculation using data from Our World in Data (Roser and Ortiz-Ospina 2021).
Note: The stringency index is a composite measure based on nine response indicators including school closures, workplace closures, and travel bans, rescaled to a value from 0 to 100 (100 = strictest). If policies vary at the subnational level, the index is shown as the response level of the strictest subregion. December data span only until the 10th of the month.

implemented its phone survey once the lockdown measures had mostly ended, almost all breadwinners who were working before the pandemic had resumed doing so. Yet the unemployment is markedly different (and higher) among the vulnerable refugee population. Although only 4 percent of Djiboutians with jobs prior to COVID-19 remained out of work, 7 percent of urban refugees and 16 percent of camp-based refugees did so.

Do work stoppages and the eventual return to work vary across the income distribution? The data from Egypt, Tunisia, Djibouti, and the West Bank and Gaza allow us to consider this more closely. For these places wealth quintiles could be constructed using data collected in the phone survey (Egypt) or in the household survey from which the phone sample was drawn (Djibouti, Tunisia, West Bank and Gaza). For Djibouti and Tunisia we can also present the data by poor and nonpoor citizens. Table 2.2 presents the results, showing specificities as well as common patterns. The table shows that at the height of the lockdown (Egypt, and Tunisia waves 1 and 2), work stoppages were common across the income distribution and affected poor and nonpoor households alike. In Egypt and the West Bank and Gaza, by contrast, those in the bottom 40 percent were affected much harder by work stoppages than households in the top quintile.

When the restrictions eased (Tunisia waves 1 and 2, Djibouti waves 1 and 2), surveys showed that respondents from the poorest quintiles were less likely to be able to return to work, with percentages of those who stopped working being twice as high for those in the bottom

TABLE 2.2

Biggest Work Stoppages Are Concentrated among Poorest Workers

Share of workers who stopped working, across quintile and poverty status (%)

		Quintile based on PMT score					Poverty status		Total
		1	2	3	4	5	Poor	Nonpoor	
Djibouti	Wave 1	25	24	22	16	—	24	21	22
	Wave 2	17	16	10	10	—	17	13	13
	Wave 3	3	4	4	3	—	5	4	4
Egypt, Arab Rep.	Wave 1	51	49	40	35	23	—	—	41
Gaza[a]	Wave 1	37	35	38	32	25	—	—	33
Tunisia	Wave 1	64	63	63	62	67	65	63	64
	Wave 2	50	39	33	32	42	51	36	38
	Wave 4	12	7	7	8	5	10	8	8
	Wave 5	12	6	10	7	7	15	7	8
West Bank[a]	Wave 1	49	48	50	46	41	—	—	47

Source: MENA Harmonized Database of High Frequency Phone Surveys.
Note: Wave 3 information not provided for Tunisia. PMT = proxy means test; — = not available.
a. Includes those who lost their job and those who maintained their job but did not work.

FIGURE 2.3

COVID-19's Impacts Hit the Construction Subsector Hardest

Work stoppages by sectors of employment pre-COVID-19 (%)

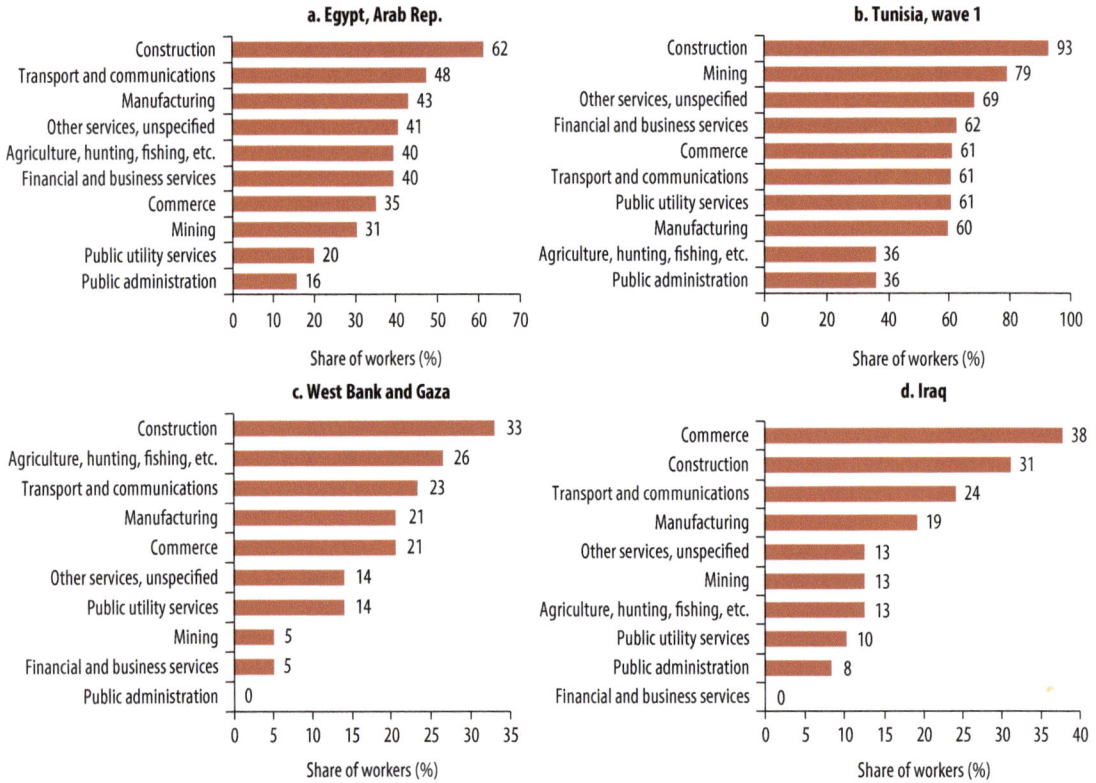

a. Egypt, Arab Rep.

Sector	Share of workers (%)
Construction	62
Transport and communications	48
Manufacturing	43
Other services, unspecified	41
Agriculture, hunting, fishing, etc.	40
Financial and business services	40
Commerce	35
Mining	31
Public utility services	20
Public administration	16

b. Tunisia, wave 1

Sector	Share of workers (%)
Construction	93
Mining	79
Other services, unspecified	69
Financial and business services	62
Commerce	61
Transport and communications	61
Public utility services	61
Manufacturing	60
Agriculture, hunting, fishing, etc.	36
Public administration	36

c. West Bank and Gaza

Sector	Share of workers (%)
Construction	33
Agriculture, hunting, fishing, etc.	26
Transport and communications	23
Manufacturing	21
Commerce	21
Other services, unspecified	14
Public utility services	14
Mining	5
Financial and business services	5
Public administration	0

d. Iraq

Sector	Share of workers (%)
Commerce	38
Construction	31
Transport and communications	24
Manufacturing	19
Other services, unspecified	13
Mining	13
Agriculture, hunting, fishing, etc.	13
Public utility services	10
Public administration	8
Financial and business services	0

Source: MENA Harmonized Database of High Frequency Phone Surveys.
Note: Industry sector includes mining, manufacturing, public utility services, and construction. Service sector includes commerce, transport and communications, financial and business services, public administration, and other services.

quintile as those in the top quintile. This presents a strong indication that COVID-19 worsened preexisting inequalities.

At the sectoral level, workplace stoppages also vary in their impact, as is evidenced by data from Egypt, Iraq, Tunisia, and the West Bank and Gaza. Although the surveys were done at different degrees of severity of the national lockdowns, the emerging patterns show that construction was among the worst affected, while public administration, utilities, and financial services were among the least affected (figure 2.3). There is also some variability at the country and economy levels. For example, in Tunisia, agriculture was one of the least affected sectors, but in the West Bank and Gaza it was one of the most affected sectors.

Another way to view these stoppages is to compare pre-COVID-19 sectoral engagement (by poverty status) with the degree of work stoppages by sector for poor and nonpoor workers, which we can do in the case of Egypt and Tunisia (table 2.3). Their data show that, prepandemic, those working in agriculture and construction are more likely to belong to the bottom 40 percent, whereas workers in service sectors (such as commerce, transport and communications, and financial and business services) are often in the top 40 percent. That fact enables us to take it a step further and see how the bottom 40 and top 40 fare during COVID-19 by sector.

We find that work stoppages due to COVID-19 affect the poor disproportionately through two channels. First, in sectors like agriculture in Egypt and construction in Tunisia, all workers were equally affected by work stoppages, but because the typical workers in these sectors are poor, the implication is that more poor people (than nonpoor) were affected. Second, in sectors like construction and commerce in Tunisia, and in manufacturing and transport and communication in Egypt, workers from the bottom 40 percent were much more likely to be affected by work stoppages than those from the top 40 percent—because those engaged in managerial and other white-collar tasks were more likely to continue working from home. The exception to this pattern is found in Tunisia, in which the top 40 percent of workers in the manufacturing sector were more likely to be affected by work stoppages than those in the bottom 40 percent.

TABLE 2.3

Construction and Agriculture Mostly Employ the Poorest Workers in Egypt and Tunisia

Distribution of workers by sector and subsector of employment pre-COVID-19 and by bottom and top 40 percent distribution

| | Pre-COVID-19 distribution of workers | | | | Percentage of work stoppages | | | |
| | Egypt, Arab Rep. | | Tunisia wave 1 | | Egypt, Arab Rep. | | Tunisia wave 1 | |
	Bottom 40%	Top 40%	Bottom 40%	Top 40%	Bottom 40%	Top 40%	Bottom 40%	Top 40%
Agriculture, hunting, fishing, etc.	66	13	55	26	38	36	41	39
Mining	26	52	54	47	—	—	—	—
Manufacturing	41	42	26	48	54	31	49	68
Public utility services	11	50	14	86	—	—	—	—
Construction	70	12	49	30	65	28	97	87
Commerce	42	39	32	38	53	24	71	45
Transport and communications	44	36	20	58	53	39	61	61
Financial and business services	47	36	22	42	49	30	—	—
Public administration	36	39	38	35	15	15	29	35
Other services, unspecified	35	36	24	53	50	32	51	80

Source: MENA Harmonized Database of High Frequency Phone Surveys.
Note: Industry sector includes mining, manufacturing, public utility services, and construction. Service sector includes commerce, transport and communications, financial and business services, public administration, and other services. — = not available.

FIGURE 2.4

Biggest Work Stoppages Are for Self-Employed and Informal Workers

Work stoppage by type of employment (%)

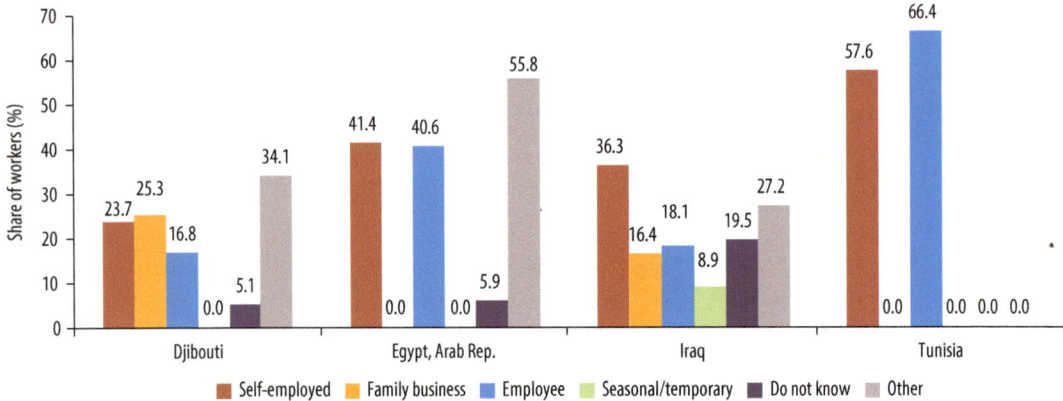

Source: MENA Harmonized Database of High Frequency Phone Surveys.
Note: The numbers for each country do not total 100 because some answers fell into multiple categories.

Yet another way to view these stoppages is in terms of contractual arrangement, as shown in figure 2.4. For example, in Djibouti and Iraq, "own-account" workers (self-employed and those engaged in a family business) experienced higher work stoppages than those in Egypt and Tunisia. These own-account workers are mostly engaged in informal jobs, lacking employment protection, health insurance, and other benefits. Because the data from Iraq and Djibouti were collected after the lockdown, and those in Tunisia and Egypt were collected at the height of the lockdown, the results are consistent with all workers having been equally affected by the lockdowns, although own-account workers have greater difficulty going back to work than employees.

Impacts on Work Intensity: Workers Working Fewer Hours

The pandemic not only reduced the number of jobs but also decreased the intensity of work, as workers ended up working fewer hours (figure 2.5). Thus COVID-19-induced lockdown measures generated changes in the labor market at both the intensive (how hard people work) and extensive (how many people work) margins. Changes at the intensive margin are more pronounced in Egypt, where 76 percent of those who worked the week before the survey reported that they worked less than usual. The phone surveys also indicate that the reduction in the intensity of work occurs more among groups in lower quintiles compared with those in the top quintile. And female breadwinners face a slightly larger decrease in their work intensity compared with their male counterparts.

FIGURE 2.5

Intensity of Work Fell Sharply during Early Months of COVID-19

Change in intensity of work by share of all workers (%)

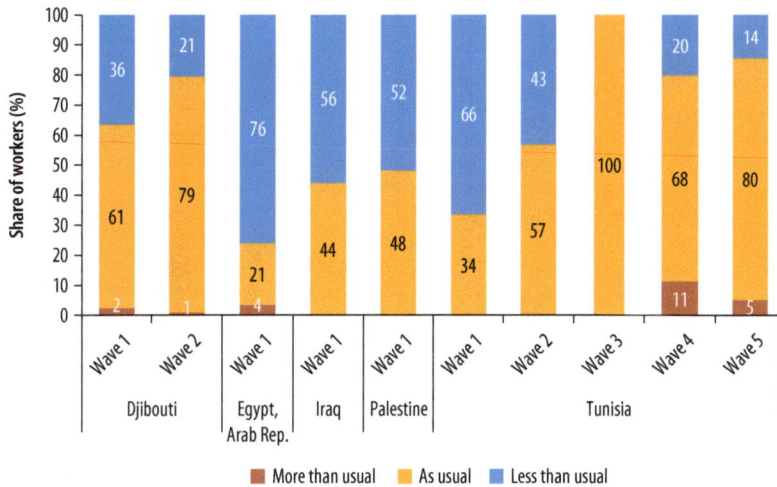

Source: MENA Harmonized Database of High Frequency Phone Surveys.

Given that the phone surveys in Djibouti occurred after the lockdown measures were discontinued—and the number stating work "as usual" is high (61 percent for the first wave and 79 percent for the second wave)—we could project that under lockdowns, workers will continue to lose working hours, thus further reducing their income. As the impacts of the pandemic continue to unfold, along with economic activity still contracted, more breadwinners will continue to be affected financially, which could reduce their household incomes to a trickle if effective policy interventions are not rapidly implemented.

Impacts on Health Care, Food Security, and Social Protection

The surveys ask to what extent the pandemic has stretched the capabilities of health systems in the MENA region, where some countries grapple with low capacity or weak health systems. Many respondents reported that they had trouble accessing health care when they needed to (figure 2.6). In the Republic of Yemen, only 47 percent of respondents could do so, while in Djibouti and Tunisia, it was 63 and 64 percent, respectively. Early on in the pandemic, COVID-19-related reasons, such as closure of roads to traffic, are why most could not access health care.

FIGURE 2.6

Respondents Report Having a Tough Time Accessing Health Care When Needed

Share reporting trouble with access to health care (%)

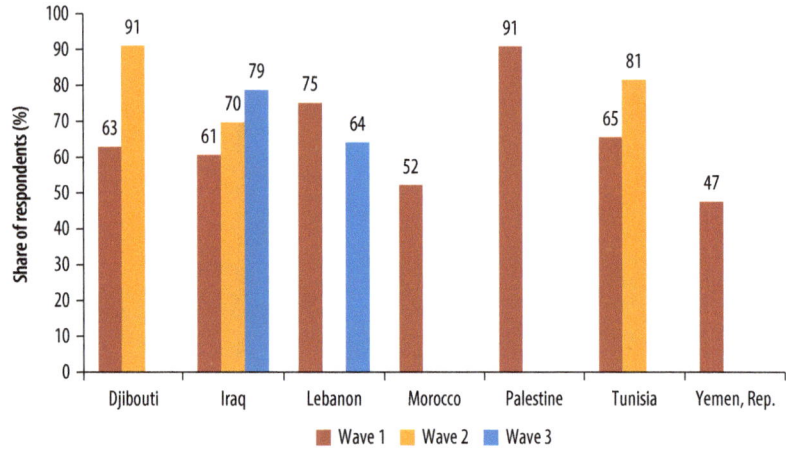

Source: MENA Harmonized Database of High Frequency Phone Surveys.

TABLE 2.4

The Wealthier Have Better Access to Health Care When Needed

Access to health facilities by welfare quintile, food consumption score, and poverty

		Quintile based on PMT score					Poverty status		
		1	2	3	4	5	Poor	Nonpoor	Total
Tunisia	Wave 1	56	72	69	61	67	51	67	65
	Wave 2	78	82	87	80	81	78	82	81

Source: MENA Harmonized Database of High Frequency Phone Surveys.
Note: PMT = proxy means test (used to proxy welfare aggregates—income or consumption). For Tunisia, the number of respondents who answered the question on access to health care is about 180 in wave 1 and about 250 in wave 2.

As time passed, access did improve, with Djibouti up to 91 percent and Tunisia up to 81 percent.

Looking at the role of income in health care access, the surveys show that in both Djibouti and Tunisia, households from higher wealth quintiles faced better odds of accessing health care when in need than those from the bottom quintile. In Tunisia, the positive differences of these values (quintile 5 and quintile 1, nonpoor and poor, and acceptable food score and poor food score) suggest some health advantage among the nonpoor (table 2.4). The surveys show that households with female breadwinners appear to be at no disadvantage with respect to their access

TABLE 2.5

MENA Countries Have Worrisome Signs of Food Insecurity

Food insecurity experience scale indicator

	Djibouti (wave 2)	Iraq (wave 1)	Lebanon (wave 3)	Palestine (wave 1)	Tunisia (wave 1)	Yemen, Rep. (wave 1)
Ran out of food	8	—	—	20	—	—
Could not eat	—	—	—	9	—	62
Went without eating a whole day	4	15	—	8	1	—
Worried about not having enough food	40	—	—	65	33	—
Unable to eat healthily	42	31	—	52	—	70
Ate only a few kinds of foods	42	—	—	62	—	—
Skipped a meal	—	—	35	46	—	64
Ate less than you thought you should	27	19	48	43	15	69

Source: MENA Harmonized Database of High Frequency Phone Surveys.
Note: — = not available.

to health care. There is no statistical support for the idea that large households experience more restricted access to health care.

As for food security, COVID-19 increased the level of concern about households' access to food, raising serious questions about potentially serious malnutrition problems ahead. In the West Bank and Gaza, 65 percent of households were worried about not having enough food to eat, as were 33 percent in Tunisia and 40 percent in Djibouti (table 2.5). It is not difficult to imagine why households are worried about not having enough food, given that they have been grappling with challenges related to their labor income and so much uncertainty about when the pandemic might end. Household worries are not merely the expression of a diffuse fear about a distant future; many already experience food deprivation. In the West Bank and Gaza, 43 percent of households reduced their food intake because of not enough resources; in Djibouti and Tunisia, the numbers were 27 and 15 percent, respectively.

For Djibouti, Iraq (excluding the Kurdistan Region of the Republic of Iraq [KRI]), KRI, Lebanon, Libya, and the Republic of Yemen, it is possible to consider food security using the Food Consumption Score (FCS). This is a commonly used indicator of food security that reflects households' dietary diversity and nutrient intake. FCS outcomes are typically presented along three categories (poor food security, borderline, and acceptable) and are primarily used by the World Food Programme to point toward households having difficulties accessing food. Figure 2.7 presents the results for the five countries and region, along with the stringency index.

FIGURE 2.7

No Apparent Link Is Seen between Food Insecurity and Stringency Measure

Food Consumption Scores (FCS) by severity of lockdown and timing of phone survey

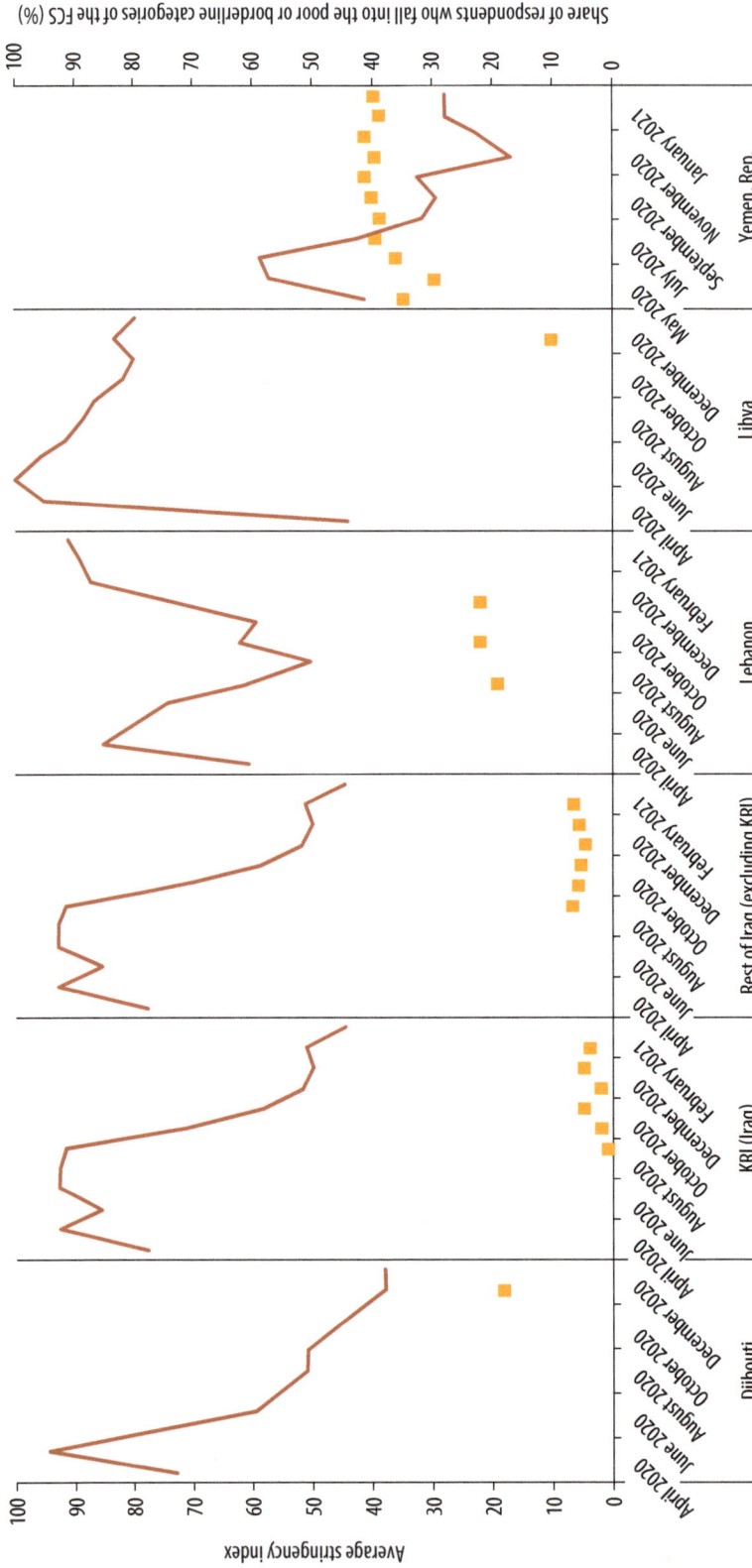

Source: World Bank calculation based on data from joint World Food Programme–World Bank phone surveys and data from Our World in Data (Roser and Ortiz-Ospina 2021).

Note: The stringency index is a composite measure based on nine response indicators including school closures, workplace closures, and travel bans, rescaled to a value from 0 to 100 (100 = strictest). If policies vary at the subnational level, the index is shown as the response level of the strictest subregion. December data span only until the 10th of the month. The FCS is calculated by inspecting how often households consume food items from the different food groups during a seven-day reference period. KRI = Kurdistan Region of the Republic of Iraq. Orange squares represent the share of respondents who fall into the poor or borderline categories of the FCS (right y-axis).

The results show concerning levels of food insecurity in Djibouti, Lebanon, and the Republic of Yemen. Food consumption scores are substantially better in Iraq, KRI, and Libya, with some variations over time. A visual inspection of figure 2.7 suggests the absence of a correlation between the stringency of COVID-19 lockdown measures and the prevalence of food insecurity. It appears that for these countries, the idiosyncrasies of their situations (high inflation in Lebanon; conflict and blockades in the Republic of Yemen) are the driving forces behind the observed high levels of food insecurity.

At this point it is worth highlighting the situation in the West Bank and Gaza, where an FCS score is not available, but a different measure employed by the Food and Agriculture Organization of the United Nations (FAO) has been calculated: the Food Insecurity Experience Scale. This measure is presented at greater length in Chapter 3. Suffice it to point out that according to this measure, food insecurity in Gaza is very high (over 50 percent of the population are food insecure), while food security has been rising rapidly in the West Bank from 9 percent pre-COVID-19 to 23 percent during the pandemic. The brunt of food insecurity is being borne by the most vulnerable: those who lost income as a result of COVID-19 and, particularly, poor households who lost income due to COVID-19. In both the West Bank and in Gaza, the incidence of food insecurity among households in the bottom 40 percent is about twice as high as food insecurity among the top 40 percent.

For Tunisia and Djibouti, too, there is evidence suggesting food insecurity is highest among the poorest households. In Tunisia, which also used the FAO's Food Insecurity Experience Scale, households from the top quintiles face lower odds of experiencing worries about not having enough food than their counterparts from the lower quintiles (table 2.6). For example, though about 63 percent in the bottom quintile worried about not having enough food, only about 16 percent in the top quintile

TABLE 2.6

Tunisia's Poorest Households Face a Disproportionately High Risk of Food Insecurity

Food Insecurity Experience Scale indicator by quintile in Tunisia

	Quintile based on PMT				
	1	2	3	4	5
Went without eating a whole day	3.2	—	—	0.6	0.3
Worried about not having enough food	62.7	49.1	33.9	24.4	15.9
Ate less than you thought you should	29.7	22.0	17.3	9.2	5.9

Source: MENA Harmonized Database of High Frequency Phone Surveys.
Note: PMT = proxy means test (used to proxy welfare aggregates—income or consumption); — = not available.

did. In Djibouti, 17 percent of the nonpoor are food insecure, versus 25 percent of the poor. Similarly, in the West Bank and Gaza, food insecurity is particularly high (around 40 percent) among those who worked less than usual as a result of COVID-19 and got paid less.

We conclude that, unlike work stoppages, which affected all countries and economies in the region, food insecurity is a problem for specific countries and economies—with the outcomes for Djibouti, Gaza, Lebanon, the West Bank, and the Republic of Yemen being of particular concern. Given the implications of malnutrition for economic and health outcomes, the situation in these countries calls for policy action. For all countries in the region, including those in which food security is less of an immediate concern, households in the bottom quintile are bearing a disproportionately high risk.

In the wake of COVID-19, another major area to watch is what occurs on the social protection front for the diverse MENA countries and economies. An attractive feature of the phone surveys is that they can collect feedback from beneficiaries of cash transfer programs. In Djibouti and Iraq, more than 30 percent of respondents indicate that they have received some assistance from the government (figure 2.8), with about

FIGURE 2.8

Most Assistance Came from Public Funding in the Region

Share of households receiving assistance from government and from other entities (%)

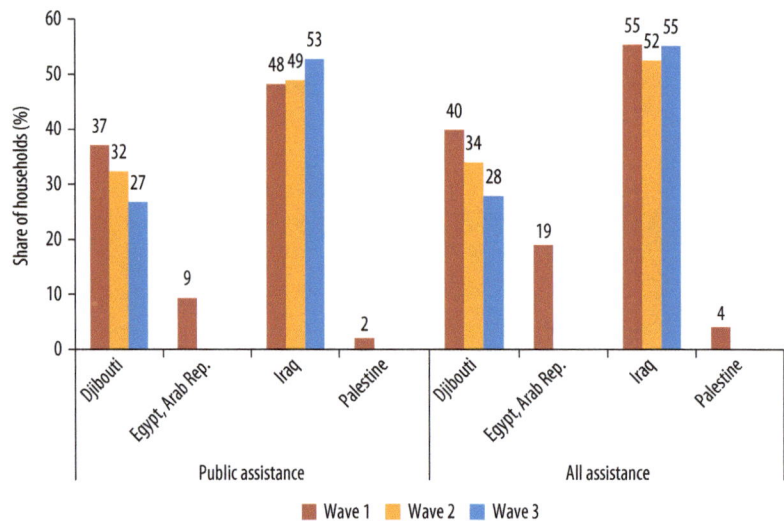

Source: MENA Harmonized Database of High Frequency Phone Surveys.
Note: For the Arab Republic of Egypt, public assistance refers to the national cash transfer program, Takaful and Karama.

2 percent of the Djibouti households receiving government cash transfers. In Egypt, 9 percent of the households were recipients of the national cash transfer program Takaful and Karama, which has been expanded since the outbreak of the pandemic. In Djibouti and Tunisia, the (cash transfer) public assistance programs appear well targeted at the poorest (table 2.7). In Tunisia in wave 1, 35 percent of respondents at the lowest quintiles indicate that they have received some public assistance from government programs—a number that is much higher than the national average (14.5 percent) and the highest quintile (4.9 percent). Although the percentage of households in the lowest quintiles are still low on average, it is relatively well targeted compared with the richer quintiles.

As for food assistance, in Egypt, a relatively large share of households benefit from food stamps or food rations, which is a widespread benefit across all income groups (89 percent for the bottom quintile and 72 percent for the top quintile). In Djibouti, around 30 percent of households from the bottom quintile receive food stamps compared with 20 percent among households from the fourth quintile. Encouragingly, food insecurity is lower among households who receive food stamps (chapter 5). And in Tunisia, receiving food assistance is more prevalent among households from the bottom quintile, with 8 percent of these households benefiting.

TABLE 2.7

Public Assistance Is Being Targeted at the Poorest

Public assistance by quintiles, by share of population (%)

		\multicolumn{6}{Quintile based on PMT score}
		1	2	3	4	5	Total
Djibouti	Wave 1	49	37	33	28	0	37
	Wave 2	37	37	30	25	0	32
	Wave 3	30	30	28	20	0	28
Egypt, Arab Rep.	Wave 1	17	9	8	5	3	10
Tunisia	Wave 1	35	25	12	10	5	15
	Wave 2	25	22	10	11	6	13

Source: MENA Harmonized Database of High Frequency Phone Surveys.
Note: For the Arab Republic of Egypt, public assistance refers to the national cash transfer program, Takaful and Karama. PMT = proxy means test (used to proxy income); — = not available.

Conclusion

In the MENA region, COVID-19 is taking a heavy toll on welfare and exacerbating long-standing structural problems such as low employment rates. And by affecting the vulnerable more, the pandemic and its impacts are increasing inequalities in a way that may take a long time to undo.

In the midst of the pandemic, HFPSs were conducted in many countries to offer a snapshot of impacts on jobs, earnings, health care, and social protection. They offer an unprecedented data collection effort aimed at producing information on the socioeconomic impact of COVID-19—and on the associated economic crisis on households and individuals in the region—at a time when more traditional data collection tools could not be employed. This chapter highlighted their key findings, which include the following:

- COVID-19 adversely affected MENA households and their members along the entire income distribution, with the hardest hit being those in the bottom 40 percent.

- Lockdown measures forced many people to stop working, and even for those who continued to work, results from HFPSs show fewer hours worked than usual and a sharp decline in their incomes.

- Once lockdown measures are lifted, many return to work and start earning an income again. Yet not all return to work, and for those who do, incomes earned are lower than before. In addition, those in the bottom 40 percent are less likely to recover fully.

- Poorer households have had less access to health care when it was needed. In the Republic of Yemen, only 47 percent of households could access health care, while in Djibouti and Tunisia it was about 63 percent.

- COVID-19 has increased the level of concern about access to food, such as in Djibouti, Gaza, Lebanon, and the Republic of Yemen, where food insecurity is widespread. Across MENA, food insecurity affects the most vulnerable in particular, and especially the poor; those affected by COVID-19-related work stoppages; and economically disadvantaged groups like refugees.

- There are promising signs that public assistance is being targeted at the poorest—as shown in Djibouti, Egypt, and Tunisia—although the numbers being reached remain low on average.

Data limitations from HFPSs make it difficult to verify the extent to which poorer households are vulnerable from the pandemic, because the surveys do not collect income and consumption information. However, in the following chapters, this report uses simulation exercises (some of which also draw on the HFPSs) to provide projections on how much poverty and inequality have increased in MENA as a result of COVID-19.

Reference

Roser, Max, and Esteban Ortiz-Ospina. 2021. COVID-19 Data Explorer (published online at OurWorldInData.org), https://ourworldindata.org/explorers/coronavirus-data-explorer.

CHAPTER 3

West Bank and Gaza: Links among Income, Jobs, and Food

Pablo Suárez Becerra, Eduardo A. Malásquez, and Jawad Al-Saleh

Key Messages

- COVID-19 affected not only the poorest Palestinian households but also those that were relatively better-off prior to the start of the pandemic, with almost 20 percent of previously employed main income earners losing their jobs from early March to late May in 2020.

- Income fell in at least 60 percent of Palestinian households across all expenditure quintiles, and 40 percent reported that their income fell by 50 percent or more.

- The pandemic has revealed how vulnerable Palestinian households are to food insecurity, even the better-off households in the West Bank, where food insecurity was low prior to COVID-19.

- Households hardest hit by higher food insecurity were those where incomes declined and the main income earner either lost their job or was unable to keep working because of restrictions.

- Access to education was limited for households of all welfare levels in the West Bank and in Gaza, but poorer households faced bigger difficulties, largely because of the lack of internet.

Introduction

COVID-19 disrupted the livelihood of Palestinian households between March and May of 2020, with the first confirmed cases reported on March 10 in the West Bank (figure 3.1). In response, the Palestinian Authority immediately declared a state of emergency, imposing restrictions that would be scaled up gradually, including suspension of educational activities, prohibition of public gatherings, closure of the Bethlehem urban area, and a halt in Palestinian employment in Israeli settlements (OCHA 2020a). Stricter measures were introduced by the Palestinian Authority on March 22, mandating people in the West Bank to stay at home, other than to purchase food and medicine and in case of emergency; and on May 25 the state of emergency was effectively ended. New measures restricting movement and activity were reintroduced later, in July, following a surge in the number of COVID-19 cases. In Gaza, educational activities were halted on March 6, and lockdown measures limiting social gatherings and business activities were introduced

FIGURE 3.1

The First Wave of COVID-19 Cases in West Bank and Gaza Peaked in Early April 2020

Daily new confirmed COVID-19 cases per million people, 7-day rolling average

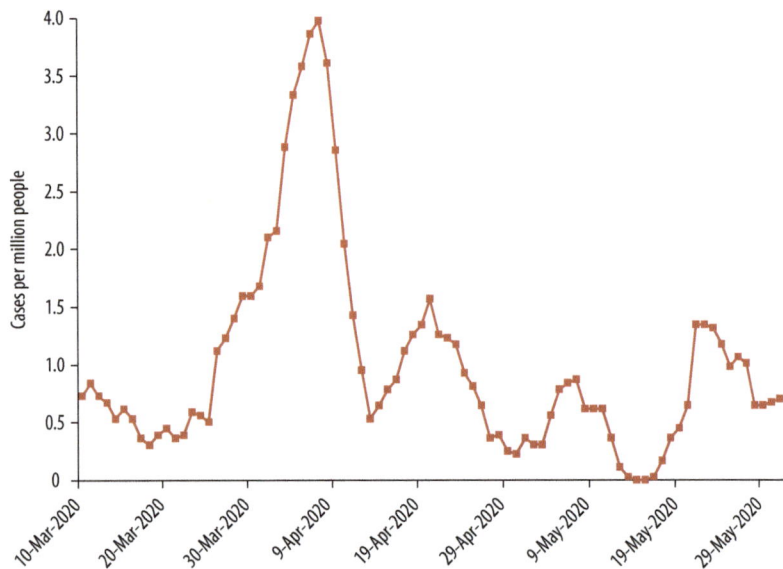

Source: Our World in Data (Roser and Ortiz-Ospina 2021).

on March 22. Business activities resumed on April 27, although the closure of schools and mosques and a ban on public gatherings continued (OCHA 2020b).

The measures adopted in both locations were successful in limiting the number of COVID-19 cases during the early months of the pandemic, despite the limited fiscal and monetary policy instruments available.[1] However, as of March 2021, the West Bank and Gaza has seen 243,479 COVID-19 cases and 2,590 deaths, which have been concentrated in two waves: one in summer 2020 and the other, more significant one, in the last quarter of 2020.

The impact of COVID-19 on the region's economy between March and May 2020 was severe, with GDP in the second quarter down by 19.4 percent compared with the same quarter in 2019, according to the Palestinian Central Bureau of Statistics (PCBS).[2] The setback aggravated an already weak economy, which before the pandemic was facing persistent fiscal deficits, high unemployment, rising poverty levels in Gaza, and declining levels of international support (World Bank 2021). In addition, a political standoff with the government of Israel disrupted clearance revenues between May and November of 2020, which affected the Palestinian Authority's ability to pay government employees' salaries during that time.[3] Preliminary PCBS estimates see a GDP contraction of 11.5 percent for the whole of 2020 compared with 2019. And World Bank projections estimate that poverty rates for the West Bank and Gaza increased from 29.3 percent in 2016 to 32.8 percent in 2019, and further to 34.7 percent in 2020 (Gansey, Aghajanian, and Al-Saleh, forthcoming).

Against this backdrop, it is vital to understand how households in the region were affected during the lockdown, especially in terms of income and employment. To bridge this information need, PCBS, together with the World Bank, United Nations Development Programme's Programme of Assistance to the Palestinian People, as well as other UN agencies (UN Women, United Nations Population Fund, United Nations Children's Fund, World Health Organization, and World Food Programme), fielded the COVID-19 Rapid Assessment Phone Survey (RAPS) between June and August of 2020, using a computer-assisted telephone interviewing approach (see box 3.1). The survey focused on households' experiences between March and May of 2020. The survey was part of an unprecedented data collection effort in the Middle East and North Africa region aimed at producing real-time information on the socioeconomic impacts of COVID-19 and the associated economic crisis on households and individuals. For some countries and economies, there was just one round (or wave); for others, multiple ones. Some began early in the pandemic, others later on.

BOX 3.1

Rapid Assessment Phone Survey (RAPS) for Palestinian Households

The 2020 RAPS draws on a probability sample of 9,910 households that were successfully interviewed in the 2018 nationally representative Socio-Economic and Food Security Survey. The response rate of the COVID-19 survey stands at 94 percent, with the total number of households interviewed being 8,709. Survey weights were designed to provide estimates that were representative at the individual level both of the West Bank and of Gaza, and the overall Palestinian households.

TABLE B3.1.1

Sample Description of Main Income Earners

| Age group | Location | | Sex of main income earner | | |
	West Bank	Gaza	Male	Female	All
24 or less	2.3	1.5	2.1	1.0	2.0
25–34	19.9	20.6	22.2	5.1	20.2
35–49	36.1	38.9	39.8	17.1	37.1
50–64	27.2	27.2	26.0	36.2	27.2
65 or more	14.4	11.8	9.9	40.5	13.5
Total	100.0	100.0	100.0	100.0	100.0
Mean age	47.6	46.6	45.6	60.0	47.3

Source: World Bank staff calculations based on the 2020 Rapid Assessment Phone Survey.

This chapter gives the phone survey results on Palestinian households between March and May of 2020, the first big lockdown period. It focuses on four themes: (a) how the pandemic affects household income, (b) how it affects food insecurity, (c) how it affects households in different parts of the welfare distribution, and (d) how changes in income and employment interact with food insecurity.

The key findings point to severe and widespread impacts on income, with almost 20 percent of previously employed main income earners losing their jobs from early March to late May in 2020. These outcomes reflect not only changes in employment status but also changes in the capacity of workers to engage in work activities. Further, COVID-19 has uncovered how vulnerable the region's households are to food insecurity, even the better-off households in the West Bank, where food insecurity was low prior to the pandemic.

A Severe, Widespread Blow to Incomes

The impact of the pandemic and associated mitigation measures on household incomes was widespread. During the lockdown, as figure 3.2 shows, two out of three households in the West Bank and Gaza suffered income losses (between March and May of 2020 compared with February 2020, the month prior to the lockdown).[4] For the West Bank, the share was 72 percent of households, and for Gaza, 57 percent. Moreover, the negative impact on income was not only widespread but also severe. Among households that reported these income drops, 40 percent said that their incomes decreased to half or less, a severity that is observed both in the West Bank (47 percent) and in Gaza (30 percent).

The results from the first wave of the RAPS (figure 3.3) show that almost two out of three main income earners in the West Bank are workers who were able to maintain their job during the period of emergency.[5] In comparison, in Gaza fewer than half (49 percent) of main income earners did. In addition, the share of main income earners who lost their work during the lockdown is slightly lower in the West Bank (13 percent) than in Gaza (15 percent). Considering that the share of main income earners not working before the lockdown is significantly higher in Gaza (36 percent) than in the West Bank (24 percent), the results would suggest that the impact of the pandemic through the labor market would have been relatively milder in the West Bank.

FIGURE 3.2

Households in the West Bank and Gaza Have Experienced Big Losses of Income

Share of households in which income decreased during lockdown (%)

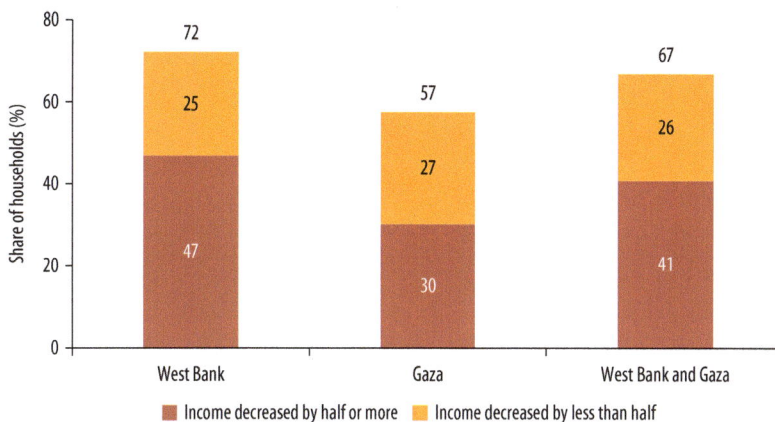

Source: World Bank staff calculations based on the 2020 Rapid Assessment Phone Survey.
Note: Data were collected between March and May of 2020 and compared with February 2020.

FIGURE 3.3

A Majority of Workers Held onto Jobs during the Lockdown
Share of main income earners employed (%)

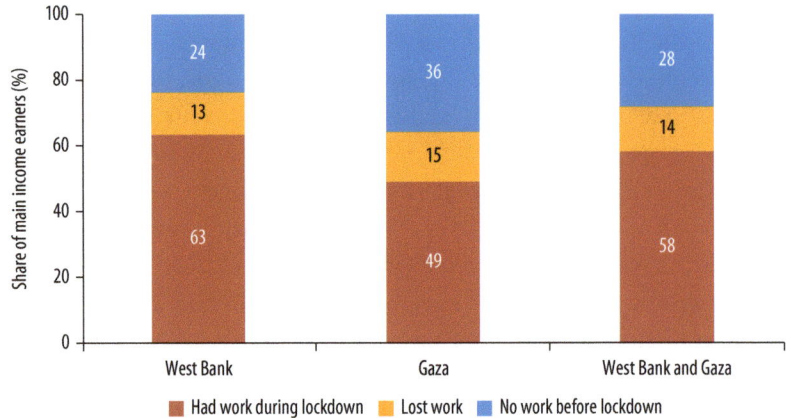

Source: World Bank staff calculations based on the 2020 Rapid Assessment Phone Survey.
Note: Data were collected between March and May of 2020 and compared with February 2020.

However, the changes in employment using the basic definition cannot explain the magnitude of the income losses. Indeed, the share of households that report income losses is much higher than the share of households whose main income earner lost their employment, as seen when comparing figure 3.2 and figure 3.3. Further, the share of households with income losses is higher in the West Bank, where the loss of employment was apparently smaller. In addition, a high share of main income earners who reported having a job during the lockdown—working as wage employees[6]—received no payments or received lower payments than usual during the period of emergency, especially in the West Bank (figure 3.4).

A possible explanation is that what explained the loss in income during the period of emergency, more than the loss of jobs, was the reduced demand for labor. To analyze how the time spent working affected Palestinian households, we break down the share of main income earners who had a job during the lockdown into three categories: (a) those who continued working the same as usual (just about 20 percent of all main income earners who had a job during lockdown); (b) those who had a job but only worked partially (about 33 percent); and (c) those who had a job but did not work at all during the lockdown (almost 50 percent).[7] Taking this approach highlights how COVID-19 had a different impact on the West Bank's labor market than it did on Gaza's. For instance, main income earners in the West Bank (34 percent) were almost twice as likely as those in Gaza (18 percent) to have had a job but not to have worked during the lockdown (figure 3.5).

FIGURE 3.4

Most Wage Workers Saw Sharp Income Drops

Share of waged main income earners whose wage payments decreased during the lockdown (%)

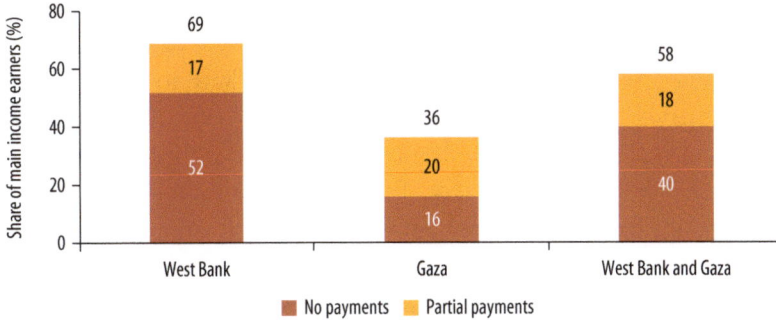

Source: World Bank calculations based on the 2020 Rapid Assessment Phone Survey.

FIGURE 3.5

West Bank and Gaza Experienced a Big Setback on Demand for Labor

Share of main income earners by work activities (%)

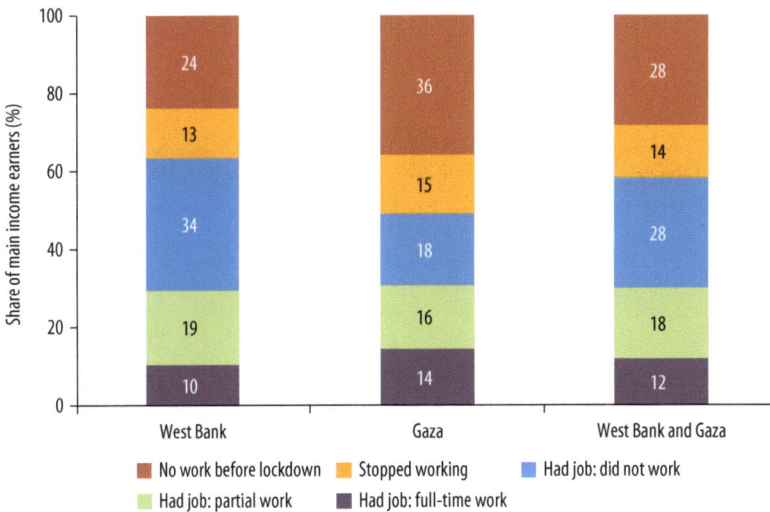

Source: World Bank staff calculations based on the 2020 Rapid Assessment Phone Survey.

Further, if we focus on the main income earners who work as wage employees, we observe a correlation between the demand for labor and changes in household income from all sources. Despite remaining employed, 61 percent of waged main income earners who were not able to work did not receive any payment during the lockdown,[8] and only about a quarter received their usual full payment (figure 3.6). In contrast, 93 percent of main income earners who worked full-time received full payments. The results suggest that having a job was no guarantee for getting paid during the lockdown.[9] Unfortunately, the 2020 RAPS did not inquire about changes in the personal income of the self-employed, although our hypothesis is that they likely followed a similar pattern (where incomes are associated with the demand for the fruits of their labor).

Thus, household income dynamics during the lockdown can be explained by the main income earners' capacity to engage in work activities. We find a strong correlation between the share of households that faced a reduction in income from all sources and the main income earner's engagement in work activities during the lockdown. Indeed, 93 percent of households whose main income earners lost their job during the lockdown faced lower incomes (figure 3.7). In contrast, less than half (42 percent) of the households where the main income earner had a job and continued working full-time experienced an income reduction. In addition, income declined for 78 percent of households where the main income earner had a job but worked less than usual (either partially or not at all). A significant share of households (about

FIGURE 3.6

Having a Job Is No Guarantee of Being Paid

Share of waged main income earners being paid during the lockdown, by work activities (%)

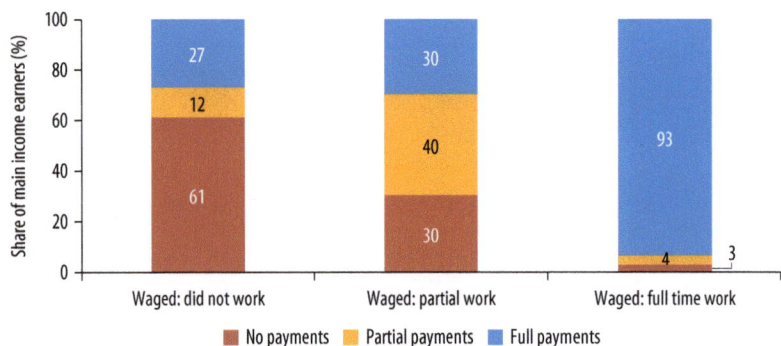

Source: World Bank staff calculations based on the 2020 Rapid Assessment Phone Survey.

FIGURE 3.7

Lower Engagement in Work Meant Lower Incomes

Share of households faced with lower income during lockdown, by main income earner's work activities (%)

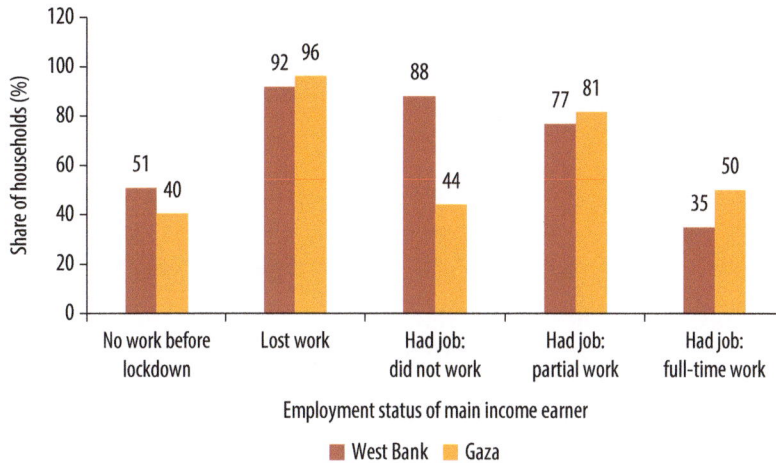

Source: World Bank staff calculations based on the 2020 Rapid Assessment Phone Survey.

40 percent) where the main income earner was not working before the period of emergency also suffered an income reduction.

Similarly, the most significant spatial differences in household income dynamics occur when the main income earner held a job during the lockdown but did not work at all. In the West Bank, 88 percent of households where the main income earner had a job but was not requested to perform work activities reported lower incomes. In contrast, the share of similar households in Gaza facing lower incomes was just 44 percent. This is significant since the share of main income earners with a job but who were not working was almost twice as large in the West Bank (34 percent) than in Gaza (18 percent).

Even when the main income earner had a job and continued working full-time during the lockdown, 50 percent of households in Gaza faced lower household incomes versus 35 percent in the West Bank. This suggests that either the labor incomes among workers in Gaza were more likely to fall than in the West Bank or that other sources of household income (besides the labor income of the main earner) had been affected during the pandemic. While 40 percent of households in Gaza where the main income earner did not have a job during the lockdown faced lower incomes, this number was higher in the West Bank at 51 percent, suggesting the relative importance of alternative sources of incomes among households in Gaza.

A Significant Increase in Food Insecurity

Besides causing big, widespread changes in income and employment, COVID-19 has taken a large toll on food security for households in the region. We use the Food Insecurity Experience Scale (FIES), a measurement metric developed by the UN Food and Agriculture Organization (FAO), to assess food insecurity.[10] The scale allows us to distinguish among various levels of food insecurity, and in our study, we use the term "food insecurity" to refer to moderate or severe food insecurity,[11] resulting in the following two findings:

- Food insecurity is many times higher in Gaza than in the West Bank, a consistent finding for both 2018 and during the lockdown.[12]

- The increase in food insecurity has been more significant in the West Bank (from 8.7 percent in 2018 to 22.8 percent in 2020) than in Gaza (from 50.2 percent to 52.9 percent) (figure 3.8).

Taken together, these two findings suggest that, despite the higher prevalence of food insecurity among households in Gaza prior to and during the lockdown, the households in the West Bank were more likely to fall into food insecurity (that is, to transition from food secure to

FIGURE 3.8

Food Insecurity Rose during the Lockdown

Prevalence of food insecurity (moderate or severe) by year (percentage of households that faced food insecurity)

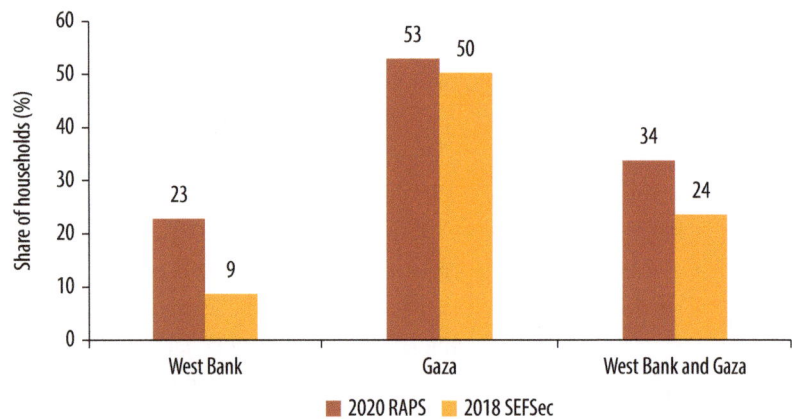

Source: World Bank staff calculations based on the 2020 Rapid Assessment Phone Survey (RAPS) and the 2018 Socio-Economic and Food Security Survey (SEFSec).

food insecure) during the lockdown period.[13] This suggestion is consistent with findings by Atamanov and Palaniswamy (2018) that, prepandemic, households in the West Bank were particularly vulnerable to welfare shocks. Alternative factors could help explain the relatively larger impact of the pandemic on food insecurity in the West Bank, such as differences in the existing social protection system or the capacity of the households to mitigate the negative shock from the pandemic.

Given this greater vulnerability to food insecurity, our findings suggest that the initial response to expand the social protection network to households in the West Bank was necessary. While almost 80 percent of households in Gaza were already beneficiaries of the social protection system before the lockdown, only 14 percent of those in the West Bank were covered. Our results underscore the significance of the expansion among households in the West Bank, which more than doubled the number of beneficiary households prior to the lockdown (figure 3.9). Overall, after the social protection expansion during the lockdown, 30 percent of households in the West Bank were beneficiaries of some type of program, while in Gaza it was 80 percent.[14]

FIGURE 3.9

The Social Protection Network in the West Bank More Than Doubled

Distribution of households receiving social protection benefits before and during the lockdown (%)

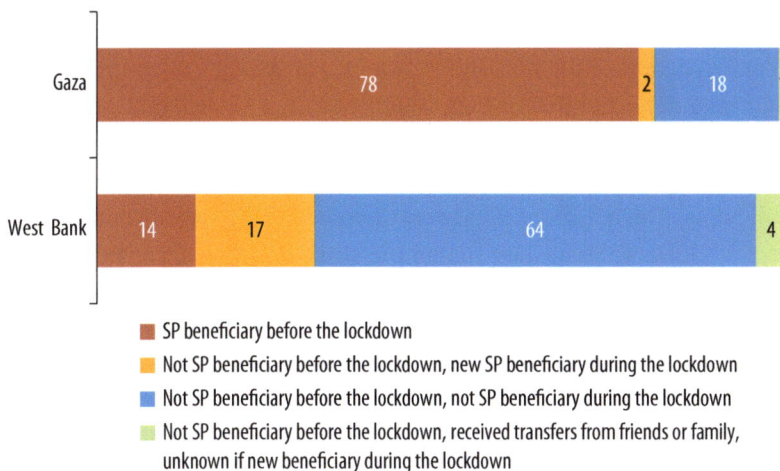

- ■ SP beneficiary before the lockdown
- ■ Not SP beneficiary before the lockdown, new SP beneficiary during the lockdown
- ■ Not SP beneficiary before the lockdown, not SP beneficiary during the lockdown
- ■ Not SP beneficiary before the lockdown, received transfers from friends or family, unknown if new beneficiary during the lockdown

Source: World Bank staff calculations based on the 2020 Rapid Assessment Phone Survey.
Note: SP = social protection.

COVID-19 Impacts on Household Welfare

So far, we have focused on how the pandemic has affected labor market outcomes (notably income and employment) in terms of scale, prevalence, and location, along with how it has affected food insecurity. Now we turn our attention to the heterogeneous impacts of the pandemic on households with different levels of expenditures. We treat each household's welfare in 2018 as a proxy of its welfare in 2020, that is, before the lockdown. We then analyze the distributional impacts of the pandemic using as a base the expenditure quintiles from the 2018 Socio-Economic and Food Security Survey (SEFSec). More precisely, our analysis uses per capita expenditure as the relevant welfare indicator to construct the quintiles.[15]

Distributional Impact of COVID-19 on Incomes

Which households, from the poorest to the richest, experienced the biggest impacts in terms of reduced incomes? Our results show that the negative impacts of the pandemic on household incomes have been prevalent among Palestinian households. Overall, income fell in at least 60 percent of the region's households across all expenditure quintiles, without significant differences across the distribution, and 40 percent reported that their income fell by 50 percent or more across the whole expenditure distribution.

Given the spatial disparities in the living standards between the West Bank and Gaza, the rest of our analysis is based on separate quintiles of per capita expenditure for each location rather than quintiles of per capita expenditure for the full population. For example, when using quintiles for the whole population in the West Bank and Gaza, we find that 44 percent of the households from Gaza belong to the lowest overall expenditure quintile (versus 6 percent in the West Bank), and about 75 percent of the households belong to the two lowest quintiles (versus 21 percent in the West Bank) (see annex figure 3A.1). Similarly, using the full population quintiles, 80 percent of households in the bottom quintile live in Gaza, while in the top quintile almost 95 percent of households are from the West Bank (see figure 3A.2). Keep in mind, though, that one-to-one comparisons between quintiles in the two locations would be misleading, since these quintiles were constructed separately and correspond to different levels of expenditure.

When we break down the results between the West Bank and Gaza we find that households in both locations experienced lower incomes at all expenditure levels (figure 3.10). However, within the West Bank and in Gaza, we find that poorer households were more likely to face a negative income shock. For instance, while more than 76 percent of

FIGURE 3.10

Poorer Households Were More Likely to Face Income Declines

Share of households with income decrease and quintile of expenditure (%)

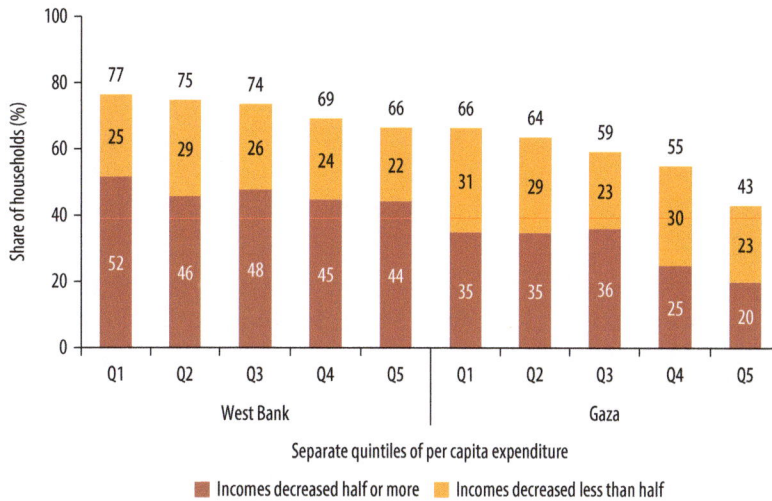

Source: World Bank staff calculations based on the 2020 Rapid Assessment Phone Survey and 2018 Socio-Economic and Food Security Survey.
Note: Expenditure quintiles calculated independently in the West Bank and in Gaza.

households in the bottom quintile faced lower incomes in the West Bank, incomes declined for only 66 percent of those in the top quintile. Similarly, while 43 percent of households in the top quintile in Gaza experienced a negative income shock, this share is higher for the bottom quintile at 66 percent. In addition, the pandemic was a major setback for the education of children in Palestinian households at all income levels, but especially for the poorest ones (box 3.2).

Further, the negative impacts of the pandemic on household incomes were not only widespread but also severe, and even more so in the West Bank. According to the RAPS, in the West Bank incomes dropped for 7 in 10 households during lockdown, and of these, two out of three households reported income decreased to half or less. In Gaza, more than half of households whose income dropped reported that it dropped by half or more.

Distributional Impact of COVID-19 on Employment

As for how the pandemic affected employment across the welfare distribution, we find that in the West Bank, main income earners at all levels were affected by job losses or lack of demand for their services (figure 3.11 and box 3.3). Further, a large share of main income earners of all levels

BOX 3.2

Children's Education Faced New Obstacles

COVID-19 severely limited the access of Palestinian children to education during the period between March and May of 2020. The lockdown coincided with the last three months of the school year in the West Bank and Gaza. The 2020 Rapid Assessment Phone Survey asks households with children ages 6–18 attending school before the lockdown (a) if their children were engaged in any education or learning activities during the period of emergency, and (b) if their children, or anyone else, were in contact with their teachers during the lockdown.

The results show that the children in half of the region's households were not engaged at all in education activities during the lockdown, with similar shares both in the West Bank and in Gaza. Further, 60 percent of households report that they were not in

contact with their children's teachers during the lockdown (the share being slightly higher in the West Bank than in Gaza).

These setbacks affected Palestinian children of all income levels, especially the poorest. Children in 60 percent of households in the lowest quintile (in both locations) were not engaged in any education activity during lockdown, while for the highest quintile in the West Bank and in Gaza, the percentage is smaller (39 percent and 35 percent, respectively), although it is still high. The main obstacle for children in the poorest households being engaged was the lack of internet (figure B3.1.1). Another major obstacle was the lack of activities by teachers, as reported by households of all income levels in the West Bank and by households in the top quintile in Gaza.

FIGURE B3.1.1

Lack of Internet and Teacher Participation Are the Main Obstacles for Education

Share of households where children stopped education during the lockdown, by separate quintile of per capita expenditure, divided by reason children stopped education (%)

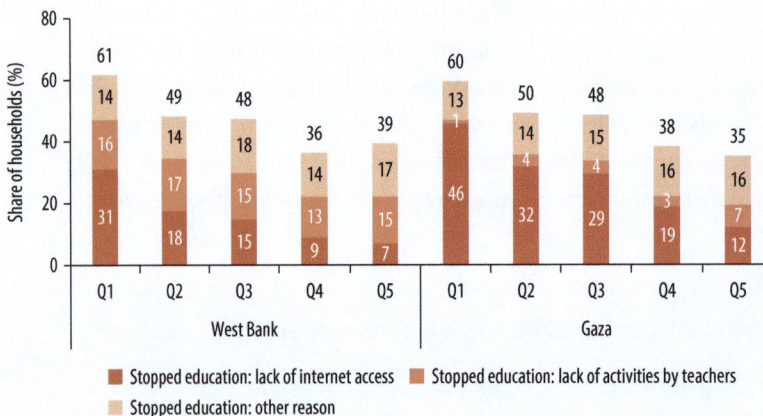

Source: World Bank staff calculations based on the 2020 Rapid Assessment Phone Survey and 2018 Socio-Economic and Food Security Survey.
Note: For children ages 6–18 in school before the lockdown.

FIGURE 3.11

Main Income Earners Experienced Job Loss or Lack of Demand for Work if They Maintained Their Jobs

Share of main income earners' engagement in work activities, by quintiles of per capita expenditure (%)

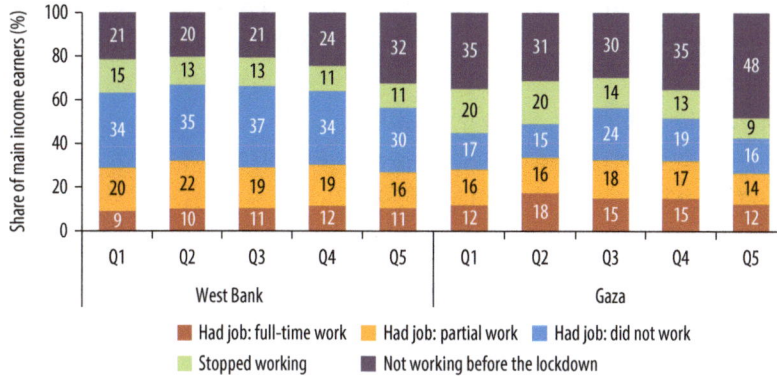

Source: World Bank staff calculations based on the 2020 Rapid Assessment Phone Survey and 2018 Socio-Economic and Food Security Survey.
Note: Expenditure quintiles are calculated independently for the West Bank and Gaza.

BOX 3.3

COVID-19's Toll on the West Bank and Gaza Labor Market

The labor market for Palestinian workers was particularly hard hit by the pandemic. In the second quarter of 2020, about 121,000 people lost their jobs compared with the first quarter of 2020, according to the Palestinian Central Bureau of Statistics (PCBS 2020). This included 25,000 Palestinian workers who cross the border to work in Israel (World Bank 2020). The loss of jobs in Israel would have especially affected West Bank residents. In 2017, almost a fifth of jobs that employed Palestinians in the West Bank were jobs in Israel and the settlements; these correspond to workers of all expenditure levels. In contrast, the share of workers in Gaza working outside Gaza was close to zero (Atamanov and Palaniswamy 2018).

However, changes in the unemployment rate do not capture the magnitude of the labor

market effect. PCBS (2020) reports that the unemployment rate in the West Bank and Gaza in the second quarter of 2020 (26.6 percent) was high but close to the unemployment rate in the second quarter of 2019 (26.0 percent). However, the labor force participation rate decreased in the second quarter of 2020 compared with the same quarter in 2019 (38.5 percent, from 44.2 percent). Further, in the second quarter of 2020, 264,100 workers—representing 29.7 percent of the employed Palestinians—reported that they were employed but absent from work.

Moreover, the results from the 2020 Rapid Assessment Phone Survey find that when focusing only on the lockdown period (March–May 2020) and on main income earners, the limitations on the capacity to work may have been even more severe.

(about 34 percent on average) report being employed but not working during the lockdown. Whether this group was able to go back to performing their usual work after the lockdown will be examined in the second round of the 2020 RAPS.

In Gaza, however, main income earners from the poorest households were more likely to suffer job loss during the lockdown. About 30 percent of main income earners in Gaza who were working before the lockdown report that they lost their job during the lockdown, calling into question their ability to return to work once the lockdown had eased. The number was lower, but still high, among main income earners in the top three quintiles, since 20 percent of main income earners who were working before the lockdown lost their job.

Distributional Impact of COVID-19 on Food Insecurity

As for food insecurity, it increased across all expenditure quintiles both in the West Bank and in Gaza, but its prevalence was especially high in Gaza. The poorest households in the region faced higher food insecurity both in 2018 and in 2020 (during the lockdown). Even before the pandemic, the levels of food insecurity in Gaza were multiple times higher than in the West Bank (figure 3.12). During the lockdown, however, moderate

FIGURE 3.12

Food Insecurity Was Far Higher in Gaza Than in the West Bank before COVID-19

Prevalence of food insecurity by per capita expenditure and year, by share of households (%)

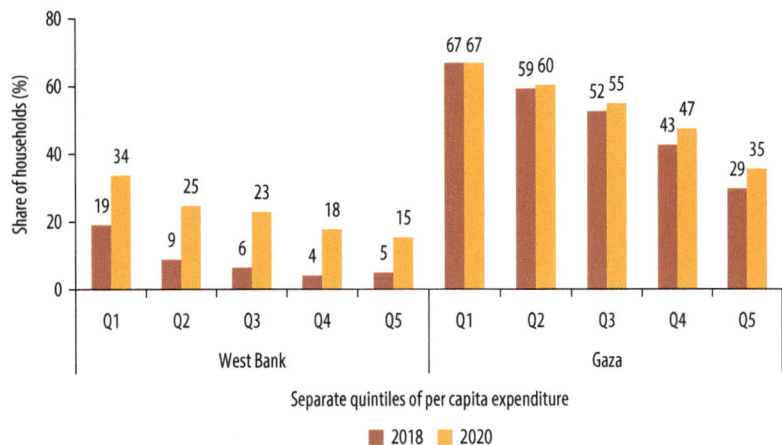

Source: World Bank staff calculations based on the 2020 Rapid Assessment Phone Survey and 2018 Socio-Economic and Food Security Survey.

and severe food insecurity increased for everyone, except for the bottom quintile in Gaza, which was already facing very high food insecurity rates. Notably, the prevalence of moderate and severe food insecurity for the bottom quintile in the West Bank is lower than food insecurity for the richest 20 percent in the Gaza in 2020.

A Complex Link: Food Insecurity, Income Loss, and Job Loss

A final question considers what might be the link between changes in income and employment and changes in food insecurity. The pandemic has shown that even the better-off households were vulnerable to food insecurity after a negative shock to incomes. Using the FAO's Food Insecurity Experience Scale, we calculate the probability of each household being food insecure in 2018 and during the 2020 lockdown, and then analyze whether changes in the household's income and in its main income earner's employment are correlated with changes in food insecurity. We used the probability of being food insecure in 2018 as a proxy for the probability of being food insecure before lockdown.

Our results show that self-reported income loss is correlated with higher food insecurity during the lockdown—across the whole expenditure distribution. Overall, food insecurity for the West Bank and Gaza increased from 23.5 percent in the 2018 Socio-Economic and Food Security Survey to 33.8 percent in the 2020 RAPS. However, food insecurity is higher among households whose income decreased, both in the West Bank and in Gaza. Within households where income decreased during the lockdown, food insecurity prevalence increased compared with 2018 levels: 18 percentage points in the West Bank and 8 points in Gaza (figure 3.13). Although the increase is stronger in the West Bank, the baseline food insecurity in Gaza was already high, at 54 percent in 2018. Food insecurity in Gaza in 2018 was higher among households whose income decreased during the period of emergency.

The increase in food insecurity during the lockdown is related to income losses across the whole expenditure distribution, even among households in the highest quintiles. Households across all expenditure levels saw their food insecurity increase in 2020 if their income decreased during the lockdown, including the richest households (figure 3.14). Almost 40 percent of households whose income decreased in the bottom quintile in the West Bank were food insecure during the lockdown. The increase in food insecurity is common to all households that lost income In Gaza, households whose income decreased also faced higher food insecurity during the lockdown than households that belong to the

FIGURE 3.13

Income Loss Goes Hand in Hand with Greater Food Insecurity

Prevalence of moderate and severe food insecurity by change in income during lockdown, by share of households (%)

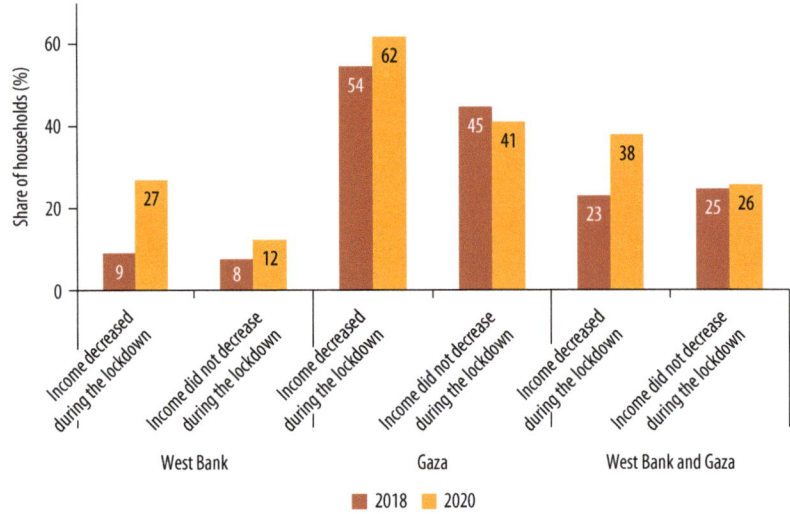

Source: World Bank staff calculations based on the 2020 Rapid Assessment Phone Survey and 2018 Socio-Economic and Food Security Survey.

FIGURE 3.14

All Households with Lower Incomes Saw Higher Food Insecurity

Share of households with food insecurity in 2018 and 2020 by change in income during the lockdown across the expenditure distribution (%)

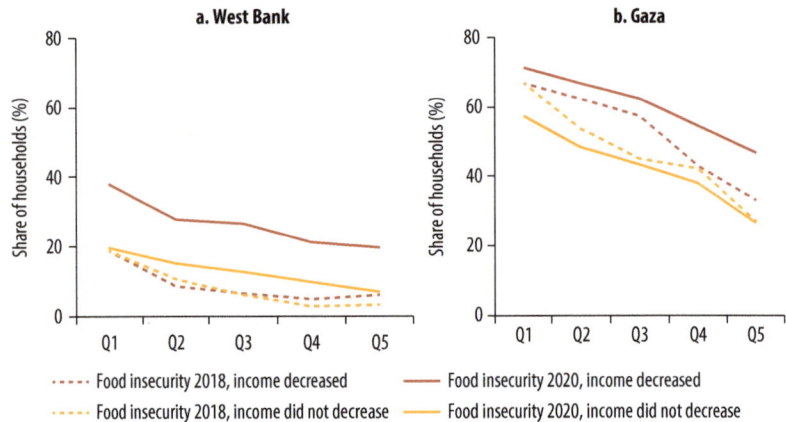

Source: 2020 Rapid Assessment Phone Survey and 2018 Socio-Economic and Food Security Survey.

same quintile but whose income did not decrease. For the second and third quintiles in Gaza, households that lost income in 2020 were also more food insecure in 2018. Overall, the pandemic has shown that even the better-off households in the region are vulnerable to food insecurity.

Food insecurity in 2020 was worse among those households whose main income earners were not able to work their usual number of hours during the period of emergency. In 2020, food insecurity in the West Bank and in Gaza was lower among households where the main income earner was able to work as usual. In the West Bank, the worse-off households were those where the main income earner (a) was not working before the lockdown, (b) lost their job, or (c) kept their job but were not able to work. In Gaza the worse-off households were those where the main income earner lost their job; 78 percent of households in this group were food insecure in 2020.[16]

A regression analysis helps clarify the relationship between changes in food insecurity, income loss, and employment. As figure 3.15 shows, the prevalence of food insecurity in 2018 in the West Bank was higher among households whose main income earner was not working before the lockdown or lost their job during the period of emergency. In addition, in Gaza, food insecurity was highest in 2018 among households whose main income

FIGURE 3.15

Ability to Keep Working Reduced the Likelihood of Higher Food Insecurity

Share of households with moderate and severe food insecurity by main income earner's engagement in work during the lockdown (%)

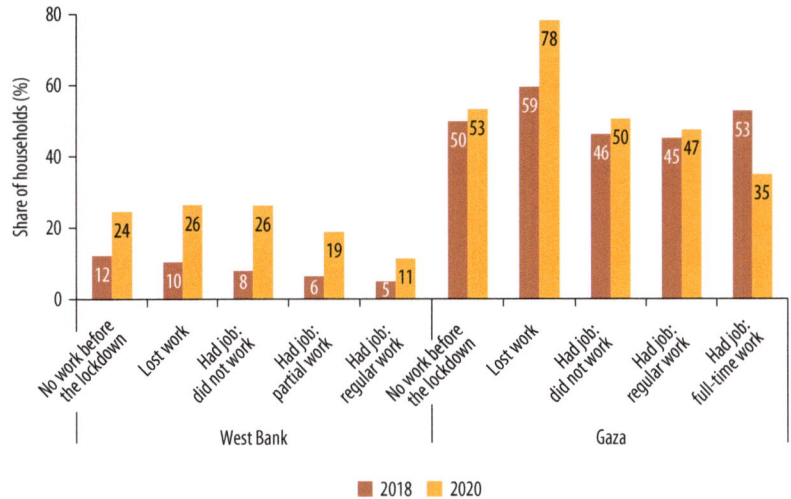

Source: World Bank staff calculations based on the 2020 Rapid Assessment Phone Survey and 2018 Socio-Economic and Food Security Survey.

earner lost their work during the period of emergency. To test the correlation between the increase in food insecurity and changes in employment and income, we propose to estimate the following linear model:

$$\Delta p_h = \alpha_0 + W_h \gamma + DI_h \theta + R_h \delta + X_h \beta + \varepsilon_h \qquad (3.1)$$

where the dependent variable, Δp_h, is the change, between 2018 and 2020, of the probability of household h being moderately or severely food insecure.[17] In equation 3.1, W_h is a set of dummy variables for each of the possible work status situations of the main income earner during the lockdown (as seen in figure 3.16). DI_h is a dummy variable that indicates if household h's income decreased during the period of emergency. R_h is a dummy indicating if the household lives in the West Bank or Gaza; and X_h is a set of control variables.[18] Finally, ε_h represents the estimation error term. The linear model is estimated using ordinary least squares, and the estimated coefficients are included in table 3A.1 in the annex.

FIGURE 3.16

The Likelihood of Being Food Insecure Was Higher in the West Bank Than in Gaza

Predicted changes in food insecurity from base scenarios, 2018 to 2020, as a result of changes in household income, work activities during the lockdown, and location

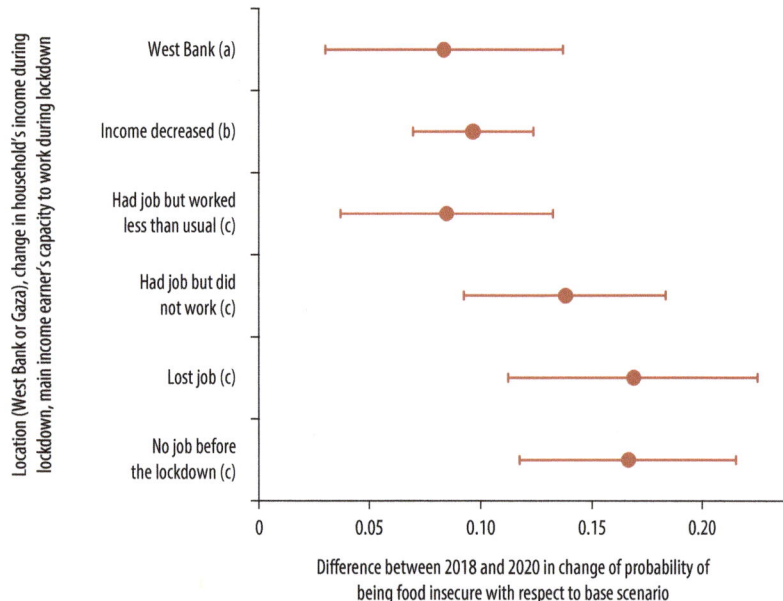

Source: World Bank staff calculations based on the 2020 Rapid Assessment Phone Survey and 2018 Socio-Economic and Food Security Survey.
Note: The base scenarios are (a) household lives in Gaza, (b) household's income did not decrease during the lockdown, and (c) household's main income earner worked as usual during the lockdown.

Changes in food insecurity driven by income shocks during lockdown differ significantly. Households that faced an income reduction during lockdown faced a 10 percentage point increase in the probability of being food insecure compared with households without income decreases. In addition, shocks in the employment of the main income earner during the lockdown help explain some of the differences in the change of food insecurity. Households whose main income earner worked less hours, stopped working, or did not work before lockdown faced higher increases in food insecurity than households whose main income earners kept working their usual number of hours during lockdown. We also find significant differences between households whose main income earner was able to work but worked less hours and households whose main income earners were not able to work, lost their job, or had no job before lockdown.

Finally, consistent with our previous analysis, we find significant differences in the change in food insecurity between the West Bank and Gaza. Even after controlling for other characteristics, the increase in the probability of being food insecure was 8.4 percentage points higher in the West Bank than in Gaza (figure 3.16 and table 3A.1 in the annex).

Conclusion

The 2020 RAPS underscores that COVID-19 seriously disrupted the livelihoods of Palestinian households through the labor market channel between March and May 2020, the period of emergency, or the lockdown. Our in-depth analysis of the phone survey and the 2018 SEFSec find that the pandemic affected not only the poorest households but also those that were relatively better-off prior to the start of the pandemic. What follows are a few key takeaways to help guide future targeted interventions.

First, our analysis suggests that although 20 percent of previously employed main income earners lost their job during the period of emergency, employment losses do not fully explain the observed income loss during the lockdown. Rather, another major factor is at work: changes in the demand for work for workers who had not lost their jobs. This helps explain some of the differences in the impacts of the pandemic on household incomes between the West Bank and Gaza. Among previously employed main income earners, less than half were able to work at least partially, and only a fraction were able to work as usual. In the West Bank, 40 percent of the previously employed main income earners reported still having a job but not being able to work. In Gaza, however, a higher share of main income earners who stopped working may have lost their jobs permanently.

Second, the pandemic has revealed how vulnerable Palestinian households are to food insecurity, even those who were better off prior to the lockdown. On the basis of the Food Insecurity Experience Scale (SDG Indicator 2.1.2), we observe that 1 out of 3 Palestinian households suffered from moderate or severe food insecurity during the period of emergency. This rate increased from about 1 out of 4 households in 2018. The West Bank saw the highest increase, with the percentage of moderate or severe food insecurity of households increasing from 8.7 in 2018 to 22.8 during the March–May 2020 period.

Third, during the lockdown, the negative impacts of the pandemic on household incomes were both prevalent and severe. They affected households across all expenditure quintiles, although the share of households with self-reported losses of income is slightly higher among the poorest quintiles, both in the West Bank and in Gaza. In the West Bank, the main income earners at all welfare levels experienced job loss or were unable to perform their work, while in Gaza, the main income earners from the poorest households were more likely to lose their job during the lockdown.

Fourth, self-reported income loss is correlated with higher food insecurity during the lockdown. This finding is true across the income distribution. For all quintiles in the West Bank and in Gaza, households whose income decreased were more food insecure than households whose income did not decrease, with differences being between 10 and 20 percentage points.

What might be future areas of inquiry? One question focuses on the differences in results between the West Bank and Gaza. Could other factors not observed in the surveys be in play, such as preexisting social protection nets? In Gaza, before the pandemic, these nets covered almost 80 percent of households, while in the West Bank, the coverage was lower, although it more than doubled during the lockdown. Our findings suggest that further studies are needed to explain the dramatic increase in food insecurity in the West Bank, beyond changes in income and work conditions.

Another line of inquiry could center on the situation of households whose main income earner was not working before the period of emergency. Our results suggest that half of these households experienced income losses during the lockdown and that, on average, food insecurity increased compared with households whose main income earner kept working as usual or continued working at least partially. The group is heterogeneous and includes, among other factors, (a) households with a retired pensioner as main income earner, (b) households whose main income earner was looking for work when the economy closed, and (c) potentially, households that report the household head to be the main income earner despite other members providing the main source of income.

Annex

Most households in the lower expenditure quintiles are located in Gaza, as opposed to the West Bank, where most households are in the third to fifth expenditure quintiles.

FIGURE 3A.1

Distribution of Households by Overall Quintile of Expenditure, by Share of Households (%)

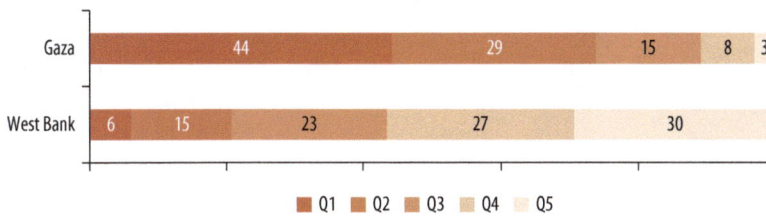

Source: World Bank staff calculations based on the 2020 Rapid Assessment Phone Survey and 2018 Socio-Economic and Food Security Survey.

FIGURE 3A.2

Most Households in the Lower Expenditure Quintiles Are Located in Gaza, as Opposed to the West Bank

Composition of overall quintiles of expenditure between the West Bank and Gaza, by share of households (%)

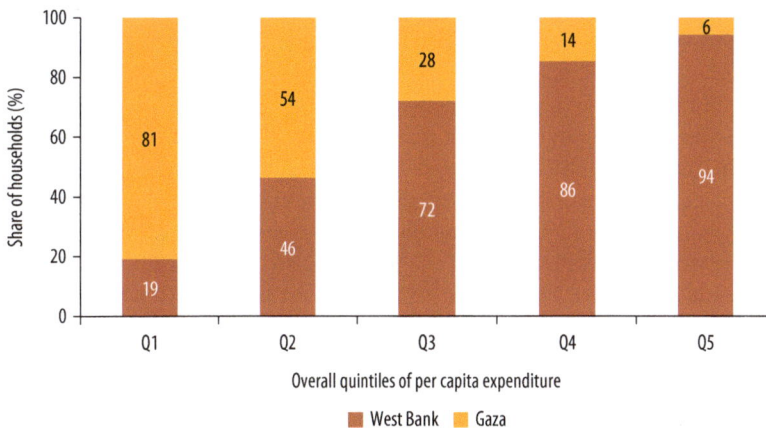

Source: World Bank staff calculations based on the 2020 Rapid Assessment Phone Survey and 2018 Socio-Economic and Food Security Survey.

TABLE 3A.1

Ordinary Least Squares Estimates of the Change in Probability of Being Moderately or Severely Food Insecure

Dependent variable: Change in probability of being moderate or severe food insecure between 2018 and 2020	(1) All variables	(2) Location only	(3) Location and work only	(4) Location and income change only
Location is West Bank	0.084	0.097	0.095	0.078
	(0.027)	(0.028)	(0.027)	(0.027)
Main income earner during the lockdown:				
did not have a job before the lockdown	0.162		0.171	
	(0.025)		(0.024)	
lost job he/she had before the lockdown	0.158		0.204	
	(0.028)		(0.026)	
had a job but did not work	0.132		0.164	
	(0.023)		(0.022)	
had a job but worked fewer hours than usual	0.081		0.114	
	(0.024)		(0.023)	
Household's income decreased during the lockdown	0.098			0.115
	(0.014)			(0.013)
Includes controls[a]	Yes	Yes	Yes	Yes
Observations	8,428	8,428	8,428	8,428
R-squared	0.048	0.024	0.040	0.037

Source: World Bank staff calculations based on the 2020 Rapid Assessment Phone Survey and 2018 Socio-Economic and Food Security Survey.
Note: Robust standard errors are in parentheses.
a. Estimates in all equations include controls for log per capita expenditure, locality (urban/rural/camps), change in household size, as well as sex, age group, refugee status, and education level of household head. Expenditure is obtained from SEFSec and corresponds to 2018. Head's education refers to the education of the head of household in 2018.

Notes

1. The number of cases of COVID-19 in the West Bank and Gaza increased during a second wave of infections in July and September of 2020. Cases peaked during a third wave of infections at the end of 2020, and then again in April 2021. The Palestinian Authority, in collaboration with the government of Israel and development partners, took proactive steps to respond to the pandemic which included community engagement campaigns, delivery of personal protection equipment, administration of COVID-19 tests, dedication of 16 hospitals to COVID-19 management, establishment of quarantine facilities, and training of health care workers. The pandemic, however, has disrupted health system financing, which requires support to face challenges in 2021 (World Bank 2021).

2. Palestinian Central Bureau of Statistics. "2015 Quarterly national accounts variables in Palestine* for the years 2019, 2020 at constant prices." http://www.pcbs.gov.ps/statisticsIndicatorsTables.aspx?lang=en&table_id=629.

3. Clearance revenues include import taxes, value added tax on bilateral trade, and revenues collected from Palestinian workers. Clearance revenues are collected by the government of Israel on behalf of the Palestinian Authority and represent half of the Palestinian Authority's revenues (World Bank 2020).

4. RAPS asks households whether—compared with their income from all sources in February 2020—their income during the period of emergency (a) increased, (b) remained the same, (c) decreased by less than half, or (d) decreased by half or more.

5. A main income earner (MIE) is classified as having work during the period of emergency if the household answers affirmatively to any of the following three questions in RAPS: (a) did MIE work for wages, salary, or other income during period of emergency even for one hour?; (b) did MIE do any work during period of emergency even for one hour in family enterprise or farm?; and (c) did MIE have, during the period of emergency, any work or enterprise for which he/she was (temporarily) absent? For MIE with a negative answer to the three questions, RAPS asks: was MIE working before the period of emergency? This question is used to identify main income earners who lost their work during the period of emergency.

6. For main income earners who reported having a job as wage employees during the lockdown, RAPS asks if they were paid, be it fully or partially, during the lockdown even if they were not working as usual. The survey does not inquire about income received during the lockdown by main income earners working as self-employed workers or employers.

7. The categories are based on a set of questions on the number of hours that the main income earner worked per week during the lockdown (which are asked regarding main income earners with work during the lockdown). Main income earners working as usual or more than usual hours per week are categorized as working full-time. Those who report working fewer hours per week than usual are considered to do partial work. Those who report working zero hours per week are categorized as having a job but not working during the lockdown.

8. For main income earners working as wage employees during the lockdown, RAPS asks if they were paid, be it fully or partially, during the lockdown even if they were not working as usual. The survey does not inquire about income received during the lockdown by main income earners working as self-employed workers or employers.

9. The payment numbers in figure 3.6 are mixed among main income earners who worked partially during the lockdown, but they do not contradict the finding that incomes were related to the actual working activities more than the employment status (that is, having a job during the lockdown).

10. The Food Insecurity Experience Scale (FIES) was developed by FAO's Voices of the Hungry Project to "provide timely information on the adequacy of people's access to food by asking them directly about their experiences" http://www.fao.org/in-action/voices-of-the-hungry/en/. Further information about FIES methodology can be found in FAO (2016). The FIES parameters were estimated and statically validated using FAO's FIES App (https://fies.shinyapps.io/ExtendedApp/). The scales in both surveys were calibrated to a global standard for comparability.

11. All households in the 2020 RAPS were previously interviewed for SEFSec in 2018. The estimates for food insecurity in 2018 in this document are limited

to households interviewed in both surveys. The weights of households in RAPS have been adjusted to guarantee representativeness of the estimates.

12. This is consistent with poverty rate estimates by Atamanov and Palaniswamy (2018); in 2017 the headcount poverty rate in the West Bank was 14 percent, and in Gaza it was 53 percent.

13. The assumption behind this conclusion is that food insecurity did not change significantly between September 2018, when SEFSec was conducted, and March–May of 2020, the recall period for RAPS.

14. In Gaza, governmental and nongovernmental social assistance in 2017 accounted for nearly a quarter of households' consumption expenditures and 45 percent of total income among Gaza's poor who are 53 percent of the population (Atamanov and Palaniswamy 2018).

15. The 2018 SEFSec asks households to provide their aggregate average monthly expenditures during the first half of 2018 on (a) food, (b) clothing and shoes, (c) home appliances, (d) house needs, (e) health care, (f) transportation, (g) communication, (h) cultural and recreational activities, (i) personal care, (j) cigarettes and tobacco, and (k) electricity. We calculate monthly total expenditure by adding these 11 elements, plus the annual expenditure on education during 2017, and dividing by 12. Our aggregate excludes expenditures on durable goods, furniture, and vehicles. SEFSec instructs households to include as part of their expenditures self-produced food and nonfood, including self-imputed rent.

16. According to Atamanov and Palaniswamy (2018), a decrease of poverty in the West Bank between 2011 and 2017 (17.8 percent to 13.9 percent) was mainly driven by improvement in labor incomes. A negative shock on the labor market like the one observed between March and May of 2020 would be expected to have negative consequences for poverty and potentially for food insecurity.

17. Both the 2018 SEFSec and 2020 RAPS include a set of eight yes or no questions about food insecurity collected to measure food insecurity based on the Food Insecurity Experience Scale (FIES). Based on a household's answers, a raw score is assigned to each; the raw score is equal to the number of questions for which the household answered yes and goes from 0 to 8. Based on its raw score, FIES assigns to each household a probability of having moderate or severe food insecurity. The probability of being food insecure is a continuous variable, but because it is based on the raw score it may take only nine possible values. To calculate these probabilities we follow FAO's methodology of standardizing and equating the scale and use FAO's tool for FIES data analysis available at https://fies.shinyapps.io/ExtendedApp/. The process is done separately for the 2018 SEFSec and 2020 RAPS. A caveat of this process is that a same raw score may be assigned different probabilities in the two surveys. In our case the probabilities assigned for the 2020 RAPS are slightly lower than those assigned for the 2018 SEFSec. This may bias our results to show a decrease in food insecurity between 2018 and 2020.

18. The set of control variables includes locality (urban, rural, and camps), change of household size between 2018 and 2020, log of per capita expenditure (in 2018), log of per capita expenditure squared (in 2018), sex of household head (in 2020), age of household head (in 2020), refugee status of household head (in 2020), and education of household head (in 2018).

References

Atamanov, Aziz, and Nethra Palaniswamy. 2018. "West Bank and Gaza Poverty and Shared Prosperity Diagnostic 2011–2017." World Bank, Washington, DC.

FAO (Food and Agriculture Organization). 2016. *Methods for Estimating Comparable Rates of Food Insecurity Experienced by Adults throughout the World.* Rome: FAO.

Gansey, Romeo, Alia Aghajanian, and Jawad Al-Saleh. Forthcoming. *Welfare and Distributional Impacts of Covid-19 in the West Bank and Gaza.* Washington, DC: World Bank.

OCHA (Office for the Coordination of Humanitarian Affairs of the United Nations). 2020a. "COVID-19 Emergency Situation Report 1, March 24." OCHA, East Jerusalem. https://www.ochaopt.org/content/covid-19 -emergency-situation-report-1.

OCHA (Office for the Coordination of Humanitarian Affairs of the United Nations). 2020b. "COVID-19 Emergency Situation Report 6 (21–28 April 2020)." OCHA, East Jerusalem. https://www.ochaopt.org/content/covid-19 -emergency-situation-report-6.

PCBS (Palestinian Central Bureau of Statistics). 2018. "Socio-Economic and Food Security Survey." https://fscluster.org/sites/default/files/documents /socio-economic_food_security_survey_sefsec_2018_full_repor_02.09t.pdf.

PCBS (Palestinian Central Bureau of Statistics). 2020. "Press Release on the Results of the Labour Force Survey Second Quarter 2020 (April–June 2020)." Palestinian Central Bureau of Statistics, Ramallah, Palestine. http://www.pcbs .gov.ps/portals/_pcbs/PressRelease/Press_Ar_9-9-2020-LF-ar.pdf.

Roser, Max, and Esteban Ortiz-Ospina. 2021. COVID-19 Data Explorer (published online at OurWorldInData.org), https://ourworldindata.org /explorers/coronavirus-data-explorer.

World Bank. 2020. "Economic Developments in the Palestinian Territories." World Bank, Washington, DC. https://www.worldbank.org/en/country /westbankandgaza/publication/economic-developments-in-the-palestinian -territories-november-2020.

World Bank. 2021. *Economic Monitoring Report to the Ad Hoc Liaison Committee.* Washington, DC: World Bank.

CHAPTER 4

Tunisia: The Link between Dropping Incomes and Living Standards

Federica Alfani, Dorra Dhraief, Vasco Molini,
Dan Pavelesku, and Marco Ranzani

Key Messages

- For about half of the Tunisian households interviewed in the five rounds of phone surveys in 2020, living standards have deteriorated compared to the pre-COVID-19 period—particularly among the poor and the bottom 40 percent.

- For about 20 percent of households (almost 40 percent in the bottom 40 percent), living standards have continued to deteriorate throughout the pandemic.

- The pandemic's negative impact seems to be attributable to changes in employment and labor income; and although employment has bounced back, it is not yet at precrisis levels.

- Although income has rebounded for private sector workers, it has not for the self-employed, largely because of the lack of customers.

- Our results call for enhanced income support to households, particularly the bottom 40 percent, until the economy has fully rebounded.

Introduction

The COVID-19 outbreak has had unprecedented negative socioeconomic effects on the lives of millions of people across the world, particularly among the most disadvantaged and vulnerable.[1] Tunisia has had to endure the human and economic costs of the COVID-19 pandemic, and the difficulties brought on by containment measures and restrictions to mobility. The first cases of COVID-19 in Tunisia were reported on March 2, 2020, and as of January 13, 2021, a total of about 165,000 cases and over 5,300 deaths have been recorded by Tunisian authorities. Following the pattern seen in other countries, the virus's spread slowed between May and July 2020, but cases rose again in the autumn, with peaks in October and November.

The public health emergency during the height of the pandemic and the introduction of lockdown measures led to a 10 percent contraction of the Tunisian economy in the first nine months of 2020, according to the National Institute of Statistics (INS). The World Bank (2020c) projects that the country's economy will contract by 9.2 percent in 2020.[2] The pandemic, the containment measures, and restrictions to mobility have led to (a) steep job losses and drops in incomes, (b) price increases, (c) decline in other income sources, and (d) disruption in the delivery of health and education services.

A serious concern is that the combined health and socioeconomic crisis of 2020 could reverse some of the progress Tunisia has made in reducing poverty and raising living standards, with an increase in the vulnerable population falling into poverty. Before COVID-19, the poverty headcount rate in Tunisia declined from 25.4 percent in 2000 to 13.8 percent in 2019, with the pace of poverty reduction fastest between 2010 and 2015. A thorough examination of trends in inequality shows a similar pattern. Particularly from 2005 onward, the Gini index fell from 0.40 in 2000 to 0.37 in 2015, and further to 0.33 in 2019.

However, monitoring the socioeconomic impact of the crisis has been challenging in the context of the COVID-19 pandemic. For that reason, several national statistical offices have resorted to high-frequency telephone surveys to replace the in-person surveys that would normally be done. Between March and October 2020, the INS, in collaboration with the World Bank, launched five rounds of these surveys to assess the socioeconomic impact of the COVID-19 pandemic on a nationally representative panel of about 1,000 households. These results have been initially published on the INS website.[3]

In addition, there has been a flurry of studies and research papers that simulate the economic impacts of the COVID-19 shock on poverty and welfare.[4] Cross-country research on the effects on the labor market shows that the magnitude of the impact of the COVID-19 shock differs, depending on the institutional context, economic structure, and work schemes in place. It particularly affects tasks that cannot be carried out remotely or by less educated workers, youth, women, and the self-employed (Adams-Prassl et al. 2020; Alon et al. 2020; Bartik et al. 2020; Blundell and Machin 2020; Cajner et al. 2020; Dingel and Neiman 2020; Mongey and Weinberg 2020; Montenovo et al. 2020; von Gaudecker et al. 2020). Other contributions (such as Alon et al. 2020) gauge the impact of COVID-19 on social norms and role models, especially in households with children, where a reallocation of duties within the household is very likely, with persistent effects on gender roles and the division of labor.

However, little evidence or data are available on the socioeconomic impacts of the COVID-19 pandemic in Middle East and North Africa (MENA) countries and economies. This chapter draws on Tunisia's recent phone surveys to shed light on the impact of COVID-19 on households' welfare during the pandemic, and particularly on the changes that occurred in the labor market—that is, employment losses and reduced labor income.[5] In particular, it shows how the declining living standards reported by households are continuing, despite the reopening of the Tunisian economy following the lockdown. Key findings include the following:

- A sizable setback in living standards, especially for the most vulnerable (the bottom 40 percent of the consumption distribution).

- A decline in welfare for about half of the households compared with before the pandemic.

- A setback in labor income especially among the self-employed, with income still below prepandemic levels.

- Deterioration in living standards resulting from an increase in food prices and a fall in remittances.

This chapter begins with detailed information on the five rounds of household telephone surveys, the data collection process, and how that process overlaps with lockdown decisions. Next, the chapter looks at the key transmission channels of an aggregate shock such as COVID-19 on living standards, examines how living standards of households have changed during the pandemic, and suggests policy recommendations.

Phone Surveys to Quickly Check on Living Standards

After the first COVID-19 cases appeared in Tunisia in early March 2020, the government announced a strict lockdown. And on May 4, it launched the first of three phases of stepwise deconfinement measures, which resulted in the gradual reopening of the economy between May 4 and June 14, 2020.

In late April, the Institut National de la Statistique (INS), in collaboration with the World Bank, launched a series of five surveys to study and monitor the socioeconomic impact of COVID-19 on the daily lives of Tunisians. The first round was conducted from April 29 to May 8—at the end of the strict lockdown and the beginning of the first reopening stage—and the fifth took place from October 4 to 16, three to four months after the end of the lockdown (figure 4.1).

The surveys were administered by telephone to a panel of 1,339 households—a subsample of the 2015 Household Budget Survey (HBS 2015). The sample makes it possible to obtain statistically significant results at the national level, as well as by rural and urban areas and households' consumption quintiles.[6] In the first round, a total of 1,032 households responded to the telephone survey, with a response rate of 77 percent. The response rate fell to 67 percent in the second round, 63 percent in the third, 59 percent in the fourth, and 53 percent in the fifth (table 4.1).

The questionnaire for all five rounds included sections on preventive health care measures and social behavior and on economic activity (table 4.2). Further, specific modules tried to capture particular sets of information: rounds 1 and 2 asked about access to goods and services,

FIGURE 4.1

Data Were Collected during Different Stages of COVID-19
Timeline of survey data collection and lockdown measures

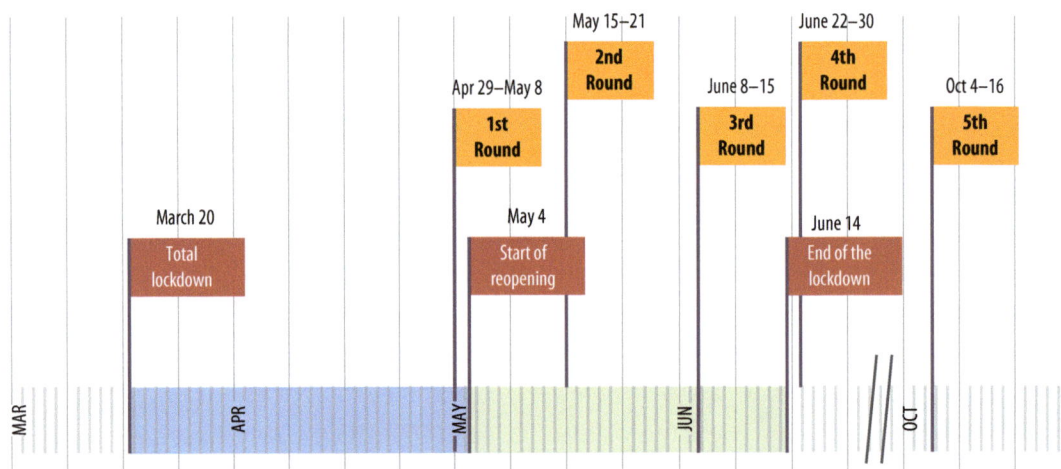

Source: World Bank calculations, based on data from Enquête téléphonique auprès des ménages pour étudier et suivre l'impact du COVID-19 sur le quotidien des Tunisiens, rounds 1–5 (survey conducted by National Institute of Statistics and the World Bank).
Note: Diagonal rules represent skipped months (July, August, and September).

TABLE 4.1

Sample Sizes and Response Rates across Five Survey Rounds

Dataset		No. of observations	Response rate (%)
Round 1	April 29–May 8	1,032	77
Round 2	May 15–21	899	67
Round 3	June 8–15	837	63
Round 4	June 22–30	789	59
Round 5	October 4–16	714	53

Source: World Bank calculations, based on data from Enquête téléphonique auprès des ménages pour étudier et suivre l'impact du COVID-19 sur le quotidien des Tunisiens, rounds 1–5 (survey conducted by National Institute of Statistics and the World Bank).

TABLE 4.2

Modules of the Survey Questionnaires by Survey Round

Section	Round 1	Round 2	Round 3	Round 4	Round 5
Preventive health care measures and social behavior	X	X			
Access to goods and services	X	X			
Economic activity	X	X	X	X	X
Financial situation of the household		X	X	X	X
Impact of COVID-19 on children's education		X			X
Access to health services				X	X
Attitudes to the targeted lockdown			X	X	
Aid	X	X			

Source: World Bank calculations, based on data from Enquête téléphonique auprès des ménages pour étudier et suivre l'impact du COVID-19 sur le quotidien des Tunisiens, rounds 1–5 (survey conducted by National Institute of Statistics and the World Bank).

preventive measures, and aid; rounds 2–5 contained modules on the financial situation of households; rounds 2 and 5 looked at the impact of COVID-19 on children's education; rounds 3 and 4 queried attitudes on targeted confinements; and rounds 4 and 5 examined access to health services.

Impact of COVID-19 on Living Standards

There are, broadly, four channels through which aggregate shocks, such as the COVID-19 pandemic and the consequent economic recession, are transmitted and affect households' welfare: (a) income from labor, (b) income from other sources, (c) prices, and (d) access to services (Figure 4.2).

- *Labor income.* The labor market is a key transmission channel, especially in countries where the poor and vulnerable rely on their labor to

FIGURE 4.2

Households' Welfare Received Short-Term Impacts Distributed in Key Transmission Channels

Labor income
- Lost earnings due to illness or to the need to attend sick family members
- Lost/reduced earnings due to job losses and reduced working hours among wage workers (formal and informal)
- Lost income among self-employed

Nonlabor income
- International remittances
- Domestic remittances

Prices
- Price increase of basic essentials
- Shortage/rationing of basic essentials
- Out-of-pocket cost of health care services
- Decrease in prices of oil and other commodities

Access to services
- Disruption in access to education (retention, learning, nutrition)
- Disruption in access to health (saturation of health system)

make ends meet. Private sector firms can experience a major shock in a pandemic. On the supply side, the lockdown and restrictions on mobility can close businesses completely and create difficulties in accessing labor and other inputs. On the demand side, lower incomes can reduce consumption to essential basic needs. Further, if enterprises lack support from banks and are unable to benefit from government assistance during the pandemic, they can experience financial distress. And limited mobility and the unavailability of home-based work, especially for low-skilled workers performing tasks that cannot be done remotely, can translate into job losses, reduced earnings, and lower living standards.

- *Nonlabor income.* Other income sources, such as public and private transfers, can be affected. Lower levels of international (and domestic) remittances are a by-product of economic contraction in countries and regions where emigrants are working. In countries with limited fiscal space, any reduction in the volume of public transfers, or in the size of the target populations after an economic downturn, can contribute to lower living standards. However, public transfers could be increased after an economic downturn, thereby helping to mitigate the impact of a crisis.

- *Prices.* Changes in prices or shortages of basic food items and medicines, caused by disruptions in international and national supply chains or domestic production contractions, can pose a problem. However, falling commodity prices (such as oil and gas) can offset some of the price increases on other goods.

- *Access to services.* The closure of schools in combination with the paucity and low quality of existing internet connections can hurt households' welfare by limiting access to education and distance learning. And the saturation of health care systems during the height of hospitalizations of COVID-19 patients can make it difficult to access health or medical services, especially where such services are weak to begin with.

Self-Reported Changes in Living Standards

Starting with changes in living standards, our study shows that more than half of the households interviewed reported that the COVID-19 outbreak led to a deterioration in living standards compared with the period prior to the outbreak, that is, March 2020 (figure 4.3). In late May (second round), 54 percent of the interviewees reported a decline in their welfare; this share declined to 49 percent in the first half of June and to 43 percent in the second half (third and fourth rounds); in the first half of October (fifth round) it rose again to 46 percent.

FIGURE 4.3

About Half of Households Report a Decline in Living Standards

Self-reported change in household living standards since before the pandemic, by survey round

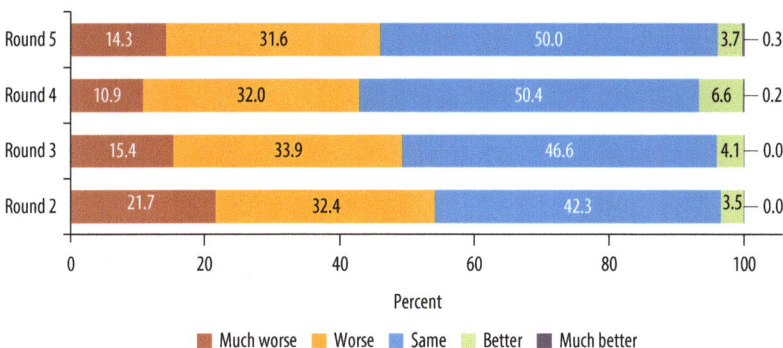

	Much worse	Worse	Same	Better	Much better
Round 5	14.3	31.6	50.0	3.7	0.3
Round 4	10.9	32.0	50.4	6.6	0.2
Round 3	15.4	33.9	46.6	4.1	0.0
Round 2	21.7	32.4	42.3	3.5	0.0

Source: World Bank calculations, based on data from Enquête téléphonique auprès des ménages pour étudier et suivre l'impact du COVID-19 sur le quotidien des Tunisiens, rounds 1–5 (survey conducted by National Institute of Statistics and the World Bank).
Note: Round 2 was conducted during May 15–21; round 3, June 8–15; round 4, June 22–30; and round 5, October 4–16.

This deterioration was seen particularly among the bottom 40 percent of the household consumption distribution (figure 4.4).[7] In May, 67–68 percent of households in the bottom 40 percent said their living standards had worsened, compared with the situation they faced in March. That share declined to 57, 47, and 37 percent among households in the third, fourth, and fifth quintiles, respectively. In the following rounds, the percentage of households that reported that their living standards were worsening was consistently higher in the bottom of the consumption distribution than at the top.

FIGURE 4.4

Living Standards Drop the Most from Prepandemic Levels for Tunisia's Bottom 40 Percent

Household-level self-reported change in living standards, by prepandemic quintile and survey round

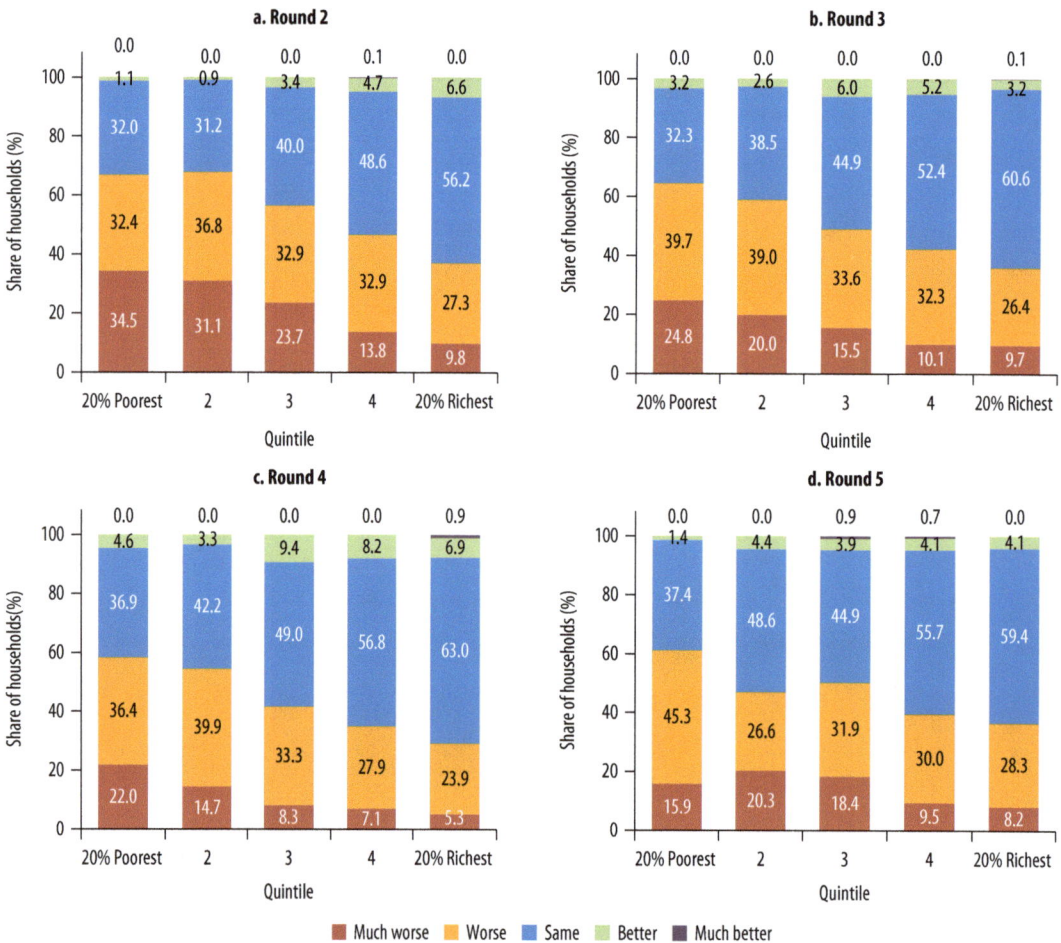

Source: World Bank calculations, based on data from the Enquête téléphonique auprès des ménages pour étudier et suivre l'impact du COVID-19 sur le quotidien des Tunisiens, rounds 1–5 (survey conducted by National Institute of Statistics and the World Bank).
Note: Round 2 was conducted during May 15–21; round 3, June 8–15; round 4, June 22–30; and round 5, October 4–16.

In the final three survey rounds, households were also asked about their welfare, as compared with the previous month, that is, once the pandemic had already had an impact on living standards. In the first half of June (third round), 24 percent of households reported a decline in their living standards compared with the month before (figure 4.5). This share decreased to about 15 percent in the second half of June (fourth round), as the lockdown was lifted, but rose again to 25 percent in the first half of October (fifth round). This evidence points to a severe decline in household welfare as the pandemic unfolded, and it extended well beyond the end of restrictions on individual mobility, as a result of a deepening economic downturn. Once again, the decline is larger at the bottom of the consumption distribution. In the October survey round, about 38 percent of households in the first quintile reported a decline in welfare; this compares with 24 percent of households in the second quintile, 29 percent in the middle of the distribution, and 23 and 16 percent in the fourth and fifth quintile, respectively (figure 4.6).

FIGURE 4.5

Households Suffer More Severe Welfare Declines as Pandemic Continues

Self-reported change in household living standards from previous month, by survey round

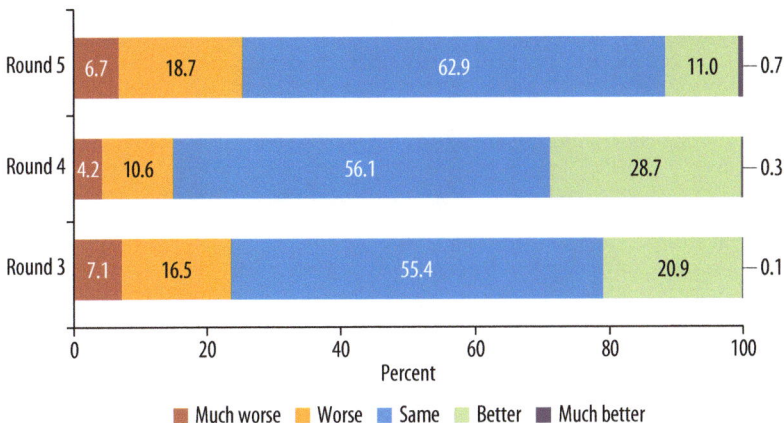

	Much worse	Worse	Same	Better	Much better
Round 5	6.7	18.7	62.9	11.0	0.7
Round 4	4.2	10.6	56.1	28.7	0.3
Round 3	7.1	16.5	55.4	20.9	0.1

Source: World Bank calculations, based on data from the Enquête téléphonique auprès des ménages pour étudier et suivre l'impact du COVID-19 sur le quotidien des Tunisiens, rounds 1–5 (survey conducted by National Institute of Statistics and the World Bank).
Note: Round 3 was conducted during June 8–15; round 4, June 22–30; and round 5, October 4–16.

FIGURE 4.6

In Later Survey Rounds, the Poorest Report a Decline in Welfare from the Month Before

Household-level self-reported change in living standards, by survey round

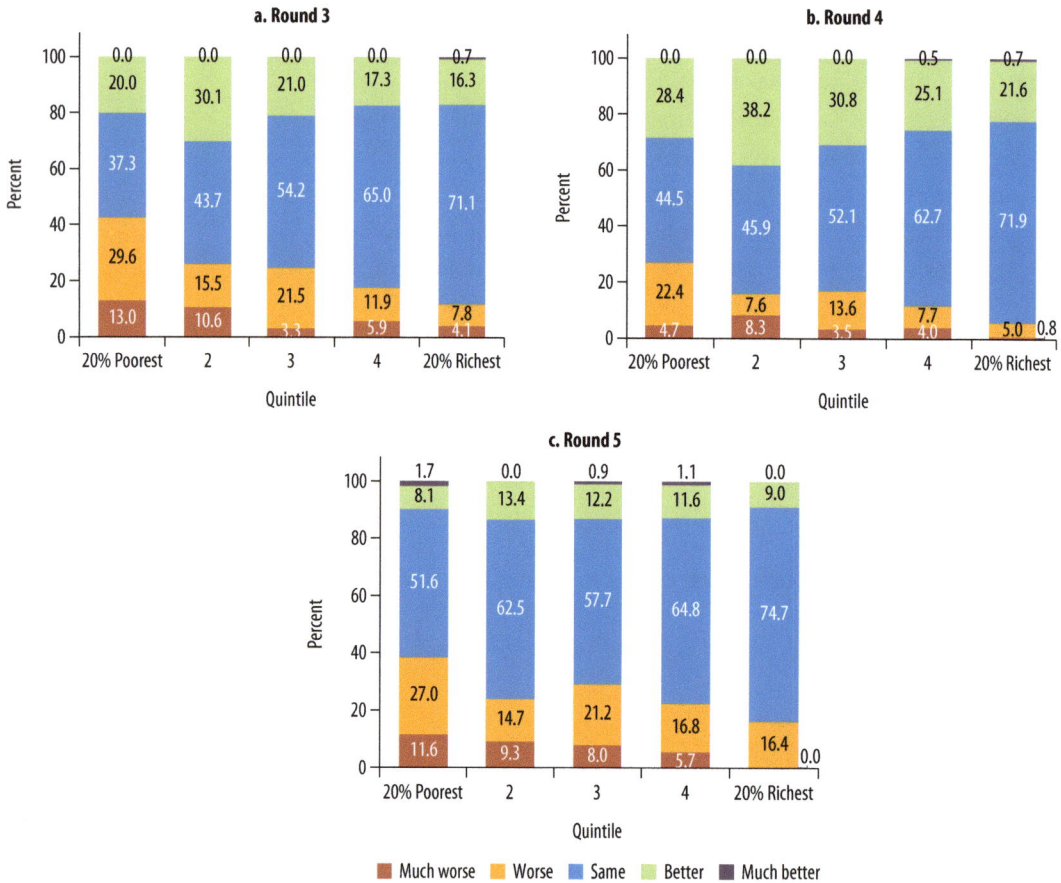

Source: World Bank calculations based on data from the Enquête téléphonique auprès des ménages pour étudier et suivre l'impact du COVID-19 sur le quotidien des Tunisiens, rounds 1–5 (survey conducted by National Institute of Statistics and the World Bank).
Note: Round 3 was conducted during June 8–15; round 4, June 22–30; and round 5, October 4–16.

Changes in the Labor Market

The labor market seems the most obvious transmission channel of aggregate shock to household welfare. This is particularly true for the bottom 40 percent in Tunisia, as they tend to live off wages and business income in the private sector. Indeed, the telephone survey showed that the deterioration in living standards appears to be due to (a) a decline in employment, particularly during the lockdown; and (b) a reduction in income from labor, which seems to continue as individuals go back to work, particularly among the self-employed.

In May, in the midst of the lockdown, employment among respondents dropped to 23 percent (figure 4.7). This is a sharp drop from an estimated employment ratio in 2017 of about 62 percent among household heads (using labor force survey data). With the lockdown coming to an end and most economic activities reopening, the share of respondents who had worked in the week preceding the interview rose from 38 percent in the latter half of May to 52 percent in the first half of June, then 59 percent in the latter half of June, and 59 percent in October. Despite this clear rebound to near precrisis levels among respondents, not everybody went back to work. Data from the Tunisia labor force survey indicate that total employment in the third quarter of 2020 was still 1.5 percent below the level estimated in the first quarter. In other words, about 54,000 jobs had been shed between quarters 1 and 3.

Unlike employment numbers, incomes have not bounced back to the level observed before the onset of the COVID-19 pandemic. At the start of the reopening in May, a rising share of private sector employees reported being paid a full salary. This share rose from 63 percent in the latter half of May to 83 percent in June with the full reopening (figure 4.8). As of October 2020, about 89 percent of private sector employees reported being paid a full wage.

FIGURE 4.7

Employment Increases after Starting Low, Even during COVID-19 Shutdowns

Share of respondents who report being employed, by survey round

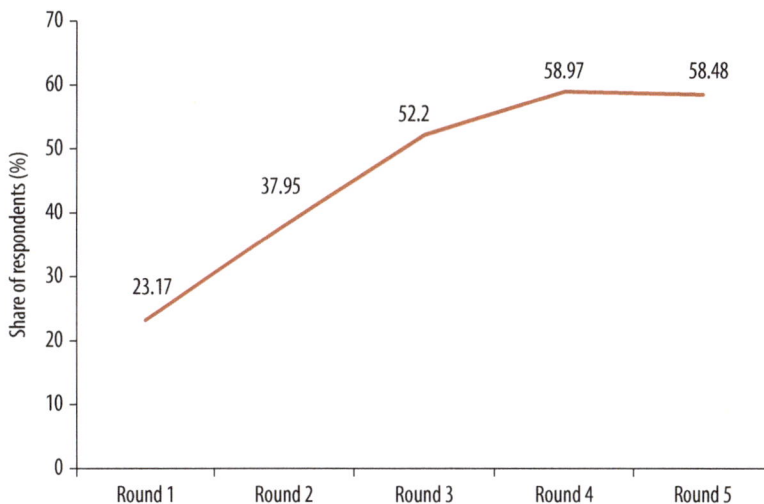

Source: World Bank calculations, based on data from the Enquête téléphonique auprès des ménages pour étudier et suivre l'impact du COVID-19 sur le quotidien des Tunisiens, rounds 1–5 (survey conducted by National Institute of Statistics and the World Bank).

Private Sector Income Increases after Its Low Level during the COVID-19 Surge

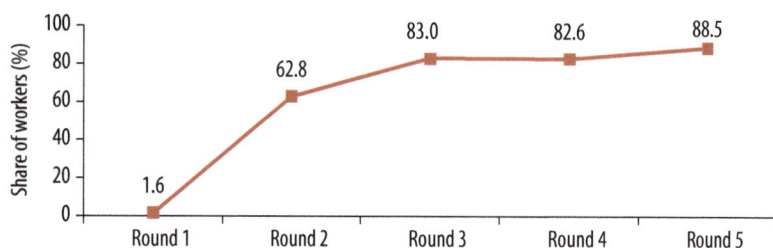

Source: World Bank calculations based on data from the Enquête téléphonique auprès des ménages pour étudier et suivre l'impact du COVID-19 sur le quotidien des Tunisiens, rounds 1–5 (survey conducted by National Institute of Statistics and the World Bank).

Among the self-employed, labor income appears to have deteriorated considerably. In March and May, the share of self-employed reporting a reduction in business income from two weeks before stood at 63 percent and 57 percent, respectively. But this share improved to 43 percent in the first half of June and to 24 percent in the first half of July and stood at 28 percent in October (figure 4.9 panel a). After the May reopening, the main factor cited for the income fall was a lack of customers (from 28.4 percent in late May to 47.6 percent in October). Before then, the main reason for lower income, cited by about half of the self-employed, was the lockdown and subsequent closure of workplaces (figure 4.9 panel b).

The phone surveys also offer a window into weighing the effects of the pandemic, while controlling for different household characteristics. By looking at the probability of a respondent declaring a worsening in living standards, we find that it is positively correlated with household heads who have a low educational level and those who are in the youngest age group (15–34) (figure 4.10). For example, a household headed by someone ages 35–44 is 10 percent less likely to see a deterioration in living standards the month before the interview than a household headed by someone under age 34. Similarly, households headed by someone with a primary (–6.3 percent), secondary (–7.1 percent), and tertiary (–10.9 percent) education are less likely to report a deterioration in living standards, compared with a household headed by someone with no education. Individuals not employed at the time of the survey, the self-employed, and contributing family workers have a higher probability of reporting a deterioration of their living standards (42.9 and 32.9 percent, respectively), compared with someone working as a civil servant (see annex for a detailed description of estimation results).

FIGURE 4.9

Self-Employed Income Falls Sharply because of the Lack of Customers

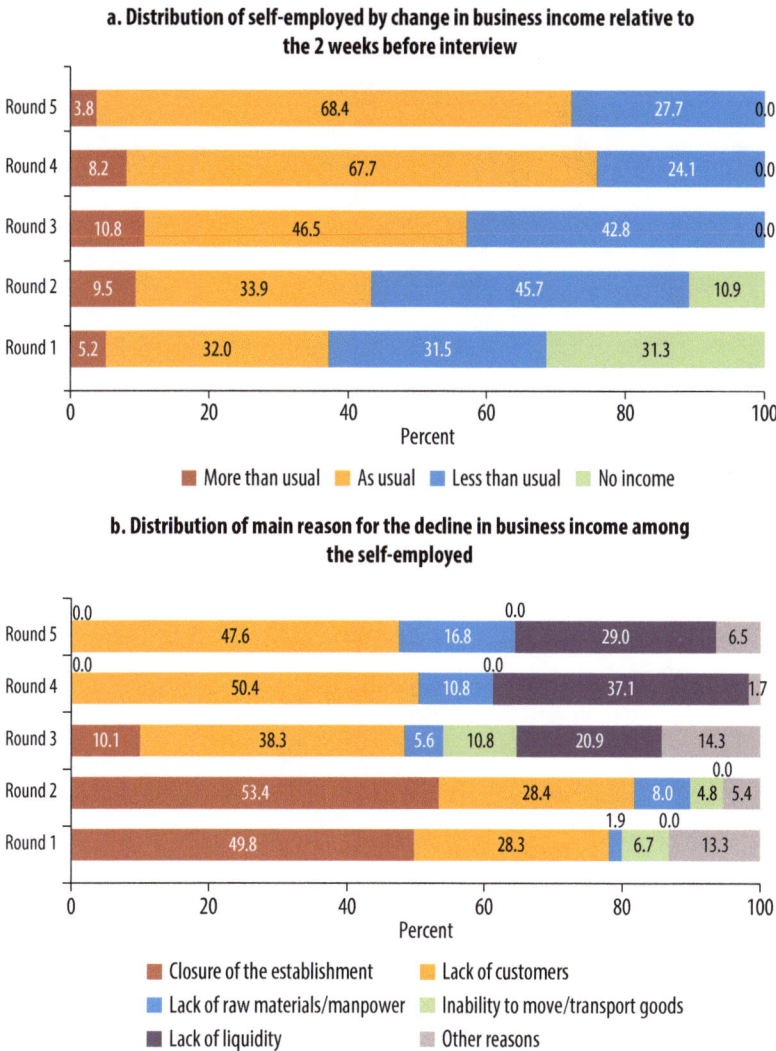

a. Distribution of self-employed by change in business income relative to the 2 weeks before interview

Round	More than usual	As usual	Less than usual	No income
Round 5	3.8	68.4	27.7	0.0
Round 4	8.2	67.7	24.1	0.0
Round 3	10.8	46.5	42.8	0.0
Round 2	9.5	33.9	45.7	10.9
Round 1	5.2	32.0	31.5	31.3

■ More than usual ■ As usual ■ Less than usual ■ No income

b. Distribution of main reason for the decline in business income among the self-employed

Round	Closure of the establishment	Lack of customers	Lack of raw materials/manpower	Inability to move/transport goods	Lack of liquidity	Other reasons
Round 5	0.0	47.6	16.8	0.0	29.0	6.5
Round 4	0.0	50.4	10.8	0.0	37.1	1.7
Round 3	10.1	38.3	5.6	10.8	20.9	14.3
Round 2	53.4	28.4	8.0	4.8	0.0	5.4
Round 1	49.8	28.3	1.9	6.7	0.0	13.3

■ Closure of the establishment ■ Lack of customers
■ Lack of raw materials/manpower ■ Inability to move/transport goods
■ Lack of liquidity ■ Other reasons

Source: World Bank calculations, based on data from the Enquête téléphonique auprès des ménages pour étudier et suivre l'impact du COVID-19 sur le quotidien des Tunisiens, rounds 1–5 (survey conducted by National Institute of Statistics and the World Bank).
Note: Round 1 was conducted April 29–May 8; round 2, May 15–21; round 3, June 8–15; round 4, June 22–30; and round 5, October 4–16.

Private sector wage workers have a lower likelihood (–7.2 percent) than civil servants of experiencing worsening living standards. As reported by respondents, the magnitude of the coefficients attached to the changes in labor income, both in wages and business income is sizable. A private sector employee receiving a partial salary, or no salary at all, has a higher probability of reporting lower living standards than a

FIGURE 4.10

Welfare Deterioration Is Revealed in a Snapshot Showing Which Households Were Most Likely to Declare Lower Living Standards

Probability of declaring a deterioration in living standards, compared with previous month

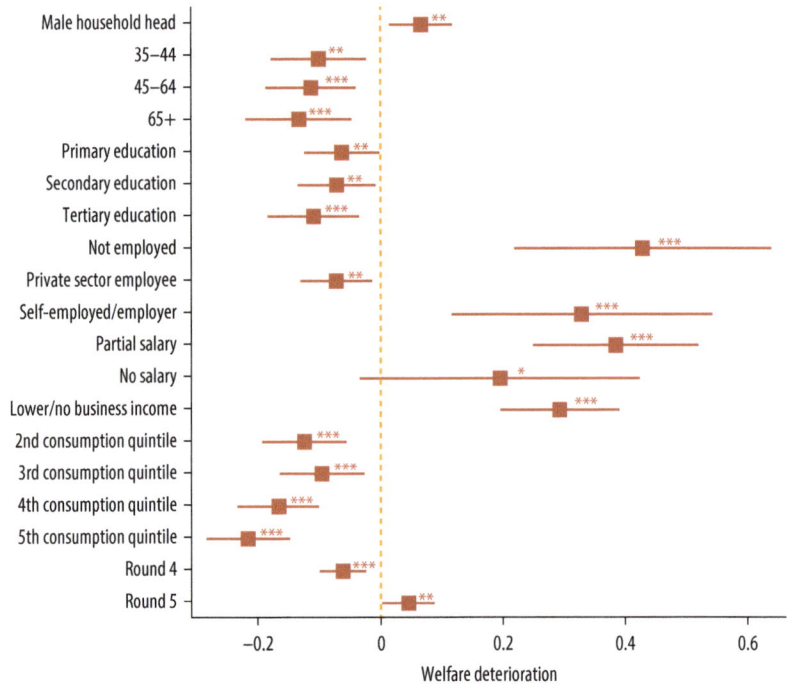

Source: World Bank calculations, based on data from the Enquête téléphonique auprès des ménages pour étudier et suivre l'impact du COVID-19 sur le quotidien des Tunisiens, rounds 1–5 (survey conducted by National Institute of Statistics and the World Bank).
Note: Figure shows estimation coefficients of the linear probability model; see annex for a description of estimation results.
Statistical significance: *$p < 0.10$; **$p < 0.05$; ***$p < 0.01$.

civil servant receiving a full salary (38.5 and 19.5 percent, respectively). Similarly, respondents employed as nonwage workers with lower than usual business income, or no income at all, have a higher likelihood of experiencing lower living standards (29.5 percent), as compared with a civil servant receiving a full salary. Finally, the household welfare measured before the pandemic, as captured by the quintile on household consumption expenditures in 2015, is highly statistically significant. More affluent households have a lower likelihood of reporting a deterioration in living standards during the pandemic after controlling for age, gender, and educational level of household heads, as well as controlling for their labor market status and reported changes in labor income. These households tend to have more access to savings or credit, which, in turn, enables them to withstand economic shocks better than poorer households.

Changes in Prices

A second mechanism that can contribute to the transmission of an aggregate shock to households' welfare is price changes, which directly affect consumption levels and may force some households to adopt negative coping strategies by reducing their consumption of specific items, including food. The consumer price index (CPI) series constructed by the Tunisia National Statistics Institute shows that in October 2020 the total CPI rose by 4 percent, compared with January 2020; over the same period in 2019, the CPI increased by 4.5 percent (figure 4.11).

Nonetheless, the price increases observed during the lockdown months of March–May are slightly higher in 2020 compared to 2019. In addition, the price index of food items increased considerably more between January and October 2020 (up 4.1 percent), compared with the same period in 2019 (up 2.9 percent). And the CPI trend for food items shows a first acceleration during the lockdown, followed by a second one beginning in September. Because less affluent households typically spend a larger share of their consumption on food items (about 40 percent among households in the bottom two quintiles, compared to 35 percent among the rest of the population), this price dynamic penalizes more households at the bottom of the consumption distribution.

FIGURE 4.11

Higher Prices for Food Items during COVID-19 Drive the Overall Price Index

Consumer price index (CPI) trends beginning January 2019 and 2020

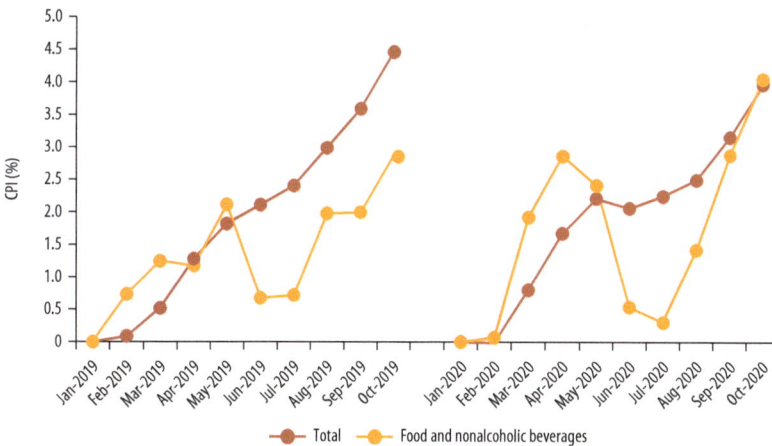

Source: Based on data from the consumer price index published by the National Institute of Statistics.

Changes in Remittances

Other sources of income, particularly remittances, can affect the living standards of households during a downturn. About 1.22 million Tunisians lived abroad in 2012, largely in Europe. These expatriates contribute to sustaining the living standards of family members in Tunisia through remittances. Although no information on the value of remittances is available at the household level, the World Bank (2020a) estimates that remittances, valued at US$1.9 billion, accounted for 4.9 percent of the country's GDP in 2019. The World Bank projects a sharp drop in remittances of about 15 percent in 2020 as a result of the COVID-19 pandemic, which has contributed to a deterioration of living standards, particularly among households that have benefited the most from this source of income (World Bank 2020b).

Public transfers, and particularly social protection systems, can provide a safety net for those who lose their job—to support their living standards and give them the means to look for new employment. Although Tunisia has a comprehensive social insurance system in place, high unemployment and levels of informality have created low coverage rates; in addition, unconditional cash transfers are poorly targeted (OECD 2015).

Shortly after the COVID-19 outbreak and subsequent lockdown, the government of Tunisia introduced short-term work schemes. These included (a) a wage subsidy of TD 200 per month in April and May, which enterprises could access by applying through a dedicated platform (helpenterprise.social.tn), and (b) a one-off cash transfer of TD 200 for microenterprises under a special tax regime (*forfaitaire*).[8]

About 110,000 microenterprises received transfers, and most firms under this regime are self-employed or have a maximum of one to two employees. In addition, 623,000 vulnerable households have received benefits from the National Assistance Program for Poor Families (Programme national d'aide aux familles nécessiteuses). And discounted health care cards (Aide medical à tarif réduit, AMG program) have been supported through two cash transfers of TD 50 and TD 60.[9] Further, a one-off cash transfer of TD 200 was credited to families hosting an elderly person, fostering children without parental support, and hosting a person with a handicap. Individuals with low retirement pensions (less than TD 180) received an exceptional monetary payment of TD 100 in April 2020. Moreover, a one-off cash transfer (TD 200) was introduced for an additional 300,000 poor and vulnerable households working in the informal sector.[10]

While these temporary compensation schemes and one-off transfers have ended, the economy is still far from a rebound. The economic contraction has meant that many Tunisian households, particularly private sector employees and the self-employed working in the sectors that have been most affected by the crisis (such as construction, manufacturing, accommodation and food services activities, and transport), will continue to experience deteriorating living standards. Strengthening and adequate targeting of social protection programs could help vulnerable households make ends meet until the economy recovers.

Conclusion

The COVID-19 outbreak and the economic crisis that followed have meant significant setbacks in living standards for millions of people, especially the poor and the most vulnerable. In Tunisia, five consecutive rounds of telephone interviews, conducted by the INS during and immediately after the lockdown, offer an opportunity to evaluate the impact of COVID-19 on Tunisian households and identify some of the transmission channels of the global pandemic on the daily life of the Tunisian people.

Survey results indicate that living standards deteriorated for about one in two households, compared with the period before the pandemic, and for over six in 10 households in the bottom 40 percent. Moreover, about one in five households reported experiencing worse living standards during the pandemic. Among the possible transmission channels, the labor market played an important role. While survey respondents reported that employment had rebounded to precrisis levels, wage workers and the self-employed indicate that their labor income is still below the levels observed prior to the pandemic. Food price increases and a sharp reduction in remittances have also contributed to the deterioration of living standards.

The government's immediate response to the crisis has included compensation schemes for private sector employees and an income support scheme for microenterprises, and both of these schemes have played an important role in limiting job destruction and income loss. Looking ahead, income support will continue to be needed for the most vulnerable households once the emergency programs have ended, especially given that an economic recovery is not expected for another one to two years. The latest World Bank projections indicate that the Tunisian economy will contract by 9.2 percent in 2020, with a large reduction in the services sector (World Bank 2020c), and it is not expected that the economy will bounce back to a precrisis level before 2022.

Particular attention will need to be paid to households that rely more than others on remittances, as well as those households with private sector employees and the self-employed working in the sectors most affected by the crisis. These households, along with the poorest, are also bearing the brunt of increasing food prices, and they will continue to experience lower living standards because of a lack of overall domestic and foreign demand. In the coming months, targeted social protection schemes will be needed for households that are being hit the hardest.

Annex

We estimated a linear probability model at the household level to simultaneously control for the effects of the factors described above, as well as for additional individual characteristics on changes in households' living standards. The dependent variable is a dummy that equals 1 if a household has reported a deterioration in living standards relative to the month before the interview. Controls are included for the sex, age group, and educational level of household heads (X_h), for a respondent's labor force status, and conditional on being employed for her employment type, and for changes in her labor income compared with the period before the pandemic (M_h) (equation A.1). We also control for the prepandemic distribution of household consumption expenditures (Q_h), and we add fixed effects for each survey round (ϑ_r).

$$Y_h = \alpha + \beta' X_h + \gamma' M_h + \theta' Q_h + \vartheta_r + \varepsilon_h \tag{A.1}$$

Table 4A.1 reports the estimates for two specifications. The first specification (M1) does not include any details on household heads' characteristics, and it contains only variables measured at the time of the survey on respondents' labor market status and change in income.

TABLE 4A.1

Correlates of the Probability of Posting a Deterioration in Living Standards Compared with the Month before the Interview—the Linear Probability Model

	M1	M2
Male household head		0.066**
Age group (years)		
35–44		−0.100**
45–64		−0.113***
65+		−0.132***
Educational level		
Primary education		−0.063**
Secondary education		−0.071**
Tertiary education		−0.109***

(continued on next page)

Correlates of the Probability of Posting a Deterioration in Living Standards Compared with the Month before the Interview—the Linear Probability Model (*continued*)

	M1	M2
Employment type		
Not employed	0.439***	0.429***
Private sector employee	−0.049*	−0.072**
Self-employed/employer/contributing family worker	0.371***	0.329***
Change in wages		
Partial salary	0.388***	0.385***
No salary	0.195*	0.195*
Change in business income	−0.088***	−0.069**
Business income lower than usual/no business income		
Quintile of household consumption	0.292***	0.294***
2nd quintile	0.357***	0.348***
3rd quintile	—	—
4th quintile	−0.135***	−0.124***
5th quintile	−0.112***	−0.095***
Survey round	−0.189***	−0.166***
Round 4	−0.253***	−0.215***
Round 5	—	—
Constant	−0.063***	−0.062***
Observations	0.043**	0.045**
R^2	−0.031	0.077

Source: World Bank calculations, based on data from the Enquête téléphonique auprès des ménages pour étudier et suivre l'impact du COVID-19 sur le quotidien des Tunisiens, rounds 1–5 (survey conducted by National Institute of Statistics and the World Bank).
Note: Reference category: 15–34 years; no education; public sector employee; full salary or business income as usual or more than usual; quintile 1; round 3. — = not available.
Statistical significance: *$p < .10$; **$p < .05$; ***$p < .01$.

The second specification (M2) adds gender, age, and educational level of household heads.[11] The estimates do not differ significantly between the two specifications.

Notes

1. Based on data collected by Johns Hopkins University, as of January 13, 2021, over 91 million cases have been confirmed worldwide, along with almost 2 million deaths.

2. Estimates of Tunisia's GDP growth rates during the first nine months of 2020 are available at the Institut National de la Statistique (National Institute of Statistics), http://www.ins.tn/en/statistiques/72.

3. Data are available on the National Institute of Statistics website, http://ins .tn/publication/suivi-de-limpact-socio-economique-du-covid-19 -sur-les-menages-tunisiens-octobre-2020.

4. Papers on this include include Sumner, Hoy, and E. Ortiz-Juarez (2020); Morsy, Balma, and Mukasa (2020); ElKadhi et al. (2020), ITES (2020); and Kokas et al. (2020) in the case of Tunisia. This literature typically identifies employment loss as the major channel of impact on household welfare and poverty (Headey et al. 2020; Josephson et al. 2020).

5. Summary notes on the Enquête téléphonique auprès des ménages pour étudier et suivre l'impact du COVID-19 sur le quotidien des Tunisiens, monitoring the socioeconomic impact of COVID-19 on Tunisian households, are available on the INS website at the following link: http://www.ins.tn/fr /recherche-publication.

6. The construction of sampling weights entailed: (a) applying the inverse of the selection probability to adjust for the subsample selection process; and (b) to adjust for non-response, modifying the design weights by a factor inversely proportional to the response rate within 12 homogeneous groups selected based on the propensity score logit model. The 12 groups, with an average of about 111 units per group, were formed by: (a) two groups based on deciles of consumption expenditures (top 40 percent and bottom 60 percent); (b) two groups based on urban/rural location of residence; and (c) three groups based on the region where they reside (that is, northern, central, or southern regions of the country).

7. The quintiles are based on the distribution of consumption expenditures in the 2015 Household Budget Survey. In 2015, the headcount poverty rate was estimated at 15.2 percent.

8. The government has recently announced the reopening of the platform to provide support to employees in the tourism sector. Microenterprises could apply through a dedicated platform (https://batinda.gov.tn).

9. In the case of the AMG program, the first transfer corresponded to TD 50 in April 2020, while the second amounted to TD 60 in May 2020.

10. Information on compensatory measures targeted to Tunisian households has been drawn from ITES (2020).

11. A household head refers to an individual who was the head of the household at the time of the 2015 household budget survey. Any changes within households (including deaths, marriages, divorces, migration, etc.) might have altered households' structure between 2015 and 2020. For this reason, we also estimate a regression that does not include household heads' demographics. We do control for the quintile of the prepandemic household welfare that partially captures returns to household heads' characteristics. By the same token though, the position of each household along the distribution of consumption expenditures might have changed since 2015. However, this is the best information available.

References

Adams-Prassl, Abi, Teodora Boneva, Marta Golin, and Christopher Rauh. 2020. "Inequality in the Impact of the Coronavirus Shock: Evidence from Real Time Surveys." *Journal of Public Economics* 189. https://doi.org/10.1016/j.jpubeco.2020.104245.

Alon, Titan, Matthias Doepke, Jane Olmstead-Rumsey, and Michèle Tertilt. 2020. "The Impact of COVID-19 on Gender Equality." NBER Working Paper 26947, National Bureau of Economic Research, Cambridge, MA.

Bartik, A. W., M. Bertrand, Z. B. Cullen, E. L. Glaeser, M. Luca, and C. T. Stanton. 2020. "How Are Small Businesses Adjusting to COVID-19? Early Evidence from a Survey." NBER Working Paper 26989, National Bureau of Economic Research, Cambridge, MA.

Blundell, Jack, and Stephen Machin. 2020. "Self-employment in the Covid-19 Crisis: A CEP Covid-19 Analysis." *CEP Covid-19 Analysis* (003). London School of Economics and Political Science, London.

Cajner, T., L. D. Crane, R. A. Decker, J. Grigsby, John A. Hamins-Puertolas, E. Hurst, C. Kurz, and A. Yildirmaz. 2020. "The US Labor Market During the Beginning of the Pandemic Recession." NBER Working Paper 27159, National Bureau of Economic Research, Cambridge, MA.

Dingel, J., and B. Neiman. 2020. "How Many Jobs Can Be Done at Home?" NBER Working Paper 26948, National Bureau of Economic Research, Cambridge, MA.

ElKadhi, Zouhair, Dalia Elsabbagh, Aymen Frija, Thouraya Lakoud, Manfred Wiebelt, and Clemens Breisinger. 2020. "The Impact of COVID-19 on Tunisia's Economy, Agri-food System, and Households." MENA Policy Note 5, International Food Policy Research Institute, Washington, DC.

Headey, Derek D., Sophie Goudet, Isabel Lambrecht, Than Zaw Oo, Elisa Maria Maffioli, Erica Field, and Russell Toth. 2020. "Poverty and Food Insecurity during COVID-19: Evidence from the COVID-19 Rural and Urban Food Security Survey (RUFSS)—June and July 2020 Round." Myanmar SSP Policy Note 27, International Food Policy Research Institute, Washington, DC.

ITES (Institut Tunisien des Études Stratégiques). 2020. *La Tunisie face à la covid-19 à l'horizon 2025. Scénarios fin 2020 et stratégie de sauvetage et de sortie de crise : quels équilibres sociaux?* https://www.realites.com.tn/wp-content/uploads/2020/11/Letude-Sociale-de-lITES-est-accessible-via-ce-lien..pdf.

Josephson, Anna, Talip Kilic, and Jeffrey D. Michler. 2020. "Socioeconomic Impacts of COVID-19 in Four African Countries." Policy Research Working Paper 9466, World Bank, Washington, DC. https://openknowledge.worldbank.org/handle/10986/34733.

Kokas, D., G. Lopez-Acevedo, A. R. El Lahga, and V. Mendiratta. 2020. "Impacts of COVID-19 on Household Welfare in Tunisia." Policy Research Working Paper 9503, World Bank, Washington, DC.

Mongey, S., and A. Weinberg. 2020. "Characteristics of Workers in Low Work-from-Home and High Personal-Proximity Occupations." BFI White Paper, Becker Friedman Institute, Chicago.

Montenovo, L., X. Jiang, F. L. Rojas, I. A. Schmutte, K. I. Simon, B. A. Weinberg, and C. Wing. 2020. "Determinants of Disparities in Covid-19 Job Losses." NBER Working Paper 27132, National Bureau of Economic Research, Cambridge, MA.

Morsy, H., L. Balma, and A. N. Mukasa. 2020. "'Not a Good Time': Economic Impact of COVID-19 in Africa." Working Paper Series 338, African Development Bank, Abidjan.

OECD (Organisation for Economic Co-operation and Development). 2015. "Tunisia: A Reform Agenda to Support Competitiveness and Inclusive Growth." Better Policies Series, March. OECD Publishing, Paris.

Sumner, A., C. Hoy, and E. Ortiz-Juarez. 2020. "Estimates of the Impact of COVID-19 on Global Poverty." UNU-WIDER Working Paper 43/2020. United Nations University World Institute for Development Economics Research. https://www.wider.unu.edu/publication/estimates-impact -covid-19-global-poverty.

von Gaudecker, H.-M., R. Holler, L. Janys, B. Siflinger, and C. Zimpelmann. 2020. "Labour Supply in the Early Stages of the Covid-19 Pandemic: Empirical Evidence on Hours, Home Office, and Expectations." IZA Discussion Paper No. 13158, IZA Institute of Labor Economics. https://www.iza.org /publications/dp/13158/labour-supply-in-the-early-stages-of-the-covid-19 -pandemic-empirical-evidence-on-hours-home-office-and-expectations.

World Bank. 2020a. "COVID-19 Crisis through a Migration Lens." Migration and Development Brief 32, April. World Bank, Washington, DC.

World Bank. 2020b. "Phase II: COVID-19 Crisis through a Migration Lens." Migration and Development Brief 33, October. World Bank, Washington, DC.

World Bank 2020c. "Rebuilding the Potential of Tunisian Firms. Tunisia Economic Monitor." World Bank, Washington, DC.

CHAPTER 5

Djibouti: Refugees More Vulnerable Than Nationals

Bilal Malaeb, Anne Duplantier, Romeo Jacky Gansey,
Sekou Tidiani Konaté, Omar Abdoulkader Mohamed,
Jeff Tanner, and Harriet Mugera

Key Messages

- A year after COVID-19 struck, Djiboutian households see an increase in the intensity of economic activity and the variety of their income sources.

- Vulnerable workers such as those from village-based refugee and poor national households are less able to catch up as inequality and job insecurity is on the rise.

- Access to basic goods and health care has improved since August 2020, but not for village-based refugee households.

- A relatively large fraction of households has an acceptable level of food consumption, unlike refugees who are more likely to experience food insecurity.

- Safety nets play a critical role in protecting the most vulnerable, particularly among village-based refugees for whom assistance from international nongovernmental organizations represents the main source of income.

Introduction

Nearly one year after recording the first case of COVID-19 in Djibouti, the rate of infection has slowed. While the daily rate of COVID-19 cases in Djibouti had been low and decreasing since August 2020, until the end of the third wave of data collection, it has seen a steady increase since February 2021. As of March 5, 2021, the World Health Organization Coronavirus (COVID-19) Dashboard (https://covid19.who.int/) reported more than 6,100 total cases and 63 COVID-19-related deaths in Djibouti; still, the daily rate of detected cases had been very low. Having initiated a lockdown policy in April 2020, the country had lifted most of the restrictive measures by the end of May 2020. However, the impacts of the pandemic and public health measures on the well-being of Djiboutian and refugee households continues. This matters greatly, given concerns that the health and socioeconomic crisis in 2020 combined could undermine progress on reducing high levels of poverty and unemployment.

Djibouti is one of the smallest countries in Africa and depends almost entirely on imports to meet its food needs. Its strength lies in its strategic position at the southern entrance to the Red Sea, making a bridge between Africa and the Middle East. Output growth is set to reach 5.5 percent in 2021 and average 6.2 percent over 2022 and 2023. Monitoring the socioeconomic impact of the crisis in the Middle East and North Africa region has been challenging in the context of the COVID-19 pandemic. In Djibouti, the statistical office resorted to high-frequency phone surveys (HFPSs) to replace the in-person surveys that would normally be done.

This chapter draws on three waves of phone survey data collected between July 2020 and January 2021 to evaluate the effects of the pandemic on households in Djibouti. The first two waves of this survey comprised a nationally representative sample of Djiboutian households and focused on the consequences of the pandemic on households' welfare, specifically in terms of breadwinners' employment, access to goods and services, and food insecurity. The third wave sought to follow the households that had been interviewed in the first two waves of data collection (with a replacement subsample), as well as a subsample of refugee households newly added to the survey. The combined results offer a rare look at the impacts of the pandemic on households over the course of the pandemic, and the survey is one of a handful to delve into the plight of refugees. In Djibouti, with a population of about 1 million, the United Nations High Commissioner for Refugees reports that there are more than 27,000 refugees and asylum seekers, mostly from Eritrea, Ethiopia, Somalia, and, more recently, the Republic of Yemen.

The objective of this chapter is to identify the trends of recovery since the onset of the COVID-19 crisis along six themes: economic activities, livelihoods and shock-coping mechanisms, safety nets, access to basic goods, access to services, and food insecurity. The results of our study suggest the following:

- Djibouti's economic recovery continues to follow a positive trend. Only 4 percent of those working before the pandemic were not working at the time of the survey. Even when counting those who were not working before the pandemic, 83 percent of all national households' breadwinners are now working, continuing strong trends from waves 1 and 2.

- In terms of refugees, village-based ones face worse employment conditions than refugees living in urban areas or urban nationals, and they are less likely to catch up. They were less likely to be employed prior to COVID-19, more likely to lose their job during the pandemic, and do not exhibit similar signs of recovery.

- A relatively large fraction of households has an acceptable level of food consumption, but refugees are more likely to experience food insecurity than nationals.

- Safety nets play an important role in protecting the most vulnerable, particularly among village-based refugees, for whom assistance from international nongovernmental organizations (NGOs) represents the main source of income.

A Snapshot of Phone Surveys

Djibouti's COVID-19 phone surveys were collected across three waves (July 2020, September/October 2020, and December 2020/January 2021). They include a three-wave panel of Djiboutian households (with replacement households), and a subsample of refugee households (only included in the third wave). Information on the households and breadwinners was provided by an adult respondent within the household.[1]

The Djiboutian subsample, referred to as *national households*, was drawn from the sampling frame of households from the Ministry of Social Affairs and Solidarity's social registry and was restricted to urban households having at least one phone number and interviewed after July 1, 2017. The third-wave dataset consisted of 1,383 interviewed national households, out of which 990 entered the survey from the first wave and 393 were added as replacement households in either the second or third wave (see table 5.1 for the respective sample sizes).

TABLE 5.1

Response Rates and Sample Sizes of the Three Waves

	National sample		Refugee sample	
	Observations	Response rate (%)	Observations	Response rate (%)
Wave 1	1,486	71.4	—	—
Wave 2	1,460	85.3	—	—
Wave 3	1,383	74.3	564	60.5

Source: World Bank calculations, based on Djibouti COVID-19 phone survey, waves 1–3. Note: Waves 1 and 2 included only national households. — = not available.

Both cross-sectional and panel weights are designed to adjust for differences in selection probability due to either design or nonresponse. Further adjustments in sampling weights were also made to ensure that results are representative of the national population, by poverty status, and by location (Balbala, the rest of Djibouti city, and urban areas outside Djibouti city). Given that the sampling frame overrepresents the poor and has an incomplete coverage of the upper distribution of income, we rely on a postcalibration approach using the household budget survey of 2017 as the reference data source to correct these biases.

Thus, the results of the national subsample are representative of the country's urban population (except the top wealth quintile). Notably, 70 percent of Djibouti's national population lives in urban areas (according to the 2009 population census).

The refugee subsample included in the third wave comprises refugees and asylum seekers from other countries and covers urban refugees and refugees residing in refugee villages, or settlements (henceforth, village-based refugees).[2] It is representative of the population of refugees and asylum seekers in Djibouti who live in the refugee villages of Ali Addeh, Holl Holl, and Markazi, as well as Djibouti City.[3] Although the sampling design does not allow disaggregation by refugee village site, differences in several characteristics (such as age) support segmenting the analysis by refugees' place of residence. Thus, whenever the sample size allows it, this subsample is disaggregated[4] into 184 urban households (33 percent of the refugees) and 380 village-based (predominantly rural) households (67 percent of the refugees). The sampling weights are designed to adjust for differences in design and nonresponse.

The potential bias in the national sample (toward poorer households) results in an expected lower bound of differences between nationals and the refugee population—meaning that as long as the excluded nationals are better off than refugees on average, as is strongly presumed, the true gap between refugee households and host is larger than exhibited here.

The majority of respondents in the third wave are male, household heads, and between 35 and 49 years of age (table 5.2). National respondents are more likely to be male, older, and breadwinners compared with the respondent for the refugee households, but they are less likely to be the household head. The breadwinners are the household head in 70.6 percent of the national households and 80.9 percent of the refugee households. In some cases, the breadwinner is not a household member (8.5 percent of the national households and 6.8 percent of the refugee households).

Impact on Economic Activities

Our study starts with a look at how COVID-19 has affected Djiboutian households on the job front. Keep in mind that pre-COVID, the labor force participation rate of the national population stood at 44.7 percent (according to the household budget survey, EDAM 2017), of which 47 percent of the active population was unemployed. Those who were employed were mostly working in the private informal sector (46.3 percent) and public sector (43.8 percent). In addition to the public branch, the economic activity of the country relied mainly on services. Regarding the refugee population, the employment rate for those ages 15 and above stood at 29 percent, with important variations across gender and location.[5]

TABLE 5.2

Characteristics of Respondents and Breadwinners

Percent

	Respondent			Breadwinner		
	Urban national	Urban refugee	Village-based refugee	Urban national	Urban refugee	Village-based refugee
Male	57.1	79.0	37.2	70.6	84.0	50.8
Age group						
18–34	28.8	28.4	42.2	20.0	27.2	38.5
35–49	44.7	52.9	37.8	49.2	53.9	38.2
50–64	20.5	16.3	17.4	24.4	17.6	20.0
65+	5.1	2.4	2.6	6.4	1.3	3.3
Relationship to the household head						
Household head	64.5	94.3	80.7	70.6	91.3	70.0
Spouse	17.3	2.9	10.2	13.3	2.1	21.7
Child	14.3	2.2	5.2	10.3	2.6	4.3
Other	3.9	0.6	3.9	5.8	4.0	4.1
Observations	**1,383**	**184**	**380**	**1,262**	**178**	**361**

Source: Djibouti COVID-19 phone survey, wave 3.

The phone surveys show that breadwinners from the national sample continue to return to work following the end of lockdowns (figure 5.1). Indeed, 83 percent of the breadwinners from the national sample (urban) worked the week before the survey, compared with 77 percent in wave 2 and 58 percent in wave 1 in June 2020. But economic activity is much lower among the refugee breadwinners, with significant disparities between urban and village-based breadwinners. Although 68 percent of urban refugee breadwinners worked before the survey, only 49 percent of village-based refugees have. In addition, 32 percent of all the refugee breadwinners reported that they were working neither in the prepandemic period nor in the week before the survey, compared with 13 percent of the national breadwinners. Thus, even before the pandemic, refugee breadwinners were less likely to participate in the labor market than the national breadwinners, although it is important to note that regional differences may exist among the refugee population that cannot be captured in the survey design.

Only a few breadwinners who were working before the pandemic have not resumed economic activity, although the rate is markedly higher among village-based refugees. And among village-based refugee breadwinners, they were more likely to not work either before the survey or before the COVID-19 crisis than urban refugees and national breadwinners.

FIGURE 5.1

Nationals Have an Especially High Rate of Getting Back to Work
Working status of breadwinners (%)

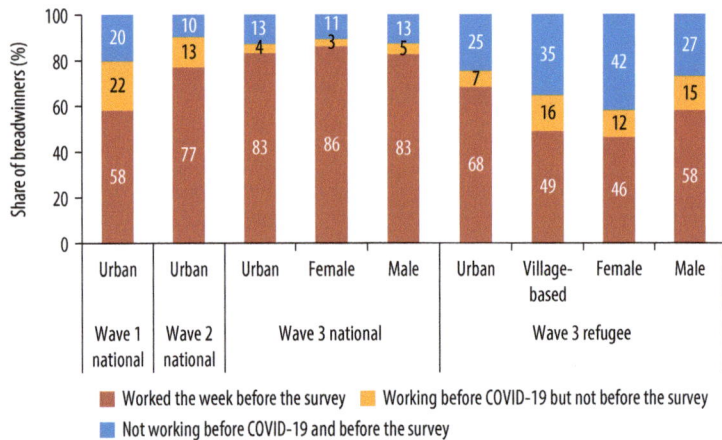

Source: World Bank calculations, based on Djibouti COVID-19 phone survey, waves 1–3.
Note: Waves 1 and 2 included only national households. Statistics are based on cross-sectional proportions and not only the longitudinal sample. The categories "female" and "male" refer to households with a female or male breadwinner. The national sample is only representative of the urban Djiboutian population.

The surveys tried to answer whether the breadwinners were in the public or private sector (formal or informal). Most of the ones who have not returned to economic activities were engaged in the informal sector.[6] Indeed, 77 percent of all the breadwinners who were working before COVID-19 but were not working before the survey were engaged in the informal sector; of these, about half were working in small businesses and the rest were mostly in public administration or large private firms. Of those breadwinners who stopped working after COVID-19 hit, about half were daily workers and the rest were self-employed and employees. Given that refugee breadwinners are much more likely to work in the informal private sector than national breadwinners (85 percent versus 49 percent, respectively), the survey results further highlight the precariousness of the refugee individuals' employment conditions.

The phone surveys point to a distinct difference between the employment sector patterns of the nationals and the refugees. Although most of the refugee breadwinners work in the informal sector (79 and 91 percent, respectively, for urban and village-based refugees), just half of the national breadwinners do (figure 5.2). Broken down by firm type, most refugee breadwinners work in small businesses (59 percent for both urban and village-based refugees),

FIGURE 5.2

Refugee Breadwinners Are More Likely to Work in the Informal Sector Than Nationals

Employment characteristics of national and refugee breadwinners who worked before the survey or before COVID-19, by share of respondents (%)

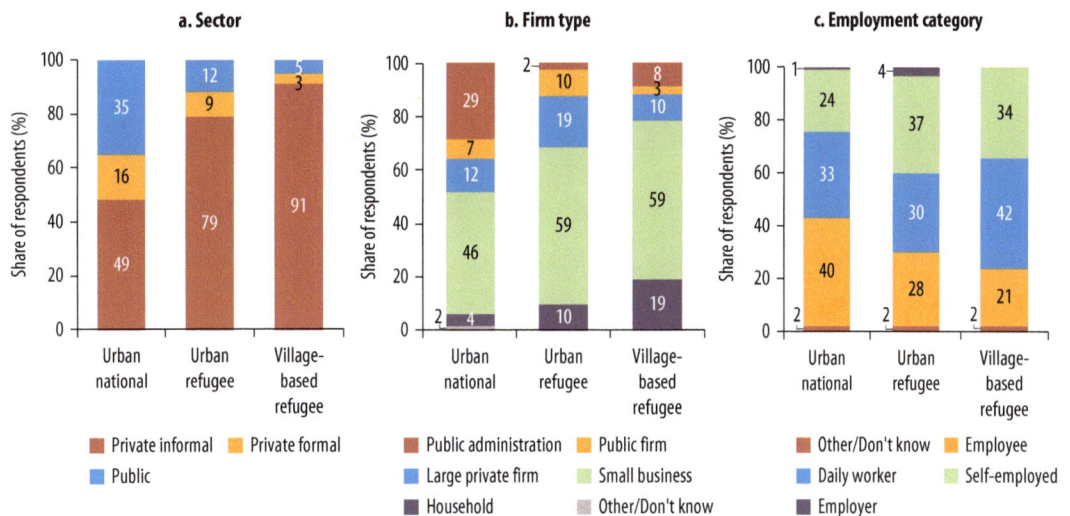

Source: World Bank calculations, based on Djibouti COVID-19 phone survey, wave 3.
Note: A small business is a sole proprietorship or cooperative; public firms are state-owned enterprises.

while urban refugees (19 percent) are more likely to work in large private firms than village-based refugees (10 percent). By employment category, urban nationals are more likely to be employees, while village-based refugees are more likely to be daily workers than both urban refugees and urban nationals. In addition, female refugee breadwinners are more likely to work in the informal sector than males (95 percent versus 83 percent, respectively), while male breadwinners are more likely to be daily laborers than their female counterparts (40 percent versus 33 percent, respectively).

As for workloads, Djiboutian breadwinners are largely returning to normal workloads. In wave 3, the percentage of national breadwinners who were working as usual was 77 percent, versus 73 percent in wave 2 and 53 percent in wave 1, and the proportion of those who worked fewer hours than usual has dropped from 31 percent in wave 1 to 9 percent in wave 3 (figure 5.3). The pattern is quite similar for the urban refugees, but the village-based refugees are much more likely to have worked less than usual. The main reason for the decrease of breadwinners' activity reported by the respondents was the stopping of their economic activity, which induced the reduction of staff and worked hours.

FIGURE 5.3

Most Djiboutians Are Returning to Normal Workloads

Reported change of workload of breadwinners who worked the week before the survey (%)

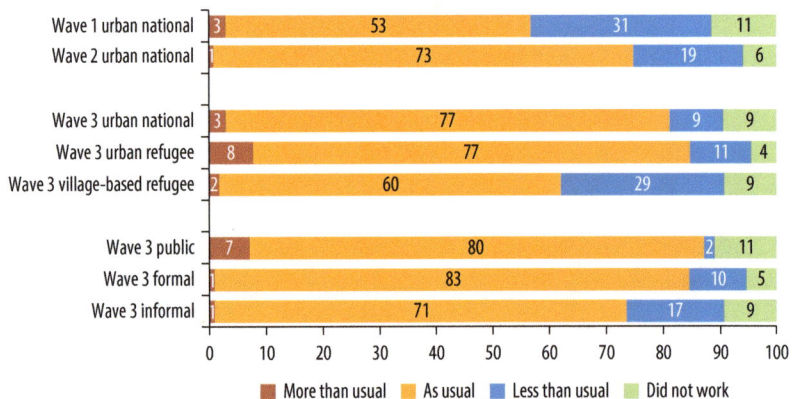

Source: World Bank calculations, based on Djibouti COVID-19 phone survey, waves 1–3.
Note: Waves 1 and 2 included only national households. Statistics are based on cross-sectional proportions and not only the longitudinal sample. The distinction by sectors of employment (public, formal, informal) concerns all the households whose breadwinner was working before the survey or whose breadwinner was working before COVID-19 but not the week before the survey. The category "formal" refers to the private formal sector and "informal" refers to the private informal sector.

Where COVID-19 still is taking a toll, however, is in the area of pay. Among those who declared having worked less than usual or not at all over the survey waves, the likelihood of receiving no pay instead of partial payment in wave 3 increased (figure 5.4)., more than half of the national breadwinners fell into this category, compared with 35 percent of the national breadwinners in wave 2. Moreover, fewer national breadwinners received partial payment compared with the previous waves (27 percent in wave 3 versus 50 percent in wave 2), while the percentage of national breadwinners who received full payment increased by 10 percentage points between wave 2 and wave 3. Therefore, it may be that some of those who were receiving partial payment in previous waves returned to their usual workload, leaving those who were least employable left behind, not working and/or not receiving payment. Further data may be required to ascertain the drivers in the dynamics of return to work.

As for the refugee breadwinners who were working less or not at all, 59 percent received partial payment, 39 percent received no pay, and 2 percent received full payment.[7] Here, the sector of employment matters. Those working in the public sector are much more likely to receive full payment (32 percent versus 12 percent in the formal sector

FIGURE 5.4

Breadwinners Still Face Big Problems in Terms of Getting Paid
Reported change in labor income among breadwinners who worked less or not at all the week before the survey (%)

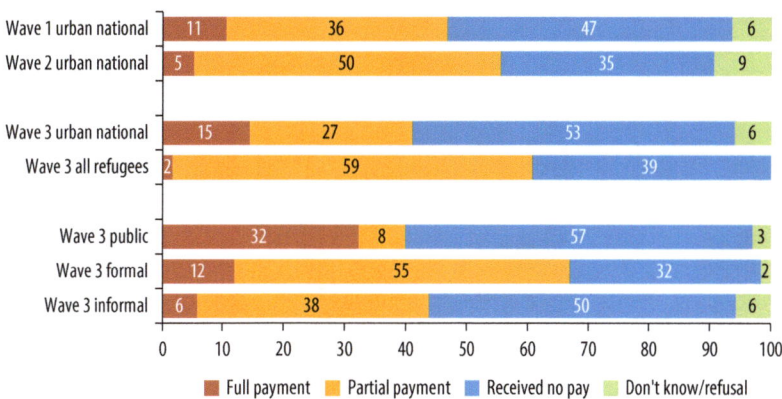

Source: World Bank calculations, based on Djibouti COVID-19 phone survey, waves 1–3.
Note: Waves 1 and 2 included only national households. Statistics are based on cross-sectional proportions and not only on the longitudinal sample. The distinction by sectors of employment (public, formal, informal) concerns all the households whose breadwinner was working before the survey or whose breadwinner was working before COVID-19 but not the week before the survey. The category "formal" refers to the private formal sector, and "informal" refers to the private informal sector. Given the small sample size after restricting it to households whose breadwinner worked less or not at all the week before the survey, it is not possible to disaggregate between urban and village-based refugees.

and 6 percent in the informal sector), but curiously they are also more likely to receive no pay at all. Breadwinners from the private formal sector appear to be the more protected, as only 32 percent of them received no pay (versus 57 percent in the public sector and 50 percent in the informal sector).

Impact on Livelihoods

Whereas in waves 1 and 2 the highest proportion in sources of income for national households is assistance from the government, in wave 3 the highest proportion is waged work and family business (figure 5.5). Refugee households in this wave rely primarily on assistance from international nongovernmental organizations. Although waged work and family business were identified as income sources for 22 percent and 43 percent of the national households in waves 1 and 2, respectively, 76 percent of nationals in the wave 3 report have it as a source of income. But government assistance remains an important source for national households, as are remittances and assistance from family or friends.

For the refugee households, the two main sources of income are assistance from international NGOs (88 percent for village-based refugees, and 62 percent for urban refugees) and assistance from family and friends

FIGURE 5.5

Family Business and Wage Work Are Back Up Strongly for Nationals

Reported sources of household's income for the last 12 months (%)

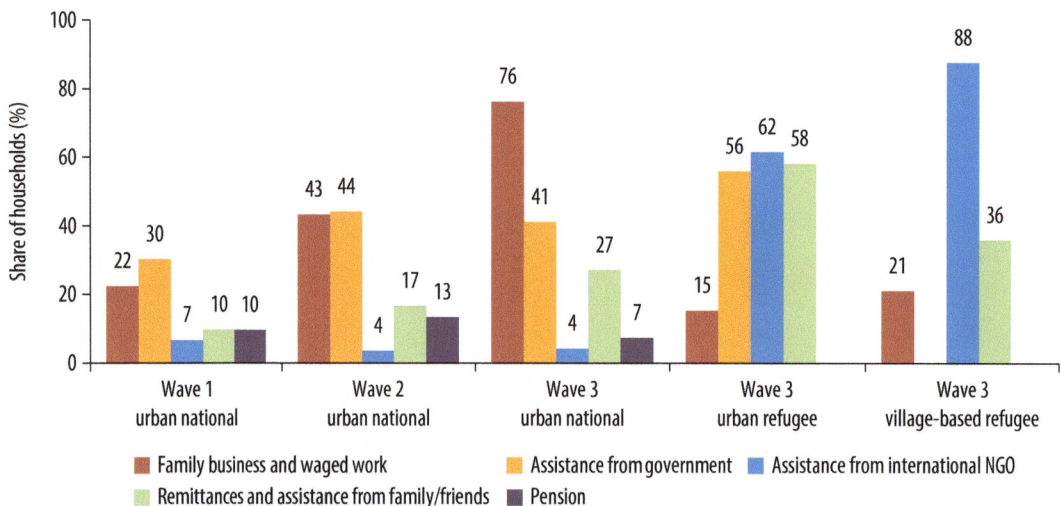

Source: World Bank calculations, based on Djibouti COVID-19 phone survey, waves 1–3.
Note: Waves 1 and 2 included only national households. Statistics are based on cross-sectional proportions and not only the longitudinal sample. NGO = nongovernmental organization.

and remittances (36 and 58 percent, respectively). Urban refugees also benefit from government assistance.[8] And both sets of refugees declared family business and waged work as a source of income (15 percent for urban-based and 21 percent for village-based), but at a far lower level than did nationals. This difference is consistent with previous results showing that refugee breadwinners are less likely to have worked the week before the survey, and when they work, refugees are likely to work less than usual compared with national breadwinners.

Compared with waves 1 and 2, fewer national households declared a decrease in all the sources of income in wave 3 (figure 5.6). Refugee households, however, are much more likely than nationals to have experienced a reduction in income from family business and waged work (37 percent versus 12 percent, respectively). That said, this difference is primarily driven by village-based refugees who had experienced a 43 percent drop in family business and waged work, compared with urban refugees (15 percent). Moreover, households with a nonworking breadwinner are more likely to suffer a reduction of all their sources of

FIGURE 5.6

Urban Nationals Have a Brighter Picture in Third Survey Round

Decrease in the reported sources of household's income for the last 30 days (%)

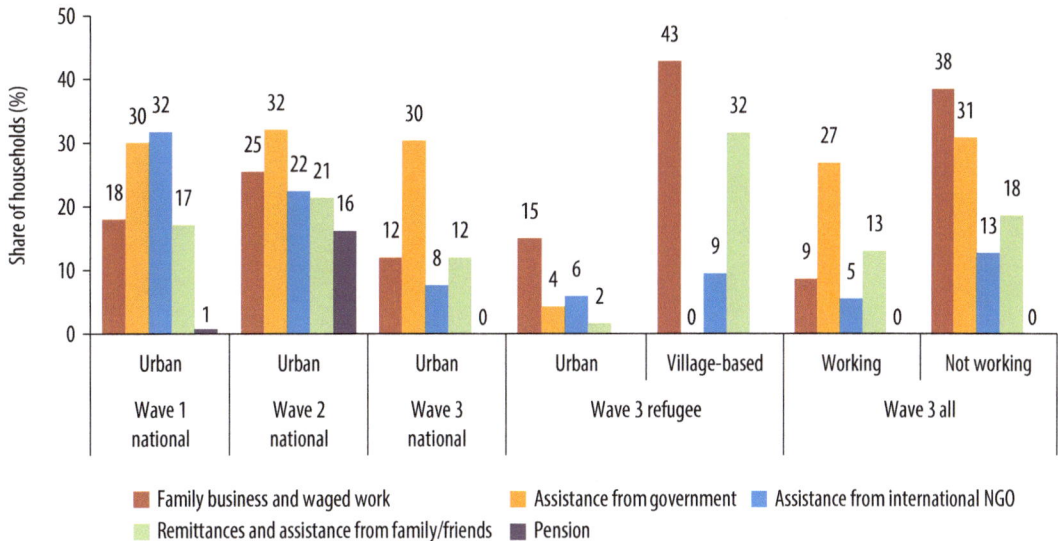

Source: World Bank calculations, based on Djibouti COVID-19 phone survey, waves 1–3.
Note: Waves 1 and 2 included only national households. Statistics are based on cross-sectional proportions and not only the longitudinal sample. The category "working" refers to the households with a breadwinner who worked the week before the survey and "not working" refers to the households with a breadwinner who did not work the week before the survey. NGO = nongovernmental organization.

income (except for remittances and assistance from family and friends) compared with households with a working breadwinner.

When facing a decline in economic activity or an income decrease, households used different strategies to cope with the situation.[9] The main ways in which national households cope is by receiving help from family or a friend (43 percent), reducing nonfood consumption (31 percent), or reducing food consumption (19 percent). For refugee households, the primary coping mechanism is getting help from an international NGO (43 percent), engaging in additional income-generating activities (37 percent), and reducing food consumption (29 percent).

However, a large proportion of households do not believe they have enough resources for the next 30 days (figure 5.7). The proportion of urban national households declaring they have enough resources has slightly decreased to 29 percent in wave 3, from 33 percent in wave 2 and 30 percent in wave 1. Among the refugees, only 10 percent of village-based households said they have enough resources for the next month, compared with 26 percent of urban refugee households. Those households that have a working breadwinner, however, are almost twice

FIGURE 5.7

Insufficient Resources Are Creating Serious Worries for the Month after the Survey

Proportion of households who declared having enough resources for the following 30 days (%)

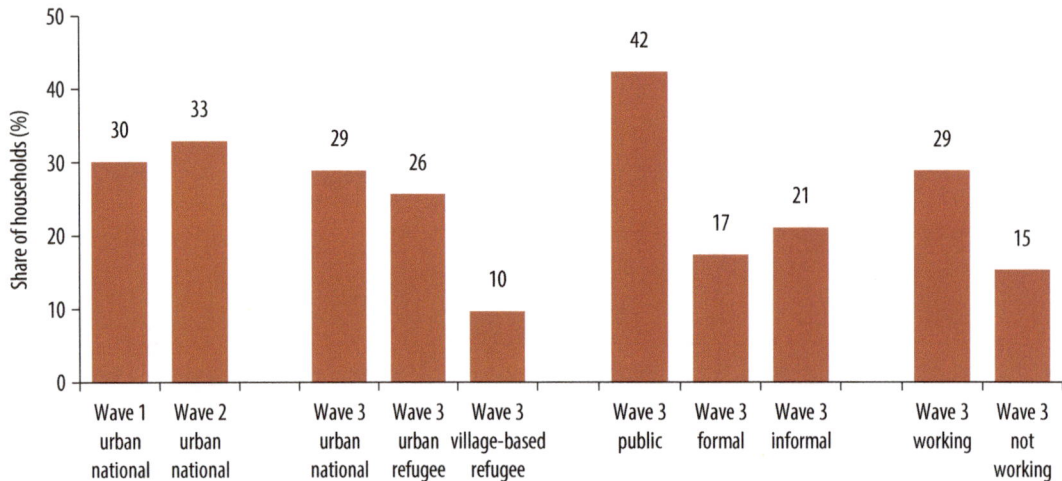

Source: World Bank calculations, based on Djibouti COVID-19 phone survey, waves 1–3.
Note: Waves 1 and 2 included only national households. Statistics are based on cross-sectional proportions and not only the longitudinal sample. The distinction by sectors of employment (public, formal, informal) concerns all the households whose breadwinner was working before the survey or whose breadwinner was working before COVID-19 but not the week before the survey. The category "formal" refers to the private formal sector and "informal" refers to the private informal sector. The category "working" refers to the households with a breadwinner who worked the week before the survey, and "not working" refers to the households with a breadwinner who did not work the week before the survey.

as likely to report enough resources for the next 30 days as those with a nonworking breadwinner. In addition, having a breadwinner who is working in the public sector seems to offer protection. Indeed, 42 percent of the households with a breadwinner employed in the public sector declared having enough resources for the next month, while less than a quarter of the other households—those with a breadwinner working in the informal sector and those in the formal private sectors—are in the same situation.

Impact on Acess to Basic Goods and Services

Access to basic goods, in general, has continued to improve since March 2020. More than 90 percent of the national households were able to have access to wheat flour, rice, cooking oil, vegetables, and hand soaps. Whereas a comparable level of access is reported by urban refugees, village-based refugees report lower access to most basic goods—notably basic medicines (for cold, cough, or fever). In particular, among the refugee households that could not access basic medicines, 89 percent reported they cannot afford them (versus 79 percent of national households).[10] Fewer national households reported a price increase on selected goods in the last 7 days before the survey in December/January than during the previous months. For example, for vegetables, 15 percent of national households declared facing a price increase in wave 3, compared with 22 percent in wave 2 and 87 percent in wave 1. In general, fewer than 35 percent of both national and refugee households reported a price increase for all the basic goods in December/January during the third wave. These findings are in line with the consumer price index evolution over time, where a price spike is observed in July 2020 (coinciding with wave 1).

The need for health care rose steadily for nationals, from 17 percent in wave 1 to 36 percent in wave 2 and 52 percent in wave 3 (figure 5.8).[11] Specifically, 25 percent of households reported needing emergency services, 20 percent immunization, and 19 percent chronic disease care. Moreover, nationals are more likely to declare a need of health services than urban refugee households, while village-based refugee households are more likely to declare being in need of health care than their urban counterparts.

As for access to health care, a positive trend is observed—that access is better among national households than refugee households compared with previous waves among the national sample: 90 percent had access when needed, compared with 85 percent in wave 2 and 60 percent in wave 1. Urban refugee households, however, report lower levels of access to health care when needed than nationals (66 percent versus 90 percent, respectively). Village-based refugees appear to have less

FIGURE 5.8

For Respondents, the Need for and Access to Health Care Is Rising
Respondents who needed and had access to health care during the last 30 days (%)

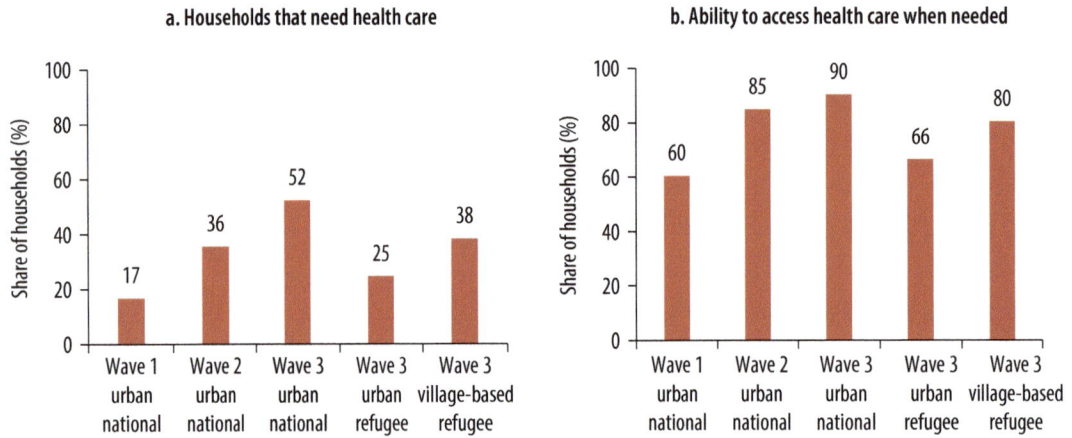

Source: World Bank calculations, based on Djibouti COVID-19 phone survey, waves 1–3.
Note: Waves 1 and 2 do not include refugee samples. Statistics are based on cross-sectional proportions and not only the longitudinal sample.

difficulty accessing health services than urban refugees, as 80 percent of them declared having access to it when needed.[12] For households that did not have access to a health service when needed, the main reasons cited by nationals are crowded health centers or hospitals (48 percent) and inability to pay the fees (24 percent), whereas refugees report as a main barrier the inability to pay fees (38 percent) and inability to afford the trip (31 percent).[13]

Impact on Food Insecurity

Food insecurity can be measured in a number of ways to assess what is going on in households. One is in terms of meals consumed. The phone surveys for wave 3 show that 85 percent of national households reported their children having three meals per day before COVID-19 and 88 percent reported that the week before the survey (figure 5.9). Children from refugee households are less likely to have eaten three meals per day than children from national households (70 percent and 81 percent for urban and village-based refugees, respectively, the week before the survey). In both samples, however, children from households with a female breadwinner are more likely to eat three meals a day than those from households with a male breadwinner. The working status of the breadwinner seems to correlate with the status of food insecurity of the households. Indeed, households whose breadwinner is not working are much less

FIGURE 5.9

Refugee Children Are Less Likely to Have at Least Three Meals a Day

Proportion of households in which children had at least three meals a day the week before COVID-19 and the week before the wave 3 survey (%)

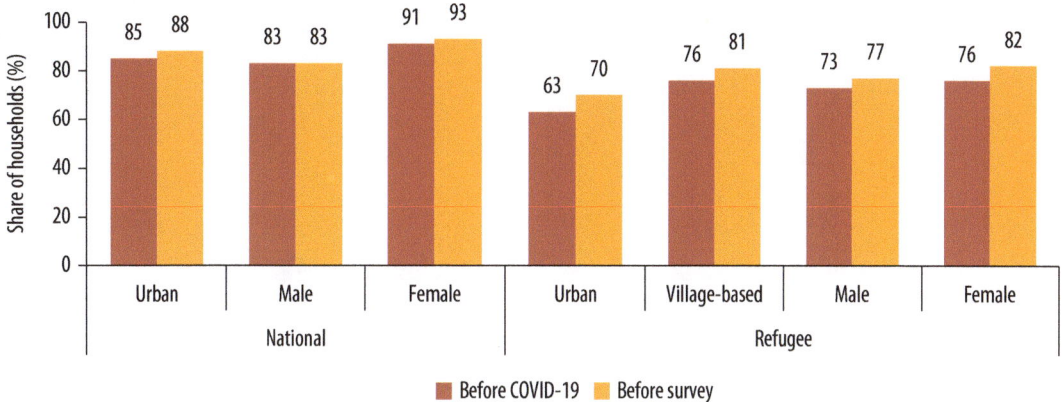

Source: World Bank calculations, based on Djibouti COVID-19 phone survey, wave 3.
Note: The categories "female" and "male" refer to households with a female or male breadwinner. Calculations are restricted to households with children.

likely to be able to offer three meals per day to their children than those with a working breadwinner (71 percent versus 87 percent the week before the survey). Moreover, children from households with a breadwinner working in the public sector are more likely to eat three meals a day during the week before the survey than others (91 percent versus 89 percent and 78 percent for private informal and private formal sectors).

A second measure of food security is whether children go to bed hungry and skipped a meal. The comparison here is whether this occurred during the last 30 days prior to the survey or during the COVID-19 crisis in April/May 2020 (figure 5.10). The results indicate that fewer children went to bed hungry and skipped a meal during the last 30 days prior to the survey. However, despite refugees receiving more assistance, differences between national and refugee households are observed. Children from refugee households, particularly those who are village-based, are more likely to go to bed hungry and to skip a meal (both during the COVID-19 crisis and during the last 30 days) than children from national households.

A third measure relates to dietary composition and adequacy. To examine this, a food consumption score based on weighted frequency indicators is calculated using the frequency of consumption of different food groups consumed by households during a 7-day recall period. This discussion draws on the World Food Programme's food consumption

FIGURE 5.10

Refugee Children Are More Likely to Go to Bed Hungry and Skip a Meal

Distribution of households according to food insecurity of children during COVID-19 and the last 30 days (%)

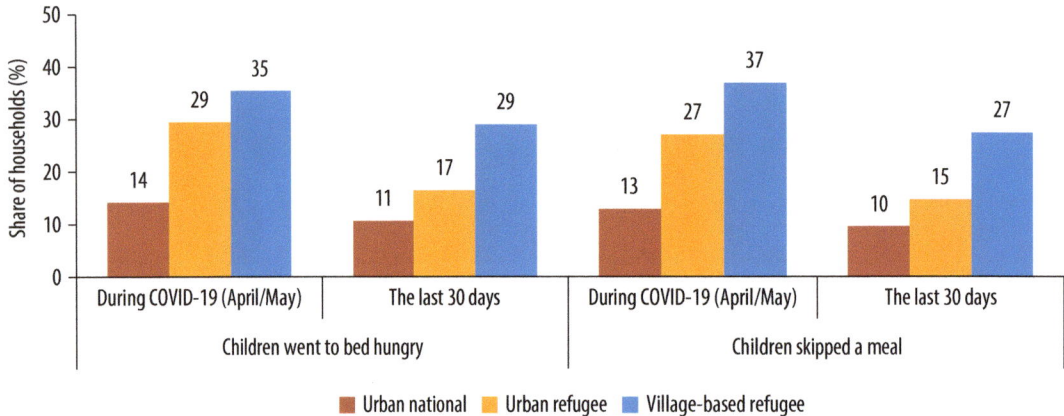

Source: World Bank calculations, based on Djibouti COVID-19 phone survey, wave 3.
Note: Calculations restricted to households with children.

score module designed to report, among other things, on food frequency and dietary diversity. Following the World Food Programme's approach, the score is recoded into a categorical indicator based on standard thresholds.[14] The phone survey results show that a relatively large fraction of households has an acceptable level of food consumption based on the food consumption score, although village-based refugees are more likely to have a low score (figure 5.11). Also, the poor national households, as identified by the social registry, are more likely to experience poor food consumption than the nonpoor.

Role of Social Safety Nets

Social safety nets play a crucial role in containing the negative effects of the pandemic on the welfare of the population. Since the early period of the pandemic, the proportion of national households who received assistance has been declining in almost all types of assistance—with around 23 percent of them receiving food stamps in wave 3, compared with 27 percent in wave 2, and 31 percent during the first wave (figure 5.12). However, 43 percent of urban refugee households reported receiving food assistance, 37 percent received food stamps, and 15 percent received cash transfers. For the village-based households, the numbers are sharply

FIGURE 5.11

Village-Based Refugees Are More Likely to Score Low on Dietary Composition

Distribution of households by food consumption groups (%)

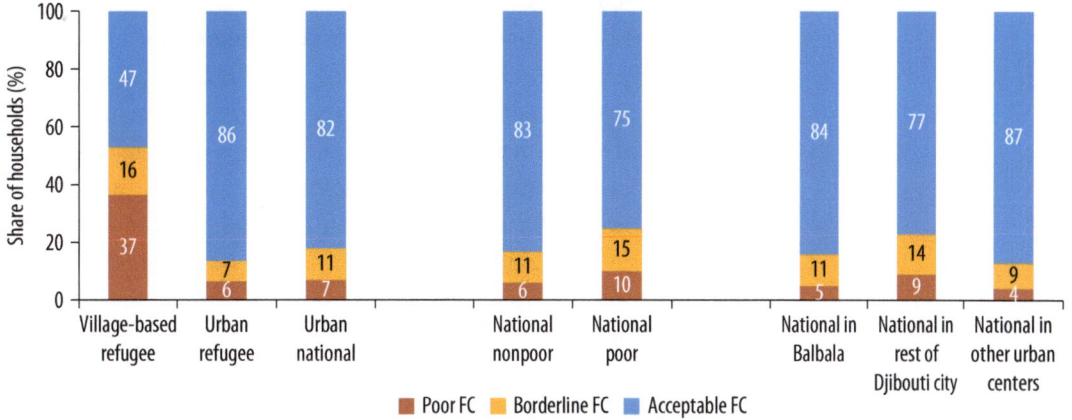

Source: World Bank calculations, based on Djibouti COVID-19 phone survey, wave 3.
Note: The food consumption (FC) of a household is considered poor if the score is inferior or equal to 28.0, borderline for a score ranging from 28.5 and 42.0, and adequate/acceptable for a score between 43.0 and 160.0. Decomposition by poverty status and location are available only for the national sample.

FIGURE 5.12

Social Safety Nets Are Still Vital for Refugees

Assistance received, by type and source, in the last 30 days before the survey (%)

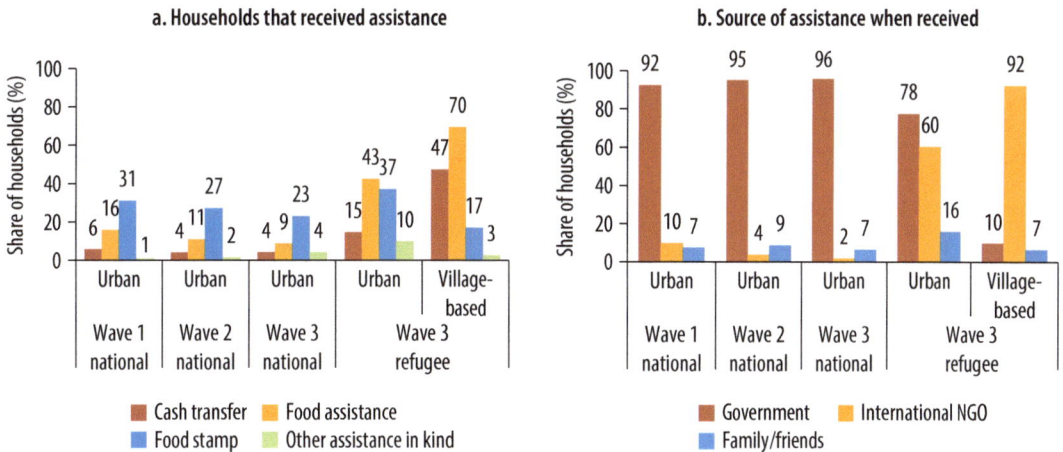

a. Households that received assistance

b. Source of assistance when received

Source: World Bank calculations, based on Djibouti COVID-19 phone survey, waves 1–3.
Note: Waves 1 and 2 included only national households. Statistics are based on cross-sectional proportions and not only the longitudinal sample. NGO = nongovernmental organization.

higher: 70 percent reported receiving food assistance, and 47 percent received cash transfers. Of those who receive assistance, its source differs according to the type of household. For nationals, the main source is the government; urban refugees rely on government and NGO assistance, and village-based refugees rely on NGOs.

Do food assistance or food stamps make a difference? The surveys show that national households that received food assistance or food stamps in the last 30 days are more likely to have an acceptable food consumption score than the ones that did not receive any assistance (figure 5.13). For urban refugee households, the assistance makes little difference. However, for village-based refugees, although 46 percent of those who received assistance have an acceptable food consumption score versus 50 percent of those who did not receive assistance, the assistance increases the percentage of those with a borderline, food consumption score. As a result, there are fewer households with poor scores among those that received assistance than among those that did not receive it.

Insight into Poor National Households

We gained additional insights into the labor market, safety nets, health care, and food insecurity by looking at the phone survey through the lens of poverty.

FIGURE 5.13

Food Assistance Boosts Food Consumption Scores

Assistance received by households according to their food consumption score (%)

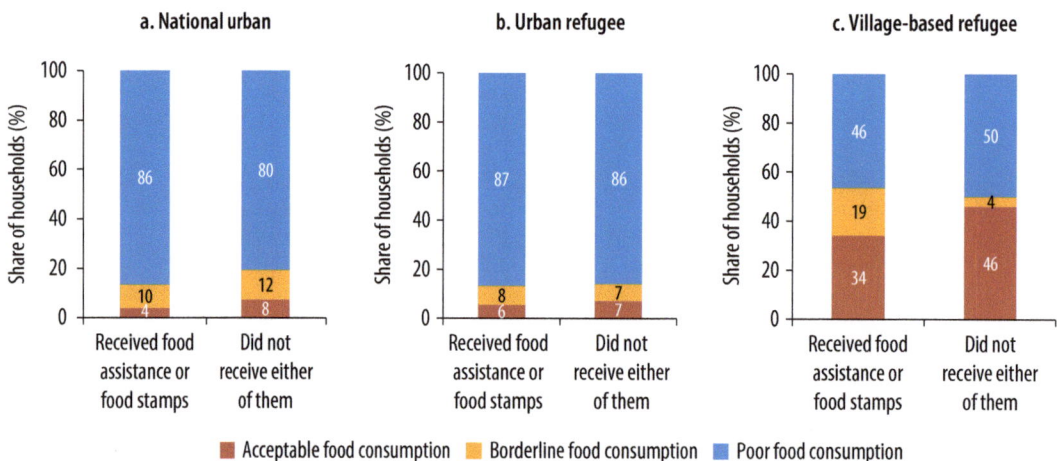

Source: World Bank calculations, based on Djibouti COVID-19 phone survey, wave 3.

Regarding the labor market, the poverty status is available only for the national sample; thus, we found that breadwinners from poor and nonpoor national households have the same probability of having worked the week before the survey (83 percent). There is also no difference between these breadwinners in the probability of working less than usual or not working at all. However, among the national breadwinners who worked less than usual or not at all the week before the survey, more of the poor households reported having received no pay compared with the nonpoor (64 percent versus 51 percent, respectively). Conversely, more of the nonpoor than the poor reported having received a full payment (16 percent versus 5 percent, respectively).

In terms of safety nets, the proportion of households that received any kind of assistance decreased for both poor and nonpoor households. Nevertheless, poor households are more likely than the nonpoor ones to receive any kind of assistance.

The need for health care has increased for all households across the three waves (figure 5.14), but poor households are more likely to need health services than the nonpoor (59 percent versus 51 percent). However, as access to health services increases, both poor and nonpoor

FIGURE 5.14

The Need for Health Services Is Rising, Especially for the Poor

Proportion of poor and nonpoor national households that needed and had access to health care (%)

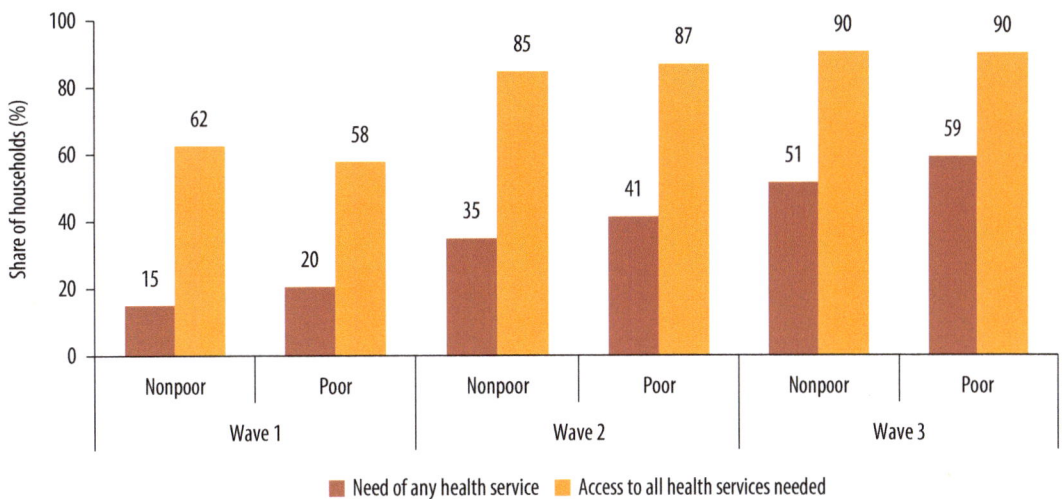

Source: World Bank calculations, based on Djibouti COVID-19 phone survey, waves 1–3.
Note: This figure includes only national households because poverty status is not available for the refugee sample. Statistics are based on cross-sectional proportions and not only the longitudinal sample.

households have a similar probability of accessing the health services when they need them.

Poor households are also more likely to face food insecurity than the nonpoor households. Around 13 percent of the poor households had children skipping a meal in the last 30 days prior to the survey, compared with 9 percent of the nonpoor ones. The same pattern is observed for households whose children went to bed hungry or had fewer than three meals per day.

Conclusion

Almost one year after the first case of COVID-19 was recorded in Djibouti, the rate of infection has slowed. Despite a return to normal life, the impacts of the pandemic continue to affect the well-being of households. The three waves of the COVID-19 phone surveys aimed to follow the recovery of the economic outcomes of the national and refugee populations in Djibouti, as well as some critical welfare results, such as access to basic goods and services or food insecurity.

Economic recovery in Djibouti continues to follow a positive trend both in terms of workload and income. In the third wave of the survey, around 83 percent of the national breadwinners worked the week before the survey versus 77 percent in wave 2 and 58 percent in wave 1. The intensity of the economic activity is also higher than in the previous waves. Moreover, fewer households reported a decrease in their sources of income compared with the previous waves. However, for the breadwinners who still suffer from the fallout of the pandemic, the situation may have worsened. The reduction of workload is more associated with no pay than during the previous waves. Moreover, fewer breadwinners received partial payment compared with the previous waves. These results suggest a situation where the fallout of the pandemic may be felt more severely by vulnerable workers.

The situation of village-based refugee households in Djibouti shows signs of being precarious. Their economic activity is much lower than among the nationals and urban refugees, with only 49 percent of breadwinners working the week before the survey (versus 83 percent for the nationals and 68 percent of urban refugees). These breadwinners were also more likely to report a lower workload than others. And they appear to be engaged in more vulnerable activities, given that most of the refugees work in the informal sector (87 percent), while only half of the national breadwinners do. Thus, it appears that the economic recovery seems to take more time for the village-based refugee households than the others, considering their vulnerable pre-COVID-19 position.

Moreover, village-based refugees' food security trails behind that of urban refugees and nationals. Among these refugees, a larger proportion reported their children having skipped a meal in the past 30 days than did national and urban refugee households. And although 82 percent of national households and 86 percent of urban refugees have an acceptable food consumption score, just 47 percent of village-based refugee households do. The safety nets in Djibouti play a vital role in protecting the most vulnerable. Indeed, especially for village-based refugees, a lower proportion of households with poor food consumption is seen among those who receive food assistance.

Notes

1. The surveyor preferably tried to interview the previous wave's respondents for the panel households, and the household head or closest related household member for the replacement in refugee households.
2. The refugee subsample is drawn from the United Nations High Commissioner for Refugees registries and identified by the National Institute of Statistics of Djibouti in a 2019 listing exercise.
3. Phone surveys are useful in the pandemic as a way to collect data without risking spread of COVID-19. However, they necessarily only include households with access to a live mobile phone line, and so may omit poor households. To overcome this, reweighting techniques were applied to bring the statistics here as close to being representative of the full refugee and urban national populations as possible.
4. However, where multiple disaggregation is necessary, the sample size may not be sufficient to draw robust conclusions.
5. The Profiling Survey Report of Refugee Villages in 2019 (Rapport d'enquête profilage dans les villages de réfugiés 2019), by the Institute of Statistics of Djibouti, Ministry of Social Affairs and Solidarity, World Food Program, and UN Refugee Agency (2020). Note that contrary to the Profiling Survey Report of 2019, which measures the employment rate, the present COVID-19 survey only captures employment of breadwinners; therefore the figures are not necessarily comparable.
6. Ideally, the pre-COVID-19 employment characteristics of the breadwinners who were working before COVID-19 but were not working before the survey would be compared with those of breadwinners who were working before COVID-19 and were working before the survey. However, the questionnaire does not ask former employment characteristics for those currently working.
7. Notice that among the 208 breadwinners who received no pay at all the week before the survey, 60 percent did not work, and 39 percent worked less than usual. Among the 167 breadwinners who did not work at all the week before the survey, 69 percent received no pay, 21 percent received a full payment, and 8 percent a partial payment.

8. According to the Ministry of Social Affairs and Solidarity, urban refugees received food vouchers on a monthly basis until March 2021. The ministry also stated that village-based refugees do not receive any assistance from the government.

9. In general, 8 percent of households experienced both an income and an activity decrease. Of the rest, 12 percent have experienced only an income decrease and 12 percent have faced only an activity decrease, while 68 percent of households have not experienced a decrease of any type.

10. Sample size does not permit disaggregation between urban and village-based refugees.

11. The reason behind the increase in need for health care is not asked in the survey. Given the low daily rates of detected COVID-19 cases in Djibouti, it is not clear whether the pandemic may have increased the need. However, it is possible that the seasonality of diseases in Djibouti partly explains these variations.

12. Because only 52 urban refugee households declared needing health care services in the last 30 days, the conclusions on their access to health care must be treated carefully.

13. Sample size does not permit disaggregation between urban and village-based refugees.

14. The cutoffs of 28 and 42 are used because of frequent use of oil. For more information, see the World Food Programme VAM Resource Centre: https://resources.vam.wfp.org/data-analysis/quantitative/food-security/fcs-food-consumption-score.

Part II: Middle East and North Africa Microsimulations

Tunisia: Poorest Households Are the Most Vulnerable

Deeksha Kokas, Abdelrahmen El Lahga, and
Gladys Lopez-Acevedo

Key Messages

- COVID-19 is going to exacerbate Tunisia's existing development challenges by reversing the trend of poverty reduction in recent years—with the risk of an increasing number of people falling below the poverty line and an increasing degree of poverty severity for the already poor.

- Our study's results show that—combining labor and price shocks simultaneously—poverty is projected to increase by 7.3 percentage points under the optimistic scenario and by 11.9 points under the pessimistic one, implying a more than 50 percent increase in poverty in the first scenario and almost a doubling of the poverty rate in the second.

- Households with per capita consumption in the poorest 20 percent of the population—which are concentrated in Tunisia's Center West and South East regions—would be hardest hit. As for the most vulnerable individuals, they are likely to be women, live in large households, lack access to health care, and are employed without contracts.

- The government's compensatory measures targeting the hardest hit are expected to mitigate some of these losses. Specifically, the increase in poverty would be 6.5 percentage points under the optimistic scenario if mitigation measures are in place versus 7.3 percentage points in their absence.

Introduction

Over the past decade, Tunisia has been struggling with several political, economic, governance, and institutional bottlenecks, which have led to a deterioration in its economic performance. Even though poverty declined significantly between 2000 and 2019, from 25.4 to 13.8 percent, spatial disparities remain between urban and rural areas (where extreme poverty remains high) and between coastal regions (where most economic activities are concentrated) and interior regions. The poor population is disproportionately concentrated in rural areas, which have one-third of the population but two-thirds of the poor, and a considerable share of the population in rural and lagging areas remains vulnerable to falling back into poverty.

Tunisia had its first confirmed case of COVID-19 on March 2, 2020. Since then, the country has recorded 90,213 cases and 2,935 deaths, according to official estimates, and even though there were signs that the spread of the disease was slowing in August, the number of cases again started to spike in October.

The effects of a rapid spread of COVID-19 in Tunisia and potential containment measures are likely to affect poverty and inequality through four broad channels: labor income, nonlabor income, direct effects on consumption, and service disruption (Molini and Lassoued 2020). The labor income impacts could be either direct, through loss of earnings due to illness, or indirect, through employment and wage shocks. Nonlabor income impacts could be driven by changes in patterns of remittances or public transfers. Consumption could be directly affected through changes in prices of items that have a significant share in household budgets or increases in out-of-pocket costs of health care. And service disruption could ultimately have severe welfare implications through school closures and saturation of health care systems (figure 6.1).

The COVID-19 pandemic is likely to exacerbate Tunisia's existing development challenges by potentially reversing the trend of poverty reduction in recent years, with the risk of increasing the number of people falling below the poverty line and increasing the degree of poverty severity of those who are already poor. Evidence generated by phone surveys reported in chapter 4 highlight this disproportionate impact of COVID-19 on the poor and vulnerable by demonstrating how household welfare was affected by rising food prices and by loss of employment. What these phone surveys were unable to reveal is the impact on poverty.

Simulation studies have been conducted to assess the impact of COVID-19 on poverty by the International Food Policy Research Institute (IFPRI) for the Middle East and North Africa, the

FIGURE 6.1

COVID-19 Can Affect Poverty and Inequality through Four Channels

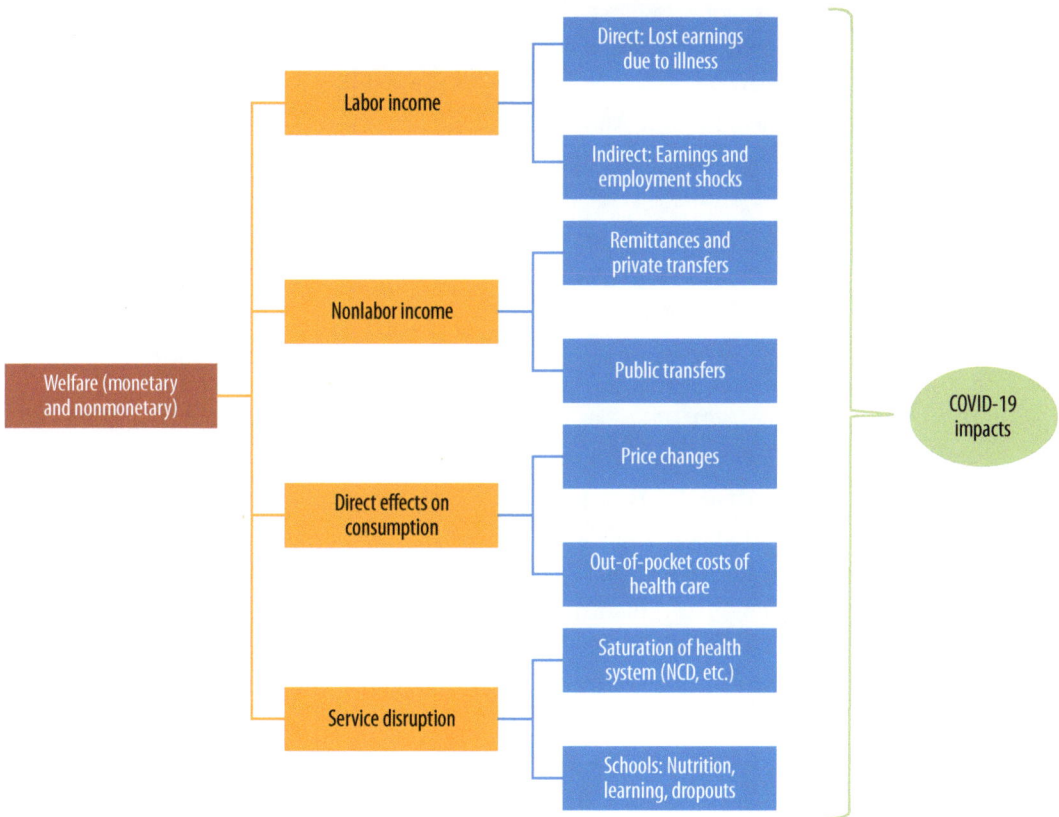

Source: World Bank 2020a.
Note: NCD = noncommunicable diseases.

United Nations Development Programme (UNDP), and the United Nations Children's Fund (UNICEF) offices in Tunisia. The results point to increasing poverty. In particular, the UNDP study simulates a post-COVID scenario (S1), which includes a decline in supply and a decline in household demand for various basic goods. The simulated drop in household demand (except for food and hygiene goods) and public investment are 40 percent compared with the baseline scenario (pre-COVID-19 scenario). The study shows the poverty rate rising to 19.2 percent from the current 15.2 percent, pulling an additional 475,000 individuals below the income poverty line. The economic recession, with a projected growth rate of –4.4 percent for 2020, is estimated (using a monetary approach) to elevate multidimensional poverty from 13.2 to 15.6 percent.

The UNICEF (2020) study showed that the two months of confinement decreed in Tunisia, during March and April 2020, led to an estimated loss of 7 percent of household income. Poverty is estimated to have increased over the same period from 14 percent to 18.5 percent, or nearly half a million new poor. Poverty among children under the age of 18 years likely rose from 19 percent to 25 percent, or nearly 900,000 poor children. And the government's mitigation measures are unlikely to have significantly countered the rise in poverty. However, the same study also shows that a universal allowance of 1 dinar per day (US$0.37) for each child not covered by social security is likely to reduce child poverty by 5 percentage points.

The potential impact on labor markets through the income and consumption channels on different population subgroups is left unanswered. Thus, the objective of this chapter is threefold: (a) assess the pre-COVID-19 situation to identify and profile population subgroups that are most vulnerable to getting infected by COVID-19 and being affected by the associated government measures; (b) simulate the impacts of COVID-19 on consumption, poverty, and inequality (based on sectoral growth performances over the whole year of 2020), and analyze the distribution of individuals expected to fall into poverty as a result of COVID-19; and (c) simulate how the impacts would vary with or without mitigation measures adopted by the Tunisian government.[1]

As highlighted by Ajwad et al. (2013), measuring real-time impacts of any crisis (financial, pandemics, or economic slowdowns) on welfare is difficult because of complex and time-consuming procedures involved in conducting household and individual-level surveys. To overcome such challenges in the short run, economists use complementary simulation techniques to conduct assessment of welfare impacts of shocks by modeling different scenarios. In general, the literature showcases a wide variety of approaches used to quantify the distributional impacts of shocks.[2]

In this chapter, we follow a methodology similar to that employed by Ajwad et al. (2013) and use a hybrid approach that combines the results of macroeconomic projections of a sectoral slowdown of the Tunisian economy in 2020 using microsimulation techniques. We focus on quantifying the magnitude of the impacts of COVID-19 on poverty and inequality in Tunisia through the labor income and consumption channels, drawing on Tunisia's household budget survey conducted in 2015 (Enquête Nationale sur le Budget, la Consommation et le Niveau de Vie des Ménages). Unlike Ajwad et al. (2013), we introduce the effect of a price increase while doing the simulations. In this regard, our study is different from those by IFPRI and UNDP, which are based on CGE (computable general equilibrium) modeling and focus mostly on the macroeconomic impact of the pandemic.

We rely on the latest round of data available in the 2015 national household budget survey. The Household Budget Survey is a quinquennial survey and the eighth survey of its kind carried out by the National Institute of Statistics (INS). The seven preceding surveys were carried out in 1968, 1975, 1980, 1985, 1990, 1995, and 2005. The survey, which covers the budget, consumption, and household standard of living in 2015, covers data on household expenditures and acquisitions during the survey period, food consumption and the nutritional situation of households, and household access to community health and education services. Although the INS has conducted a 2019 household budget survey, the official estimates are not yet published, and the data are not yet widely available and do not include consumption data.

This chapter begins with a comprehensive description of Tunisia's precrisis situation, including trends in poverty, labor markets, and demographics. It then describes the data and the empirical methodology to simulate the impacts of COVID-19 on labor income and consumption, along with the magnitude of impacts in the presence of mitigation measures. It concludes with key findings and policy implications.

Precrisis Situation: Poverty and Labor Markets

Which population subgroups are most vulnerable to getting infected by COVID-19 and most heavily affected by the associated government mitigation measures? In the pre-COVID period, the poverty headcount rate in Tunisia declined—from 25.4 percent in 2000 to 13.8 percent in 2019 (figure 6.2, panel a). The pace of poverty reduction was fastest between 2010 and 2015. A thorough examination of trends in inequality shows a similar pattern. Particularly from 2005 onward, the Gini index fell from 0.40 in 2000 to 0.37 in 2015, and further to 0.33 in 2019. Urban areas registered a higher Gini index, but between 2015 and 2019 the gap between the Gini index in urban and rural areas seemed to be declining.

Overall, economic growth has been pro-poor, with the bottom 40 percent benefiting the most. Figure 6.2, panel b, shows Tunisia's growth incidence curve (GIC), which displays the annualized increase in consumption per capita by percentage of the consumption distribution (the left side of the horizontal axis is the poorest and the right side is the richest). It shows that the poorest experienced the largest percentage increase in consumption, and that the increase declines as one moves

FIGURE 6.2

Economic Growth Has Been Pro-Poor with Some Inequality Gains

a. Poverty headcount

b. Growth incidence curve 2000–15

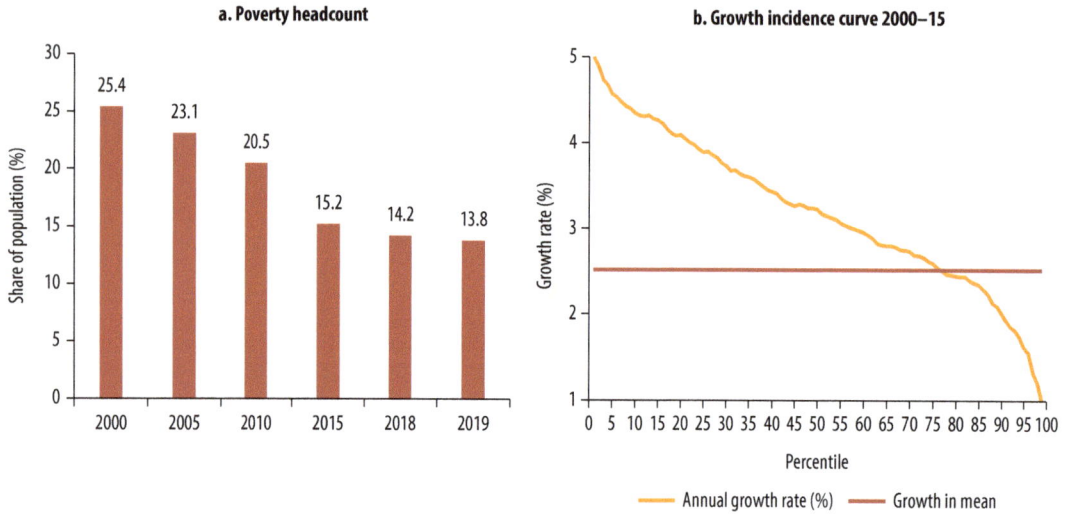

Source: World Bank calculations.
Note: The growth incidence curve shows the annualized increase in consumption per capita by percentile of the consumption distribution (the left side of the horizontal axis is the poorest and the right side is the richest).

along the consumption distribution to richer households. These massive gains in poverty reduction between 2010 and 2015 seem to be driven by greater gains for rural areas.

Against this backdrop of progress and the need for continued efforts on the poverty and inequality fronts, there are five key ways in which COVID-19 and associated containment measures could affect labor market outcomes.

First, there are six high-risk sectors that are more likely to get affected. These include (a) tourism or hotels, cafes and restaurants; (b) textiles; (c) mechanical and electric industry; (d) transport; (e) commerce; and (f) construction or civil engineering and building. These sectors employ a large share of the population, ranging from 47 percent of those employed among the poorest decile to between 53 and 54 percent among the fourth, fifth, and sixth deciles (figure 6.3). The Center East and North East region workers are most likely to see a sharp decline in income, given the large percentage of those employed in these high-risk subsectors. About 46 percent of those employed in the Grand Tunis region also work in high-risk sectors. And a high percentage of women employed in the textile sector and men employed in construction are likely to be hurt.

FIGURE 6.3

High-Risk Sectors Are More Likely to Be Affected

Share of employed in each sector, by consumption decile, gender, and region

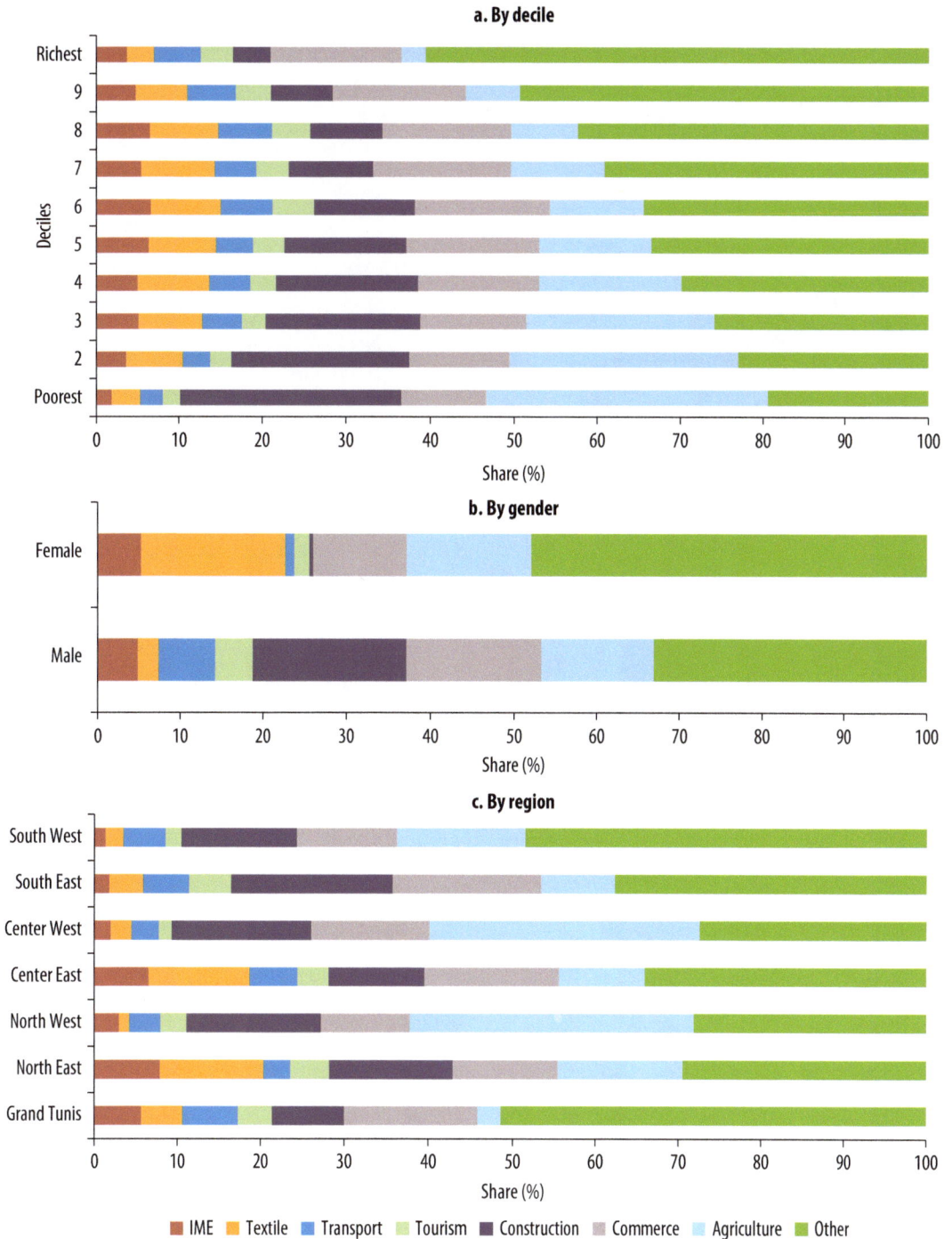

Source: World Bank calculations, based on 2015 Household Budget Survey.

Note: IME = mechanical and electric industry.

Second, a high proportion of workers are engaged in informal work. Informal employment—defined as those employed and not affiliated with social security (Caisse National de Securite Social—is widespread in Tunisian labor markets. It tends to be higher for lower consumption deciles, ranging from 56 to 71 percent in the lowest three consumption deciles in contrast with 19 to 34 percent for the highest three consumption deciles (figure 6.4). There are substantial variations among regions, with an average share of informal jobs at 54 percent in the North West region and 62 percent in the Center West region. Interestingly, even

FIGURE 6.4

A High Proportion of Workers Are Still in Informal Jobs
Share of workers in informal jobs

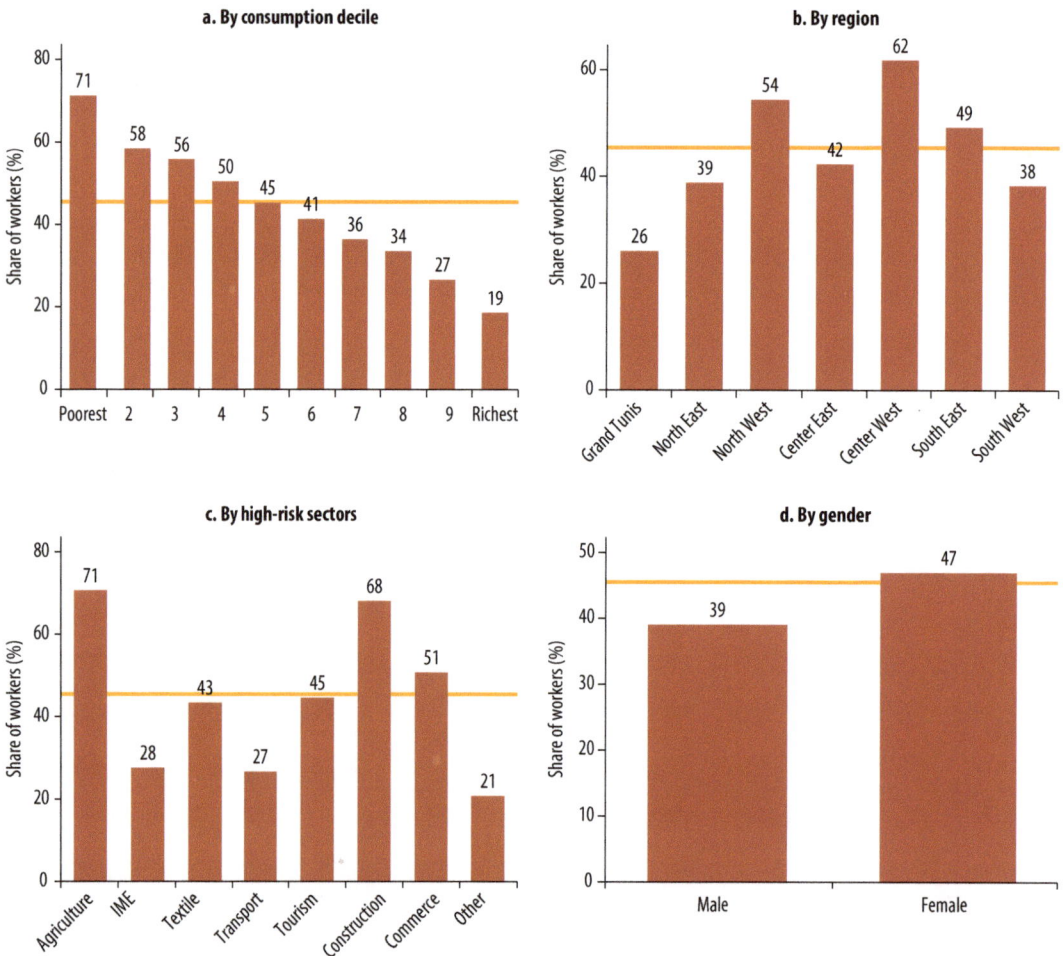

Source: World Bank calculations, based on 2015 Household Budget Survey.
Note: The orange line represents the total share of workers in informal jobs. IME = mechanical and electric industry.

among the six high-risk sectors, informal employment is widespread, with the highest in construction (68 percent), commerce (51 percent), tourism (45 percent), and textiles (43 percent). Informal employment also tends to be higher for women (47 percent) than men (39 percent).

Third, there is a high use of public transport by commuters. Not only could labor mobility be limited during the outbreak, but there is also a higher risk of contracting the infection while using public transport, because of contact with fellow commuters. On average, about 43 percent of those employed in Tunisia rely on public transport to get to work (figure 6.5). The more well-off individuals are, the more likely they are to use public transport, because a high share of the poor walk to work. Looking at regions, as expected, about two-thirds of those employed in Grand Tunis use public transport.

Fourth, a significant proportion of the labor force works at home. Dingel and Neiman (2020) compute a score measure of teleworking or home-based work (HBW) that illustrates the possibility of working from home. Hence, workers with the lowest HBW scores may be the most likely to immediately lose their job due to COVID-19. An analysis using this approach shows that most jobs in sectors such as education, finance, and communication could plausibly be performed at home. But very few jobs in agriculture and industries (such as textiles and mechanical and electrical) can be performed at home, putting workers engaged in these

FIGURE 6.5

The Higher People's Incomes, the More They Use Public Transport for Commuting
Share of workers using public transportation, by decile and region

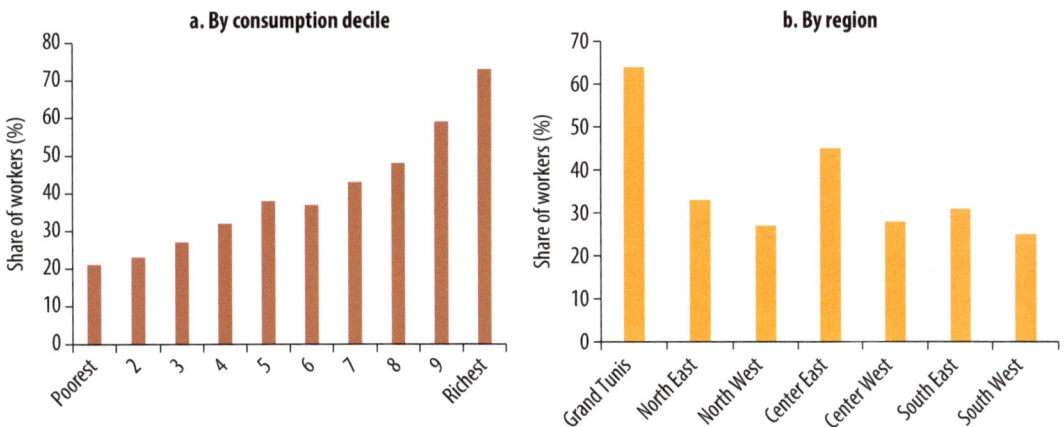

Source: World Bank calculations, based on 2015 Household Budget Survey.
Note: Public transport is defined as the use of any of the following to go to work: metro, train, bus, taxi, driver car, or passenger car.

sectors at a greater risk of job loss. In addition, the ability to work from home tends to be greater for higher-consumption deciles in contrast to lower consumption deciles.

Fifth, food expenditures constitute a major part of the household budget for Tunisians, and more so for the poor. Not surprisingly then, it is the households that spend a lot of money on food items that are more likely to be affected by price increases stemming from the pandemic. Figure 6.6 shows the share of food expenditures in total expenditure of Tunisian households by consumption decile and region. Share of food expenditure tends to be higher for households in the poorest deciles. Across regions, the average share of food expenditure is highest for the North West and the Center West, at 39 and 37 percent, respectively.

Besides factors affecting labor market outcomes, several demographic or living characteristics of the Tunisian population make the poor more vulnerable to COVID-19. One is overcrowded living conditions and low access to health insurance, which put the Tunisian poor at a higher risk to get infected or not be able to seek health care if they contract COVID-19. Poor households tend to live in more densely populated environments, ranging from 7 to 28 percent in the three poorest deciles, in contrast to 1 percent or less in the three richest deciles.

FIGURE 6.6

The Poorest Spend a Higher Share of Their Household Expenditures on Food

Share of average food expenditure, by decile and region

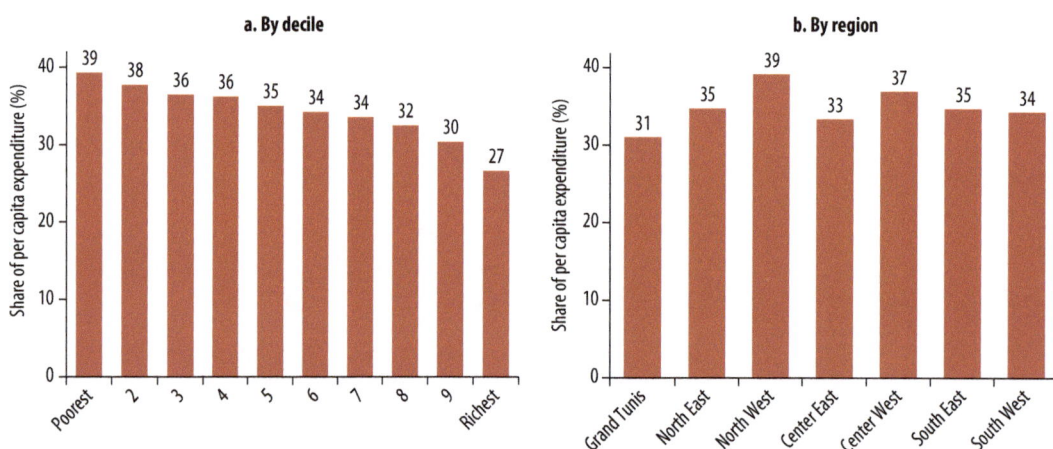

Source: World Bank calculations, based on 2015 Household Budget Survey.

Another characteristic is living in intergenerational households—defined as those that include at least one member below the age of 18 and one member above the age of 64—meaning that older household members are more likely to be in closer contact with the younger household members. Overall, 10 percent of the population lives in an intergenerational household. Nevertheless, this type of household is disproportionately represented among the poor, ranging from 14 to 17 percent in the three poorest deciles. Intergenerational households are also more prevalent in the South East region, followed by the North West and South West regions.

How the Study Is Conducted

Our study uses a methodology similar to that employed by Ajwad et al. (2013). It employs a hybrid approach that combines the results of macroeconomic projections of a sectoral slowdown of the Tunisian economy during 2020 using microsimulation techniques. Combining information on GDP growth projections by sector and employment elasticity in the growth of each sector (to capture how elastic employment is to changes in sectoral GDP), we estimate the loss of employment in each sector. Using household survey data, we then identify individuals who are likely to lose their jobs based on regression analysis and simulate the impact on consumption under various assumptions. With this, we can identify a new distribution of postpandemic consumption and assess impacts on poverty and inequality.[3] To simulate price shocks as a result of COVID-19, we use the published consumer price index (by INS) by product categories. We then apply new prices on household consumption and simulate the decline in real disposable income and consumption. We also assume that this trend of change in prices will continue during the rest of the year.[4] We account for heterogeneity of consumption patterns across households, in particular between poor and nonpoor households, by using information on consumption of products collected in the household survey.

These impacts are assessed under two scenarios: The first (optimistic) scenario uses recent World Bank estimates with –8.8 percent real GDP growth, at constant factor prices.[5] The second (pessimistic) simulates a growth of –11.9 percent; that is, the economy achieves the same growth as that achieved during the first half of the year. Below we provide a detailed methodology of how these impacts are estimated.

Estimation of Loss of Income

Suppose that the economy is partitioned into S sectors ($s = 1, \ldots S$), the level of activity is observed before the pandemic period 0 and after the pandemic period 1.

Let g_s be the sectoral growth rate during the pandemic period, and g be the growth rate of the economy. Let E be the total employment in the economy and E_s the employment in sector s.

The growth elasticity of employment is given by ε_s.

We first estimate the sectoral growth of the economy. Our starting point is the sectoral projection of growth g_s ($s = 1, \ldots S$) carried out by the World Bank projections according to several scenarios of the evolution of the pandemic.

This is followed by estimating the loss of employment at the level of each sector: The loss of employment at the level of each sector is given by $L_s = E_s \times g_s$.

The next step is to identify individuals who will lose their jobs, and in this step a logit model is estimated to predict the probability that each worker in the household loses his or her job depending on four variables (education, age, gender, region of residence). Individuals with the lowest predicted probabilities are assumed to leave the labor market.[6] At this level, several hypotheses are adopted: each household has a certain amount of savings or employment insurance (even informal) that allows it to smooth its consumption. Some households can liquidate certain assets to finance current consumption. Thus, in each sector of activity we find two types of individuals: those who have managed to preserve their jobs and those who have lost them. For the first group, the impact of the pandemic on the household of an individual i who continues to work in sector s is given by $I_s^i = C_s^i \times g_s$, where C_s^i and I_s^i stand for precrisis and postcrisis consumption, respectively, of the household of individual i and working in sector s. For the second group, postpandemic per capita consumption is set at the same level as the mean of the consumption[7] of a household whose head is unemployed (in their area of residence). Note that we assume that public sector workers (including state-owned enterprises) and retirees will not suffer any loss of income generated by the pandemic. This methodology allows us to estimate the impact of the pandemic on household consumption levels.

Estimation of Price Changes on Household Welfare

Let x_i be the per capita total expenditure of household $i (= 1, \ldots N)$ on $q (1 \times K)$ goods at price p_0 $(1 \times K)$. All prepandemic prices are normalized to 1. Let p_1 $(1 \times K)$ be the vector of postpandemic prices. $p_{k,1}$ denotes the price of good k $(=1, \ldots K)$.

The simplest way to estimate the loss of purchasing power is to use the published consumer price index (CPI) and define the postpandemic purchasing power as

$$\Gamma_i = \frac{x_{i1}}{CPI} = \frac{x_{i0}(1 + I_i)}{p_1} \tag{6.1}$$

where I_i is the pandemic impact on household i consumption.

Such an approach ignores the heterogeneity of consumption patterns across households, in particular between poor and nonpoor households. For more precise estimates of the impact of price increases, it is important to estimate a price index at the household level. To do so, we rely on the approach adopted by King (1983) and define the equivalent income. Under the budget constraint defined by $(p_1, x_{i,1})$, the equivalent income is defined as the income level that, in the reference price system p_1, generates the same level of utility as the level of utility achieved under $(p_1, x_{i,1})$:

$$v(p_0, \Gamma_i(p_0, p_1, x_{i1})) = v(p_1, x_{i1}) \tag{6.2}$$

where $v(\cdot)$ denotes the indirect utility function, and $\Gamma_i(\cdot)$ denotes the equivalent income function of household i.

Given that all households face the same price p_1, $\Gamma_h(\cdot)$ can be considered as a monetary measure of utility $v(p_1, x_{i1})$, given that $\Gamma_h(\cdot)$ is a monotonic transformation of $v(\cdot)$. Inverting the indirect utility function, the equivalent income can be derived as:

$$\Gamma_{i0} = \Gamma_i(p_0, p_1, x_{i0}) = x_{i0} \tag{6.3}$$

$$\Gamma_{i1} = \Gamma_i(p_0, p_1, x_{i1}) = x_{i0} - EL_{i1} \tag{6.4}$$

where Γ_{i0} and Γ_{i1} denote pre- and postpandemic equivalent incomes, and EL_{i1} is the equivalent loss. The price effect of the pandemic on household i is estimated by the EL_{i1}.

Suppose that consumer preferences are represented as the Stone-Geary utility function. The corresponding indirect utility function is given by:

$$v(p, x) = \frac{x - \sum_{k=1}^{K} p_k \gamma_k}{\prod_{k=1}^{K} p_k^{\beta_k}} \tag{6.5}$$

with $\sum_{k=1}^{K} \beta_k = 1$, γ_k is the subsistence need of good k, and β_k is the share of residual income (i.e., $x - \sum_{k=1}^{K} p_k \gamma_k$) devoted to consuming good k after the minimum expenditure $p_k \gamma_k$ is incurred.

Based on equations 6.2–6.4, the equivalent income function for the household i, facing the pandemic, is given by:

$$\Gamma_i\left(p_0, p_1, x_{i1}\right) = \sum_{k=1}^{K} p_k \gamma_k + \frac{x_{i1} - \sum_{k=1}^{K} p_{1,k} \gamma_k}{\prod_{k=1}^{K} \left(\frac{p_{1,k}}{p_{0,k}}\right)^{\beta_{k,i}}} \tag{6.6}$$

The equivalent income function given in (6) has a clear interpretation in terms of real income. Indeed, if $\sum_{k=1}^{K} p_{1,k} \gamma_k$ represents the subsistence expenditures, only the residual income $x_{i1} - \sum_{k=1}^{K} p_{1,k} \gamma_k$ is available for the discretionary allowance, which is deflated by a household-specific price index, $\pi_{1i}^0 = \prod_{k=1}^{K} \left(\frac{p_{1,k}}{p_{0,k}}\right)^{\beta_{k,i}}$. If one then adds the initial cost of subsistence needs to the actual residual income, we obtain the equivalent income.

One can further simplify and assume that subsistence needs are low (converging to 0), in which case $\beta_{k,i}$ becomes the budget share devoted to good k, and the equivalent income function is reduced to that generated by Cobb-Douglas preferences.

$$\Gamma_i\left(p_0, p_1, x_{i1}\right) = \frac{x_{i1}}{\pi_{1i}^0}$$

On the basis of this exercise, we could generate postpandemic consumption and estimate the effects of the crisis on poverty and inequality.[8]

Crisis Situation: Poverty and Labor Markets

How large will the employment losses be across Tunisia's sectors as a result of COVID-19? We combine projected estimates of slowdown in growth across sectors with employment growth elasticities to estimate the projected employment losses. Our results (table 6.1) show that the percentage decline in employment in scenario 1 should be the greatest for (a) tourism or hotels, cafes and restaurants (28.63 percent); (b) construction (21.47 percent); and (c) textiles (21.25 percent). For the pessimistic scenario 2, the top ones are: (a) building and civil engineering (64.22 percent); (b) tourism or hotels, cafes and restaurants (47.4 percent); and (c) transport (31.7 percent).[9]

TABLE 6.1

Some Sectors Are Expected to Experience Significant Declines in Employment
Estimated percentage decline in employment across sectors

Sector	Scenario 1	Scenario 2
Building materials, ceramics and glass industry	−17.30	−23.5
Mechanical and electrical industry	−16.59	−22.50
Textile, clothing and leather industry	−21.25	−28.80
Miscellaneous industries	−15.21	−20.60
Construction (building and civil engineering)	−21.47	−64.22
Commerce	−4.63	−7.70
Transport	−19.10	−31.70
Tourism (hotels, cafés and restaurants)	−28.63	−47.40
Various merchant services	−9.99	−16.60

Source: World Bank estimates and calculations.
Note: We have used sectoral growth projections estimated by the World Bank, combined with growth elasticity of employment, to generate projected employment contraction across sectors.

In light of these projected employment contractions, we find that overall, poverty is projected to increase by 7.3 percentage points under scenario 1, and by 11.9 percentage points under scenario 2 (table 6.2). This implies a more than 50 percent increase in poverty in scenario 1 and almost a doubling of the poverty rate in scenario 2, thus reversing the trend of declining poverty over the past decade. What is worse, many more are expected to lose income and become vulnerable to falling into poverty in the future. The poverty gap, which measures the poverty deficit of the entire population, would increase from 3.2 to 4.4 percent under scenario 1, and to 5.0 percent under scenario 2. Income inequality is also expected to modestly increase as a result of the sustained crisis, with the Gini coefficient rising from 37.2 to 39.4 under scenario 1 and to 41.4 under scenario 2. Overall, we observe the economy to be hit hard by the pandemic and the associated shutdown.[10]

Not surprisingly and in line with global estimates,[11] the poor in Tunisia are more likely to suffer the most in the wake of the COVID-19 pandemic. To analyze the subgroups of the population along the welfare distribution that are most likely to be affected by an economic slowdown, we plotted density and GIC. Figure 6.7 panel a shows the precrisis and postcrisis consumption distribution under the two scenarios, along with the poverty line (blue line). One can see that the poor will become poorer as a result of the economic shock induced by COVID-19. The GIC curve presents this information in a different way, plotting the

TABLE 6.2

Poverty and Inequality Could See Setbacks Post-COVID-19

Projected impacts on poverty and inequality, as share of population

	Pre-COVID-19	Post-COVID-19 scenario 1	Difference scenario 1	Post-COVID-19 scenario 2	Difference scenario 2
Extreme poverty rate (%)	2.9	7.4	4.5	11.8	8.9
Extreme poverty gap (%)	0.5	0.8	0.2	0.9	0.3
Poverty rate (%)	13.7	20.9	7.3	25.6	11.9
Poverty gap (%)	3.2	4.4	1.2	5.0	1.8
Gini coefficient	37.2	39.4	2.2	41.4	4.2

Source: World Bank calculations, based on 2015 Household Budget Survey.
Note: Extreme poverty is defined as living on less than US$1.90 a day. The poverty gap measures the poverty deficit of the entire population.

growth rate of consumption per capita across two time periods (pre- and postcrisis) under the two scenarios, for each percentile of the distribution. Figure 6.7 panel b shows that for almost all subgroups of the population along the welfare distribution, there is expected to be a decline in consumption per capita (see that GIC is below 0). Households with per capita consumption in the poorest 20 percent of the distribution are simulated to be hit the hardest, experiencing large declines.

Using the pre- and postcrisis consumption, we identify individuals who have fallen into poverty as a result of the shock induced by COVID-19. We also identify individuals who have faced the largest declines in their consumption (in the population, we identify those with 20 percent as having the largest losses). We find that although 38 percent of the population live in North East and Center East regions, 49 percent of those have the 20 percent largest losses. And although 21 percent of the country's population live in Center West and South East regions, about 30 percent of the individuals who have fallen into poverty as a result of the shock are from these regions. Individuals who have fallen into poverty as a result of the shock induced by the pandemic are more likely to be women, live in large households, be employed without contracts, and lack access to health care, as compared with national averages.

In an effort to mitigate some of these impacts of the pandemic, the government of Tunisia, on March 21, 2020, announced, enacted, and gradually implemented an exceptional social and economic emergency plan, which targets the poorest and most vulnerable, covering almost 1.1 million people. Table 6.3 provides a comprehensive description of the compensatory measures, including the amount of support; period of support; and target number of needy families, families with limited

FIGURE 6.7

Consumption Levels Are Expected to Decline in the Wake of COVID-19, Especially for the Poorest

Distribution of per capita consumption pre- and post-COVID-19 (kernel density), and growth incidence curves, under two scenarios

a. Kernel density, scenario 1

b. Anonymous absolute pro-poor curves, scenario 1

c. Kernel density, scenario 2

d. Anonymous absolute pro-poor curves, scenario 2

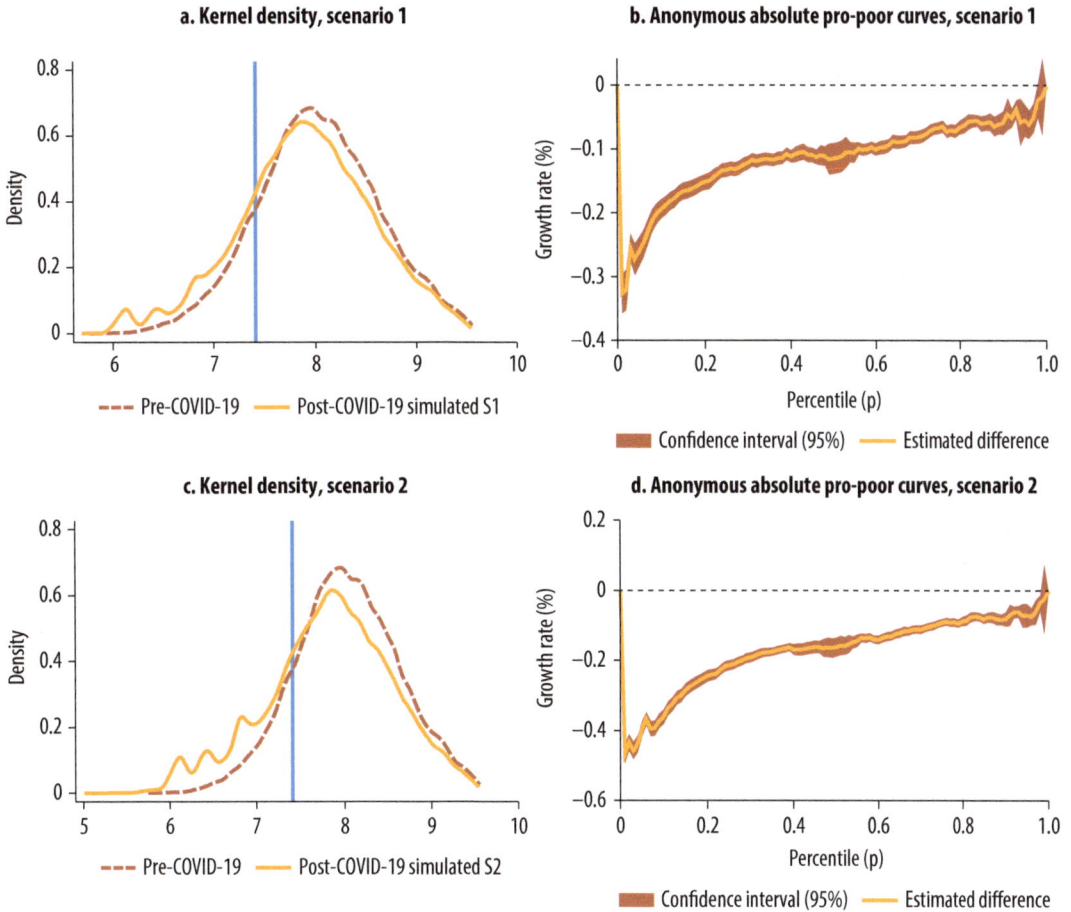

Source: World Bank calculations, based on 2015 Household Budget Survey.
Note: The growth incidence curve displays the annualized increase in consumption per capita by percentile of the consumption distribution (the left side of the horizontal axis is the poorest and the right side is the richest). GIC below 0 shows a decline.

income, families caring for a person without family support, those with low retirement pensions, and families without a limited income.

Simulating the impacts of the pandemic on welfare in the presence of all the above mitigation measures announced,[12] we observe that under scenario 1, there would be a positive impact on poverty. Specifically, the increase in poverty would be 6.5 percentage points with the mitigation measures in place, whereas in their absence, the increase in poverty

TABLE 6.3

Tunisia Is Enacting Compensatory Measures for Mitigating COVID-19 Impacts

Target population	Amount of support	Period	Target number (in theory)
Needy families (PNAFN/AMG1)	TD 50 (US$15)	April 2020	260,000 households
	TD 60 (US$17)	May 2020	
Families with limited income (AMG2)	TD 200 (US$70)	April–May 2020	370,000 households
Families caring for a person without family support	TD 200 (US$70)	April 2020	779 households
Low retirement pensions (less than TD 180 (US$60)	TD 100 (US$30)	April 2020 (pension increased to TD 180 in August 2019)	140,000 households
Istimarat families (families that did not necessarily need aid but received it, excluding families with limited income)	TD 200 (US$70)	May 2020	301,149 households

Source: World Bank compilation of data from Ministry of Social Affairs.
Note: Emergency measures announced by the government of Tunisia on March 21, 2020. AMG (AMG1 and AMG2) = Assistance Medicale Gratuite (free medical assistance); PNAFN = Programme National d'Aide aux Familles Nécessiteuses (National Assistance Program for Needy Families).

TABLE 6.4

Mitigation Measures Are Estimated to Decrease the Impact of COVID-19 in Tunisia
Impact of COVID-19 with mitigation measures for the optimistic scenario

	Before COVID-19	After COVID-19	After mitigation measure	Difference (without mitigation measure)	Difference (with mitigation measure)
Extreme poverty	2.9	7.4	6.9	4.5	4.0
Poverty	13.7	20.9	20.2	7.3	6.5
Poverty gap lower	0.5	2.0	0.7	1.5	1.3
Poverty gap upper	3.2	6.4	4.2	3.2	1.0
Inequality	37.0	39.5	39.2	2.5	2.2

Source: World Bank calculations, based on 2015 Household Budget Survey.
Note: Simulations are based on the announced measures; there is no access to information on actual spending under these measures.

would be 7.3 percentage points (table 6.4).[13] Similarly, extreme poverty, the poverty gap, and inequality would all fare better than without the measures.

Conclusion

Our findings show that the COVID-19 pandemic is likely to have a large impact on household welfare, with the risk of an increasing number of people falling below the poverty line and an increasing degree of poverty severity for the already poor.

Which households are hardest hit will depend on the socio-economic characteristics of the population, sector of employment, and location. The poor, who are more likely to be living in over-crowded conditions, and those with chronic diseases are at greater risk to contract the infection, while those without health insurance (largely the poor and those in informal sectors) are faced with a greater inability to access health care. Those who spend more on food as a share of their consumption expenditure—notably, the poor—will be most affected by price shocks. And workers in tourism and construction are the most vulnerable.

Against this backdrop, our analysis combines the labor shock and price shock induced by COVID-19 simultaneously and simulates post-pandemic consumption. Our estimates indicate that poverty is expected to increase by 50 percent from the pre-COVID-19 levels under the optimistic scenario and to almost double under the pessimistic scenario, thus reversing the trend of declining poverty over the past decade. At the same time, inequality is expected to increase slightly. In fact, our simulations show that households with per capita consumption in the poorest 20 percent of the distribution will be hit the hardest.

Using the postcrisis welfare distribution, this analysis also helps identify the individuals who are expected to fall into poverty as a result of COVID-19. They are likely to disproportionately reside in the Center West and South East regions, and they are more likely to be women, live in large households, be employed without contracts, and lack access to health care. While transfer measures enacted by the government targeted at the poor and the most vulnerable could mitigate some of these negative effects, setbacks to welfare outcomes will persist. These findings underscore that it is extremely important to ensure that economic growth benefits the poor and the vulnerable—and enacting measures to protect this large, vulnerable subgroup should be a top priority for the government.

Notes

1. In terms of this chapter's scope, we seek to estimate the impact of COVID-19 and not the determinants of contamination in Tunisia by COVID-19.
2. Refer to Ajwad et al. (2013) for a detailed review.
3. According to the National Institute of Statistics (INS), the national rate translates to 15.2 percent using the 2015 data. Given this, we first update the 2015 data to create a new distribution of consumption and observe a pre-COVID-19 (2019) poverty rate. We then use growth projections to identify the distribution of postpandemic consumption and assess impacts on poverty and inequality.

4. We do not observe the evolution of prices over the whole year. Thus, we use the inflation rate observed up to the date of the simulation (September) and we assume that for the rest of 2020 we observe the same trend.

5. These are recent World Bank projections estimated by the Macro, Trade and Investment team at the World Bank Group using the MFMod model and information from government and other sources to inform the forecast.

6. Consider a sector that will lose 20 percent of jobs (according to the estimated elasticity). Thus, we assume that 20 percent of those with the lowest predicted probability will lose their jobs. The imputed level of consumption for those who lost their job will be equal to the average observed consumption of an unemployed person. The calculation is made for workers in the household, adopting the simplifying assumption that they contribute equally to household consumption.

7. Consumption surveys provide information only on consumption and not on income.

8. Although our methodology uses historical elasticities, an important caveat of this approach is that the impact of the growth shock due to COVID-19 could affect unemployment trends differently from past shocks.

9. These are calculated based on recent World Bank projections estimated by the Macro, Trade and Investment team at the World Bank Group using the MFMod model and information from government and other sources to inform the forecast.

10. We have also considered the growth of certain sectors in our simulations (such as agriculture). In some African countries such as Uganda, the remittances have increased according to their central bank estimates. In the case of Tunisia, we do not know which way remittances would move. Intuition suggests that given the economic situation in Europe, remittances would probably decrease, but there is no evidence of an increase or decrease in remittances. Hence, we do not consider this in our simulations.

11. According to World Bank (2020b), the COVID-19 pandemic is estimated to push an additional 88 million to 115 million people into extreme poverty this year, with the total worldwide rising to as many as 150 million by 2021, depending on the severity of the economic contraction. Extreme poverty, defined as living on less than US$1.90 a day, is likely to affect between 9.1 percent and 9.4 percent of the world's population in 2020.

12. We provide a description of the government measures announced on March 21, 2020. The simulations are based on the announced measures; there is no access to information on actual spending under these measures.

13. The data used to estimate these welfare impacts in the presence of mitigation effects do not allow us to focus on a region; hence we do not provide estimates of these impacts across regions. Moreover, the activities targeted by government measures are more concentrated in coastal regions. The South Region, where some of the riots are concentrated, is characterized by the oil extraction industry and some chemical industries, which do not employ a large workforce.

References

Ajwad, M. I., M. A. Aran, M. Azam, and J. Hentschel. 2013. "A Methodology Note on the Employment and Welfare Impacts of the 2007–08 Financial Crisis." *Development Analytics Research Paper Series* (1303).

Dingel, J., and B. Neiman. 2020. "How Many Jobs Can Be Done at Home?" NBER Working Paper 26948, National Bureau of Economic Research, Cambridge, MA.

King, M. A. 1983. "Welfare Analysis of Tax Reforms Using Household Data." *Journal of Public Economics* 21 (2): 183–214.

Molini, Vasco, and Adnen Lassoued. 2020. "How the Coronavirus Affects the Poor in Tunisia: First Findings." *World Bank Blogs*, June 3, 2020. https://blogs .worldbank.org/arabvoices/how-coronavirus-affects-poor-tunisia-first -findings.

UNICEF (United Nations Children's Fund). 2020. "Tunisie: Impact des mesures de confinement associées à la pandémie COVID-19 sur la pauvreté des enfants." July 2020. https://www.unicef.org/tunisia/rapports/impact-des -mesures-de-confinement-associ%C3%A9es-%C3%A0-la-pand %C3%A9mie-covid-19-sur-la-pauvret%C3%A9-des.

World Bank. 2020a. "Poverty and Distributional Impacts of COVID-19: Potential Channels of Impact and Mitigating Policies." World Bank, Washington, DC. https://www.worldbank.org/en/topic/poverty/brief/poverty-and -distributional-impacts-of-covid-19-potential-channels-of-impact-and -mitigating-policies.

World Bank. 2020b. *Reversals of Fortune: Poverty and Shared Prosperity 2020*. Washington, DC: World Bank. doi:10.1596/978-1-4648-1602-4.

CHAPTER 7

West Bank and Gaza: Emergence of the New Poor

Romeo Jacky Gansey, Alia Jane Aghajanian, and Jawad Al-Saleh

Key Messages

- For the West Bank and Gaza, our microsimulations paint a picture of worsening poverty—up to 35.6 percent in 2020—driven by income shocks that have been further exacerbated by COVID-19.

- Although inequality does not seem to be as affected by COVID-19, there is an emergence of the "new poor"—those who were not poor in 2016 but have become poor since.

- Their characteristics differ from those of the traditionally poor in that they are more concentrated in the West Bank, are in rural areas, are more likely to have tertiary education, and are more likely to belong to female-headed households.

- Interestingly, the new poor are more likely to live in households above the first two income deciles—a finding that is analogous to the World Bank's global report *Poverty and Shared Prosperity*, which indicated 82 percent of the new poor will live in middle-income countries (World Bank 2020).

- Further, unless households are able to continue smoothing consumption, poverty could dramatically increase for households in Gaza, reaching levels close to what was observed in Gaza in 2016.

Introduction

As of March 2021, the West Bank and Gaza have seen 243,479 COVID-19 cases and 2,590 deaths, which have been concentrated in two waves; see the World Health Organization (WHO) Coronavirus (COVID-19) Dashboard (https://covid19.who.int/). The Palestinian Authority was relatively swift in implementing a series of restrictions (figure 7.1), which included stay-at-home orders and restriction of movement. In addition, the border between the West Bank and Israel was closed, which further limited the ability of the West Bank labor force who work in Israel or the settlements to work over this period.[1] In March the Palestinian Authority started to deliver vaccines supplied through the international Covax scheme. However, although Israel has seen the highest inoculation rate globally, vaccine delivery is relatively low in both the West Bank and Gaza.

The disruption caused by the pandemic comes at a time when living conditions, particularly for those living in Gaza, have been declining. The latest poverty figures in the Palestinian Expenditure and Consumption Survey (PECS 2016/17) show that 29.3 percent of the population live in

FIGURE 7.1

Stringent Restrictions on Movement Were Quickly Put in Place
Selected indicators for the COVID-19 response in the West Bank and Gaza

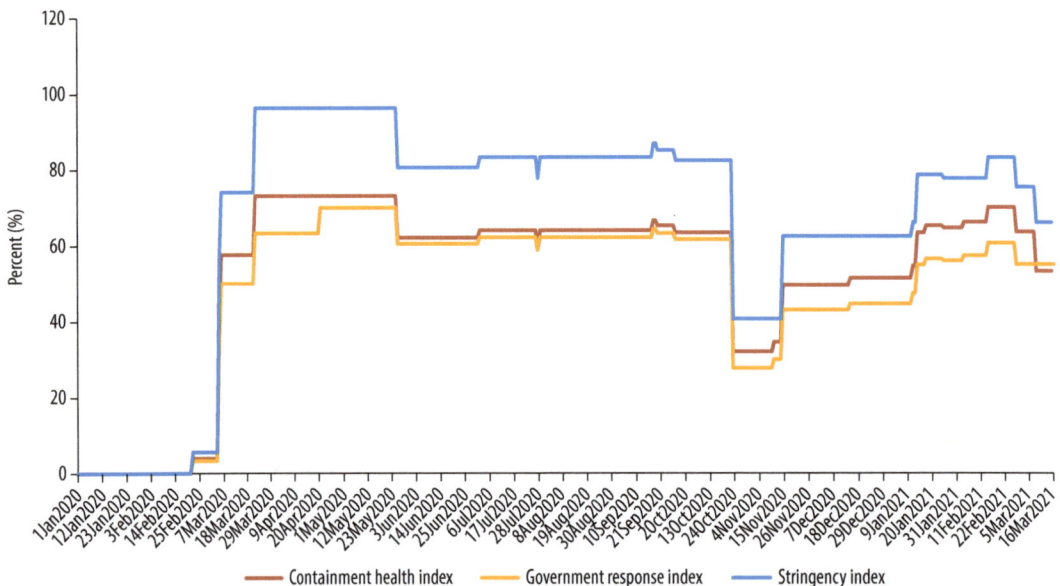

Source: Oxford COVID-19 Government Response Tracker (Hale et al. 2021).

poverty, using the official global extreme poverty line of around US$1.90 per person per day.[2] But this masks the diverging situation between the West Bank and Gaza, where poverty is at 13.9 percent and 53.0 percent, respectively. If using the international US$5.50-a-day poverty line, 22 percent of the region's residents live in poverty. Similarly, the situation is worse for refugee-headed households and those living in refugee camps (figure 7.2). Moreover, in 2019, the West Bank and Gaza had a very low labor force participation rate (about 37 percent) and low employment rate (about 28 percent of the working-age population), with a large youth population badly in need of jobs. Growth was just under 1 percent of GDP.

As COVID-19 enters its second year, analysts have been taking stock of how the health crisis, government restrictions, and economic downturn have affected the poor and vulnerable. Most of the studies that have been conducted rely on various assumptions of macroeconomic growth and how those assumptions translate into changes in household income and welfare. Some of their assumptions are restrictive, and they do not exploit the variation in household or individual characteristics that could determine exposure to the pandemic and mobility restrictions. Macroeconomic projections are also dependent on expectations of how the economy will recover, which, in turn, depends on the highly unpredictable rollout of vaccines.

FIGURE 7.2

Almost a Third of the Population of West Bank and Gaza Live below the Poverty Line

Share of population living below the poverty line, by household type (%)

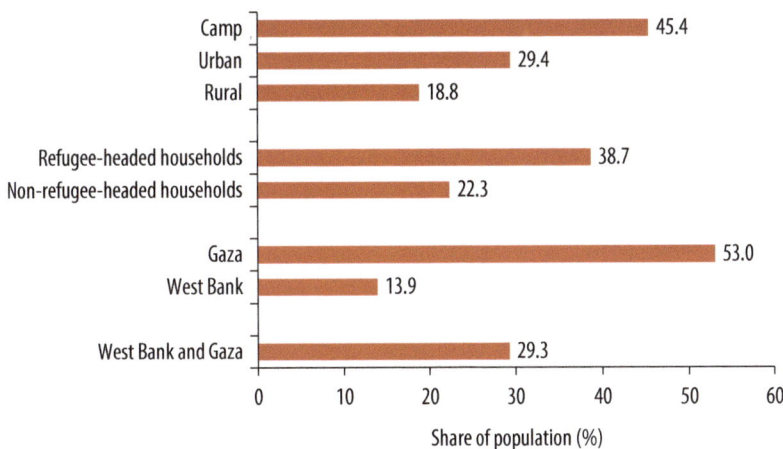

Source: Palestinian Expenditure and Consumption Survey (PECS) 2016/17.
Note: The national poverty line was updated in 2010 and stands at NIS 2,470 or US$671 for the reference household (two adults and three children) in 2017.

How have COVID-19, the economic downturn, and lockdowns affected the welfare of households in the West Bank and Gaza? This study takes an innovative approach to simulating the effects of COVID-19 on poverty and other welfare indicators in these locations, relying mostly on microdata collected before and after the pandemic. It takes advantage of two recent sources of information on employment and wage income: the quarterly labor force survey collected by the Palestinian Central Bureau of Statistics (PCBS), and the rapid assessment phone survey conducted by PCBS, the World Bank, the United Nations Development Programme of Assistance to the Palestinian People, and other UN agencies (UN Women, United Nations Population Fund, United Nations Children's Fund, the World Health Organization, and the World Food Programme). It draws on behavioral models that predict households' likelihood of experiencing income and employment shocks. And it accounts for not only government and nongovernment responses to the economic downturn but also estimated remittance flows. These changes are simulated onto the PECS 2016/17 to estimate the change in income, consumption, poverty rate, and inequality.

The study's key results show that poverty would increase from 33.4 percent in 2019 to 35.6 percent in 2020, or an increase of 2.2 percentage points—the equivalent of pushing more than 110,000 Palestinians into poverty as a result of COVID-19 alone—while inequality would be little changed. In fact, rather than reinforcing previous vulnerabilities, the analysis shows an emergence of the "new poor," predominantly located in the West Bank. The future path hinges on targeted programs to help Palestinians smooth consumption and weather the welfare shocks.

As new sources of information become available, this microsimulation model can be adapted to reflect changes to the labor force and household welfare. At the time of writing, violence between Israel and the residents of the West Bank and Gaza has escalated, particularly in Gaza. Household welfare is likely to be further eroded, and this model has been set up in a way that will act as a living model, to be updated with the changing situation.

How the Pandemic Could Influence Welfare

There are five main ways that the COVID-19 pandemic could affect household welfare—labor income, international remittances, social support, changes in prices, and access to services:

FIGURE 7.3

Big Impacts on Household Welfare Occur through Lost Wages

Impact of COVID-19 on payments received by main income earner by location, sex of main income earner, and area of residence

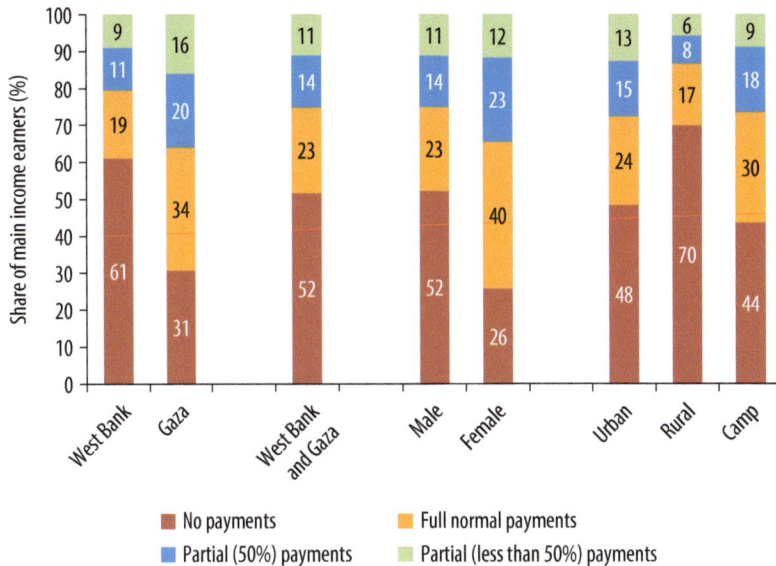

Source: Rapid Assessment Phone Survey 2020 (PCBS 2020).

- Labor income will be adversely affected through loss of employment and wages, because government restrictions have led to firms reducing working hours or laying off workers. In the West Bank and Gaza, phone surveys in 2020 show that 52 percent of workers received no payments (figure 7.3).

- International remittances would be reduced, because most of the global economy has been affected by the crisis.

- Regarding social support, the government and various organizations have compensated for the restrictions by setting up social protection programs, most notable of which are cash transfers implemented by the United Nations Relief and Works Agency for Palestine Refugees in the Near East (UNRWA) and the Palestinian Authority. However, UNRWA has faced funding cuts since 2016, and changes to older programs could be felt. To mitigate these effects, the World Bank has supported Palestinian households and firms through at least two programs: (a) the Waqfit Izz fund to provide small and medium-size enterprises with liquidity and boost labor demand, and (b) the cash transfer program.

FIGURE 7.4

No Major Changes Are Seen in the Consumer Price Index

Monthly consumer price index for the West Bank and Gaza, 2016–19

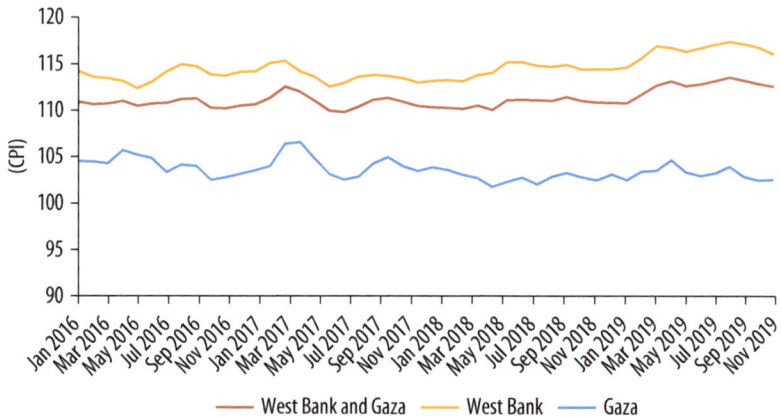

Source: Palestinian Central Bureau of Statistics, https://www.pcbs.gov.ps/site/lang__en/695/default.aspx.
Note: Base year = 2010. CPI = consumer price index.

- Changes in prices could affect household purchasing power, but so far there have not been large or significant changes in the West Bank and Gaza (figure 7.4). In fact, there might be an improvement in the relative prices that would favor consumers as a result of slow or negative growth in the consumer price index (CPI) and appreciation of the local currency.[3]

- Regarding access to services, any cuts in access to key services, such as health and education, would affect household welfare directly and indirectly.[4]

As for the impact of COVID-19 on individual households, that will vary greatly depending on the shares of labor income and nonlabor income in total household income. The poorest quintiles are more likely to be affected by changes in nonlabor income (in the form of governmental and nongovernmental aid). For example, the bottom three deciles rely on transfers that make up 23, 11, and 9 percent of their income, respectively, and on international remittances for just 1 percent of their income (figure 7.5). Labor income forms the majority of household income sources, and this increases as a percentage of total income as households become richer.

FIGURE 7.5

Poorest Households Are the Most Vulnerable to Changes in Nonlabor Income

Composition of household income, by welfare decile

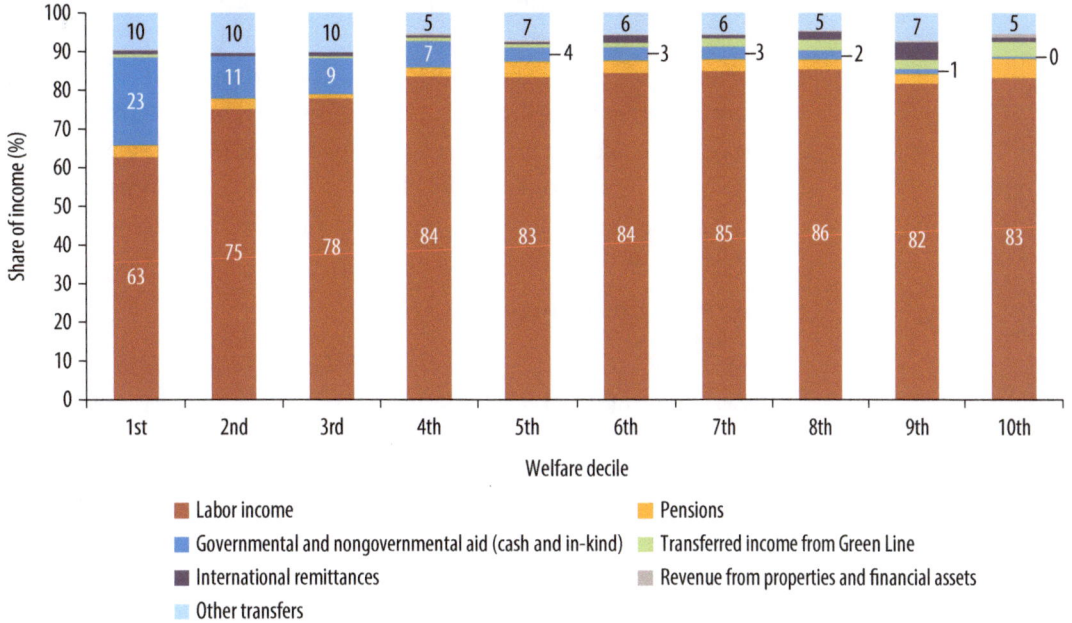

Source: Palestinian Expenditure and Consumption Survey (PECS) 2016/17.
Note: The Green Line refers to the demarcation lines, rather than permanent borders, between Israel and the West Bank.

Chief Data Sources

This study relies on three main sources of microdata: the Palestinian Expenditure and Consumption Survey of 2016/17, the Palestinian labor force surveys from 2016 to 2020, and the first round of the rapid assessment phone survey of 2020.

Palestinian Expenditure and Consumption Survey 2016/17

PECS is the main expenditure and consumption survey conducted in the West Bank and Gaza and is used to estimate official poverty estimates. Besides household consumption expenditure, it collects information on socioeconomic conditions, (labor and nonlabor) income, and employment status. The 2016/17 PECS was collected over 12 months, starting in September 2016, to account for seasonal changes in consumption. Consumption was collected using a registration book (diary) to record daily food consumption and expenditures over one month, and fieldworkers visited the households 8–10 times to ensure completeness and quality of the data.

The sampling frame was based on the 2007 census, which was updated as part of the 2014 Palestinian Multiple Indicator Cluster Survey. The completed sample was 3,739 households from 391 enumeration areas stratified over governorates and locality type (urban, rural, and refugee camps), resulting from a response rate of 71.4 percent (PCBS 2018). The average household size is 5.5, the average age of the head of the household is 47, and 71 percent of household heads are employed—primarily in the private sector (see table 7A.1 in the annex for more household details).

Palestinian Labor Force Survey (LFS)

The Palestinian Central Bureau of Statistics conducts the LFS every quarter to collect information on the size and structure of the region's labor force. To understand changes to employment since the last time poverty was estimated, the surveys from 2016, 2019, and 2020 were used. The sample is stratified by governorate and type of locality (urban, rural, and refugee camps) and drawn from 494 enumeration areas of the master sample. The enumeration areas remain fixed over time, but 50 percent of households are replaced each round. Some key trends from 2016 to 2020, as table 7.1 shows, have been a declining labor force participation rate and declining employment rate (of the working-age population), from their already low levels.

The definitions used for labor force and employment status changed in 2018, following international standards. Unemployment was more strictly defined to consider only those who are actively searching for work and available to start work immediately. For this reason, the increases in the employment rate from 2018 could be overestimated because the number of unemployed becomes smaller as a result of the more restrictive definition. Similarly, reductions in the employment rate from 2016 to 2019 will be underestimated. To address this issue, the

TABLE 7.1

Sample Size and Key Statistics from the Palestinian Labor Force Survey

Year	Sample size (no. of households)	Response rate[5] (%)	Labor force participation rate (%)	Employment rate of labor force (%)	Employment rate of working-age population (%)
2016	23,884	86.7	38.6	73.0	28.2
2019	24,487	83.4	37.4	74.7	27.9
2020	25,653	75.7	34.5	76.7	26.5

Source: Data are from the Palestinian Labor Force Survey.

model relies on changes in the number of employed rather than changes in the employment rate.

Rapid Assessment Phone Survey 2020

The Palestinian Central Bureau of Statistics, with support from the World Bank and UN agencies, conducted a rapid household survey to assess the impact of COVID-19 on socioeconomic conditions (PCBS 2020). The interviews were conducted by mobile phone from June 15 to July 30, 2020. The reference period for most of the questions was over the first lockdown period from March 5 to May 25, 2020.

The sample consisted of the list of households that responded to the 2018 Socio-Economic Conditions Survey, which has been stratified at the governorate and locality-type level. The sample size was 8,709 households (completed), with a response rate of 93.6 percent. The data show that the average age of the household head was 39.6 years, that 6.3 percent of households are headed by females, and that 46.2 percent of respondents had been working before the lockdown period.

An Innovative Methodological Approach

The analysis presented in this study relies on a microsimulation model to evaluate the welfare impacts of the COVID-19 pandemic. It focuses on the (labor and nonlabor) income transmission channel, as this channel is expected to dominate the short-run impact on households' welfare for at least two reasons. First, labor income represents a large share of household income (figure 7.5); second, the lockdown has caused a disruption in employment across all economic sectors.

Design of the Microsimulation Model

The microsimulation model draws on data from multiple waves of the LFS to estimate behavioral models based on the PECS 2016/17 and the rapid COVID-19 phone survey. It builds on previous approaches to microsimulation described in Walsh (2020) and Cereda, Rubiao, and Sousa (2020). The model links employment shocks to changes in income and predicts drops in labor income using the results from the COVID-19 phone survey. In sum, the model has four main steps that account for the following: (a) a change in employment from the LFS; (b) a change in labor income resulting from a growth of productivity and a reduction in working hours over the COVID-19 period; (c) a change in nonlabor income (aid and remittances); and (d) a corresponding change in consumption. These steps are summarized in figure 7.6.

FIGURE 7.6

Simulations Were Estimated to Predict Labor Income Caused by Employment Shocks

Overview of microsimulation model and steps to determine changes in household welfare

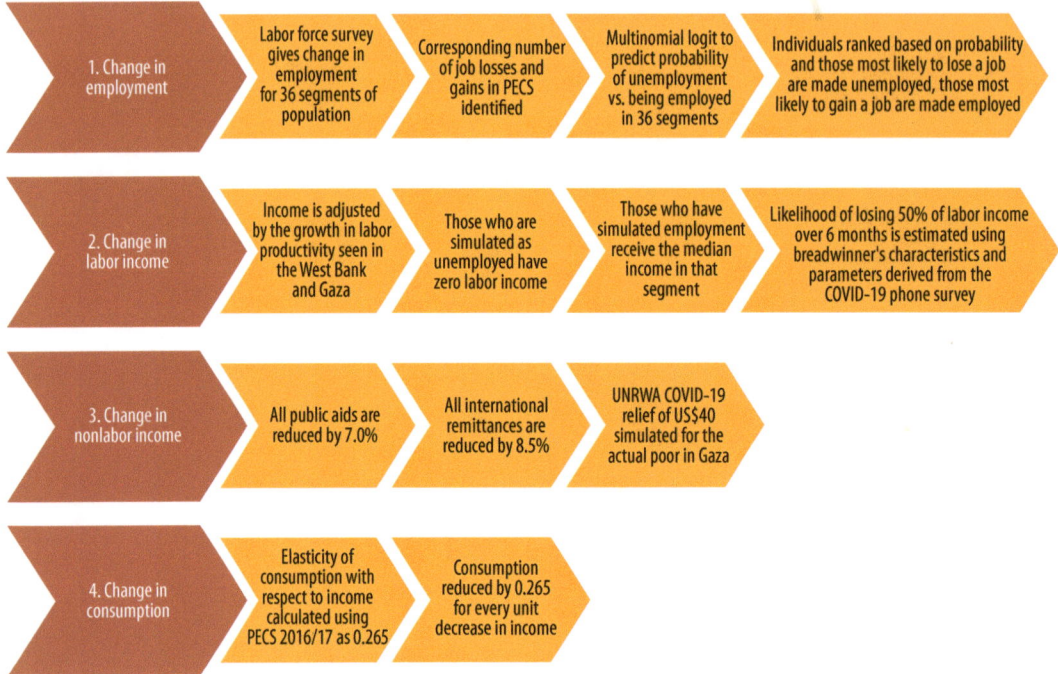

1. Change in employment	Labor force survey gives change in employment for 36 segments of population	Corresponding number of job losses and gains in PECS identified	Multinomial logit to predict probability of unemployment vs. being employed in 36 segments	Individuals ranked based on probability and those most likely to lose a job are made unemployed, those most likely to gain a job are made employed
2. Change in labor income	Income is adjusted by the growth in labor productivity seen in the West Bank and Gaza	Those who are simulated as unemployed have zero labor income	Those who have simulated employment receive the median income in that segment	Likelihood of losing 50% of labor income over 6 months is estimated using breadwinner's characteristics and parameters derived from the COVID-19 phone survey
3. Change in nonlabor income	All public aids are reduced by 7.0%	All international remittances are reduced by 8.5%	UNRWA COVID-19 relief of US$40 simulated for the actual poor in Gaza	
4. Change in consumption	Elasticity of consumption with respect to income calculated using PECS 2016/17 as 0.265	Consumption reduced by 0.265 for every unit decrease in income		

Source: World Bank.
Note: PECS = Palestinian Expenditure and Consumption Survey; UNRWA = United Nations Relief and Works Agency for Palestine Refugees in the Near East.

Specifically, the microsimulation exploits changes in the relative share of workers in various segments of the population, defined by intersecting location of residence (West Bank or Gaza), economic sector of activity, and refugee status.[6] Segments are grouped to provide sufficient within-group homogeneity, while having large between-group heterogeneity. Contractions in the proportions working in each segment are interpreted as a reduction in the number of workers in that segment, while expansions are seen as an increase in the size of the segment's workers, who are drawn from the pool of the unemployed. The COVID-19 phone survey was used to further model a reduction in labor income resulting from a decrease in work intensity in the wake of the COVID-19-induced lockdown.

Step 1: Change in employment

The LFS data suggest that from 2016 to 2019 employment increased for most segments in the West Bank, while it decreased in most segments in Gaza, indicating the grim economic prospects facing this area (figure 7.7).

FIGURE 7.7

Some Sectors in the West Bank and in Gaza Suffered Bigger Employment Losses Than Others

Percentage change in employment by segment, from 2016 to 2019 and 2019 to 2020

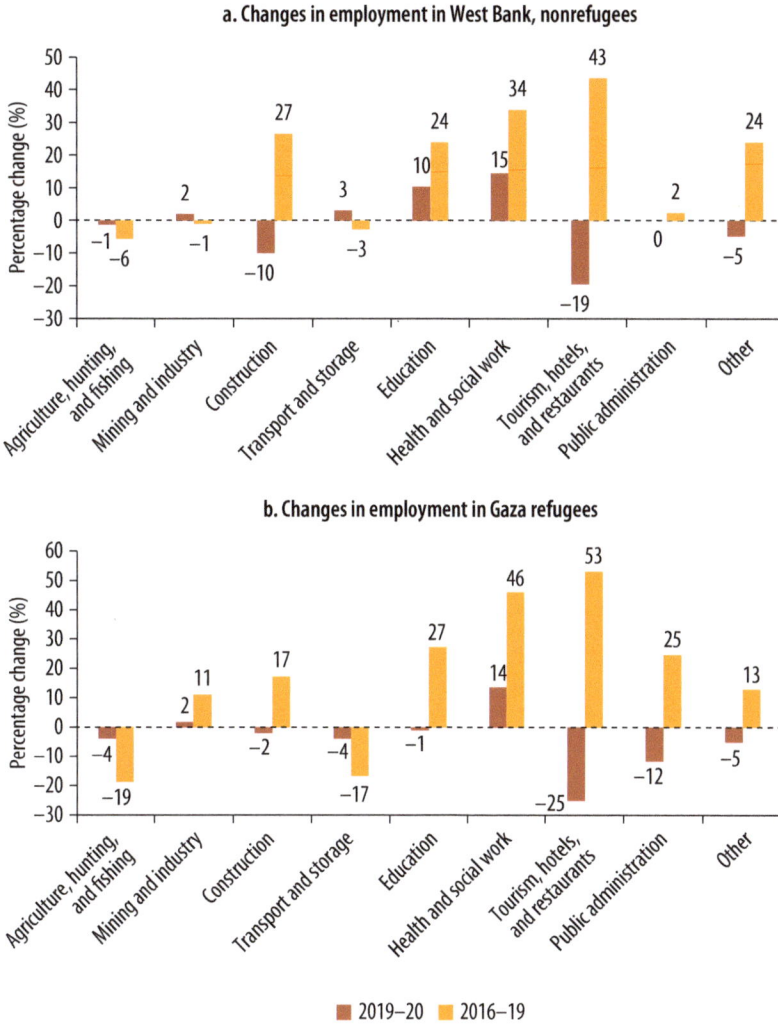

a. Changes in employment in West Bank, nonrefugees

b. Changes in employment in Gaza refugees

■ 2019–20 ■ 2016–19

Source: Original calculations from Palestinian labor force surveys, 2016–20.
Note: Share of employed is the proportion of the working-age population that is employed.

Then in 2020, most sectors contracted, likely because of the COVID-19 pandemic and its associated lockdown. The tourism, hotel, and restaurant industries are the most affected by a reduction in employment, in both the West Bank and Gaza.

The analysis begins with the production of a 2019 baseline by updating the work status of household members participating in the labor force in the PECS 2016/17 data. It then uses relative changes in sectoral labor productivity between 2016 and 2019 to adjust household labor income, given that from 2016 to 2019, labor productivity changed differently by economic sector of activity, sometimes eroding household income.[7] Next, annual LFS data is used to examine changes in employment status between 2019 and 2020. Changes in employment status are derived by selecting individuals who will either gain or lose a job. To identify the workers who are more likely to be laid off or recruited when a sector contracts or expands, a Mincer type multinomial logit regression was run on workers' observable characteristics (such as years of schooling, age and its square, and selected household assets).

Then, for each worker a propensity score, representing the likelihood that an individual with a given set of observables would be working in each segment, is generated. The propensity score of working in their current segment is stored. It is assumed that workers would be laid off sequentially beginning from the one with the lowest propensity of working in that segment until the number of those employed in that segment matches what is observed in the LFS. The approach is slightly modified when it comes to job expansion. When a segment expands, it is assumed that new recruits would enter the pool of workers, starting from those with the highest propensity among the unemployed. All workers who lose their jobs are assumed to receive no labor income, while those who gain a new job would receive the median annual income of their segments.

Step 2: Change in labor income

Furthermore, the COVID-19 phone survey provides data on variations in wages among workers who saw a change in their work intensity. This could help identify workers who did not necessarily lose their job but still saw a loss of income as a result of reduced working hours or profit. The data were used to identify main income earners who lose a fraction of their labor income in the PECS dataset. To do that, we modeled the likelihood of losing the totality or fraction of income in the phone survey data.[8] Then, with the estimated parameters, the likelihood of losing income is generated in the updated PECS data. Main income earners who lose some income are identified by ranking their estimated propensity.[9]

Step 3: Change in nonlabor income

This exercise draws on the World Bank's estimates of changes in the flow of remittances (Ratha et al. 2020) and of income from public transfers, with estimates modified to be consistent with data from the

World Bank on public spending and donor aid.[10] Information on social protection packages used to mitigate the economic consequences of COVID-19 is also used. It includes a one-time payment to poor refugees living in Gaza delivered by UNRWA (NIS 138), a one-time emergency cash transfer (NIS 700) from the Palestinian Authority to laborers and the poor, and a three-month top-up cash transfer (NIS 17) delivered by the World Food Programme to nonrefugees who are food insecure and extremely poor.[11]

The microsimulation estimates the income distribution at different points in time to derive changes to household welfare. Consistent with past work, the income of household member i at time t is defined as:

$$Y_{it} = YL_{it} + YG_{it} + YR_{it} + YO_{it} \tag{7.1}$$

where Y_{it} stands for individual i's income, YL_{it} is the labor of the household member, and YG_{it} and YR_{it} are, respectively, net public transfer received and remittance received by individual i. The income from all other sources is YO_{it}.

The microsimulation exercise assesses the change in YL_{it}, YG_{it}, and YR_{it} based on five scenarios after updating household income to 2019. The results also consider the following:

- A "2020 without COVID" scenario that projects forward lower labor productivity, assuming a similar trend since 2016.

- In the first scenario, only the employment shifts between 2019 and 2020 are simulated to assess their impacts on labor income.

- The second scenario compounds the effects of employment shifts with information about loss in labor income, with breadwinners assumed to lose half their income for one quarter.

- The third scenario assumes that the 50 percent income loss occurs during two quarters.

- The fourth scenario adds an 8.5 percent decrease in international remittances to the setup of the third scenario.

- The fifth scenario alters the third one to incorporate COVID-19 transfers, and it is the most plausible one because it closely mirrors households' living conditions.

In the remainder of this chapter, only results of the scenario 2020 without COVID and the fifth scenario are presented, with results from other scenarios shown as a sensitivity analysis. Finally, equipped with these changes to individual incomes, the model generates total household income and per capita income.

Step 4: Change in consumption

The implications of changes in income for household consumption are examined by using income elasticity of consumption. It is estimated from the PECS data by regressing log-consumption on log-income, controlling for a set of household and household head characteristics. These characteristics include age, years of schooling, working in agriculture, working in manufacturing, ownership of certain assets, and the location of the household. Elasticity is estimated to be 0.265.

Model Assumptions and Limitations

A few assumptions and limitations are associated with our method. First, the use of the updated household data as a baseline may not be optimal because the changes in welfare could potentially stem from other factors acting simultaneously in the economy. Second, the simulation model draws on behavioral models built on past data that reflect the precrisis structure of the labor market and household incomes. In particular, that data includes the relationship between income and consumption and the estimated elasticity. Hence, the model assumes these structural relationships to hold during the time span of the analysis. The longer the analysis period, the more questionable this assumption becomes.

Third, the model implicitly accounts for demographic growth by adjusting income for changes in sectoral labor productivity. Regarding public transfers in the pre-COVID-19 era, changes are assumed to affect all households in the same way, although this assumption is likely to be violated because transfers are probably targeted in a way that accounted for specific household characteristics. Yet the absence of precise information about various assistance programs prevents the development of a more refined model.

Fourth, the model does not allow for mobility of labor across space and economic sectors. Thus, all individuals are assumed to remain in their initial place of residence (a reasonable assumption) and their sector of employment (less likely to hold true).

Fifth, the model has little ability to account for changes in relative prices between different commodity groups resulting from external shocks. However, as mentioned earlier, empirical evidence suggests little change in relative prices, especially for commodities (like food) that matter most for the poor. In fact, there might be an improvement in the relative prices that would favor consumers, due to slow or negative growth in the CPI and an appreciation of the local currency.[12]

Finally, the change in employment from 2016 to 2019 could be underestimated as a result of the change in methodology employed by

PCBS in 2018. This will have the effect of underestimating the decrease in poverty, so results presented are likely to be a lower bound.

How COVID-19 Affects Household Welfare

What are the key findings of our microsimulations for the households in the West Bank and Gaza? We start with the overall results for changes in income, poverty, and inequality between the end of 2019 and 2020, before turning to a breakdown of changes across different groups.

Changes in Income

The first finding, on changes in income, shows that there will be a small reduction in income (1.5 percentage points) in 2020 from 2019. Between 2016 and 2019, consistent with trends recorded elsewhere,[13] per capita income declined, with differences by location (figure 7.8); mean annual per capita income dropped by 20.4 percent, reaching about NIS 7,140 in 2019. Importantly, per capita income is simulated to decrease faster in Gaza than the West Bank (24.8 percent versus 19.2 percent).

FIGURE 7.8

Income Was Expected to Remain Steady in 2020 before COVID-19 Effects

Changes in mean annual per capita income by location

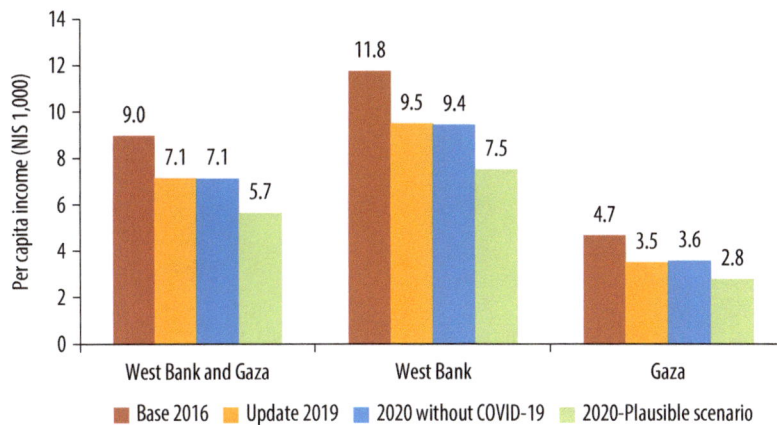

Source: World Bank.
Note: 2020-Plausible scenario = 2020-Employment shift + 50 percent income loss of breadwinner for two quarters + COVID-19 transfers (UNRWA aid to Gazan refugees, World Food Programme one-time transfer to poor nonrefugees, and the Palestinian Authority's one-time cash assistance in the West Bank).

During the pandemic, changes in income are projected to be felt differently in the West Bank and in Gaza. According to the most plausible scenario—which adds to the employment shift a reduction in the labor income of the main income earner and induced income changes resulting from UNRWA aid to Gazan refugees—the simulated drop in per capita income is 20.8 percent in the West Bank and 20.4 percent in Gaza, or 20.8 percent overall. As expected, the various transfers slightly dampen the adverse impacts on income.[14]

The divergence of these results is also explained in chapter 3 in this report, drawing on a forthcoming World Bank report (Suarez, Malásquez, and Al-Saleh forthcoming). While individuals in Gaza are more likely to have lost employment because of the pandemic, in the West Bank workers are more likely to forgo income because of reduced hours and inability to perform work-related activities.

Changes in Poverty and Inequality

The second finding shows an expected rise in poverty, although with no real change in inequality. Before the COVID-19 pandemic, poverty had worsened between 2016 and 2019, with simulated poverty rates for the West Bank and Gaza rising from 29.3 to 33.4 percent (figure 7.9). Gaza experienced a sharper increase in poverty (from 53.0 to 59.4 percent)

FIGURE 7.9

After Already Rising in Recent Years, Poverty Is Up Again in Response to COVID-19

Changes in poverty by location, adjusting for income elasticity

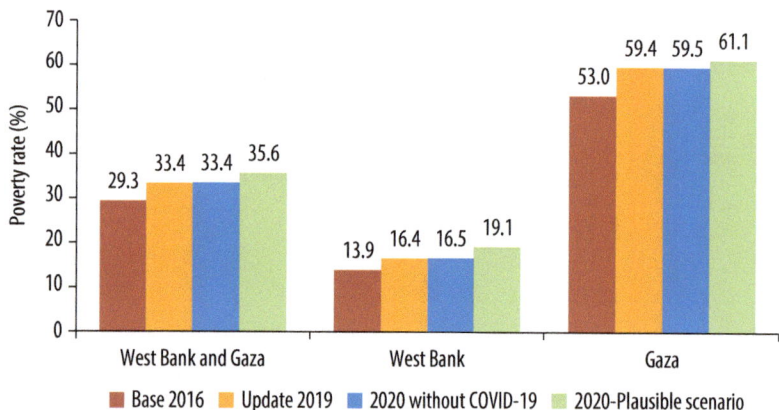

Source: World Bank.
Note: 2020-Plausible scenario = 2020-Employment shift + 50 percent income loss of breadwinner for two quarters + COVID-19 transfers (UNRWA aid to Gazan refugees, World Food Programme one-time transfer to poor nonrefugees, and the Palestinian Authority's one-time cash assistance in the West Bank).

than the West Bank (from 13.9 to 16.4 percent). However, inequality remained almost unchanged between 2016 and 2019, as the Gini index increased slightly from 33.7 to 33.9 percent. Changes are small across all scenarios and between the West Bank and Gaza.

Then, in 2020, as shown in figure 7.9, the simulated poverty rate in the West Bank and Gaza rose by 2.2 percentage points to reach 35.6 percent, the equivalent of more than 110,000 new poor as a result of the pandemic. Simulated poverty is on the rise in both the West Bank (from 16.4 to 19.1 percent) and in Gaza (from 59.4 to 61.1 percent), albeit at a more rapid pace in the West Bank compared to Gaza. And once again, there was no real change in inequality (figure 7.10).

As for the poverty gap, it is projected to rise from 10.0 to 10.7 percent between 2019 and 2020, pointing to the greater need for resources to lift people out of poverty (figure 7.11). Much of this increase would be driven by changes in the West Bank, where the simulated poverty gap rose to 4.5 percent from an updated value of 3.8 percent in 2019, with almost no change in the poverty gap in Gaza at 19.7 percent and 20.3 percent. Interestingly, this finding is not on par with some literature pointing to a widening gap and a reinforcement of existing poverty and vulnerabilities (Hill and Narayan 2020; Oxfam 2021; Serkez 2021).

FIGURE 7.10

Inequality Is Expected to Remain Steady Even after COVID-19

Gini index (%) adjusting for income elasticity

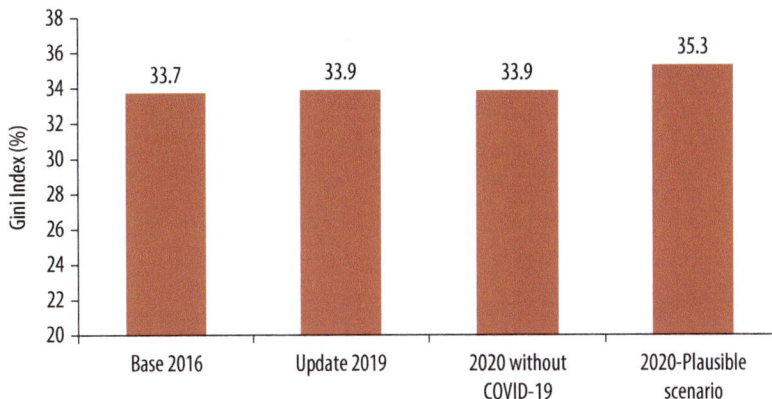

Source: World Bank.
Note: 2020-Plausible scenario = 2020-Employment shift + 50 percent income loss of breadwinner for two quarters + COVID-19 transfers (UNRWA aid to Gazan refugees, World Food Programme one-time transfer to poor nonrefugees, and the Palestinian Authority's one-time cash assistance in the West Bank).

FIGURE 7.11

Poverty Gap Is Expected to Increase with COVID-19

Poverty gap (%) by location, adjusting for income elasticity

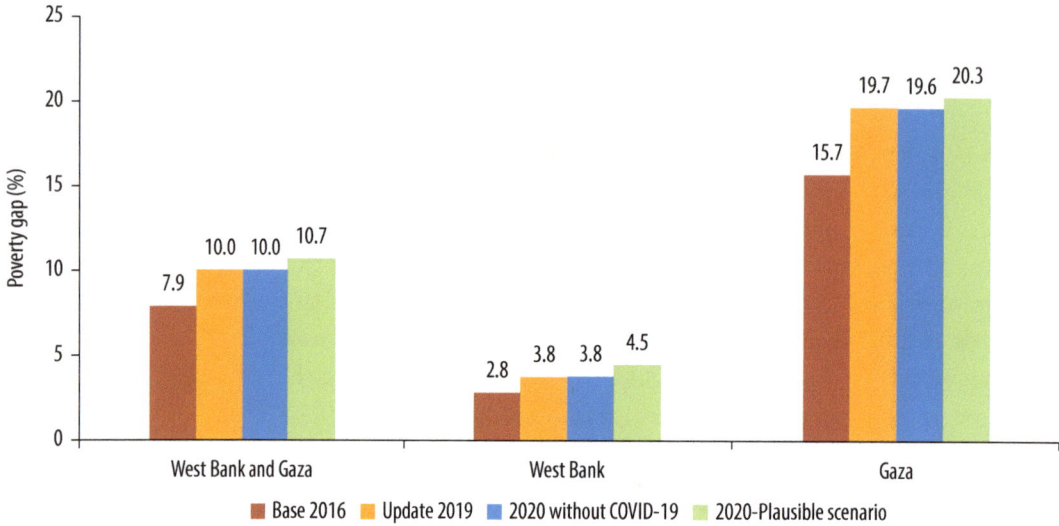

Source: World Bank.
Note: 2020-Plausible scenario = 2020-Employment shift + 50 percent income loss of breadwinner for two quarters + COVID-19 transfers
(UNRWA aid to Gazan refugees, World Food Programme one-time transfer to poor nonrefugees, and the Palestinian Authority's one-time cash
assistance in the West Bank).

Distributional Analysis

The third simulation shows that the impact of the pandemic on poverty will be felt differently across groups. Starting with educational attainment, the study finds that households with a more educated household head experience a smaller increase in poverty (up 1.8 percentage points) compared with households whose heads have no education (with poverty up 3.7 percentage points) (figure 7.12).

As far as industry is concerned, the study shows that households with heads working in the industry sector experience the largest simulated increase in the poverty rate, whereas the services sector is projected to have a relatively small increase in poverty (figure 7.13). Although the services sector was more affected by the pandemic, this result is likely due to the fact that those employed in the services sector were already poorer compared to those in the industry sector. Among households whose heads are not in the labor force, poverty actually decreases in 2020, probably reflecting the effects of various programs targeting the poor during the COVID-19 pandemic.

Turning to gender, between 2019 and 2020, poverty is simulated to increase faster among male-headed households compared with female-headed ones (figure 7.14). But it is worth mentioning that poverty rates

FIGURE 7.12

Different Educational Attainment Groups Are Estimated to Experience Different Impacts

Estimated poverty rates (%) by educational attainment

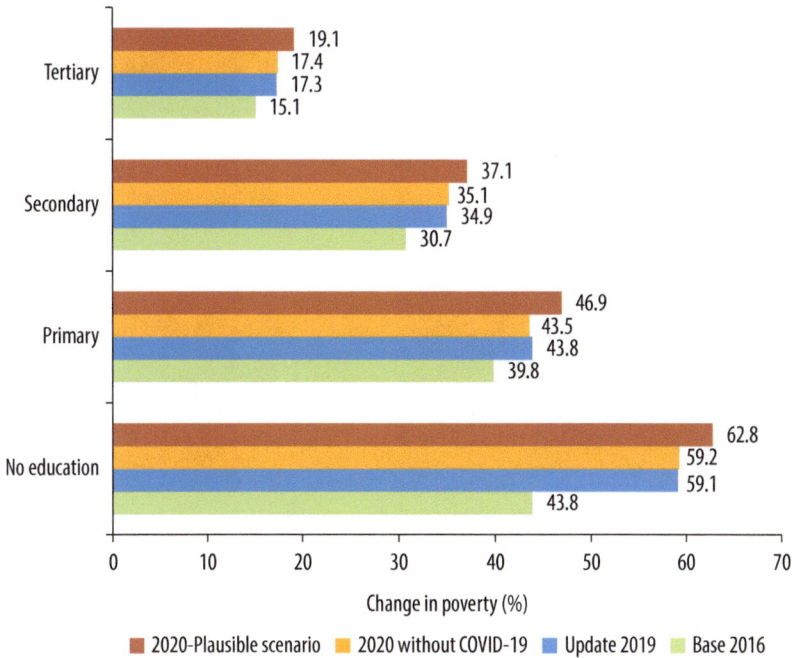

Source: World Bank.

Note: 2020-Plausible scenario = 2020-Employment shift + 50 percent income loss of breadwinner for two quarters + COVID-19 transfers (UNRWA aid to Gazan refugees, World Food Programme one-time transfer to poor nonrefugees, and the Palestinian Authority's one-time cash assistance in the West Bank).

are higher among female-headed households in 2016 and in the simulated scenarios. More worrying is that the poverty rate for female-headed households has increased much more from 2016 to the plausible 2020 scenario, with a 12 percentage point increase for women compared to the 6 percentage point increase for men. This implies that the poverty rate for female-headed households had been increasing, but the gap has narrowed because male-headed households are being more affected by the COVID-19 pandemic.

As for refugee-headed households, in 2016 they were more likely to be in poverty than non-refugee-headed ones, and this disparity still holds in the simulated estimates of poverty in 2020 (figure 7.15). However, a faster impoverishment rate is under way between the two subpopulations, as poverty increases more rapidly among non-refugee-headed households (2.5 percentage points) compared to the refugee-headed ones (1.9 percentage points).[15]

FIGURE 7.13

The Most Affected Households Are Those with Heads Working in Industry Rather Than Services

Estimated poverty rates (%) by industry

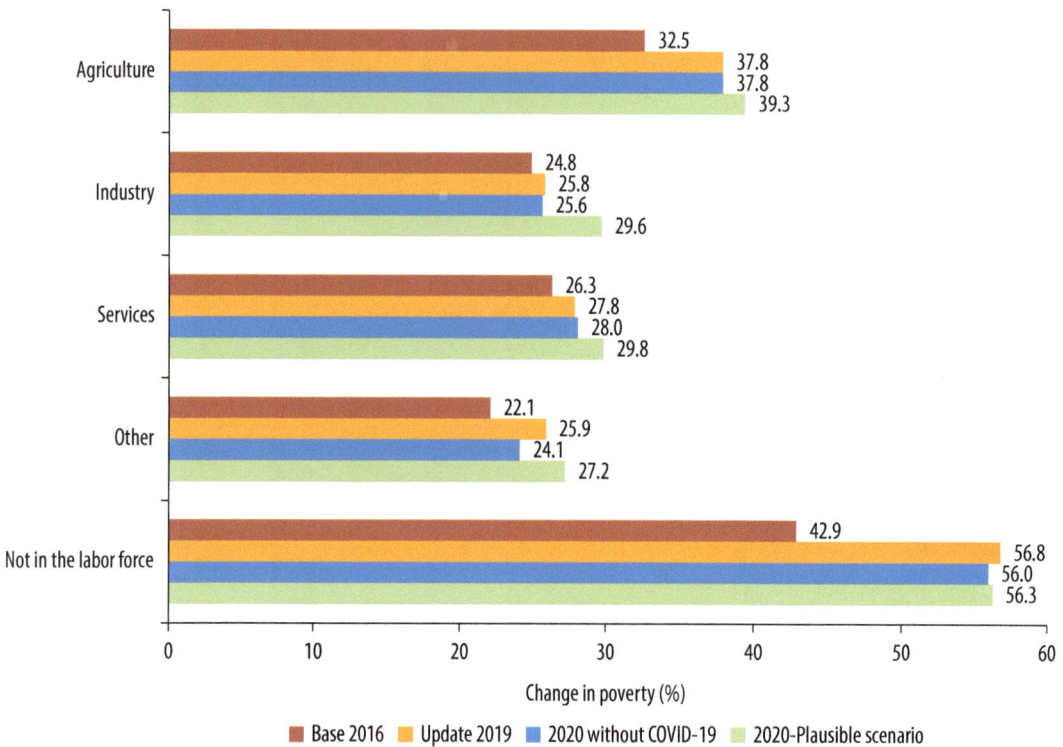

Source: World Bank calculations.
Note: 2020-Plausible scenario = 2020-Employment shift + 50 percent income loss of breadwinner for two quarters + COVID-19 transfers (UNRWA aid to Gazan refugees, World Food Programme one-time transfer to poor nonrefugees, and the Palestinian Authority's one-time cash assistance in the West Bank).

Impact Incidence Analysis

One of the advantages of microsimulation is that it allows for the possibility of exploiting impact incidence curves to investigate how changes are distributed between locations and across income groups. The impact incidence curves in figure 7.16 plot deciles of per capita income from the PECS 2016/17 data against simulated changes in per capita income by decile. Importantly, income deciles are computed separately in the West Bank and in Gaza, as the distributions are quite different between these locations.

The simulated employment shocks and disruption to economic activities are expected to translate into an income reduction across much of the income groups for the West Bank and Gaza overall, in addition to location levels. Except for the first decile in Gaza, all deciles saw a drop in their incomes. At the national level, the entire distribution

FIGURE 7.14

Male-Headed Households Take a Bigger Hit Than Female-Headed Households

Estimated poverty rates (%), by gender

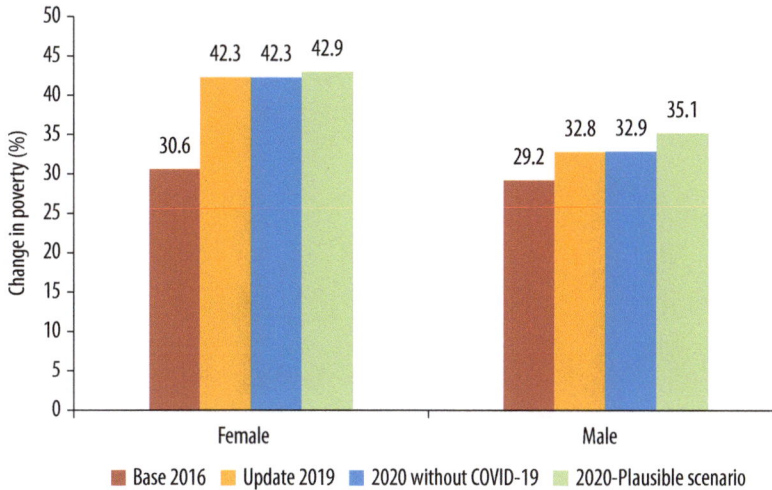

Source: World Bank calculations.
Note: 2020-Plausible scenario = 2020-Employment shift + 50 percent income loss of breadwinner for two quarters + COVID-19 transfers (UNRWA aid to Gazan refugees, World Food Programme one-time transfer to poor nonrefugees, and the Palestinian Authority's one-time cash assistance in the West Bank).

FIGURE 7.15

Refugee-Headed Households Are More Likely to Be in Poverty

Estimated poverty rates (%), by refugee status

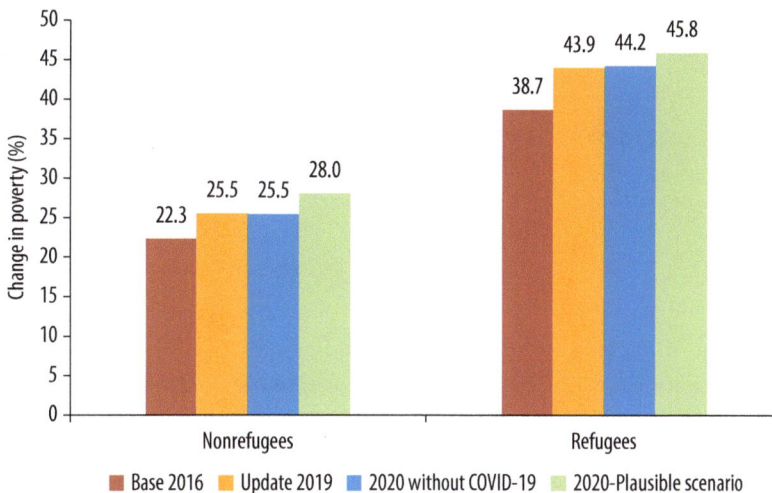

Source: World Bank.
Note: 2020-Plausible scenario = 2020-Employment shift + 50 percent income loss of breadwinner for two quarters + COVID-19 transfers (UNRWA aid to Gazan refugees, World Food Programme one-time transfer to poor nonrefugees, and the Palestinian Authority's one-time cash assistance in the West Bank).

FIGURE 7.16

Households in the Second and Third Deciles Feel the Brunt of COVID-19

Impact incidence curves by location

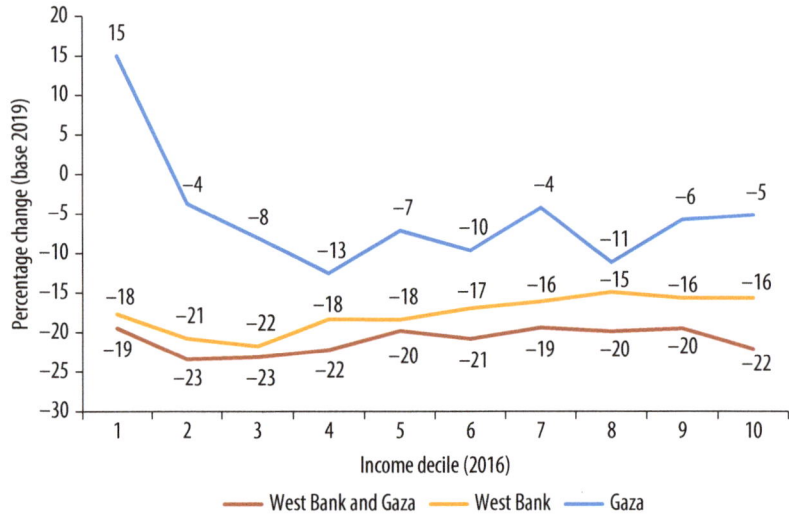

Source: World Bank.

suffers welfare losses. However, the income decline does not affect all deciles in the same way. Households from the second and third deciles experience the largest reduction in income (23 percent each).

Income losses affect households differently in the West Bank and in Gaza. Per capita income losses are largest among households in the second and third deciles in the West Bank, with losses ranging between 21 and 22 percent. In Gaza, these losses are felt more among households in the fourth through eighth deciles, with households from the fourth decile suffering the largest loss (13 percent).

New Poor

Given that the microsimulation approach enables us to examine the distribution of households that are likely to suffer from the economic fallout of the COVID-19 crisis along socioeconomic dimensions, it also helps us to investigate the characteristics of the new poor. Although the COVID-19 crisis has unevenly affected various groups, a change in the profile of the poor was already under way before the outbreak.

The new poor appear to be different from the traditionally poor in several ways (table 7.2). The West Bank is expected to host relatively more new poor than Gaza. These individuals are much more likely to live in rural areas than in camps. They appear to mostly come from

TABLE 7.2

Characteristics of the New Poor

percentage

Characteristics	Traditionally			New poor without COVID-19 impacts
	All samples	Poor	New poor	
West Bank	60.7	28.7	64.8	65.0
Gaza	39.3	71.3	35.2	35.0
Rural	16.8	10.8	16.7	16.0
Urban	73.0	73.4	72.8	72.4
Camp	10.2	15.8	10.5	11.6
No education	2.9	4.3	4.4	5.9
Primary	17.8	24.2	18.5	17.9
Secondary	57.4	60.2	52.1	54.3
Tertiary	21.9	11.3	25.0	21.9
Male	93.9	93.6	89.4	84.5
Female	6.1	6.4	10.6	15.5

Source: World Bank.

either end of the distribution of education; in other words, they are more likely to hold either no education or secondary or tertiary education. They have a greater likelihood of belonging to female-headed households. And women are more affected by new waves of impoverishment than men.

Sensitivity Analysis

So far, we have presented only the results from our 2020-plausible scenario—the one that exploits a 2020 employment shift, a 50 percent income loss of the breadwinner for two quarters, and the COVID-19 transfers. Although it appears to be a realistic depiction of the national context, a comparison with our four other scenarios would help give bounds to the results and provide an alternate set of estimates.

As shown in figure 7.17, although COVID-19 pushed many into unemployment, its adverse impact on poverty is felt through its impact on labor income, with lower employment rates in the first quarter in most sectors increasing poverty by 0.8 percentage points. But when the time span is extended to two quarters, poverty worsens another 0.8 points—for a total of 1.6 points from the pre-COVID-19 level. Any drop in remittances would make only a small difference in household income and thus have only a small effect on the level of poverty.

Since the poverty rate is dependent on household consumption, which is calculated using the imputed consumption to income elasticity, we explore how the results could change using different levels of elasticity. As shown in figure 7.18, the poverty rate could be 33.4 percent if

FIGURE 7.17

COVID-19's Impact on Poverty through Labor Income Continues into Second Quarter
Changes in poverty by scenario and location

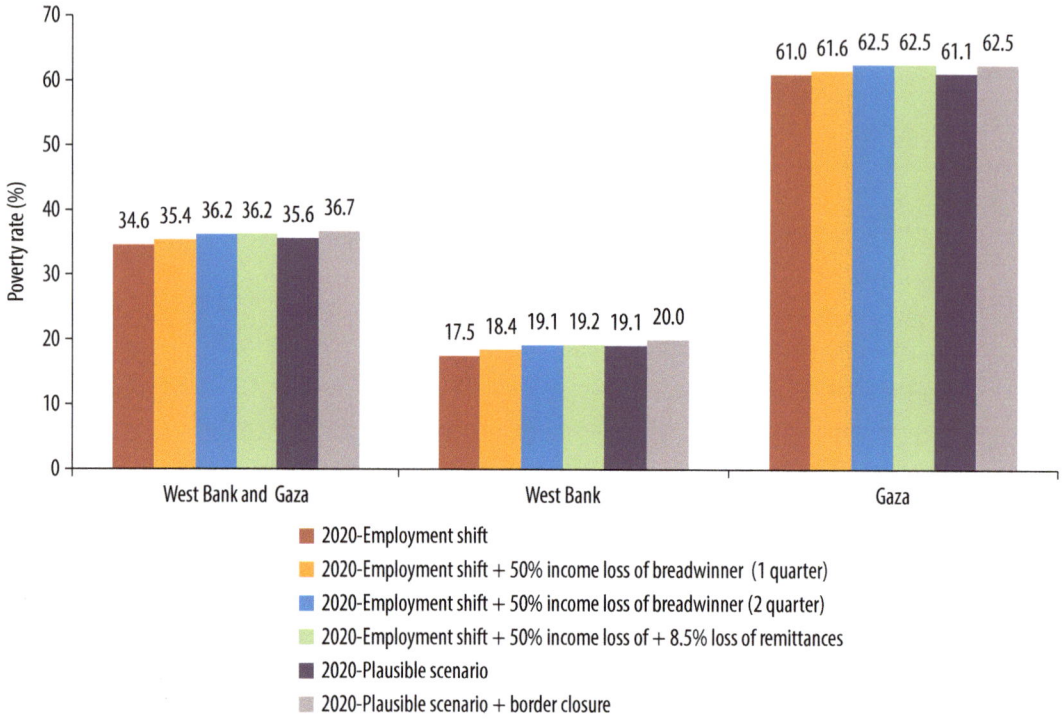

Legend:
- 2020-Employment shift
- 2020-Employment shift + 50% income loss of breadwinner (1 quarter)
- 2020-Employment shift + 50% income loss of breadwinner (2 quarter)
- 2020-Employment shift + 50% income loss of + 8.5% loss of remittances
- 2020-Plausible scenario
- 2020-Plausible scenario + border closure

Source: World Bank.

FIGURE 7.18

Poverty Rate Is Sensitive to Consumption to Income Elasticity
Poverty rate, by elasticity and location

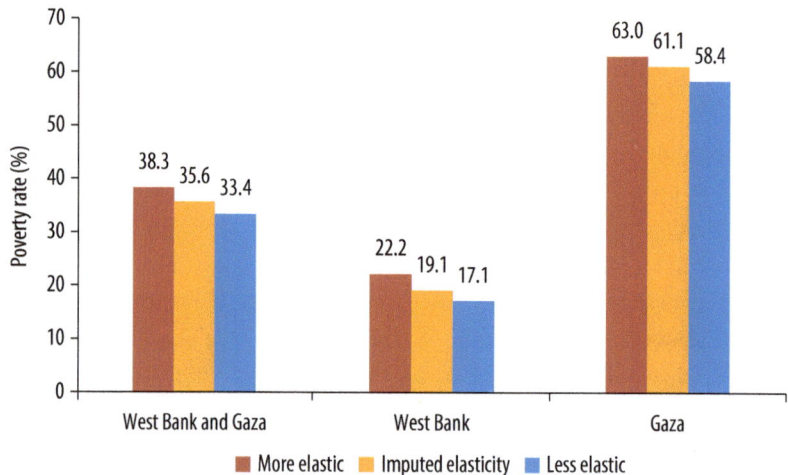

Legend:
- More elastic
- Imputed elasticity
- Less elastic

Source: World Bank.

elasticity is 10 percentage points less than the computed rate, or 38.3 percent if elasticity is 10 percentage points higher.

Future Scenarios

Recovery in the West Bank and Gaza will depend on the rollout of vaccines and the likelihood of another wave of COVID-19. It is difficult to determine whether a recovery will take place and to what extent. Even macroeconomic forecasts will be sensitive to many assumptions that are unpredictable at the moment. Instead, this section considers three possible scenarios:

A pessimistic scenario. The West Bank and Gaza sees another wave of COVID-19 cases and is forced to implement another series of mobility restrictions. Those who have lost their jobs will remain out of work, and those who have seen reduced working hours will also see a continued reduction in income. However, while households might have had an arsenal of coping strategies to deal with the income shocks in the first wave, it is likely that they will run out of coping strategies. Households might have been able to rely on using savings, selling assets, or borrowing, but as time goes on they are unlikely to smooth consumption, leading to a perfectly elastic relationship between income and consumption. Evidence from the COVID-19 phone surveys also suggests a limited ability to smooth consumption. For example, the majority of households living in rented housing units reported not being able to pay their rents in the month following the phone survey. In this scenario, a 1 percentage point decrease in income will yield a 1 percentage point decrease in consumption, driving overall poverty to 55.8 percent.

A slight recovery. In this scenario, as businesses have reopened properly, those who have seen reduced hours of work will return to full working hours and their income will recover. However, it will take more time for new jobs to be created to allow those who have lost their jobs to return to work. As the economy in the Middle East and North Africa region and globally also starts to recover, international remittances could slightly bounce back to around 96 percent of 2016 levels. Overall poverty will be around 33.9 percent.

A very optimistic recovery. In addition to those who have seen a reduction in working hours when they return to work, half of the newly unemployed could find work and become employed again. Remittances could return to normal as the economy improves in other countries. Poverty will be 32.3 percent, just under the simulated 2019 level.

FIGURE 7.19

The Optimistic Scenario Is Estimated to Return Poverty Rates to Their Previous Levels

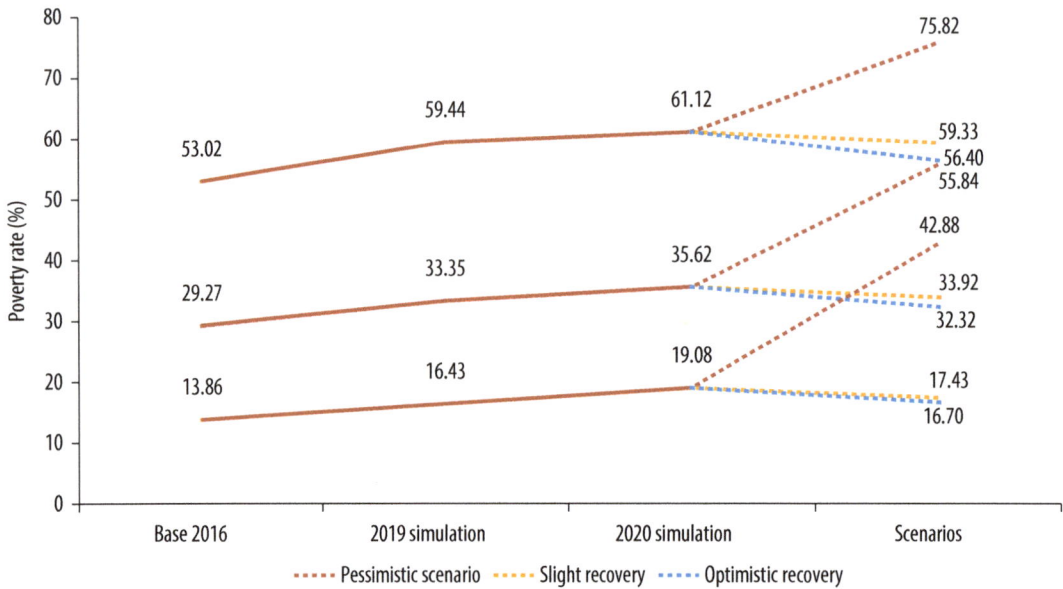

Source: World Bank.

Figure 7.19 demonstrates the potential trajectory of poverty in the West Bank and Gaza and by other locations (see table 7A.4 for the full results refugee status, including the Palestinian territories).

Conclusion

To better understand the COVID-19 pandemic's impact on the welfare of households in the West Bank and Gaza, our study develops an innovative approach to simulating the effects of poverty in the region—one that mostly relies on microdata collected before and after the pandemic, largely from rapid assessment phone surveys and the quarterly labor force survey. This approach allows for a simulation model that is grounded in data rather than assumptions and allows us to model household behavior. In so doing, we are able to convey a diversity across households in their experience of income and employment shocks, which can then be used to understand the profiles of the new poor and the segments of society most affected by COVID-19. Another advantage of this approach is its flexibility to incorporate new data and changing events. A potential next step will be to incorporate the effects of the escalating violence between Israel and the residents of the West Bank and Gaza.

Taken together, the results of this microsimulation exercise can paint a picture of worsening poverty driven by income shocks that is further exacerbated by the COVID-19 pandemic. In our most plausible scenario, poverty in the West Bank and Gaza is estimated to be 35.6 percent in 2020, which is 2.3 percentage points higher than what would have occurred in 2020 had there been no pandemic. The increase in poverty is felt more strongly in the West Bank than in Gaza—which could reflect Gaza's preexisting high levels of poverty, the stricter COVID-19 restrictions and border closures in the West Bank, and the fact that the income shock was felt more strongly in the richer deciles than in the bottom two deciles.

Although there is little change in inequality reflected in the simulations, the results point to an emerging new poor—those who were not poor in 2016 but have become poor since. Their characteristics are in fact different from the traditionally poor: (a) a greater concentration in the West Bank, (b) a greater concentration in rural areas, (c) a greater likelihood of having no education or secondary/tertiary education, (d) a greater likelihood of belonging to female-headed households, and (e) a greater likelihood of women being more affected by new waves of impoverishment.

Further, analysis of impact incidence curves indicates that the bottom 20 percent are less affected by income shocks than higher deciles—a finding that is analogous to the World Bank global report *Poverty and Shared Prosperity*, which indicates that 82 percent of the new poor will live in middle-income countries (World Bank 2020). This is an important result, and programs targeting the poor will need to weigh how the distribution of the poor has changed, especially between the West Bank and Gaza.

Of course, there are still many unknowns, notably the size of the economic recovery, which will depend on the rollout of vaccines and the likelihood of another wave of COVID-19. For that reason, our study also considers three additional scenarios: a pessimistic scenario, a slight recovery, and a very optimistic recovery. In the worst case, in which households are unable to continue smoothing consumption, poverty could rise to 56 percent in the West Bank and Gaza, close to what was observed in Gaza in 2016. But in the best case, poverty returns to 32 percent, just below the simulated 2019 level.

Considering the impact of past UNRWA interventions on the welfare of low-income households, the current pledge by the United States to provide aid to the Palestinians is timely and would help to counteract the fallout of the COVID-19 pandemic for the most vulnerable. The ripple effect of such a relief package, in eliciting funding from other donors, would also enable many households to weather the various shocks to welfare.

Annex

FIGURE 7A.1

Sectoral Growth of Output Per Worker in West Bank and Gaza between 2016 and 2019

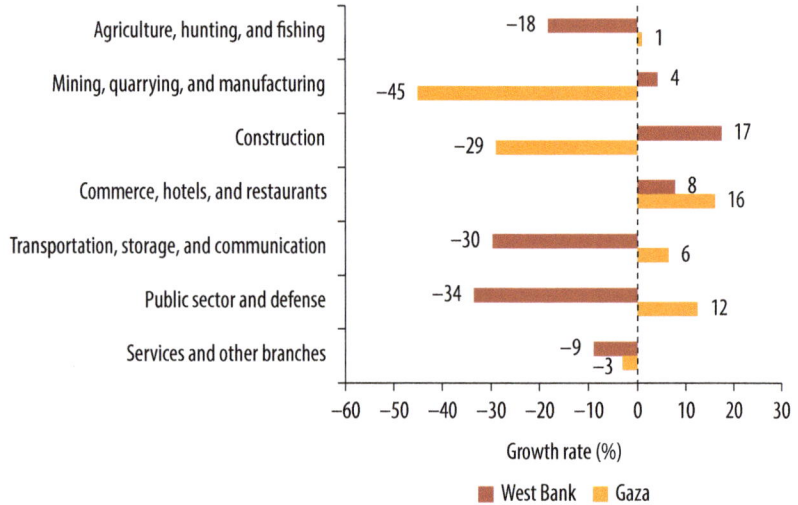

Source: Palestinian Central Bureau of Statistics, https://www.pcbs.gov.ps/site/lang__en/695/default.aspx.

TABLE 7A.1

PECS 2016/17 Respondent Household Characteristics

Variable	Household percentage distribution	Average household size	Number of households in the sample
West Bank and Gaza	100	5.5	3,739
West Bank	64.5	5.2	2,411
Gaza	35.5	6.1	1,328
Locality Type			
Urban	73.1	5.5	2,732
Rural	17.4	5.4	652
Camp	9.5	5.9	355
Employment status of head of household			
Employed	71.1	5.8	2,697
Unemployed	3.3	6.1	116
Out of labor force	21.1	4.6	764
Student/retired	4.4	4.2	156
Source of income			
Agriculture	2.0	6.3	75
Other household business	12.5	5.6	467
Wages and salaries from public sector	18.7	6.2	698
Wages and salaries from private sector	30.9	5.6	1,157

(continued on next page)

TABLE 7A.1

PECS 2016/17 Respondent Household Characteristics *(continued)*

Variable	Household percentage distribution	Average household size	Number of households in the sample
Wages and salaries from Israeli sector	11.5	5.9	431
Wages and salaries from international organizations	2.1	6.2	77
Transfers/assistances	20.2	4.6	757
Property income/other sources	2.1	3.8	77
Refugee status of head of household			
Refugee	41.8	5.6	1,563
Nonrefugee	58.2	5.4	2,176
Sex of head of household			
Male	89.9	5.8	3,363
Female	10.1	3.3	376

Source: Palestinian Expenditure and Consumption Survey (PECS), 2018.

TABLE 7A.2

Employment Shift by Segment (of Total Population)

Segment	Total employed (2016)	Total employed (2019)	Total employed (2020)	Shift 2020–2019	Shift 2019–2016	Shift 2020–2019 (%)	Shift 2019–2016 (%)
West Bank Agriculture, hunting and fishing; Not a refugee	38,582	39,108	41,429	(527)	(2,321)	−1	−6
West Bank Agriculture, hunting and fishing; Refugee	9,421	9,798	12,049	(377)	(2,251)	−4	−19
West Bank Mining and industry; Not a refugee	83,783	82,216	83,053	1,568	(837)	2	−1
West Bank Mining and industry; Refugee	26,126	25,677	23,107	448	2,570	2	11
West Bank Construction work; Not a refugee	121,177	134,548	106,358	(13,371)	28,190	−10	27
West Bank Construction work; Refugee	37,269	38,012	32,447	(742)	5,564	−2	17
West Bank Transport and storage work; Not a refugee	22,905	22,241	22,857	664	(616)	3	−3
West Bank Transport and storage work; Refugee	7,362	7,648	9,163	(286)	(1,515)	−4	−17
West Bank Education; Not a refugee	54,382	49,278	39,770	5,104	9,508	10	24
West Bank Education; Refugee	20,044	20,225	15,887	(181)	4,338	−1	27
West Bank Health and social work; Not a refugee	20,972	18,316	13,681	2,656	4,635	15	34
West Bank Health and social work; Refugee	9,119	8,026	5,495	1,092	2,531	14	46
West Bank Tourism, hotels, and restaurants; Not a refugee	13,883	17,221	12,001	(3,339)	5,220	−19	43
West Bank Tourism, hotels, and restaurants; Refugee	5,634	7,512	4,907	(1,877)	2,605	−25	53
West Bank Public administration; Not a refugee	42,912	43,016	42,029	(104)	987	0	2
West Bank Public administration; Refugee	20,577	23,270	18,670	(2,693)	4,600	−12	25
West Bank Other; Not a refugee	144,176	151,262	122,025	(7,085)	29,236	−5	24
West Bank Other; Refugee	51,924	54,718	48,462	(2,794)	6,256	−5	13
Gaza Strip Agriculture, forestry, and fisheries; Not a refugee	7,111	7,054	8,702	57	(1,648)	1	−19
Gaza Strip Agriculture, forestry, and fisheries; Refugee	5,678	5,298	6,984	380	(1,686)	7	−24
Gaza Strip Mining and industry; Not a refugee	6,914	7,381	7,519	(468)	(138)	−6	−2
Gaza Strip Mining and industry; Refugee	8,446	8,814	10,617	(368)	(1,803)	−4	−17
Gaza Strip Construction work; Not a refugee	4,425	5,082	6,611	(657)	(1,529)	−13	−23

(continued on next page)

TABLE 7A.2

Employment Shift by Segment (of Total Population) *(continued)*

Segment	Total employed (2016)	Total employed (2019)	Total employed (2020)	Shift 2020–2019	Shift 2019–2016	Shift 2020–2019 (%)	Shift 2019–2016 (%)
Gaza Strip Construction work; Refugee	5,098	6,015	14,340	(918)	(8,325)	−15	−58
Gaza Strip Transport and storage work; Not a refugee	6,381	7,781	7,444	(1,399)	336	−18	5
Gaza Strip Transport and storage work; Refugee	9,069	11,043	9,267	(1,974)	1,775	−18	19
Gaza Strip Education Not a refugee	7,891	8,957	9,058	(1,066)	(101)	−12	−1
Gaza Strip Education; Refugee	25,769	30,779	26,154	(5,010)	4,625	−16	18
Gaza Strip Health and social work; Not a refugee	3,871	4,771	3,152	(899)	1,619	−19	51
Gaza Strip Health and social work; Refugee	11,071	10,673	11,924	398	(1,251)	4	−10
Gaza Strip Tourism, hotels, and restaurants; Not a refugee	1,620	2,606	2,333	(986)	273	−38	12
Gaza Strip Tourism, hotels, and restaurants; Refugee	2,609	3,604	4,357	(995)	(753)	−28	−17
Gaza Strip Public administration; Not a refugee	17,635	20,588	21,282	(2,953)	(694)	−14	−3
Gaza Strip Public administration; Refugee	40,099	43,319	54,944	(3,220)	(11,625)	−7	−21
Gaza Strip Other; Not a refugee	25,689	30,503	31,385	(4,814)	(882)	−16	−3
Gaza Strip Other; Refugee	37,113	47,081	50,165	(9,968)	(3,084)	−21	−6
Total	**956,738**	**1,013,440**	**939,628**	**(56,703)**	**73,812**	**−6**	**8**

Source: Palestinian Labor Force Surveys, 2016–20.

TABLE 7A.3

Poverty Rates by Location, Area of Residence, and Refugee Status

Percent

Region	Base 2016	Update 2019	2020-Employment shift	2020-Employment shift + 50% income loss of breadwinner (1 Qtr)	2020-Employment shift + 50% income loss of breadwinner (2 Qtr)	2020-Employment shift + 50% income loss of breadwinner + 8.5% loss of remittances	2020-Plausible scenario
West Bank and Gaza							
Rural	18.8	21.6	22.3	23.0	23.4	23.4	22.9
Urban	29.4	33.4	34.8	35.6	36.6	36.6	36.0
Camp	45.4	52.7	53.7	54.1	54.7	54.7	53.8
Nonrefugees	22.3	25.5	26.7	27.5	28.1	28.2	28.0
Refugees	38.7	43.9	45.3	46.0	47.1	47.1	45.8
West Bank							
Rural	15.9	18.5	19.2	20.1	20.4	20.4	20.4
Urban	12.3	14.8	15.9	17.0	17.8	17.8	17.7
Camp	22.5	26.3	26.9	27.3	28.7	28.7	28.7
Nonrefugees	13.2	15.7	16.8	17.9	18.5	18.6	18.5
Refugees	15.6	18.3	19.3	19.7	20.7	20.7	20.7
Gaza							
Rural	60.9	67.0	66.4	66.4	66.4	66.4	60.1
Urban	51.6	57.5	59.2	59.8	60.9	60.9	59.7
Camp	58.4	67.8	69.0	69.4	69.5	69.5	68.1
Nonrefugees	51.1	56.5	58.0	58.0	58.5	58.5	58.4
Refugees	54.0	61.0	62.6	63.5	64.7	64.7	62.6

Source: World Bank.

TABLE 7A.4

Poverty Rates for Three Potential Future Scenarios

Percent

	Base 2016	2019 simulation	2020 simulation	Pessimistic scenario	Slight recovery	Optimistic recovery
Palestinian territories	29.27	33.35	35.62	55.84	33.92	32.32
Nonrefugees	22.31	25.50	28.04	49.36	26.58	25.90
Refugees	38.65	43.93	45.84	64.58	43.81	40.98
Rural	18.82	21.59	22.95	45.74	21.86	21.00
Urban	29.43	33.36	36.01	56.01	34.06	32.63
Camp	45.36	52.74	53.77	71.31	52.78	48.83
West Bank	13.86	16.43	19.08	42.88	17.43	16.70
Nonrefugees	13.20	15.71	18.45	41.16	16.69	15.99
Refugees	15.56	18.28	20.67	47.28	19.31	18.51
Rural	15.95	18.49	20.41	43.31	19.25	18.52
Urban	12.29	14.75	17.70	41.70	15.88	15.10
Camp	22.48	26.34	28.72	54.24	26.93	26.81
Gaza	53.02	59.44	61.12	75.82	59.33	56.40
Nonrefugees	51.12	56.49	58.35	75.28	57.84	57.24
Refugees	54.04	61.03	62.62	76.11	60.13	55.95
Rural	60.94	66.97	60.08	81.39	60.08	57.37
Urban	51.65	57.47	59.74	74.56	57.63	55.35
Camp	58.43	67.83	68.08	81.07	67.56	61.42

Source: World Bank.

Notes

1. The ability to work in those areas was limited by 18 percent, according to the 2019 Palestinian Central Bureau of Statistics labor force survey.
2. The official poverty line is based on a "deep poverty line," which reflects a budget needed for a family of two adults and three children to cover food, clothing, and housing. This line is increased based on the spending habits of those under the deep poverty line on health care, education, transportation, personal care, and housekeeping.
3. World Bank Economic Outlook on the West Bank and Gaza. http://pubdocs .worldbank.org/en/887141603047349535/pdf/13-mpo-am20-palestinian -territories-pse-kcm.pdf.
4. The rapid assessment phone survey shows households are still able to access health services to a certain extent. Given that the reduction in access to services is small, and that accounting for such a reduction in welfare is difficult, the microsimulation model does not consider changes in access to services.
5. The sampling weights adjust for non-response cases.

6. An individual is considered a refugee if he or she belongs to a household headed by a refugee. Both registered and unregistered refugee status are considered.

7. See figure 7A.2 in the annex for further information on declining labor productivity. Labor productivity is likely to have been declining in the West Bank and Gaza since 2011, coinciding with the start of the Arab Spring and the decline in external funding.

8. Although the phone survey provides a detailed categorization of income loss, the simulation only makes the simplifying assumption of a 50 percent loss. It is further assumed that income loss affecting wage workers reflects losses among all workers, excluding those in public administration, whose labor income is thought to suffer no shock in the microsimulation.

9. Because many households have a single income earner, extending the analysis to all workers at the household level has only a negligible effect on the results.

10. These data are extracted from the World Development Indicators database at https://datatopics.worldbank.org/world-development-indicators/.

11. While there are more social transfers, they were not considered because they were too small or not enough information was available at the time of writing.

12. World Bank Economic Outlook on the West Bank and Gaza.https://thedocs .worldbank.org/en/doc/169601538076901007-0280022018/original /mpoam18palestinianterritoriespseks913fin.pdf.

13. World Bank Economic Outlook on the West Bank and Gaza, http://pubdocs .worldbank.org/en/887141603047349535/pdf/13-mpo-am20-palestinian -territories-pse-kcm.pdf; International Labour Organization (2020).

14. Without COVID-19 transfers, income would have been reduced by 15.4 percent total in both the West Bank and Gaza, 17.2 percent in the West Bank and 8.5 percent in Gaza.

15. The breakdown of the poverty impact by location, area of residence, and refugee status is presented in table 7A.3 in the annex.

References

Cereda, Fabio, Rafael M. Rubiao, and Liliana D. Sousa. 2020. "COVID-19, Labor Market Shocks, Poverty in Brazil: A Microsimulation Analysis." World Bank, Washington, DC. https://openknowledge.worldbank.org/handle/10986 /34372.

Hale, Thomas, Noam Angrist, Rafael Goldszmidt, Beatriz Kira, Anna Petherick, Toby Phillips, Samuel Webster, Emily Cameron-Blake, Laura Hallas, Saptarshi Majumdar, and Helen Tatlow. 2021. "A Global Panel Database of Pandemic Policies (Oxford COVID-19 Government Response Tracker)." *Nature Human Behaviour* 5: 529–38. https://doi.org/10.1038/s41562-021-01079-8.

Hill, Ruth, and Ambar Narayan. 2020. "Covid-19 and Inequality: A Review of the Evidence on Likely Impact and Policy Options." Working Paper. Centre for Disaster Protection, London.

ILO (International Labour Organization). 2020. "Impact of the COVID-19 Pandemic on the Labour Market in the Occupied Palestinian Territory:

A Forecasting Model Assessment." International Labour Office, Geneva. https://www.ilo.org/wcmsp5/groups/public/---arabstates/---ro-beirut /documents/publication/wcms_774731.pdf.

Oxfam International. 2021. "The Inequality Virus: Bringing Together a World Torn Apart by Coronavirus Through a Fair, Just and Sustainable Economy." Methodology note. Oxfam International. https://oxfamilibrary.openrepository .com/bitstream/handle/10546/621149/tb-inequality-virus-methodology -note-250121-en.pdf.

PCBS (Palestinian Central Bureau of Statistics). 2018. "Main Findings of Living Standards in Palestine (Expenditure, Consumption and Poverty), 2017." 2368. Ramallah, Palestine: Palestinian Central Bureau of Statistics.

PCBS (Palestinian Central Bureau of Statistics). 2020. "Impact of COVID-19 Pandemic (Coronavirus) on the Socio-Economic Conditions of Palestinian Households Survey (March-May)." Palestinian Central Bureau of Statistics, Ramallah, Palestine.

Ratha, Dilip, Supriyo De, Eung Ju Kim, Sonia Plaza, Ganesh Seshan, and Nadege Desiree Yameogo. 2020. "Migration and Development Brief 33: Phase II: COVID-19 Crisis through a Migration Lens." KNOMAD-World Bank, Washington, DC. https://www.knomad.org/sites/default/files/2020-11 /Migration%20%26%20Development_Brief%2033.pdf.

Serkez, Yaryna. 2021. "Opinion: We Did Not Suffer Equally." *New York Times*, March 11, 2021. https://www.nytimes.com/interactive/2021/03/11/opinion /covid-inequality-race-gender.html.

Suarez, Pablo, Eduardo Malásquez, and Jawad Al-Saleh. Forthcoming. "The Distributional Impact of COVID-19 on Incomes, Labor Markets and Food Security among Palestinian Households." World Bank, Washington, DC.

Walsh, Brian. 2020. "A Bayesian Approach to Identifying Households Affected by Labor Market Shifts." Unpublished. World Bank, Washington, DC.

World Bank. 2020. *Poverty and Shared Prosperity 2020: Reversals of Fortune.* Washington, DC: World Bank. doi:10.1596/978-1-4648-1602-4.

CHAPTER 8

The Islamic Republic of Iran: Battling Both Income Loss and Inflation

Laura Rodriguez and Aziz Atamanov

Key Messages

- Iranians in the bottom half of the welfare distribution—working in services and high-contact economic sectors—are disproportionately affected by income losses.

- Rural households and those in the Zagros region have been the worst affected by inflation. Urban households, especially those in the Tehran metropolitan area, have experienced the lowest price rise in their consumption basket.

- The study's microsimulations show that poverty rates will rise substantially—by more than 20 percentage points—as a combined result of income losses and a reduction in how much households can afford, after accounting for higher inflation. Inequality will increase by 2 points in the Gini index.

- Government cash transfers aimed at informal poor workers can mitigate about a third of the increase in poverty, while a broader targeted consumption loan has a potentially larger mitigating effect on poverty, but at a higher fiscal cost.

Introduction

The Islamic Republic of Iran has been hit hard by the COVID-19 pandemic, which has claimed more than 60,000 lives and infected more than 1.7 million people, as of March 2021. At the same time, the economic ramifications of the shock have been raising concerns about the welfare of Iranians, including the possibility of major setbacks on the poverty front. The main channels through which the COVID-19 outbreak has affected household welfare in many countries are reductions in income and increases in the cost of living. Problems with supply chains, restrictions to labor mobility, and lower global demand have been reflected in higher agriculture prices and food price inflation. This inflation, especially rising prices for food and other basic commodities, has further lowered household living standards, with particularly worrisome implications for the cost of living of the poor and vulnerable.

Before the COVID-19 pandemic, the country was already amid economic tumult. The Islamic Republic of Iran had been in economic contraction after the reintroduction of US sanctions in 2018. The growth rate in GDP per capita was –7.0 percent in 2018/19 and –7.7 percent in 2019/20 (World Bank 2020a), although some recovery is expected for 2020/21.[1] Meanwhile, inflation, which had started to come down from the 2018 spike, rose again in 2019/20 as the rial sharply depreciated. The exchange rate passed RI 120,000 per US dollar in the parallel market, and the depreciation rate in April–June 2020 was equal to that of the entire previous year (figure 8.1). These changes increased import prices, which in turn pushed up the domestic price of goods. Among the top five imported products in the Islamic Republic of Iran are maize, rice, and soybeans; vegetables are 15 percent of total imports.[2] Because many key staples are imported, food prices are especially exposed. The COVID-19

FIGURE 8.1

GDP Growth Had Been Falling, and Currency Lost Much of Its Value

GDP per capita growth rate and parallel market exchange rate

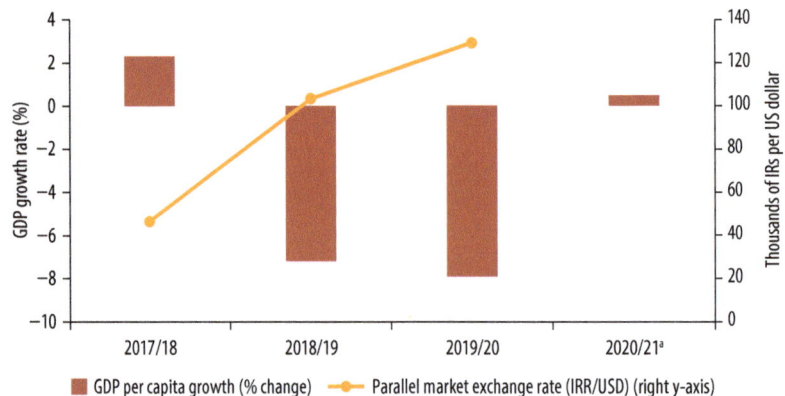

Source: World Bank staff calculations from Central Bank of Iran.
Note: GDP = gross domestic product; IRR = Iranian rial.
a. Estimated given that 2021 is not over.

pandemic—which reached the Islamic Republic of Iran early in 2020—heightened these pressures. The consumer price index (CPI) increased by 10 percentage points to 41.2 percent in 2019/20, and inflation continued to accelerate in 2020, reaching the highest month-to-month increase in almost two years in October 2020.

In response to the pandemic, the Iranian government unveiled new rounds of cash transfers and consumption loans for lower income deciles and households without a permanent source of income. But what can Iranian policy makers do to better direct resources to assist households during a crisis and prevent the emergence of hard-to-escape poverty traps? This study aims to help answer this question by assessing the short-term impacts of the pandemic on household welfare and poverty in the Islamic Republic of Iran, emphasizing the role of cost-of-living changes (resulting from inflation) that intensified throughout the pandemic. It also highlights the differences in impacts occurring for households at different points in the welfare distribution and in different parts of the country.

Policy makers need prompt and reliable information to make better informed decisions. Public health measures put in place to contain the spread of the disease—such as lockdowns, curfews, and limits to social and work interactions—upended traditional data collection methods to obtain the required information. In many countries, the World Bank launched frequent monitoring phone surveys to learn how the pandemic was affecting households. But in the absence of such alternative data for the Islamic Republic of Iran, the analysis of potential scenarios using household survey data from before the pandemic can be a useful tool to understanding the vulnerabilities of households and the likely impacts of the pandemic on poverty.

The results of our analysis show that in the short run, the combined fall in household incomes and high inflation during the COVID-19 pandemic will push more Iranian households into poverty—with poverty rising by up to 21 percentage points and inequality rising by 2 points. Hardest hit will be Iranians in the bottom half of the welfare distribution, working in services and high-contact economic sectors, and those in rural areas. As for the impact of the government's pandemic measures, the study finds that the measures help compensate for the income shocks, mitigating much of the poverty impact. But while they partly ease pressures on the poor, they also place an additional burden on fiscal balances and thus can be better targeted.

This chapter starts with a review of how the pandemic fits into the literature on the price changes and inflation that result from shocks. Then it describes how the study was done, followed by the results on cost-of-living increases, impacts on household welfare and poverty, and the government's new compensatory measures. It concludes with thoughts on the main findings, especially in terms of how they could help policy makers design mitigation measures.

How This Study Fits into the Literature on Economic Shocks

Given the most recent growth prospects, the World Bank estimates that the COVID-19 pandemic will increase the number of poor people around the world, and that lower labor incomes and higher unemployment are putting welfare at risk for many. In developing countries, phone surveys conducted by the World Bank show that income losses in International Development Association (IDA) countries are more prevalent than in non-IDA countries, but households in IDA countries are less likely to suffer job stoppages during COVID-19 than those in non-IDA countries (Yoshida, Narayan, and Wu 2020).

Within countries, there is empirical evidence that workers are more likely to stop working in services and industry sectors than in agriculture (Khamis et al. 2021). Incomes for self-employed workers in the services and high-intensity contact sectors that are difficult to do from home are being the hardest hit. This is consistent with findings from skills surveys from 53 countries, which reveal that workers in hotels and restaurants, construction, agriculture, and commerce are less likely to be able to work from home (Hatayama, Viollaz, and Winkler 2020). Phone surveys in developing countries also show that women and lower-educated workers are more likely to lose their jobs, especially in industry and service sectors (Sanchez-Paramo and Narayan 2020). Similar findings have been echoed in the United States, United Kingdom, and Germany (Adams-Prassl et al. 2020).

In many places, prices have risen during the pandemic. According to Food and Agriculture Organization data, food prices in the Islamic Republic of Iran—as well as in the Arab Republic of Egypt, Kuwait, Lebanon, Morocco, Qatar, Saudi Arabia, the Syrian Arab Republic, Tunisia, and the Republic of Yemen—have risen by more than 20 percent since February 2020. There is a considerable literature assessing the impact of price changes, particularly food and agricultural prices, on poverty. Ivanic, Martin, and Zaman (2012) estimate the first-order impacts of the 2006–08 food price crisis for a large number of developing countries and find an overall poverty increase of 1.1 and 0.7 percentage points in low- and middle-income countries, respectively. Similarly, de Hoyos and Medvedev (2011) find that rising food prices can increase poverty by 1.7 percentage points at the global level, even after accounting for the rise in incomes of agricultural producers, and by 0.6 points when incorporating potential higher wages in the biofuels industry. Various country-level studies also attest to the severe impact of large food price increases on households (for example, de Janvry and Sadoulet 2010; Fujii 2013; Rodriguez-Takeuchi and Imai 2013; Vu and Glewwe 2011).

This chapter is also related to a few studies that focus on the heterogeneous impact of depreciation-driven inflation on households' living standards. For Egypt, Kraay (2007) and Alazzawi and Hlasny (2019) estimate the impact of two currency depreciation episodes on household welfare. They start by estimating the pass-through of the depreciation to consumer inflation and then focus on the welfare impacts via household consumption. Kraay (2007) finds that the average welfare loss is 7.4 percent of initial household expenditures, and that most of that loss is accounted for by the direct effect, that is, before households make substitutions to their consumption patterns. A similar direction, but stronger impacts, are found by Alazzawi and Hlasny (2019) for the most recent depreciation of 2016.

For Mexico, a study by Cravino and Levchenko (2017), which focuses on the country's 1994 hyperinflation episode, highlights how inflation is felt differently across the income distribution, depending on two aspects of households' consumption patterns. First, poorer households spend more on tradable goods, making them more exposed to price fluctuations associated with a devaluation. Households in the lower deciles of the distribution consequently experience increases in their cost of living that are 1.25 times the rise experienced by those in the higher deciles. Second, within products, low-income households spend more on lower quality (and thus lower priced) items, which the authors also find rose disproportionally in Mexico compared with high-quality varieties.

As for economic shocks, the literature distinguishes between the immediate and the later impacts. In the medium and long run, households might be able to adjust by purchasing cheaper goods, and by switching agricultural household production to crops with higher returns, and further derive higher labor incomes if wages in certain production sectors rise. Ivanic and Martin (2014) compare the short- and long-run impacts of food price increases in a sample of developing countries. They find that while the estimated long-run impacts are in fact smaller, there are still some groups of households (low-educated, female-headed, and urban ones) for whom poverty increases even after accounting for second-order effects. It is not surprising that the urban poor are more vulnerable to price surges and less likely to benefit from increases in agricultural household production, as they tend to do little of this activity. But even most rural households, especially the poorest, are net consumers of food items and are likely to be negatively affected by price changes (Barrett and Dorosh 1996; de Janvry and Sadoulet 2010).

Moreover, it is relevant for policy makers to analyze the short-run impacts, especially of large shocks. The COVID-19 pandemic and inflation shocks occurred in the context of a preexisting prolonged crisis in the Islamic Republic of Iran, and thus the ability of households to adjust or use coping mechanisms was already constrained. Even short-lived shocks can compromise dietary diversity and nutrition intake (Skoufias, Tiwari, and Zaman 2012), for instance, by pushing households into hard-to-escape poverty traps. Also, the use of coping strategies in the short run might be less than fully effective and bring later negative consequences (Paxson and Alderman 1992), for instance, if households accumulate debt or deplete their savings.

How the Study Is Conducted

Data

Data come from the 2018/19 Iranian Household Expenditures and Income Survey (HEIS), an annual nationally representative survey collected by the Statistical Center of Iran (SCI). HEIS is stratified by province and by urban and rural areas. It contains detailed information of a household's sources of labor and nonlabor income, as well as consumption across a range of goods and services. Additionally, consumption shares derived from the 2016/17 HEIS are used to build price indexes. The structure and content of both survey rounds is similar.

The SCI collects official price data to construct the CPI. Prices are reported for the 31 provinces and 12 large categories of goods and services, which are matched to those in HEIS.[3] Prices are also available for 10 subcategories of food expenditures and three subcategories of housing expenditures.[4] SCI reports CPI for deciles and provinces. By contrast, the group-specific indexes constructed in our study are further disaggregated for intersections of those groups (for example, rural areas in a specific province), allowing a more detailed analysis. Further, they are adapted to the welfare aggregate used for the poverty measurement, excluding durable items and health expenditures.

The poverty measurement follows well-established international standards, which requires defining an indicator to measure welfare or living standards. This study uses both household consumption and household income (expressed per person), in line with standard procedures, to construct the aggregates and implement price adjustments to ensure comparability within and across survey years (see Deaton and Zaidi 2002;

Haughton and Khandker 2009). The consumption aggregate excludes expenditure on health and durable goods and is intertemporally and spatially deflated to account for changes in prices during the survey period and for spatial variations in prices.[5] In the absence of an official national poverty line, the poverty threshold—the minimum level below which a person is considered to be poor—is the international upper-middle-class poverty line of US$5.50 expressed in 2011 purchasing power parity (PPP) terms for household final consumption expenditures (Jolliffe and Prydz 2016).[6] PPP rates correspond to the May 2020 CPI revision.[7]

Microsimulation Analysis

In the context of the global pandemic, where health concerns and mobility restrictions may limit traditional data collection by national statistical offices, microsimulations are a useful tool to understand how the shocks are affecting people's welfare. In the Islamic Republic of Iran, where high-frequency phone data are not being collected, this work helps to shed light on the impacts of COVID-19 on households in the country. The analysis is based on the simulation of scenarios in which various sources of household income are reduced, depending on the degree of the pandemic's impact. It is a partial-equilibrium assessment that captures the first-order effects of the shock on various sources of household income. The COVID-19 pandemic can affect welfare through changes in labor and nonlabor incomes (such as remittances and transfers), consumption changes stemming from cost-of-living increases, higher health care and other expenses, and service disruptions (particularly to health and education).

This chapter focuses on the short-term impacts of the shock and assesses changes to monetary welfare. As such, it omits possible long-term impacts on household welfare that arise from human capital shocks and service disruptions. Further, monetary impacts occur primarily through labor and some sources of nonlabor income. Although the analysis emphasizes the impacts generated by price changes, it omits other changes in consumption patterns (such as those potentially derived from higher health care costs).

Labor incomes may suffer as a result of work restrictions or loss of earnings and working hours associated with lower aggregate demand, direct illness, household caring needs, quarantines, or social distancing behaviors. The impacts are likely to be starker in certain sectors—such as construction; retail; transport; hotels and restaurants; communications; real estate; administrative and support activities; and entertainment and art. Within sectors, individuals who are self-employed are more vulnerable to layoffs or income reductions than those with a salary.

On the other hand, the income of public sector workers is much less volatile. And remittances, which typically rise during crises, will most likely be a limited source of consumption smoothing this time, as the pandemic's effects are felt across the country and globally.[8]

As a first-order approximation, the microsimulation does not account for a potential increase in labor incomes that arise from the possibility of switching jobs to work activities that are less affected by the pandemic. For example, in Uganda, there was a shift in employment from services and industry to agriculture during the pandemic (World Bank 2020b). However, in the recessionary context of the Islamic Republic of Iran, such impacts are likely limited. Also, when accounting for price changes, the assumption is that households are affected by higher prices as consumers but not as producers, who could benefit from higher prices. This means that the assessment is a potential higher-bound estimate of the long-run impacts—but likely a better approximation of short-run impacts.

The income effects that are modeled vary by employment income type (wage or self-employment) and economic sector of employment, as shown in table 8.1, which displays the parameters (with 1 indicating no change in income after the shock). For instance, self-employment income is assumed to decline to 80 percent of the preshock annual level. We could think of this as a fall in this type of income for two-and-a-half months of the year. Labor income changes are adjusted by province of residence to account for some regions of the country being more heavily affected by the pandemic than others.[9] There is an additional small shock to private household transfers (domestic and international remittances), which have

TABLE 8.1

Self-Employed and Workers in Hard-Hit Sectors Suffer the Biggest Income Losses

Parameters by type of income and economic sector of occupation

Income source	Scenario parameters
	Share of initial income (%) over months without income
Self-employment general	80 (2.4 months)
Self-employment – selected sectors[a]	50 (6 months)
Salary – public sector	1 (no change)[b]
Salary – private sector general	90 (1.2 months)
Salary – private sector – selected sectors[a]	70 (3.6 months)
Household transfers (remittances)	95 (1 month)
Pensions	1 (no change)[b]

a. Selected sectors are construction; retail; transport; hotels and restaurants; communications; real estate; administrative and support activities; entertainment and art; other services.
b. 1 indicates no change in income after the shock.

fallen during the pandemic.[10] These income changes (as a share of initial household income) are then applied to the welfare aggregates used to estimate poverty: total consumption per capita per day (in 2011 PPP dollars) and total income per capita per day (in 2011 PPP dollars).

The second step of the simulation addresses the added impact of inflation, providing an estimate of how much households can now afford given the new prices. This is done by deflating the resulting household welfare aggregate with the inflation rate in the year. An innovation of this study is that households are matched to group-specific price indexes, by region and by rural or urban location of the household, to account for the impact of price changes on welfare, instead of using the national CPI as is commonly done in other microsimulation analyses.[11]

Since the data used in the microsimulation are from the 2018/19 HEIS, they need to be updated to the beginning of the pandemic period. The welfare aggregates are nowcasted to March 2020 (the beginning of the Iranian calendar year) by applying nominal private consumption per capita growth, deflated with the group-specific price indexes to obtain their value in the same baseline year. With these updates, the baseline poverty rates are 15.2 percent (consumption per capita poverty) and 20.4 percent (income per capita poverty).

Group-Specific Price Indexes

The degree to which purchasing power declines with inflation depends on the items consumed as well as spatial variations in price increases. The group-specific price indexes facilitate capturing such variations in the estimation of welfare impacts, by reflecting the change in the cost of living for a subgroup of households, for instance, by location (rural or urban) or place in the welfare distribution. Rising living costs are strongly connected to declining socioeconomic well-being, but not everyone is equally affected.

Unlike a generic price index—such as the national CPI, which weights price increases for different goods and services using a common basket for the whole country—a group-specific price index accounts for variations in consumption baskets, incorporating, for instance, the higher share of expenditures on food by poorer households, or higher rent expenses by urban ones.

The Laspeyres indexes are calculated by weighting price indexes for disaggregated expenditure categories g, with the shares of expenditure on such items ω in the baseline period (t_0), for each subgroup of households h.[12] The expenditure categories included are 10 large groups of goods and services, 10 subcategories of food expenditures, and three subcategories of housing expenditures. The baseline period is chosen to be 2016/17 since it predates the inflationary pressures in the Islamic Republic of Iran.

$$\hat{P}_t^b = \sum_g \omega_g^b * \hat{P}_{g,t}^b \tag{8.1}$$

where $\omega_g^b = \dfrac{P_{g,t_0}^b * q_{g,t_0}^b}{\sum_g P_{g,t_0}^b * q_{g,t_0}^b}$.

Cost-of-Living Increases by Welfare and Region

Rising living costs are strongly connected to declining socioeconomic well-being, but not everyone is equally affected. The degree to which purchasing power declines with inflation depends on the items consumed as well as spatial variations in price increases. In recent years, the highest increases in the overall CPI in the Islamic Republic of Iran have been for food, beverages, and tobacco (figure 8.2), with prices for many other items—such as furnishings and household equipment, recreation and culture, and transportation—also quite high. Tobacco expenditures are only 1 percent of the total household budget,[13] so a large price increase would be minimally felt by most. However, higher food costs have deeper

FIGURE 8.2

Inflation Has Been Picking Up in Recent Years, Led by Food, Beverages, and Tobacco

National CPI by type of goods and services, by percent change year-over-year, 2016–20

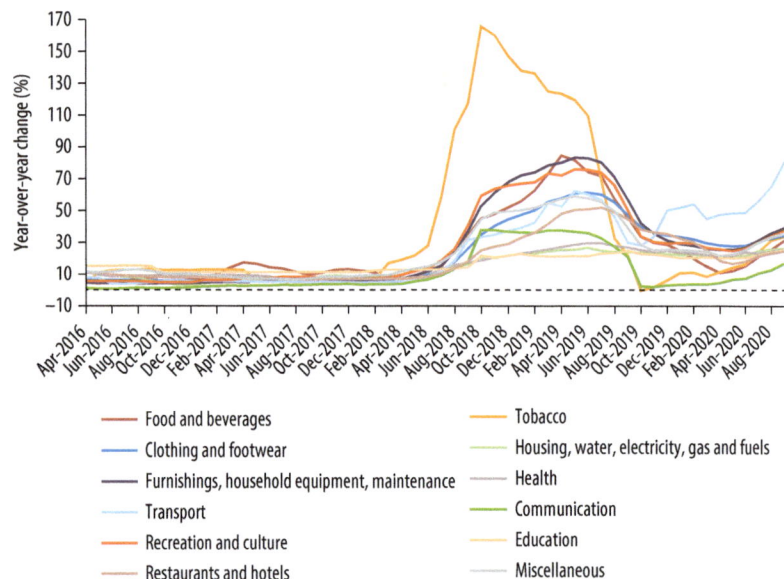

Source: World Bank staff calculations, based on Statistical Center of Iran.
Note: CPI = consumer price index.

implications, especially for the poor, given that food shares are as high as 46 percent of the household budget in rural areas and for households in the lowest welfare decile (figure 8.3). Rent inflation most heavily affects the middle class and even the more affluent urban households, as housing cost shares are large in urban areas (32 percent of total expenditure) and in the top decile (38 percent). Transport costs represent 5–6 percent of expenditures, without much variation across the distribution.

Which households, by income and location, were most affected by the pickup in inflation? On average nationally, by October 2020 the consumption basket was 2.6 times more expensive compared to April 2016. Rural households across the income distribution were the hardest hit (figure 8.4 panels a and b). The rural poor experienced the biggest increase, 2.8 times by October 2020, with richer rural households close behind. For urban households, the cost-of-living increase was overall smaller, but with variations across the welfare distribution—a 2.7 times increase for those in the poorest welfare decile compared with a 2.5 times increase for those in the richest one, which was even lower than the national average.

FIGURE 8.3

Poor and Rural Dwellers Spend More on Food

Expenditure shares by type of goods and services (%), by rural/urban and welfare decile

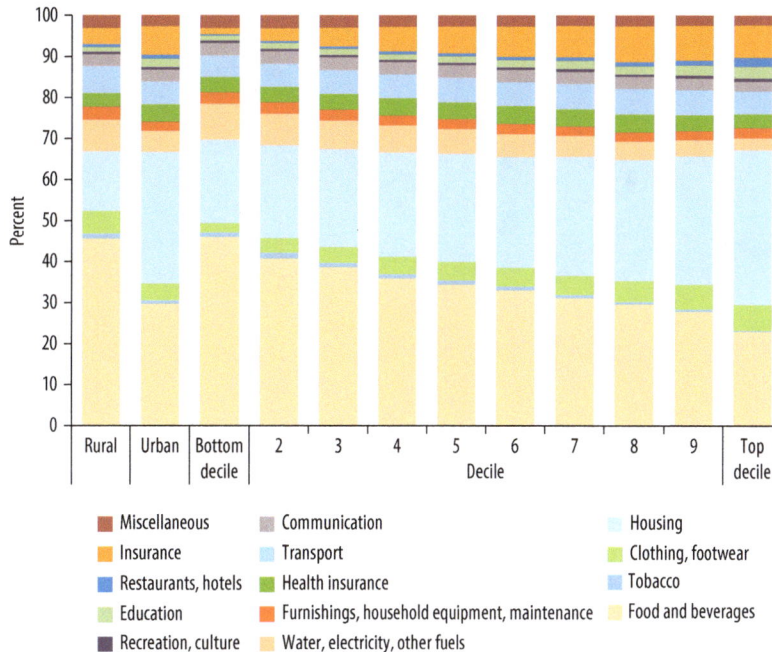

Source: World Bank staff calculations, based on HEIS 2016/17.
Note: Deciles based on consumption per capita in the base period. The figure excludes health expenditures other than health insurance. See figure 8A.1 in the annex for shares including all health expenses.

FIGURE 8.4

Rural Households across the Income Distribution Experienced the Worst Inflation

Group-specific price index from December 2019 to October 2020, by welfare decile and urban or rural location; and by region and urban or rural location (April 2016 = 1)

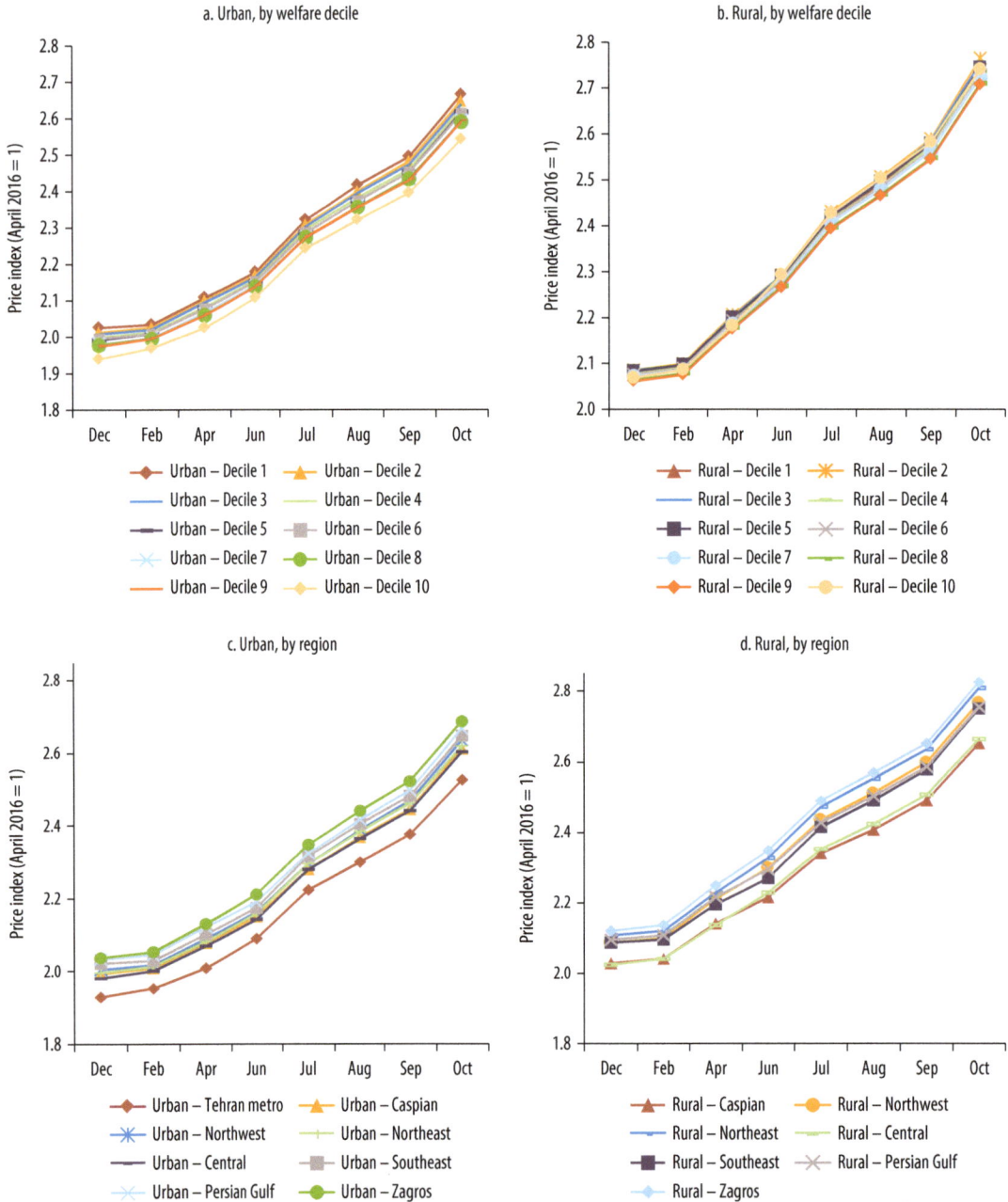

Source: World Bank staff calculations, based on HEIS 2016/17 and consumer price index from Statistical Center of Iran.
Note: Deciles are based on consumption per capita in the base period. Provinces are grouped in the following regions: Tehran metro (urban parts of Tehran and Alborz); Caspian (Gilan, Golestan, Mazandaran); Northwest (Ardebil, East and West Azarbaijan, Zanjan); Northeast (Khorasan Razavi, North and South Khorasan, Semnan); Central (Fars, Isfahan, rural parts of Tehran and Alborz, Markazi, Qazvin, Qom); Southeast (Kerman, Sistan and Baluchestan, Yazd); Persian Gulf (Bushehr, Hormozgan, Khuzestan); Zagros (Bakhtiari, Hamadan, Ilam, Kermanshah, Kohkiloyeh, Kurdestan, Lorestan).

At the regional level, some areas were more heavily affected than others. Figure 8A.2 in the annex shows the price indexes for each province separately. For ease of presentation, figure 8.4 (panels c and d) groups provinces into regions and shows the price indexes separately for the urban or rural areas of each region. At the upper end, households in rural Zagros (Bakhtiari, Hamadan, Ilam, Kermanshah, Kohkiloyeh, Kurdestan, and Lorestan) experienced the largest price increases (2.8 times), although those in the urban parts also experienced high inflation (2.7 times).[14] At the other end, households in the Tehran metropolitan area saw the lowest price rise in their consumption basket (2.5 times increase). Among urban households, those in the Persian Gulf (2.6 times) and the Southeast (2.6 times) saw relatively high inflation compared with those in other regions. From a poverty perspective, the most worrisome areas are the provinces of South Khorasan in the Northeast and Baluchestan and Sistan in the Southeast regions, which had high initial poverty at the beginning of the pandemic, with households experiencing price increases of over 2.7 times by October 2020 (figure 8A.3 in the annex).

How robust are these results? Our inflation analysis estimates the change in cost-of-living increases for households if they were to keep their consumption habits constant. But as a response to high inflation, households may change the composition of their budgets, choosing to consume cheaper goods. Hence, the method overestimates the potential welfare impact because the possibility of consumption substitution is not incorporated. The welfare effect after substitution is approximated in a robust analysis by calculating the price index using the expenditure shares calculated from the end-line survey (2018/19), after households have adjusted their consumption patterns (Paasche index).

The expenditure shares in the end-line period are in figure 8A.4 in the annex, but they reveal only minimal differences in expenditure patterns compared with the baseline period.[15] Consequently, the price indexes also show magnitudes similar to those in the main results (figure 8A.5 in the annex). This result suggests that the ability to substitute consumption was not large enough to offset the differences in the experienced inflation across households in different parts of the country.

Impacts on Household Welfare and Poverty

The impact of the COVID-19 shock depends on the preexisting exposure of households to shocks, which depend on their income sources and where they are across the welfare distribution. Of workers in the poorest 20 percent of the population, 60 percent are employed in the sectors expected to be affected the most during the pandemic, a large proportion of them because they work in the construction sector. The poorer are also less likely to work in the public sector and rely more on private earnings, whereas those in the middle of the distribution rely more on self-employment income (table 8.2).

As for the labor income and remittances shocks, the simulations show an average reduction of 14.5 percent in total household income. Households in the bottom half of the welfare distribution face a loss ranging from 15 to 17 percent, while the total income loss for those in the top 50 percent ranges from 10 to 14 percent (figure 8.5). The larger falls for poorer households are associated with their relying more on self-employment and being in sectors such as construction, retail, transport, and hotels and restaurants, which are the most affected by the economic shock and by the restrictions imposed to curb the pandemic. As a result of these income losses, poverty rises by 10 percentage points from the baseline when measured with the consumption aggregate and by a similar magnitude when measured with the income aggregate (figure 8.6). Since the model of the welfare distribution is close to the poverty line (figure 8A.6 in the annex), the poverty gap also rises significantly, from 7 to 11 percentage points as a result of the income shock (figure 8.7). Inequality, as measured by the Gini index, rises by 2 points (figure 8.8).

The fall in incomes through the pandemic is exacerbated by high inflation. Because inflation reduces how much households can afford with a given income, accounting for the rise in the cost of living further increases poverty—by 11 percentage points in the case of the consumption poverty measure and by 9 percentage points using the income

TABLE 8.2

Poorest Workers Are Less Likely to Work in the Public Sector and More Likely to Work in Sectors Affected during the Pandemic

Household income sources by welfare decile (share of total household income, %)

Income source	Lowest decile	2	3	4	5	6	7	8	9	Highest decile
Self-employment	18.6	25.8	29.5	29.8	28.5	25.3	23.9	24.0	22.0	20.4
Self-employment: hard-hit sectors	9.3	14.2	18.1	18.7	19.0	16.5	16.1	16.0	14.8	13.0
Salaries	39.9	41.6	40.1	40.4	41.4	43.4	43.8	42.8	44.2	41.4
Salaries (public sector)	0.8	2.1	3.4	4.4	7.6	8.4	12.1	15.6	18.7	20.1
Salaries (private sector)	39.1	39.6	36.7	36.1	33.8	35.0	31.7	27.2	25.6	21.2
Salaries (private): hard-hit sectors	26.2	25.3	22.3	20.4	20.3	18.3	16.2	13.6	11.2	9.6
Social assistance	26.2	16.1	13.2	11.7	10.5	9.2	8.0	6.5	5.1	3.1
Private transfers	9.7	7.2	5.9	3.9	4.8	3.7	3.3	3.8	3.0	3.0
Pension	3.2	6.6	8.5	10.8	11.7	14.6	17.0	19.2	21.4	26.1
Other incomes	2.4	2.6	2.7	3.3	3.2	3.8	4.0	3.7	4.3	6.0

Source: World Bank staff calculations, based on HEIS 2018/19.
Note: Hard-hit sectors are construction; retail; transport; hotels and restaurants; communications; real estate; administrative and support activities; entertainment and art; other services.

FIGURE 8.5

Households in the Bottom Half of the Income Distribution See a Larger Income Fall

Income reduction across per capita consumption, by decile (% change)

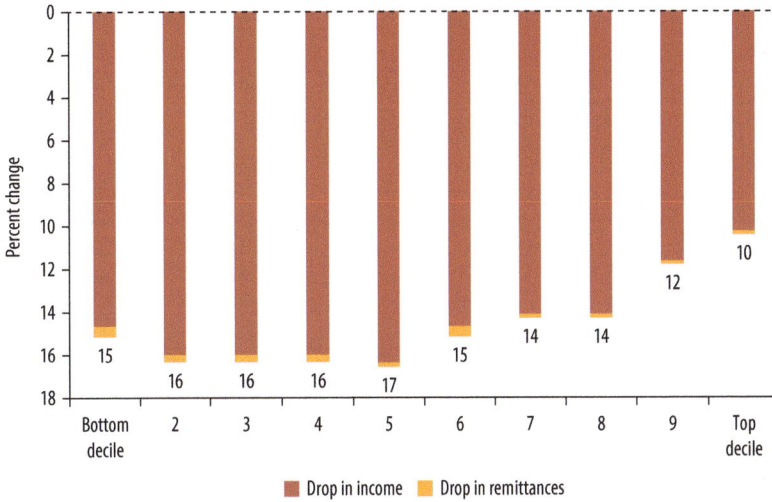

Source: World Bank staff calculations, based on HEIS 2018/19.

FIGURE 8.6

Inflation on Top of Income Loss Further Increases Poverty

Simulated poverty impacts (US$5.50 2011 PPP), per capita change (%)

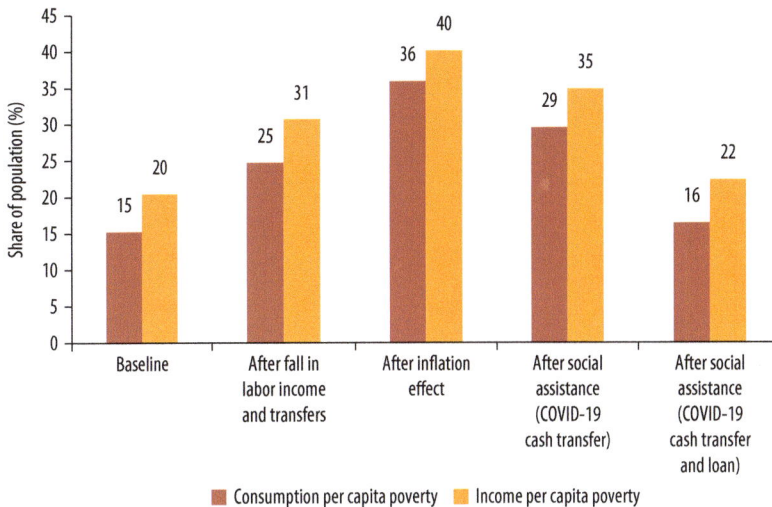

Source: World Bank staff calculations, based on HEIS 2018/19.
Note: PPP = purchasing power parity.

FIGURE 8.7

Income Shock Widens the Poverty Gap

Simulated poverty impacts, by poverty gap (US$5.50 2011 PPP)

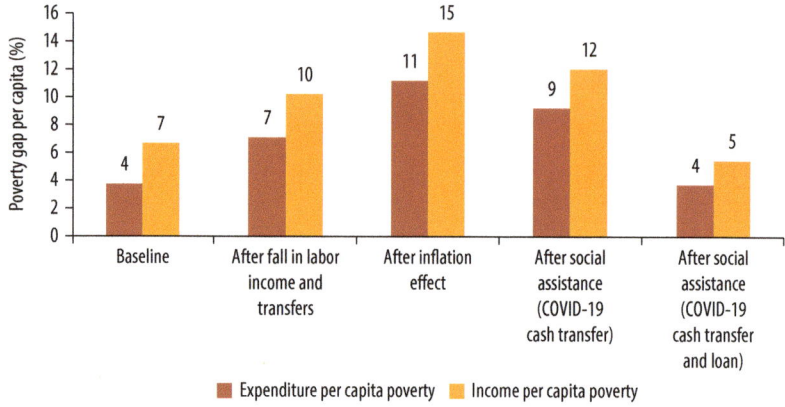

Source: World Bank staff calculations, based on HEIS 2018/19.

FIGURE 8.8

Inequality Increases by Two Percentage Points

Simulated inequality impacts (Gini index)

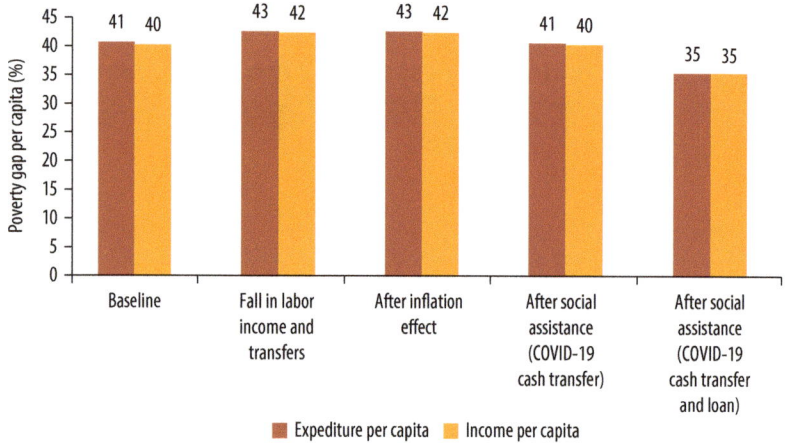

Source: World Bank staff calculations, based on HEIS 2018/19.

poverty measure. The 2020 inflation does not alter inequality, because the gaps in purchasing power emerged earlier (in late 2018 and early 2019) and did not change much in 2020.[16]

The impacts have considerable geographic variation (figure 8.9). The increase in poverty in provinces such as Qom and Semnan happens primarily because of the fall in incomes; however, especially in the provinces

FIGURE 8.9

The Inflation Effect Is Dominant in Provinces with Higher Baseline Poverty Rates

Simulated poverty impacts by province, by headcount poverty rates (US$5.50 2011 PPP)

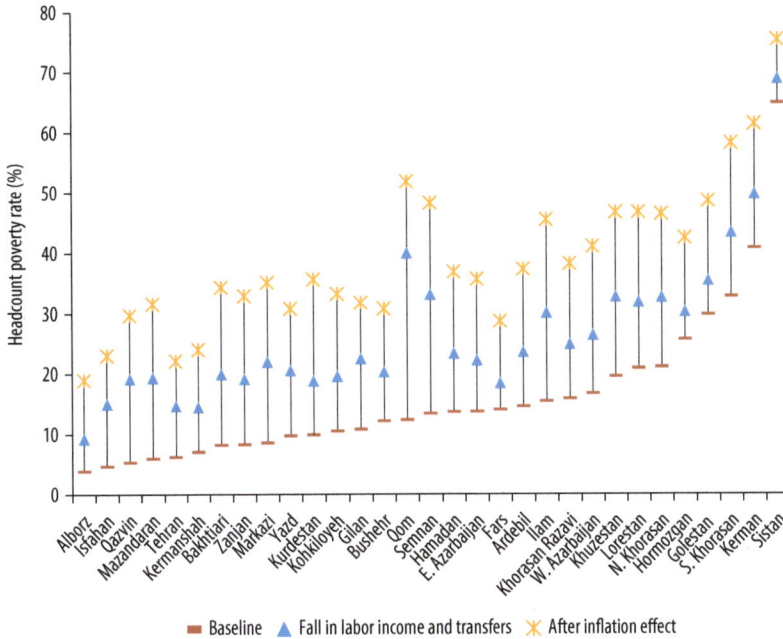

Source: World Bank staff calculations, based on HEIS 2018/19.

with higher baseline poverty rates, the inflation effect is the dominant one. This is consistent with the fact that poorer households spend more on food and other goods that had higher inflation.

During the pandemic—and despite limited public resources—the government of the Islamic Republic of Iran has adopted a series of measures to mitigate the negative impacts of the shocks. Two social assistance measures have been adopted so far to respond to the crisis: (a) a cash transfer to 3 million poor households without a formal income before the pandemic, and (b) a low- or no-interest loan to about 21 million households across the country.[17] This study also simulates these responses to assess their potential impact (table 8.3). The study finds that despite being a relatively small program, the first measure can mitigate about 6 percentage points, or about a third, of the increase in consumption poverty because of its narrower targeting at the bottom of the distribution, and the measure can mitigate almost a fifth of the increase in income poverty. The consumption loan adds 13 percentage points of mitigation, bringing poverty closer to the pre-COVID-19 baseline. Because the loan

TABLE 8.3

Social Assistance Responses Are Expected to Mitigate COVID-19's Impact

Social assistance	Scenario parameters	
	Recipient allocation in survey	Amount (IRR per household/year)
COVID-19 cash transfer (four rounds)	About 3 million households without formal wage, pension, or property income and in the bottom seven deciles of the household consumption distribution.	IRR 2 million plus IRR 1 million for each additional household member, up to IRR 6 million for households with five or more members.
Consumption loan	About 21 million households receiving existing social assistance transfers, excluding those in the top decile of the household consumption distribution.	IRR 10 million; no interest repayments.

Source: World Bank.
Note: IRR = Iranian rial.

is intended to be repaid as lower cash handouts as part of future subsidy reforms, its mitigation impact might be somewhat reversed if the crisis is prolonged.

Conclusion

Against a backdrop of economic contraction and high inflation, the economic consequences of COVID-19 for households have been severe. Our study shows that, overall, poverty substantially increases by up to 21 percentage points, as a combined result of the fall in household incomes and high inflation through the pandemic, and inequality rises by 2 points. Of the poverty total, income loss accounts for 10 points and inflation 11 points. Moreover, Iranians in the bottom half of the welfare distribution—those working in services and high-contact economic sectors and those in rural areas—are disproportionately affected.

Although inflation associated with the sharp fall in the currency value has been widespread, some households, depending on their baseline consumption patterns, have experienced larger rises in their cost of living. For instance, rural households across the welfare distribution saw the highest rise in the price of their consumption basket. By region, households in the Tehran metropolitan area saw the lowest rise, while those in the provinces of rural Zagros saw the highest. On average nationally, by October 2020 the consumption basket was 2.6 times more expensive compared to April 2016.

Even if in the long run these impacts are mitigated as households find ways to cope and adjust their employment, production, and consumption patterns, it is important for policy makers to analyze the short-run impacts—especially of such a large shock—to identify those in greatest need and better target resources to prevent hard-to-escape poverty traps. This study also estimates the potential effect of two social assistance mitigation measures adopted by the government during the pandemic. It finds that a cash transfer aimed at informal poor workers can mitigate about a third of the increase in consumption poverty, while a more broadly targeted consumption loan has a potentially larger mitigating effect on poverty, but at a higher fiscal cost.

As the COVID-19 pandemic continues to unfold in a harsh economic environment, protecting households from further deterioration of their economic well-being is paramount. In late November 2020 the parliament approved an additional, broadly targeted social assistance transfer to further help mitigate the economic impact of the pandemic on households. At an estimated cost of RI 300 trillion (US$7.1 billion), it is intended to reach 60 million Iranians. These mitigation measures will further help to offset the strain on household incomes, but as happened with previous cash transfers in the Islamic Republic of Iran (Hayati et al. 2018), the strength of social assistance measures to halt the poverty increase will be limited if cost-of-living increases diminish the real value of the transfers.

Annex

FIGURE 8A.1

Expenditure Shares Including Health by Type of Goods and Services, by Rural and Urban and by Welfare Decile (%)

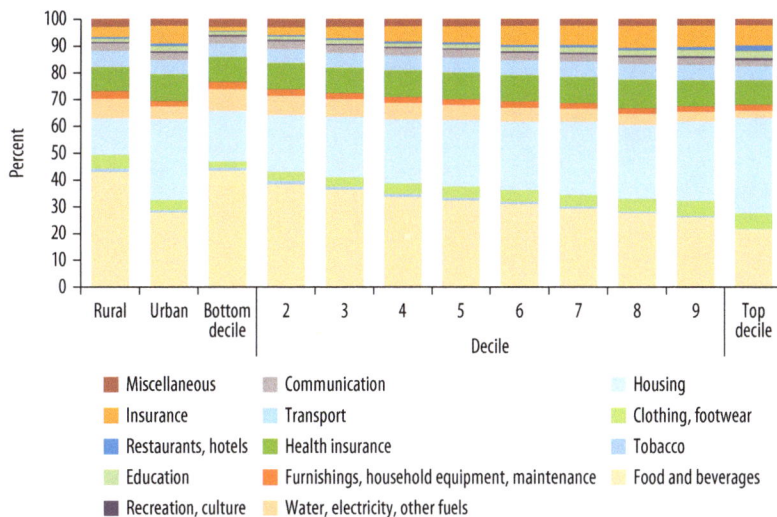

Source: World Bank staff calculations, based on HEIS 2016/17.
Note: Deciles based on consumption per capita in the base period.

FIGURE 8A.2

Group-Specific Price Index (April 2016 = 1), by Province

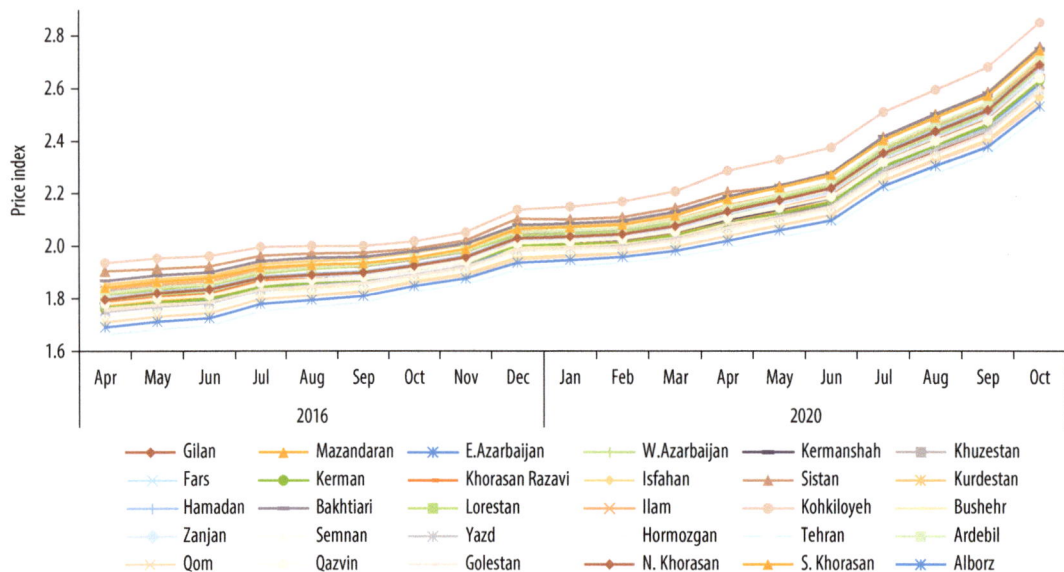

Source: World Bank staff calculations, based on HEIS 2016/17 and consumer price index from Statistical Center of Iran.

FIGURE 8A.3

Baseline Poverty Rates and Price Index (April 2016 = 1) of Provinces, by October 2020

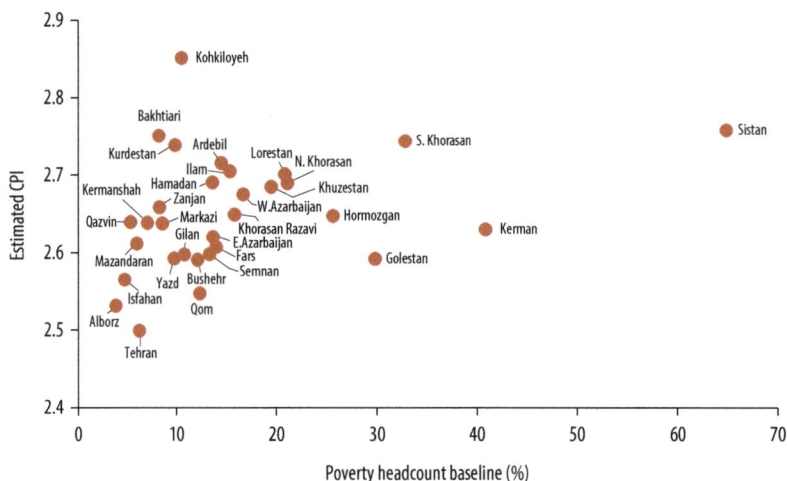

Source: World Bank staff calculations, based on HEIS 2016/17, 2018/19 and consumer price index (CPI) from Statistical Center of Iran.
Note: Poverty headcount based on consumption per capita.

FIGURE 8A.4

Expenditure Shares in End-Line Period, by Type of Goods and Services, by Rural and Urban, and by Welfare Decile (%)

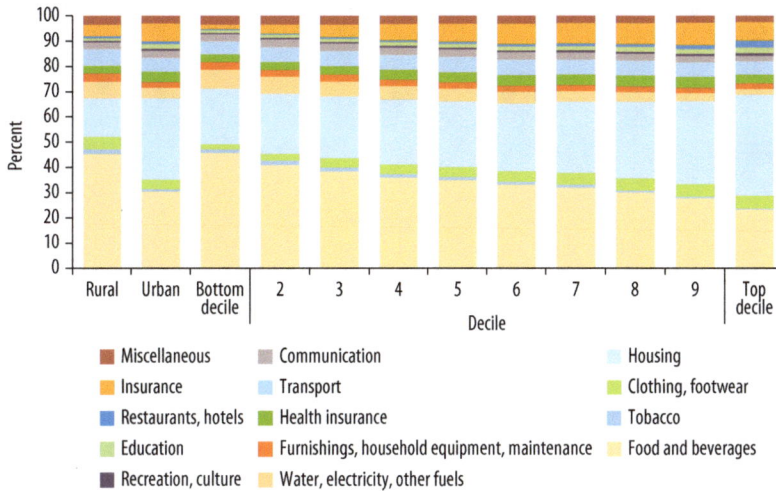

Source: World Bank staff calculations, based on HEIS 2018/19.
Note: Deciles based on consumption per capita in the end-line period.

FIGURE 8A.5

Group-Specific Price Index (April 2016 = 1), by Region, and by Rural and Urban with Substitution Effects

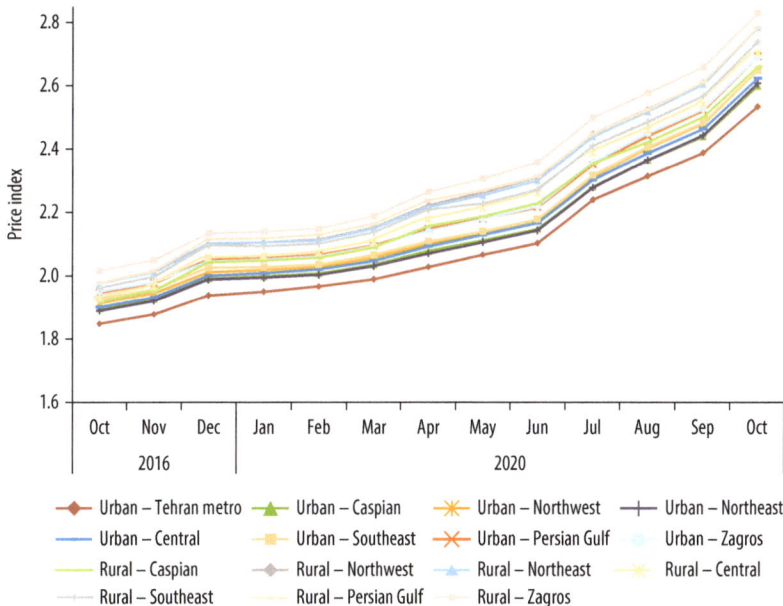

Source: World Bank staff calculations, based on HEIS 2018/19 and consumer price index from Statistical Center of Iran.

Welfare Distributions before and after the Shocks and Mitigation Measures

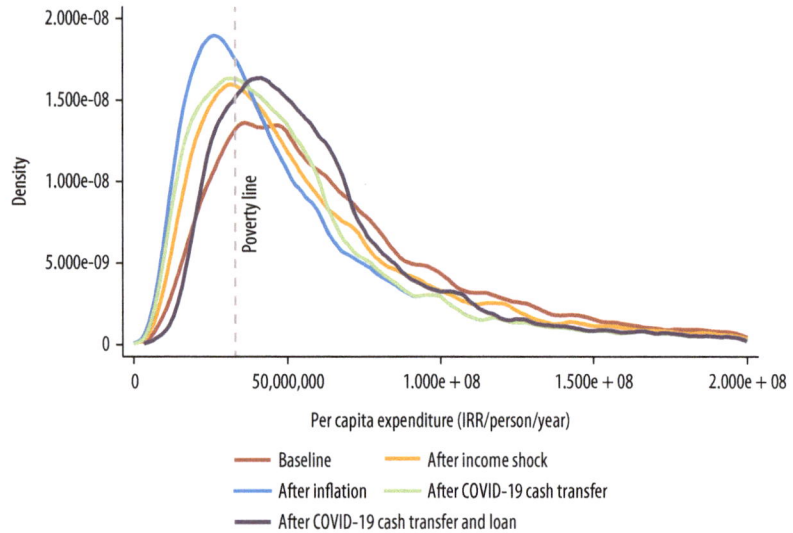

Source: World Bank staff calculations, based on HEIS 2018/19.
Note: The poverty line is very close to the highest point of the probability curve (or mode)—the expenditure per capita that occurs most frequently in the population.

Notes

1. Yearly figures in the paper are based on the Persian calendar, which bridges two years in the Gregorian calendar, starting and ending in March.
2. Data for 2017 from the World Integrated Trade Solution. Software is available online by registering at the website: https://wits.worldbank.org/.
3. Food and beverages; education; tobacco; clothing and footwear; housing, water, electricity, gas; furnishings, household equipment and maintenance; health; transport; communication; recreation and culture; restaurants and hotels; miscellaneous.
4. Food expenditures include bread and cereals; red meat and poultry; fish and seafood; dairy products and eggs; oils and fats; fruits and nuts; vegetables and pulses; sugar, jam, honey, chocolate, confectionary; other food products; and beverages. The three categories of housing expenditures are rent; maintenance and repair services; water, electricity and other fuels.
5. The CPI rates used to convert figures to 2011 values come from SCI. See Atamanov et al. (2020) for a detailed explanation of the methodology to construct the consumption aggregate.
6. The most common US$1.90 poverty line is not used because extreme poverty at this level is almost nonexistent in the country. The levels of poverty are slightly different than those reported by the World Bank for global poverty monitoring. The main difference comes from the way the welfare aggregate is created.

7. As in many other countries and global estimates, poverty increased with the revised 2011 PPP figures (Atamanov et al. 2020).

8. Household savings and borrowing are also likely to be a limited source of consumption smoothing. Because of the prolonged economic deterioration in the Islamic Republic of Iran, most households are likely to have few liquid assets that they can use to cushion the impact of income losses, and many had already borrowed before the current shock, limiting their ability to do so now.

9. The province-specific parameters are calibrated between 0 and 1 from the intensity of COVID-19 cases in March 2020, when the latest official subnational estimates were available. Since then, the government of the Islamic Republic of Iran has released a list of classifications of provinces as red, orange, and yellow, without specifying the provincial caseloads. The parameters reflect this classification system from October 2020 to further adjust the province parameters.

10. Ratha et al. (2020) estimate a 5 percent fall in international remittance inflows to the Islamic Republic of Iran in 2020 compared with 2019. It is not possible to distinguish domestic from international remittances in HEIS.

11. An alternative would be to draw on household-specific shares of each consumption category and shock households, using a household-specific price increase. But in the absence of panel data starting in a baseline period before the inflationary episode began, the household shares of consumption would already incorporate some substitution effect, and the resulting welfare change would likely be underestimated. Although they would be more detailed, the overall results are unlikely to be substantially different if the consumption patterns of households within groups are similar.

12. The Laspeyres index follows closely Cravino and Levchenko (2017), but because of data limitations, only the changes in welfare attributed to the variation of prices for households that consume different types of goods (across variation) are identified—not those owing to the within variation.

13. Budget shares are for 2016/17 before the inflationary pressures began in the Islamic Republic of Iran. Shares exclude durables and health expenditures, which are not part of the consumption aggregate. Health insurance is included. See figure 8A in the annex for shares including all health expenses.

14. Provinces are grouped in regions. See note in figure 8.4. Province price indexes are in figure 8A.2 in the annex.

15. However, it is possible that the aggregate nature of the consumption groups hides some variation within categories of goods. Estimating weights based on consumption patterns *during* the pandemic would be more accurate but is complicated as consumption patterns might be fluctuating (see Reinsdorf 2020) and data collection efforts are stalled or disrupted.

16. For instance, the ratio in the price indexes of the groups with the lowest and highest inflation were 1.09 in January and 1.12 in October 2020, respectively.

17. The cash transfers were distributed in four rounds between April and June 2020. The loan was available for households that were receiving the existing energy subsidy reform compensation transfer. Of the eligible households, about 21 million households applied for it.

References

Adams-Prassl, Abi, Teodora Boneva, Marta Golin, and Christopher Rauh. 2020. "Inequality in the Impact of the Coronavirus Shock: Evidence from Real Time Surveys." *Journal of Public Economics* (189). https://doi.org/10.1016/j.jpubeco.2020.104245.

Alazzawi, Shireen, and Vladimir Hlasny. 2019. "Disparities in the Cost of Living Changes after a Large-Scale Devaluation: The Case of Egypt 2016." ERF 26th Annual Conference, 277. Topics in Middle Eastern and African Economies, *Proceedings of Middle East Economic Association* 21 (1).

Atamanov, Aziz, Christoph Lakner, Daniel Gerszon Mahler, Samuel Kofi Tetteh Baah, and Judy Yang. 2020. "The Effect of New PPP Estimates on Global Poverty: A First Look." Global Poverty Monitoring Technical Note 12, World Bank, Washington, DC.

Barrett, Christopher B., and Paul A. Dorosh. 1996. "Farmers' Welfare and Changing Food Prices: Nonparametric Evidence from Rice in Madagascar." *American Journal of Agricultural Economics* 78 (3): 656–69. https://doi.org/10.2307/1243283.

Cravino, Javier, and Andrei A. Levchenko. 2017. "The Distributional Consequences of Large Devaluations." *American Economic Review* 107 (11): 3477–3509. https://doi.org/10.1257/aer.20151551.

Deaton, Angus, and Salman Zaidi. 2002. "Guidelines for Constructing Consumption Aggregates for Welfare Analysis." LSMS Working Paper 135, World Bank, Washington, DC. https://openknowledge.worldbank.org/handle/10986/14101.

de Hoyos, Rafael E., and Denis Medvedev. 2011. "Poverty Effects of Higher Food Prices: A Global Perspective." *Review of Development Economics* 15 (3): 387–402. https://doi.org/10.1111/j.1467-9361.2011.00615.x.

de Janvry, Alain, and Elisabeth Sadoulet. 2010. "The Global Food Crisis and Guatemala: What Crisis and for Whom?" *World Development* 38 (9): 1328–39. https://doi.org/10.1016/j.worlddev.2010.02.008.

Fujii, Tomoki. 2013. "Impact of Food Inflation on Poverty in the Philippines." *Food Policy* 39: 13–27. https://doi.org/https://doi.org/10.1016/j.foodpol.2012.11.009.

Hatayama, Maho, Mariana Viollaz, and Hernan Winkler. 2020. "Jobs' Amenability to Working from Home: Evidence from Skills Surveys for 53 Countries." Policy Research Working Paper 9241, World Bank, Washington, DC. http://hdl.handle.net/10986/33753.

Haughton, Jonathan, and Shahidur R. Khandker. 2009. *Handbook on Poverty and Inequality*. Washington, DC: World Bank.

Hayati, Fayavar, Majid Kazemi Najaf Abadi, Maria Reinholdt Andersen, Aziz Atamanov, Matthew Grant Wai-Poi, Mohammadhadi Mostafavi Dehzooei, and Djavad Salehi Isfahani. 2018. "Iran Economic Monitor: Weathering Economic Challenges. Special Focus Topic: Understanding the Latest Poverty Trends in Iran (2009–2016)." World Bank, Washington, DC.

Ivanic, Maros, and Will Martin. 2014. "Short- and Long-Run Impacts of Food Price Changes on Poverty." Policy Research Working Paper 7011, World Bank, Washington, DC. https://doi.org/10.1596/1813-9450-7011.

Ivanic, Maros, Will Martin, and Hassan Zaman. 2012. "Estimating the Short-Run Poverty Impacts of the 2010–11 Surge in Food Prices." *World Development* 40 (11): 2302–17. https://doi.org/10.1016/j.worlddev.2012.03.024.

Jolliffe, Dean, and Espen Beer Prydz. 2016. "Estimating International Poverty Lines from Comparable National Thresholds." Policy Research Working Paper 7606, World Bank, Washington, DC.

Khamis, M., D. Prinz, D. Newhouse, A. Palacios-Lopez, U. Pape, and M. Weber. 2021. "The Early Labor Market Impacts of COVID-19 in Developing Countries: Evidence from High-Frequency Phone Surveys." Policy Research Working Paper 9510, World Bank, Washington, DC.

Kraay, Aart. 2007. "The Welfare Effects of a Large Depreciation. The Case of Egypt, 2000-05." Policy Research Working Paper 4182, World Bank, Washington, DC.

Paxson, Christina H., and Harold Alderman. 1992. *Do the Poor Insure?: A Synthesis of the Literature on Risk and Consumption in Developing Countries*. Washington, DC: Agriculture and Rural Development Department, World Bank.

Ratha, Dilip, Supriyo De, Eung Ju Kim, Sonia Plaza, Ganesh Seshan, and Nadege Desiree Yameogo. 2020. "Migration and Development Brief 33: Phase II: COVID-19 Crisis through a Migration Lens." Washington, DC: KNOMAD and World Bank. https://www.knomad.org/sites/default/files/2020-11/Migration%20%26%20Development_Brief%2033.pdf.

Reinsdorf, Marshall. 2020. "COVID-19 and the CPI: Is Inflation Underestimated?" IMF Working Paper No. 224. International Monetary Fund, Washington, DC. https://www.imf.org/en/Publications/WP/Issues/2020/11/05/COVID-19-and-the-CPI-Is-Inflation-Underestimated-49856.

Rodriguez-Takeuchi, Laura, and Katsushi S. Imai. 2013. "Food Price Surges and Poverty in Urban Colombia: New Evidence from Household Survey Data." *Food Policy* 43 (C): 227–36. https://doi.org/10.1016/j.foodpol.2013.09.017.

Sanchez-Paramo, Carolina, and Ambar Narayan. 2020. "Impact of COVID-19 on Households: What Do Phone Surveys Tell Us?" *Voices* (blog), November 20, 2020. https://blogs.worldbank.org/voices/impact-covid-19-households-what-do-phone-surveys-tell-us?cid=ECR_E_NewsletterWeekly_EN_EXT&deliveryName=DM85808.

Skoufias, Emmanuel, Sailesh Tiwari, and Hassan Zaman. 2012. "Crises, Food Prices, and the Income Elasticity of Micronutrients: Estimates from Indonesia." *World Bank Economic Review* 26 (3): 415–42. https://doi.org/10.1093/wber/lhr054.

Vu, Linh, and Paul Glewwe. 2011. "Impacts of Rising Food Prices on Poverty and Welfare in Vietnam." *Journal of Agricultural and Resource Economics* 36 (1): 14–27.

World Bank. 2020a. "Iran Economic Monitor, Fall 2020: Weathering the Triple-Shock." World Bank, Washington, DC. https://openknowledge.worldbank.org/handle/10986/34973.

World Bank. 2020b. "Uganda Economic Update, 16th Edition, December 2020: Investing in Uganda's Youth." World Bank, Washington, DC.

Yoshida, N., Ambar Narayan, and H. Wu. 2020. "How COVID-19 Affects Households in Poorest Countries—Insights from Phone Surveys." *Voices* (blog), December 10, 2020. https://blogs.worldbank.org/voices/how -covid-19-affects-households-poorest-countries-insights-phone-surveys.

CHAPTER 9

Lebanon: Sharply Increased Poverty for Nationals and Refugees

Bilal Malaeb and Matthew Wai-Poi

Key Messages

- Against the backdrop of a particularly fragile moment for a country already grappling with severe economic, financial, and political crises—exacerbated by the Port of Beirut blast in August 2020—COVID-19 and the compounded crises have had devastating effects on the Lebanese and refugee communities.

- The microsimulation results show that poverty is rising sharply for both the host communities and Syrian refugees. For the Lebanese, the increase is an estimated 13 percentage points for 2020 from the 2019 baseline, and 28 percentage points for 2021, using the international poverty line. For the refugees, the increase is an estimated 39 percentage points for 2020 and 52 percentage points for 2021.

- These changes will translate into an additional 2.3 million individuals being pushed below the international poverty line by end-2021 (of which 1.5 million are Lebanese and 780,000 are Syrian refugees).

- The drivers of changes in poverty are primarily linked to high inflation rates, with headline inflation averaging 84 percent in 2020 and reaching highs of 145 percent in certain months.

- The crises are expected to leave refugees, who are already poorer than the host community, much poorer, reflecting inequalities in the transmission of the shock.

Introduction

By now it is no surprise that the COVID-19 pandemic and its ensuing confinement policies have wreaked havoc in world economies. While some countries had the fiscal and economic resources to lessen the impact of the pandemic, lessening its severe consequences on their population, other countries were in an acutely fragile position even before the pandemic struck, leaving them particularly vulnerable to its ramifications. Lebanon is one of the countries in which COVID-19 compounded already severe economic, financial, and political crises.

By the end of 2019, Lebanon had plunged into crisis—marked by currency and banking crises, increasing unemployment, and soaring levels of inflation—which was brought about by a drop in capital inflows and poor governance. It had been running a current account deficit since the early 2000s, and the net negative foreign currency position of the balance sheets of the sovereign, the central bank, and the commercial banks stood at 90 percent of GDP at end-2019 (Moubayed and Zouein 2020). Further, the debt-to-GDP ratio is estimated at around 187 percent for 2020, up from 171 percent in 2019, and unemployment is at 40 percent (World Bank 2021). In tandem, the government had resigned following the broad-based demonstrations of October 2019, and a new government, formed in January 2020, had defaulted on its debt obligations in March 2020. These conditions, together with the pandemic, saw the currency's value plummet and a parallel exchange market established.

Within Lebanon, Syrian refugees had been grappling with poor living conditions since their arrival after the onset of the 2011 Syrian war. Lebanon hosts an estimated 1.5 million Syrian refugees out of its nearly 7 million population, making it the nation with the highest number of refugees per capita in the world. Although this situation reflects the remarkable generosity of the Lebanese people, it has also led to tensions between the host community and the refugees, who tend to live mostly in cities and villages, and in some cases in informal settlements, because of the government's decision to establish refugee camps (UNDP and ARK 2019).

The following describe the deplorable living conditions of these refugees:

- As of 2020, the Vulnerability Assessment of Syrian Refugees conducted by the United Nations High Commissioner for Refugees (UNHCR), United Nations Children's Fund (UNICEF), and World Food Programme (WFP) indicated that refugees live in conditions that do not meet humanitarian standards, such as overcrowding and dangerous shelter conditions.

- Over half of these refugees suffer from poor food consumption levels, and 88 percent of them cannot afford the Survival Minimum Expenditure Basket, compared with 55 percent at end-2019 (Hohfeld et al. 2020).

- Among refugee children, most students did not attend school in 2020, including remotely, and the primary and preprimary attendance rates stood at 16 percent in 2020, similar to that in 2019.

Moreover, an explosion in the Port of Beirut in August 2020 rocked the city, leaving more than 200 people dead, causing rampant damage, and displacing as many as 300,000 individuals (WHO 2020). Despite the concentration of the material damage in Beirut, the economic impact of the explosion was felt throughout the country, given the Port of Beirut's position as the main point of entry and exit of traded goods, the small and open nature of the economy, and the demographic and economic concentration in the capital (World Bank 2020a). The damages in housing and culture sectors, which touched the lives of both affluent and poorer neighborhoods of the city, are estimated at US$3.8–4.6 billion, with losses in economic flows estimated at US$2.9–3.5 billion. The government of Lebanon resigned soon after the explosion and continues in its caretaker capacity to this date,[1] amid a political deadlock.

How will the pandemic, compounded by preexisting crises, affect both the Lebanese and refugee populations' poverty levels? To answer that, we conducted an analysis that estimates the changes in poverty since the onset of COVID-19 in Lebanon, and explores the inequalities that the shocks may have propagated among Syrian refugee and host communities. It considers the two crises together, because of their entangled nature, without attempting to identify the impact of each one separately. Understanding the magnitude of the impact of these crises, including that of COVID-19, has implications for the policies that governments and international organizations may need to adopt as the pandemic unfolds and during the recovery period.

In light of the restrictions in collecting face-to-face data from households, the lack of existing data (the most recent welfare survey fielded by the Central Administration of Statistics dates from 2012), and limited ability of phone surveys to measure household consumption and poverty, this study uses a microsimulation model to project the changes in household welfare after the onset of COVID-19. It analyzes the baseline poverty and labor market characteristics of host and refugee households and simulates the effects of the macroeconomic sectoral trends and forecasts on these characteristics. To do that, the study relies on a unique survey that is comparable between refugees and host communities, combined with the latest macroeconomic growth and inflation projections and related labor market characteristics of hosts and refugees.

This chapter begins with a discussion of how households are affected by the combination of economic crises and a health crisis, before detailing how the study was done and its findings on poverty and the "new poor." The analysis uses two poverty lines: the national line, which is often context specific and reflects the consumption baskets at the national level, and the upper-middle-income international poverty line of US$5.50 per person per day.

Our key findings are that poverty is rising sharply for both populations within Lebanon:

- For the host community, using the international poverty line, the increase is an estimated 13 percentage points for 2020, from the 2019 baseline, and 28 points for 2021. For Syrian refugees, the increase is an estimated 39 percentage points for 2020 and 52 points for 2021.

- For the host community, at the national poverty line, the increase is an estimated 33 percentage points for 2020, from the 2019 baseline, and 46 points for 2021. For Syrian refugees, the increase is an estimated 24 percentage points for 2020 and 29 points for 2021. The refugees' baseline is 24 percentage points higher than that of the Lebanese.

- Moreover, because of the inequalities in the transmission of the shock, the crises are expected to leave refugees, who are already poorer than the host community, much poorer. And the impact of the pandemic on Lebanon's large informal market is also expected to be marked.

Transmission Channels

The combined COVID-19 and economic crises have affected household welfare in a number of ways. The impacts are often monetary, because of a loss in income or of price changes, as well as nonmonetary, such as service disruptions in health, education, and other sectors. This study focuses on the monetary impacts on consumption, the welfare aggregate used to measure poverty. Perhaps the most direct impact is a reduction in labor income as a result of contracting the illness, but the more salient impacts are those on the economic sectors in which individuals are employed, causing earnings and employment shocks.

Besides direct losses to labor income, households face negative effects on nonlabor income, such as a decline in remittances owing to the global economic slowdown. In addition, disruptions in supply chains, employment, and changes in demand have affected prices in the Middle East

FIGURE 9.1

Inflation Has Soared, Especially for Food Prices
Year-over-year monthly changes in inflation in Lebanon for 2020 (%)

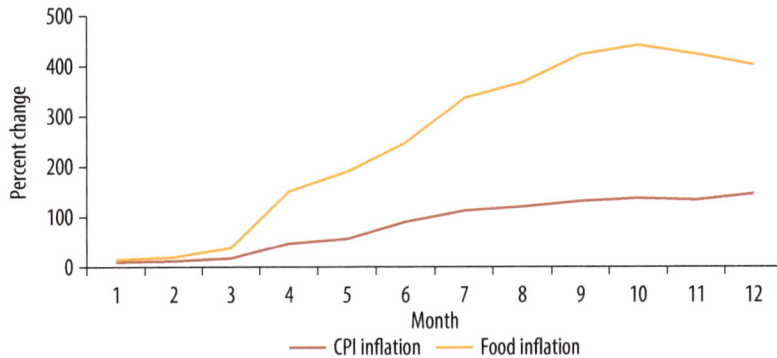

Source: World Bank staff calculations, based on consumer price index (CPI) 2020 data from the Central Administration of Statistics Lebanon.

and North Africa (MENA) region, with some countries experiencing an increase in the price of staples by more than 20 percent from February to October 2020. Lebanon has experienced a big increase in price levels, reaching around 145 percent by the end of 2020, and even higher food price inflation (at 402 percent), largely due to its import dependence and currency devaluation, on top of the effects of the COVID-19 crisis (figure 9.1). Given that the share of food expenditures is higher among poorer households, the increase in food prices can have significant effects on their welfare, a big reason why this study uses inflation levels as a key component of the microsimulation models.

How the Study Is Conducted

This analysis relies on the Syrian Refugees and Host Communities Survey (SRHCS) undertaken by the World Bank in 2015/16. The SRHCS collects information on households' sources of income and assistance, and provides information on labor market characteristics of randomly chosen individuals within these households. The survey was designed to be comparable for Syrian refugees and host communities and used a unified survey module. The SRHCS data is complemented with auxiliary macroeconomic data. In Lebanon, because of the lack of a recent and reliable sampling frame, the data were collected based on a frame that consists of the universe of enumeration areas in the country, with associated estimates of population. The survey was representative of host communities and Syrian refugees. Figure 9.2 shows the distribution of refugees and host communities, those in wage labor or working on their own account, across economic sectors according to the SRHCS 2015/16.[2] Refugees are concentrated in wholesale and retail trade and in construction, and the Lebanese community is concentrated in wholesale and retail trade and in education.

FIGURE 9.2

Lebanese Workers Are Mostly in Wholesale and Retail Trade and in Education, and Syrian Refugees Are in Construction and in Wholesale and Retail Trade

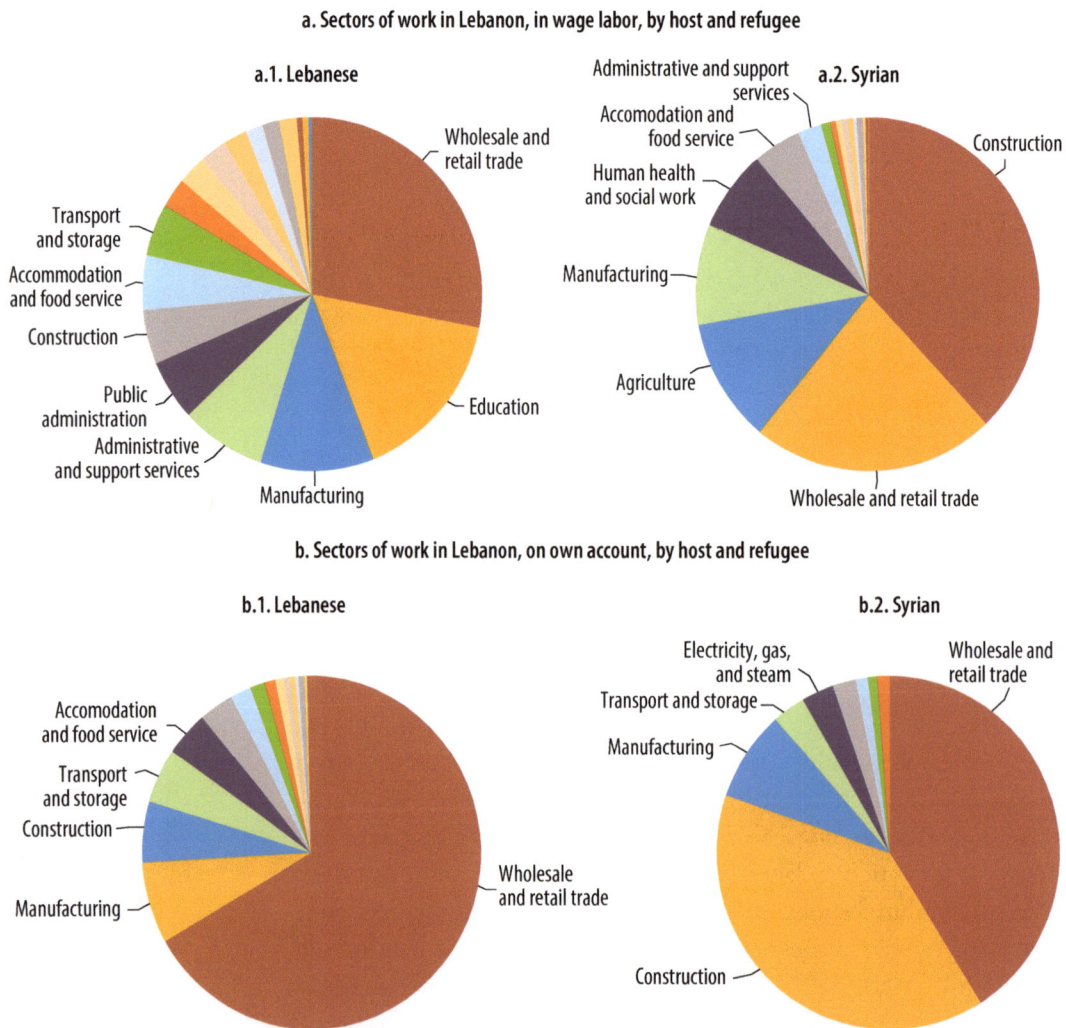

a. Sectors of work in Lebanon, in wage labor, by host and refugee

b. Sectors of work in Lebanon, on own account, by host and refugee

Source: World Bank staff calculations, based on SRHCS 2015/16.

On the welfare side, there are observable differences between host communities and refugees when we compare the consumption distribution against both the international poverty line for upper-middle-income countries (US$5.50/day) and the national poverty line.[3] These distributions reflect the household per capita expenditure distribution at end-2019, because they are nowcast based on growth and inflation from the year of the survey. The analysis begins by examining the pre-COVID-19 baseline distributions. Figure 9.3 shows the density distribution of household per capita expenditures and reflects the proportion of households under the poverty line; that is, the area underneath the curve to the left of the poverty line is the fraction of households that are considered poor by that poverty line. In Lebanon, although the refugee distribution still lies to the left of the host community's distribution, the modes (the highest points) are at similar levels. As a consequence, many refugees are under the poverty lines, and more refugees than members of host communities are under the poverty lines.

FIGURE 9.3

More Refugees Than Host Community Members Are under the International and National Poverty Lines

Baseline density expenditure (per capita) distribution of poverty in Lebanon

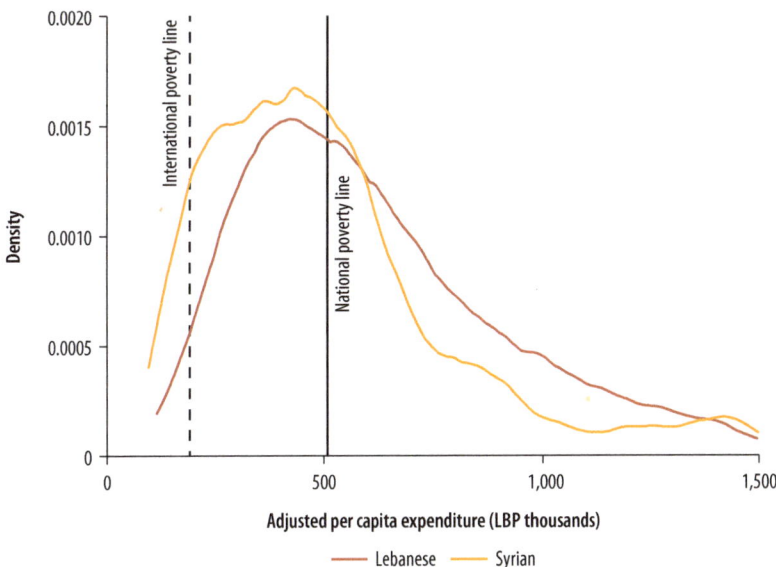

Source: World Bank staff calculations, based on SRHCS 2015/16.
Note: LBP = Lebanese lira.

Methodological Choices

The SRHCS is a dataset that is highly suitable for this exercise, primarily because it is more recent and comparable between the refugees and their host communities. As such, for the purposes of our analysis that compares these two communities, it provides clear advantages over other datasets, which may either be older than the SRHCS or capture only one of the two communities, or sacrifice representativeness of the underlying population. In addition, the data include an income module that captures eight different income source groups: wage income; business earnings; pensions; asset earnings; government, UN, and nongovernmental organization assistance; remittances; autoconsumption; and other income sources.

One drawback in relation to this analysis, and to the effort to produce credible poverty estimates, is that the SRHCS lacks a consumption module. To address this impediment, the income distributions in the SRHCS were transformed to reflect relevant consumption distributions obtained from the 2012 household budget survey (HBS) in Lebanon. One option is to transform the distributions using survey-to-survey imputation techniques. For example, regression analysis of per capita consumption could use the common indicators of welfare in both HBS and SRHCS, and the resulting coefficients would then be used to predict the per capita consumption in SRHCS. One drawback with this approach is that the predicted distributions tend to be more compact than the true distribution, which affects the poverty estimates derived from the predicted distribution.

As an alternative, a more mechanical transformation was applied, whereby a scaling factor is calculated for each percentile of the SRHCS income distribution to expand it to match the same percentile of the national survey consumption distribution. The scaling factor can be defined as follows:

$$s_p = \frac{mean\_cons_p^{NatSurvey}}{mean\_income_p^{SRHCS}}$$

where s is the scaling factor, p is the percentile subscript, *mean_cons* and *mean_income* are the mean consumption and income in that percentile, respectively. This process, while not analytically grounded, produces an accurate replication of the consumption distribution and preserves the rank order of the income distribution. The application of household-specific shocks (based on a mix of income sources and sector and formality of employment) to the transformed household per capita consumption then rests on the assumption that, although the SRHCS income distribution is far more compressed than the national survey consumption distribution, it provides a much more comparable rank ordering of the households. This is not a very strong assumption given the lack of savings in the poorer half of the distribution (and especially in Lebanon pre-COVID-19 and post-economic crisis). This transformation is implemented separately for host communities and refugees, whose distribution is mapped onto the non-Lebanese distribution of HBS 2012. The comparison between the distributions is shown in figure 9.4, where the adjusted expenditure distribution is nearly identical to that of the HBS 2012.

FIGURE 9.4

Distribution of Adjusted and Unadjusted Income and Expenditure

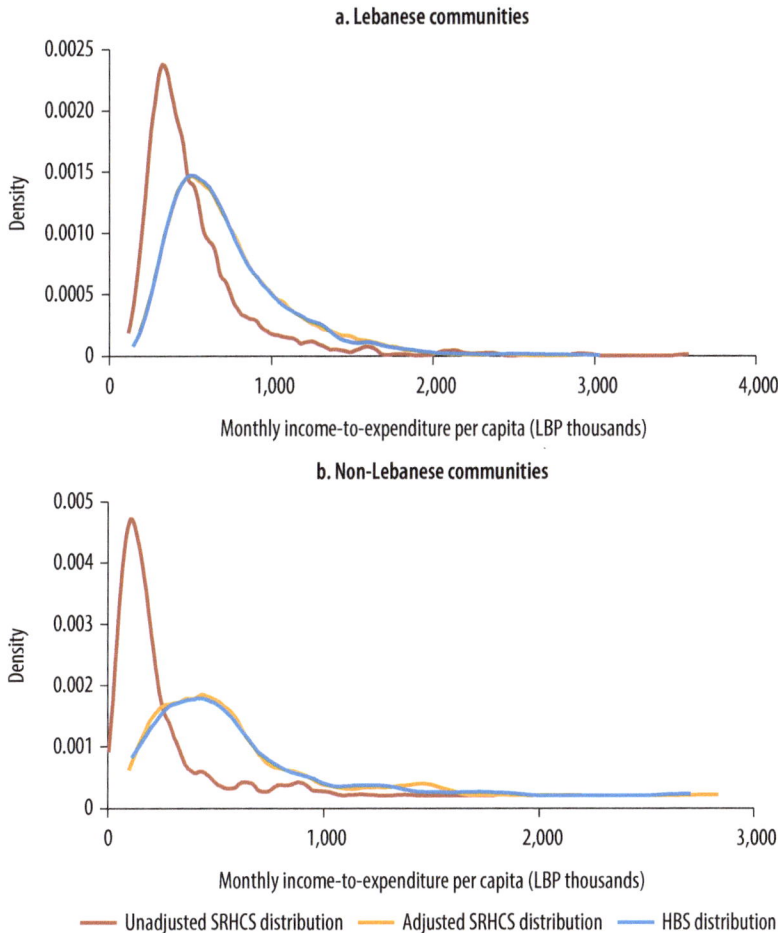

Source: World Bank staff calculations, based on SRHCS 2015/16 and HBS 2016.
Note: This graph uses HBS 2012 (nowcast to 2019), moves the PC expenditure distribution to start at zero, and stretches the HBS distribution to it assuming 1:1 income-to-consumption relationship. HBS = household budget survey; LBP = Lebanese lira.

As for the economic sectors, the SRHCS dataset includes information about the households' sources of income, including wage income and income from own-account work. Because the microsimulation models are based on the macrosectoral shocks, it is necessary to make assumptions on households' main sector of work to determine the level of macroeconomic shock that they face. The survey includes two modules (for wage work and own-account workers) collected for two randomly selected adults within the household, where they are asked about their current employment status and the sector in which they work. For most households, only one of the two randomly selected adults reports working. As such, the household is assigned the sector of that individual. Where two of the individuals report their employment, and they differ on sector, one of the two individuals' sector was randomly selected. For some households, if neither of the two individuals reports working, and the household is reported to have wage income or own-account income, their sector of work is imputed based on observable characteristics (age, sex, nationality, and education of the randomly selected adults) using a multinomial logit model. The same logic is followed for determining informality of the household, where informality is defined as having a contract or having insurance.

Macroeconomic Assumptions

Methodologically, this study (a) takes the baseline consumption aggregate of each household and introduces to it the nominal GDP growth rate of its economic sector and informality, (b) reflects changes in the remittances based on the currently available macroeconomic trends, and (c) adjusts the poverty line according to the changes in inflation rate. It is important to note that, although the values in table 9.1 show a positive nominal growth across most sectors, the levels of inflation mean that the real GDP growth is negative. Further, the analysis does not model employment changes but rather translates predicted income changes into changes in consumption. The macroeconomic trends are based on the macroeconomic projections, Macro Poverty Outlook, of the World Bank (2021). The contraction in real terms is expected be –20.3 percent on average in 2020 and –9.5 percent in 2021, and the pass-through of income into consumption, calculated as the ratio of private consumption growth to GDP growth, is estimated at 50 percent in 2020 and 75 percent in 2021.

The World Bank estimates an 8.5 percent decline in remittances to low- and middle-income MENA countries as a result of the pandemic in 2020, followed by a fall of 7.7 percent in 2021 (World Bank and KNOMAD 2020). Naturally, the rebound in remittances to precrisis

TABLE 9.1

Positive Nominal Growth Is Expected across Most Sectors, but Real Growth Will Be Negative

Changes in nominal value added by sector relative to first quarter of 2020 (%)

Sector	2020			2021			
	Q2	Q3	Q4	Q1	Q2	Q3	Q4
Agriculture, forestry and fishing	125	175	200	231	262	294	325
Mining and quarrying	121	164	185	214	243	272	301
All manufacturing	109	128	138	159	181	203	224
Electricity, gas, steam and air conditioning supply	101	103	104	121	137	154	170
Water supply; sewerage, waste management and remediation activities	113	139	151	175	199	223	247
Construction	87	61	49	56	64	71	79
Wholesale and retail trade; repair of motor vehicles and motorcycles	123	169	192	222	252	283	313
Transportation and storage	123	170	193	224	254	285	315
Accommodation and food service activities	64	–9	–45	–53	–60	–67	–74
Information and communication	127	182	210	243	276	309	342
Financial and insurance activities	145	236	282	326	371	415	460
Real estate activities	108	125	133	154	175	196	217
Professional, scientific and technical activities	122	167	189	219	249	279	309
Public administration and defense; compulsory social security	98	95	93	108	123	138	152
Education	107	122	129	149	170	190	210
Human health and social work activities	106	118	125	144	164	183	203
Administrative and support services	118	154	172	199	227	254	281
Arts, entertainment and recreation	118	154	172	199	227	254	281
Other service activities	118	154	172	199	227	254	281
Activities of households, other goods and services	118	154	172	199	227	254	281
Extraterritorial organizations and bodies	118	154	172	199	227	254	281

Source: World Bank staff calculations, based on World Bank 2020a, 2021.
Note: The results take the trends that are predicted by using computable general equilibrium modeling used in the Beirut Rapid Damage and Needs Assessment (World Bank 2020a), then they are calibrated to the overall growth trends as provided by the Macro Poverty Outlook (World Bank 2021). Although the nominal GDP changes are positive, the real growth trends show a reduction in GDP of 20.3 percent in 2020 and of 9.5 percent in 2021. These are assumed to be economywide effects, and the formal sector is assumed to have performed 10 percent better than average while the informal sector is assumed to have performed 10 percent worse.

levels will depend on the global economic recovery. Further, non-labor income may be affected, including private transfers as well as property, asset, and other business income. An initial 10 percent drop in international remittances is assumed, as well as a 50 percent drop in domestic remittances and a gradual recovery (figure 9.5). Given that

FIGURE 9.5

Remittances to MENA Countries Are Expected to Fall for 2020–21
Assumptions on the changes in remittances

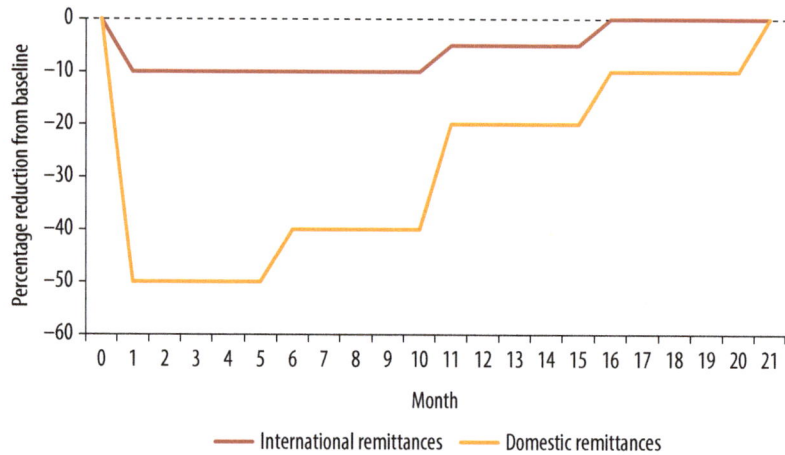

Source: World Bank staff calculations

the microdata on the source of remittances, domestic or international, are not available, the models assume an average remittances shock for each month.

Caveats

It is important to note here that the study's results are far from definitive, as many assumptions are necessarily being made in the absence of accessible and reliable data. For instance, no data are available on the changes in consumption patterns that households had to take in the face of the inflation shocks. It may be that households have had to adjust their consumption baskets and, therefore, absorb varying levels of inflation across and within the deciles of the consumption distribution. It is reasonable to assume that households' share of food consumption out of the overall consumption basket has increased, but the degree to which households have been able to protect themselves from inflation is unclear. Adjustments could have been made, such as a substitution of the nature of the goods (local versus imported), a reduction in total food consumption, or a shift toward lower quality of calories consumed. The current models inherently treat any such changes as welfare losses that translate into simulated poverty levels.

In addition, the pass-through of GDP into consumption is assumed based on the changes in private consumption relative to GDP based on macroeconomic data, which necessarily ignores the differences across the distribution. Though less likely given the macroeconomic trends of the economy, any shifts in households' employment and sources of livelihood cannot be captured without frequent data that monitor the evolution of the crises.

Finally, despite the SRHCS 2015/16 being useful in conducting this analysis, the absence of a recent official household budget survey, on the basis of which the consumption distribution can be calibrated and accurately capture the consumption distribution of refugees, is a serious limitation. As such, the results of this analysis are treated as indicative of the expected losses in welfare as a result of changes in the country's macroeconomic conditions, but these results do not necessarily reflect measured poverty.

Large Poverty Setbacks

For a country with an already high level of poverty for both the host and the refugee communities, what kind of a setback might occur as a result of the pandemic? The results show that there will be a sharp rise in poverty levels for both the Lebanese population and the Syrian refugees (figure 9.6). In addition, there will be a large number of new poor (those who were not poor in the first quarter of 2020 but became poor after) for both groups, for a combined total of about 2.3 million individuals by end-2021.[4] Using the international poverty line, the analysis shows the following:

- For the Lebanese population, the rise is estimated at about 13 percentage points from the 2019 baseline by end-2020, and 28 points by end-2021, meaning that the number of poor Lebanese is expected to increase by about 1.5 million by then.

- For Syrian refugees, the rise is estimated at about 39 percentage points from the 2019 baseline by end-2020, and 52 points by end-2021, meaning that the number of poor refugees is expected to increase by about 780,000 by then. Note that the baseline for this group is 8 points higher than that of the Lebanese.

The poverty trend is much the same if the national poverty line is used:

- For the Lebanese population, the rise is estimated at about 33 percentage points from the 2019 baseline by end-2020, and 46 points by end-2021, meaning that the number of poor Lebanese is expected to increase by about 2.5 million by then.

FIGURE 9.6

A Sharp Rise in Poverty Is Expected for Both the Lebanese Population and Syrian Refugees

Changes in poverty after the onset of COVID-19, using overall CPI inflation

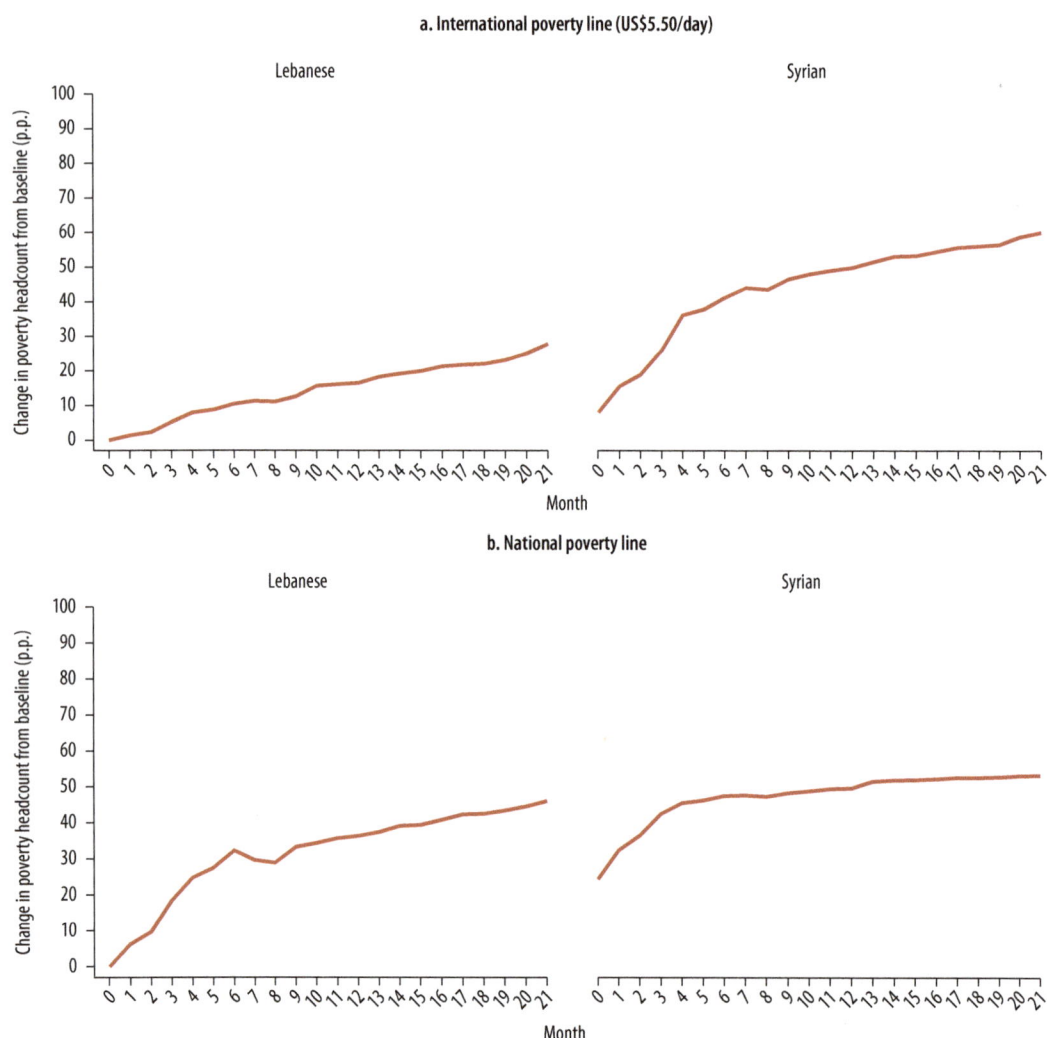

a. International poverty line (US$5.50/day)

b. National poverty line

Source: World Bank staff calculations, based on SRHCS 2015/16 and overall CPI inflation.
Note: The lines show the changes month by month from period 0 until the end of 2021. Period 0 is the first quarter of 2020, month 1 is April 2020, and month 21 is December 2021. CPI = consumer price index; p.p. = percentage point.

- For Syrian refugees, the rise is estimated at about 24 percentage points from the 2019 baseline by end-2020, and 29 points by end-2021, meaning that the number of poor refugees is expected to increase by about 432,000 by then. Note that the baseline for this group is 24 points higher than that of the Lebanese.

Finally, a direct comparison of the changes in poverty from baseline between the national and international lines may not be very useful. Because the national line is a higher poverty line, poverty at the baseline is expected to be higher than that of the international poverty line, as shown in table 9.2. Further, changes in prices (inflation) yield varied changes in poverty rates, depending on the position of the poverty line in the underlying consumption distribution.

For the MENA region, economic losses are estimated at around 7.7 percent of the region's GDP in 2019, relative to a no-crisis counterfactual, and poverty is estimated to have increased by roughly 12–15 million people in 2020 alone, at the upper-middle-income country poverty line of living on US$5.50 per day. This estimate could rise to upward of 23 million people by the end of 2021. Within this headline figure, there is also great variability. In Lebanon, GDP losses exceed the regional average by almost a factor of three, with an estimated GDP loss in 2019 of as much as 25 percent; the impact on poverty is concomitantly worse than elsewhere in the region. Inflation, in particular, played a central role in the poverty increases in Lebanon.

As a result of the ongoing economic crisis in Lebanon, the government has had limited resources to provide any form of social assistance to its citizens, as has been the case in other countries around the world. Refugees continue to receive assistance from international organizations (such as UNHCR and WFP), which have scaled up their assistance in response to the crisis. However, because of the low official exchange rate of the Lebanese currency in relation to its market rate, assistance toward

TABLE 9.2

Large Numbers of New Poor Will Accompany Higher Poverty Rates

Predicted changes in poverty and population for the Lebanese community and Syrian refugees

		Lebanese		Syrian	
		International poverty line	National poverty line	International poverty line	National poverty line
December 2020	Percentage point change	+12.6	+33.4	+38.5	+23.9
	Change in number of poor people (thousands)	+674	+1,786	+577	+358
December 2021	Percentage point change	+27.9	+46.1	+52.0	+28.8
	Change in number of poor people (thousands)	+1,495	+2,468	+780	+432

Source: World Bank staff calculations, using SRHCS 2015/16.
Note: Changes presented are relative to a simulated poverty estimate at baseline (Q1 2020) of each group. Syrian refugees' poverty is higher at baseline than that of the host communities.

refugees has not kept up with the soaring levels of inflation, leading to minimal mitigation of the effects of the crises.

Another issue is that Lebanon has large informal markets, with poorer workers in precarious employment conditions. Informal enterprises often have limited financial cushioning and would naturally resort to wage cuts and job cuts or suspensions in times of crisis (ILO 2020). Where governmental regulation may offer support to workers, informal workers fall outside the remit of such benefits. Given its ubiquity, unemployment in the informal sector affects the most vulnerable, including refugees. While some refugees have benefited from expansions in humanitarian cash assistance and food programs, which may have partially buffered the impact of the crises, most refugees have been forced into increased borrowing and reduced consumption.

Sensitivity Analysis

Since food price inflation is considerably higher in Lebanon than overall CPI inflation (figure 9.1), and because the food consumption share of the consumer basket is likely to have become larger as a result of the economic downturn, this study also uses food price inflation to present an upper-bound projection of the change in poverty. The results at the higher food price inflation show a larger increase in poverty than overall CPI inflation (figure 9.7). Indeed, they suggest that at this upper bound, poverty among the Lebanese population would have increased by around 35 percentage points and 47 points at the international and national poverty lines, respectively, by the end of 2020, and by 47 and 51 percentage points, respectively, by the end of 2021, compared with the baseline. These correspond to an increase of 1.8 million poor individuals by the end of 2020, up to 2.5 million poor individuals by the end of 2021, at the international poverty line compared with the baseline. At the national poverty line, these correspond to an increase of 2.5 million poor individuals among the Lebanese population in 2020, and 2.7 million by the end of 2021.

For the Syrian refugees, under this scenario, poverty is expected to increase by 58 percentage points at the international poverty line and 29 points at the national poverty line by 2020, and 68 points and 31 points, respectively, by the end of 2021, compared with the baseline. In population terms, these numbers suggest that 863,000 more Syrian refugees fell under the international poverty line by the end of 2020, and up to a million did so by the end of 2021. At the national poverty line, an increase of around 440,000 poor individuals is expected by the end of 2020, and around 457,000 poor individuals by end of 2021, compared with the baseline.

FIGURE 9.7

Sensitivity Analysis Using Food Price Inflation Shows an Increase in Poverty

Changes in poverty after the onset of COVID-19

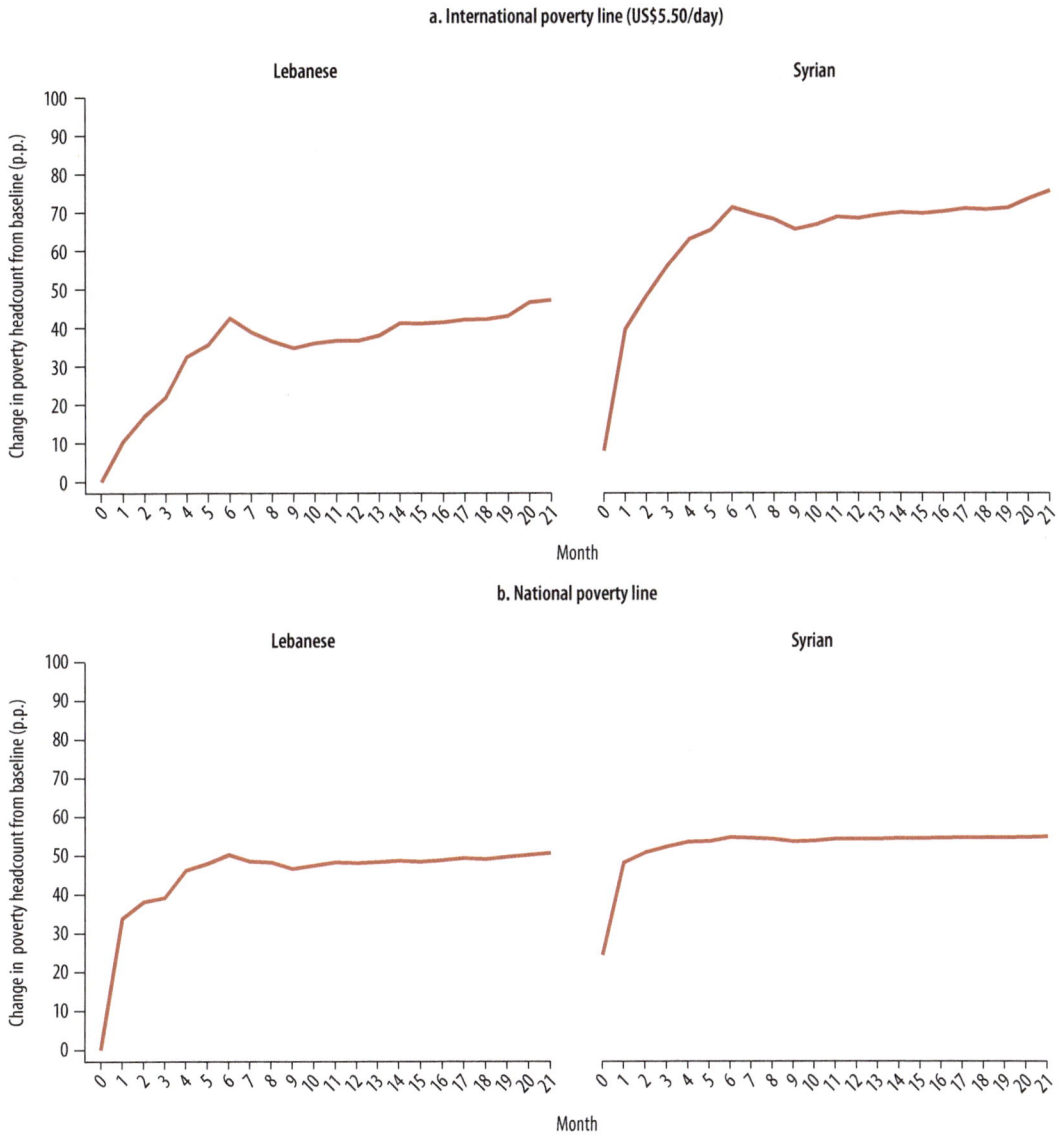

a. International poverty line (US$5.50/day)

Lebanese

Syrian

b. National poverty line

Lebanese

Syrian

Source: World Bank staff calculations, based on SRHCS 2015/16 and the consumer price index on food price inflation.
Note: The lines show the changes month by month from period 0 until the end of 2021. Period 0 is the first quarter of 2020, month 1 is April 2020, and month 21 is December 2021. p.p. = percentage point.

Characteristics of the New Poor

A central question in this analysis is understanding who the new poor are, that is, those who were not poor in the first quarter of 2020. First, we group the individuals into their sector of employment and select two points in time: December 2020 (month 9) and December 2021 (month 21).[5] As table 9.3 shows, most of the new poor in December 2020, under the international poverty line (US$5.50 per person per day), are in the accommodation and food service sector (45.2 percent)

TABLE 9.3

The New Poor Initially Concentrate in the Accommodation and Food Service Sector

Characteristics of the new poor by sector of employment (%)

	International Poverty Line				National Poverty Line			
	December 2020		December 2021		December 2020		December 2021	
	Lebanese	Syrian	Lebanese	Syrian	Lebanese	Syrian	Lebanese	Syrian
Agriculture	0.9	12.2	0.7	12.7	1.3	6.4	1.1	6.1
Mining	—	—	—	0.1	0.8	2.0	0.6	1.7
Manufacturing	5.4	3.7	11.6	8.0	4.9	13.0	4.4	15.4
Electricity, gas, steam, etc.	—	—	—	0.3	0.6	0.5	1.9	0.4
Water supply, sewerage, waste management	0.3	0.5	2.6	0.3	0.6	0.1	0.5	1.4
Construction	22.4	57.6	12.1	49.3	3.6	32.9	2.7	29.5
Wholesale and retail trade	7.7	7.4	12.9	10.8	25.7	20.4	27.1	21.2
Transport and storage	0.6	—	0.4	—	11.7	0.4	8.9	0.3
Accommodation and food service	45.2	10.3	23.8	7.7	9.0	13.3	6.8	10.8
Information and communication	—	—	—	—	1.3	—	1.2	—
Financial and insurance	—	—	—	—	—	—	1.7	—
Real estate	—	0.5	—	1.4	0.2	0.5	0.1	0.4
Professional, scientific, and technical	—	—	0.1	—	0.9	—	0.8	—
Administrative and support service	1.3	0.3	6.4	0.3	15.2	—	15.2	—
Public administration	4.2	—	16.8	—	3.9	—	3.5	—
Education	8.3	—	7.7	0.1	13.7	—	13.8	4.0
Human health and social work	0.3	6.7	0.7	8.2	1.0	8.0	3.5	6.7
Arts, entertainment, and recreation	3.0	0.3	3.9	0.2	2.1	0.5	2.5	0.4
Other services	0.5	0.7	0.3	0.6	3.8	2.1	3.9	1.7
Total	100	100	100	100	100	100	100	100

Source: World Bank staff calculations, based on SRHCS 2015/16.
Note: — = not available.

and construction (22.4 percent). By end-2021, when more new people are expected to have become poor, although the majority remain in the accommodation and food service sector (23.8 percent), around 17 percent of the new poor work in public administration, 13 percent work in wholesale and retail, and 12 percent work in construction. For Syrian refugees, the majority are in the construction sector (57.6 percent in 2020 and 49.3 percent in 2021).

However, using the national poverty line, a greater number of people have fallen into poverty compared with the international poverty line, but the new poor are more evenly distributed across sectors. The Lebanese are concentrated in wholesale and retail (25.7 percent and 27.1 percent in 2020 and 2021, respectively), in administrative and support services (around 15 percent), and in education (around 14 percent), for both years. The Syrian refugees below the national poverty line are mainly in construction (32.9 percent in 2020 and 29.5 percent in 2021), wholesale and retail (20.4 percent in 2020 and 21.2 percent in 2021), and manufacturing (13.0 percent and 15.4 percent in 2020 and 2021, respectively).

The following are other key characteristics of the new poor that were observed:

- *Head of household.* The simulations found that for the Lebanese, 93 percent of the new poor are male-headed households in 2020, and 96 percent for the Syrian refugees (using the national poverty line). The distribution is similar in 2021 (94 percent among the Lebanese and 92 percent among the Syrian refugees). Using the international poverty line, around 90 percent of both host community households and refugee households are male headed in 2020, and 91 percent in 2021.

- *Size of household.* Larger households have a higher probability of becoming poor.

- *Education.* More years of schooling for the household head is associated with a lower likelihood of falling into poverty among the Lebanese host community but not among the Syrian refugees.

- *Subjective poverty.* The SRHCS 2015/16 also asked households about their subjective poverty. Among the newly poor Syrian refugee households at the international and national poverty lines, respectively, 98 percent and 79 percent of the newly poor considered themselves subjectively poor at the time of the survey. Notably, only 20 percent of newly poor Lebanese households at the national poverty line considered themselves poor, and 38 percent of those at the international poverty line considered themselves as new poor.

Conclusion

At the onset of the COVID-19 pandemic, Lebanon had been grappling with a severe economic and financial crisis and serious political instability. The cumulative effects of these crises had led to a contraction in the real value added in the various economic sectors and to soaring levels of inflation. What further impact will the pandemic have on the welfare of households in the host community and of the Syrian refugees?

This chapter contends that there will be a significant increase in poverty from an already high base. Using the international poverty line, poverty for the Lebanese will rise by about 28 percentage points from the 2019 baseline by end-2021, and for the Syrian refugees poverty will rise by about 52 points. These increases will result in large numbers of individuals for both groups falling into poverty by end-2021, to total about 2.28 million (of which 1.5 million are Lebanese and 780,000 are Syrian refugees).

While the results suggest that the crises have affected both communities, they also reveal inequalities in the transmission of the shock. First, the crises are expected to leave refugees, who are already poorer than the host community, much poorer. Second, the poorer households' share of food expenditures before the crisis was so high that their susceptibility to changes in food prices is expected to be marked. After the economic deterioration, this effect is likely to be even more pronounced. Notably, food and nonalcoholic beverage prices have increased four times in 2020 alone.

The analysis highlights the need for better, more accessible, and more reliable data in Lebanon. Notably, strong assumptions had to be made to carry out the microsimulations, which should be indicative of the welfare losses incurred by the people of Lebanon as a result of the crises, yet those assumptions are not likely to reflect measured poverty. Indeed, as the crisis unfolds, the importance of data and monitoring cannot be overstated in addressing the poverty and economic concerns that ensue. To better prepare for the future, "under crisis conditions, reliable poverty data are even more important for guiding response and recovery policies that will not leave vulnerable groups behind" (World Bank 2020b, 3).

The results suggest that an economic recovery in Lebanon is not expected under the current macroeconomic outlook. They also highlight that a response commensurate with the magnitude of the crisis is necessary. While structural reforms—including curbing the increase in prices and reigniting economic activity—are crucial in the path to recovery, social protection programs are necessary in the immediate term to lessen the impact of the overlapping crises. Further, any response to the crises will need to be broad and inclusive, given the inequalities that the crises have reinforced and propagated.

Notes

1. As of April 2021, Lebanese officials continue to struggle to reach consensus on the formation of a new government.
2. A household's sector is based on the sector reported by randomly chosen individuals within the household. Where this information is not available, despite a household reporting wage labor or own-account income, it has been imputed based on observable characteristics.
3. The SRHCS survey does not include a consumption module but does include an income module. The resulting income distributions have been transformed into national consumption distributions.
4. The population figures are calculated based on a population of 6,855,713, according to UN population statistics, which includes an unofficial estimate of 1.5 million Syrian refugees.
5. The self-employment sector is not analyzed because of the low sample size, which does not allow further decomposition by poverty status.

References

Hohfeld, Lena, Cinzia Papavero, Susanna Sandstrom, Anaïs Dalbai, and Simon Renk. 2020. "Minimum Expenditure Basket for Syrian Refugees in Lebanon: Rights-Based Versus Expenditure-Based Approaches" March. World Food Programme, Geneva. https://reliefweb.int/report/lebanon/minimum -expenditure-basket-syrian-refugees-lebanon-rights-based-versus-expenditure.

ILO (International Labour Organization). 2020. "COVID-19 Crisis and the Informal Economy: Immediate Responses and Policy Challenges." ILO Briefing Note, May 2020, International Labour Organization, Geneva. https:// www.ilo.org/wcmsp5/groups/public/---ed_protect/---protrav/---travail /documents/briefingnote/wcms_743623.pdf.

Moubayed, Alia, and Gerard Zouein. 2020. "Finding a Way Out of Lebanon's Crisis: The Case for a Comprehensive and Equitable Approach to Debt Restructuring." https://lebanoneconomics.net/finding_a_way_out_of_lebanons _crisis.pdf.

UNDP (United Nations Development Programme) and ARK. 2019. "Regular Perception Surveys on Social Tensions throughout Lebanon, Wave VI." August. https://data2.unhcr.org/en/documents/details/71599.

WHO (World Health Organization). 2020. "Beirut Port Blast Emergency Strategic Response Plan." http://www.emro.who.int/images/stories/lebanon/who -lebanon-strategic-response-plan-27.9.20.pdf?ua=1.

World Bank. 2020a. "Beirut Rapid Damage and Needs Assessment." https://www .worldbank.org/en/country/lebanon/publication/beirut-rapid-damage -and-needs-assessment-rdna---august-2020.

World Bank. 2020b. *Reversals of Fortune: Poverty and Shared Prosperity 2020*. Washington, DC: World Bank. doi:10.1596/978-1-4648-1602-4.

World Bank. 2021. *Macro Poverty Outlook: Country-by-Country Analysis and Projections for the Developing World*. Lebanon Country Notes. Washington, DC: World Bank. https://www.worldbank.org/en/publication/macro-poverty -outlook.

World Bank and KNOMAD (Global Knowledge Partnership on Migration and Development). 2020. "Phase II: COVID-19 Crisis through a Migration Lens." Migration and Development Brief 33, October 2020. World Bank, Washington, DC. https://www.knomad.org/sites/default/files/2020-11/Migration%20 %26%20Development_Brief%2033.pdf.

www.ingramcontent.com/pod-product-compliance
Lightning Source LLC
Chambersburg PA
CBHW050818220326
41598CB00006B/245